THE ROYAL WITHIN

Twisted Branches

VOLUME I

House of Coningsby

GHP

**Grosvenor House
Publishing Limited**

This book is published by
Grosvenor House Publishing Ltd
Link House
140 The Broadway, Tolworth, Surrey, KT6 7HT.
www.grosvenorhousepublishing.co.uk

A CIP record for this book
is available from the British Library

ISBN 978-1-80381-398-1

PREFACE

A NOTE FROM A FAMILY MEMBER

This book shows the journey of discovery of our ancestors that we found through our research.

The reason for writing this book was to share the lives and times of our influential family members, combining all records, archives, and interesting information in one place.

A record to show how each of these characters connect to each other, and how they also connect to us.

Some of these historical characters have been sadly forgotten, or worse, hardly known and almost wiped from our history books.

We wanted to breathe life back into the people that they once were, showing a real sense of their character and how they played a large and important part in our history.

The family decided over 15 years ago to undertake this mammoth task of finding relatives, having spent their childhood – from the age of six months to adulthood – within the care system. This branch of the family did not have an easy life growing up; in fact, this is quite an understatement.

They were born in Edgware in London, and my mother was the youngest of four children born within her parents' marriage. She and an older sibling were constantly moving between a nunnery, children's homes, their grandparent's homes, then later into foster placements. They themselves had their own five minutes of fame as children, both in a documentary and starring on stage at the Royal Albert Hall before the age of seven.

Even though they had an incredibly harsh childhood, I am proud to say that my mother turned out to be a decent person.

The genealogy journey started in 2008, so let's go back to then when my mother opened an Ancestry account in a bid to find more information about our family history, for herself and the rest of the family.

Neither of her parents were willing to speak about their parents or any other relatives, if indeed they even knew of any family history.

In the hopes of gaining more knowledge, my mother signed up for Ancestry, using the very limited information she already knew about our family, her parents, and grandparents. To make it more complicated, her own father had been put up for adoption as a baby by his Irish mother, to a very loving Irish couple.

Going on a little information from one of her Irish cousins when she visited them in Ireland, she started to build the family tree.

She then took a DNA ancestry test in the hope of opening more doors and began to build the family tree using research and cross-referencing documents, which included studying local parish archives.

This in itself is a very long and slow process, making sure that everything is record checked and correct. But slowly and surely, our family tree began to take shape and grow in time, as more people were added.

My mother and one of her siblings started travelling to Ireland to research their father and, with the help of the adoptive Irish cousins, were able to meet their biological family and gain more knowledge and documents about the family, including a family bible and photographs when they visited their great-grandparents' family farm in Tullamore, Ireland.

It is at this point that things started to get more interesting, and we had our first big discovery. We found that some of our Irish family descended from the Sheehan's and the Condon's, who had owned castles in the distant past.

The Condon's had descended from William the Conqueror, and there is a book *The Condon Family of County Waterford* by Christopher Condon, regarding this branch of the family.

One such castle stands in Moorpark, Kilworth, Cloghleagh, and North Cork in Ireland. It is a very tall castle tower made of grey stone, which was the Condon's' stronghold and ancestral home.

This was an exciting find for us all, and we Googled the images of the now ruined castle, which was a shame but no less exciting.

From there my mother carried on working on other parts of the tree for the next few years, with no other mentions of castles, but by this point our tree had reached around 10,000 people and was still climbing – with no sign of stopping.

My mother spent hours poring over various documents, making sure everything she added to the tree was correct, checking birth, death, and marriage certificates as well as wills and censuses. She also studied historical documents from various local parishes and archives, and other research resources.

During this time the tree was growing fast, but it is only within the last couple of years that things started to yet again get very interesting. As she turned her attention back to my maternal grandmother's line, she started to find ancestors with money and/or larger houses than the average person of that time would have had. Wondering where and how these ancestors would have gained these, my mother continued up the tree to see if she could find the source.

It was in 2017 when my mother discovered the surname Bunyan, through her 2nd great-grandparents, William Matthews and Maria Butterfield. The discovery of this surname was through Maria Butterfield's mother, Catherine Bunyan, and led us to the author John Bunyan, our 11th great uncle who wrote the famous book *The Pilgrim's Progress*.

This got us all rather excited, and we bought his books and read up a little information on him, learning that *The Pilgrim's Progress* is regarded as one of the most significant works of religious English literature, and that it has been translated into over 200 languages.

In Bedfordshire there is a John Bunyan Museum dedicated to his life and works, there have also been two film adaptations: *The Pilgrim's Progress* (1978), and *Pilgrim's Progress: Journey to Heaven* (2008), with a further film made in 2019.

A rather sad extract from *The Pilgrim's Progress* describes how his mother Margaret, and later his fourteen year-old sister, who he nursed, died of the plague in 1644 in Elstow. The Queen Elizabeth II speech in 1952 made reference to John Bunyan.

Following up from the Bunyan's took us to John Bunyan's mother Margaret and her Bentley line. Here we came across Captain James Bentley and his father George Bentley ESQ of Monmouth, who married Barbara Watts of Hawkesdale, our 15th great-grandmother.

Continuing up through Barbara's father brings us to the Coningsby line and our very first hint of nobility with our great-grandfather, Sir Ralph Coningsby MP, born 1555.

We ourselves are direct descendants of Sir Humphrey Coningsby (our 20th great-grandfather), of Hampton Court Castle, through Elizabeth Coningsby (1575-1655).

A funny story we came across was of one of our cousins, the 1st Earl Thomas Coningsby, born 1656, which we can relate to very well.

Thomas, who had fought to get back the family estate, had a very special and important room within the castle which he called 'the evidence room' where he kept all of his documents regarding anything and everything family-related. Thomas was also obsessed with the idea that he was descended from royalty, and he wanted to prove this fact.

Unfortunately, the room no longer exists, which is a real shame, as perhaps many of his documents may have helped us in our family search. The reason we can relate to this is due to the number of documents we have acquired in our family research, and we jokingly refer to where we keep ours as 'the evidence room'.

Following up the Coningsby line gives us connections to families such as Throckmorton; Boteler; Frowick; Lewknor; Devereux; Berkley; and Fereby, to name just a few, who lived at Hampton (Court) Castle. We will go into detail in a later book in this series.

The Coningsby's, Matthews, Butterfields and Todd's are related to a great many royal households, including Her Majesty Queen Elizabeth II of England, Northern Ireland, Scotland, and Wales. Many of these historical figures would make a fine television drama – a change from the usual characters you often find in them.

Moving on up further through the line, we come to Lady Elizabeth Frowick, our 18th great-grandmother, born in 1516. She married Sir John Coningsby ESQ, and it is through her line we now carry on briefly.

Lady Elizabeth's father was Lord Mayor Sir Henry Frowyke (another spelling of the name) of London and old Ford Manor, South Mimms. Sir Henry's line takes us to his grandfather, Henry Frowyke of old Ford, who married Eleanor Throckmorton, also spelt Throgmorton.

Eleanor's parents were Mary Margaret Whorwood of Putney and Thomas Throckmorton of Coughton, the MP of Warwickshire. Thomas's great-grandmother was Catherine Anna Parr, her parents the 1st Baron Nicholas Vaux of Harrowden, and his wife Lady Elizabeth Fitzhugh, grandmother to The Queen Consort Catherine Parr.

Through Lady Elizabeth Fitzhugh, her parents 5th Baron Lord Henry Fitzhugh of Ravensworth and his wife Lady Alice

Neville – daughter of the Earl Richard Neville of Salisbury and 5th Countess Lady Alice Montague van Salisbury – this is where things again start to become interesting. If we follow up the Earl Richard Neville's line, we come to his parents Ralph Neville 1st Earl of Westmoreland and his wife Countess Joan Beaufort Plantagenet!

Countess Joan Beaufort, who we are also related to through my mother's great-grandmother Todd's line (the Lundon (Loudoun) line), makes Countess Joan Beaufort our 17th great-grandmother.

At that point, we started getting extremely excited on seeing the name Plantagenet, and we continued up through the tree in silent amazement and shock as we came to John of Gaunt. It is highly controversial as to who his birth father was, and we think it has since been proven that he was not King Edward III's son, however his mother was the granddaughter to King Philip III of France! And we were excited to have found our first royal line!

Having discovered this, my mother was straight onto the phone in utter excitement to her sibling, telling her what she had found, which my aunt couldn't fully believe. In fact, it took them both a little while to get their heads around it, but they soon came around once more royal lines were discovered.

Following on along the French line, King Louis XIV of France is our 4th cousin x12 removed through King Manuel 1st The Fortunate, the great Avis of Portugal and Algarve.

Going back to the Coningsby's, we decided to take on their name as they were the very first royal line we discovered, so we wanted to honour them and their part within history.

Being that this line is mainly MPs, Lords, Barons, and Countesses, it was a lot easier to find information about them and our ancestral home. Many of the MPs we could find on the History of Parliament's website, but we were also able to find records and documents at the British Library, The National

Archives, and Parliament, when we made trips to London to look at these very old records.

Looking at the records themselves in person was an amazing experience, knowing that our ancestors had touched as well as written these very papers. Reading these documents and personal letters gave us a clear insight into their lives and to what their lives entailed.

We also learnt of the infamous Coningsby temper that was well known by fellow members of Parliament.

Through our great-grandmother's line, we discovered that our 9th great-grandfather was John Tinker, the Captain of *Saint Andrew's* ship. He was not to be the last in this occupation, but this line brought us down to the Dean of Westminster Abbey, Arthur Penrhyn Stanley.

Having found information, we headed back up to London on another family heritage hunting trip to Westminster Abbey. We had been wanting to go for a little while knowing that many of our relatives are buried there including, Sir Isaac Newton our 4th cousin x10 removed.

We managed to get to Westminster Abbey just in time before they closed, but there was still quite a long queue waiting to get in. Unfortunately, we didn't have enough time to look at St Margaret's Church, where there is a stained-glass window commemorating the marriage of King Henry VIII and Catherine of Aragon.

Sir Winston Churchill was also married here, and it is also where he brought the House of Commons to pray for thanksgiving for the end of the Second World War.

Once we had conquered the queue and taken a few pictures of the Abbey, we finally made it inside where it was rather packed and continued our quest of finding relatives who are buried there.

We slowly made our way around and excitedly whispered to each other when we found another relative, as it was incredibly silent inside the Abbey. As we made our way around past Earl Edmund's cross, back to our 28th great-grandfather, we came to one of the partially closed-off sections. Going inside, we found more relatives.

In one of these sections around the Abbey, we were reading the text on the marble stone of one of our relatives when we got a little curious as to whether it was really marble. We had already noticed that there were no signs to say that you couldn't touch anything, so we gently touched it.

It was at this moment that a rather rude lady in the crowd shouted very loudly, 'Don't touch!' That made a few people around, including us, jump, bearing in mind that the whole Abbey was silent, as many people were wearing headsets. She was not an employee of the Abbey so we were confused about why she did this.

After having made our way around the entire building and visiting all the chapels, there was one particular person we were having a hard time locating.

We spotted a clergyman – a verger – and we enquired to where Dean Stanley's effigy would be. He then took us to the back of the Abbey where, in a corner, stood Dean Arthur Stanley's resting place. We were permitted by one of the vergers to take a photograph due to being family.

The verger told us a few interesting facts about Dean Stanley, who was the dean from 1864 to 1881. He was incredibly passionate about the Abbey and his work, he was the author of *The Historical Memorials of Westminster Abbey*. A full account of all the tombs and memorials in the Abbey was first published in 1867.

The verger asked if we would like to walk down the central aisle, which was currently closed to the public. We eagerly agreed, and we were in awe whilst we were walking down the aisle, especially when suddenly the grand organ started to play and echoed around the cathedral before we reached the Throne of Britain.

CHAPTERS

CHAPTER ONE

THE MATTHEWS' HISTORY

Our grandfather George Matthews was the second of four children born to George Matthews and Lucy Alice Todd, his birth was on a cold London winter's day in 1918, during the time of the First World War.

His younger brother, John, later emigrated to South Africa before 1947, to pan for gold and invest in diamond mines. He and his young children would often go to the mountains, where there were lions and many other wild beasts. Upon speaking to relatives, it sounds as though John was something of an Indiana Jones-type of character.

Their births were from the direct descendent line of the Earls of Llandaff and the Lords of Cardigan.

The Matthews have a lengthy recorded genealogy as an ancient Welsh landed family, directly descended from the Earls of Llandaff and the Lords of Cardigan. Their pedigree even carries back to King Gwaythooed of Cardigan (Ceredigion), whose recorded coat of arms displayed one lion sable regardant.

During the fourteenth century, the Matthews family held posts as seneschals – a steward or principal administrator in a royal or noble household.

There are many notable characters descending from this branch, including Cecilia Matthews, heiress to the Hensol fortune, and who married 1st Baron Charles Talbot. Their descendants produced the current 8th Earl Thomas Frances Dermot Pakenham-Tyson of Longford; Baroness Caroline Elizabeth Anne Rice-Trevor Bateson of Deramore; ESQ Daniel Matthews of Clandon Park; 5th Viscount William George

Monckton-Arundell of Galway, and Hon. Judge James Mathews Griggs.

This line also produced Jane Elizabeth Austin Lefroy (1793-1872), an author and the daughter of Jane Austin's nephew, the Reverend James Leigh Austin, and our tenth distant cousin Anne Matthews. Jane spent a lot of time with her famous aunt.

Other relatives of note include pioneer Nancy Josephine Cooper *(nee Ham)*; inventors Harry Grindell Matthews and Gordon Matthews, actors Alfred Edward Matthews, Lester Matthews, and Jessie Matthews; and several sporting legends and artists.

One ancestor was the 5th-century founder and progenitor of the royal dynasty of the North Welsh kingdom of Gwynedd (Edinburgh), King Cunedda Wledig, who originated in Manaw Gododdin in South Central Scotland (Firth Area). Land in Wales was a reward in return for ousting Irish raiders he had invaded, and he settled along the Welsh coastline in the 4th century.

King Cunedda's paternal ancestors were Roman, including Padarn Beisrudd. Paternus, a latinised version of his name. He was more famously known as 'of the scarlet robe' and his family possibly ruled the north of Hadrian's wall. His father Tegid ap Lago, born in A.D. 400, was most likely a high-ranking Roman officer – to which his red robe suggests – in command of now Scotland. Padarn descendants became the early Welsh kings of Gwynedd, and include Isabel of Mar, wife to King of Scotland, Robert the Bruce.

His maternal grandmother is thought to have been the granddaughter of Conan Meriadoc, heir to the Welsh King Eudaf Hens.

The Llandaff senior line was quietly Royalist, which later then became Whig within politics. This descends down to our 15th great grandfather, Lord Dafydd Matthews – a well-known Marcher Lord of his time.

LORD DAFYDD MATTHEWS (1400-1484)

Lord Dafydd of Llandaff was born in 1400 at Llandaff Court, and was one of four sons. His father, Mathau Ableuan, was a follower of an unsuccessful leader, Owain Glyndwr, against the English rule. Their revolt failed, but Sir Mathau *(Mathew)* was pardoned, and the family retained Llandaff in Cibwr holdings. Upon his death, he left his inheritance in property which was divided between his sons. Welsh inheritance believed that properties and money should be divided equally amongst both legitimate and illegitimate children, unlike the English where only the eldest son inherited.

This branch of the family dominated South Wales from the Medieval times down to the Tudor era.

When Lord Dafydd was a small child, he witnessed an unsuccessful revolt that involved his father, and the success of English power. As an adult, he became a Welsh knight and a Marcher Lord. Marcher Lords were the strategy used by William the Conquer for the English-Welsh borders. Marcher Lords, or Marquis as they came to be called, had the palatine powers of a minor king where they enjoyed special privileges from those that were Earls or Barons. These privileges included the right to hold court, build castles, and raise armies.

He was also a key supporter of both King Richard II and King Edward IV, and part of his role would include receiving a summons to arms only from the King.

There is a description of Lord Dafydd, describing him to be very tall – 6ft 7 inches, when at the time an average male was around 5ft 5 – with a strapping build, broad-shouldered, black hair, and a long, thin face. Our grandfather was similar in build and structure – not as tall, but did have the characteristic long face. Dafydd was reputed to be a man of such splendid build and stature that he was even able to use a two-handed sword with amazing power.

Dafydd married Gwendoline Herbert, a descendent from the Earls of Pembroke, in 1428. Her first cousin was Sir William ap Thomas, otherwise known as the Blue Knight of Gwent.

They had one surviving daughter and seven sons that founded several cadet branches.

He owned 2,232 acres of land from King Henry VI in St Fagans, and from Earl William of Pembroke, lands in Pentyrch, Wales. He also had lands in Llandaff, Canton, Ely, Coity, and Cardiff amongst others. With Sir John Neville, another Marcher Lord, he received conjointly the grant of the crown, Manors of Glaspool and Peteron-on-Ely, during the reign of Henry VII. When King Edward IV reigned, he further received a gift of lands.

Dafydd was an eminent military leader of his day and a zealous supporter of the Yorkist white rose cause during the War of the Roses. The white rose stands for the briar rose, rose of the field, symbolising a flower from the old roots of British royalty to which the Plantagenet dynasty and Saxon lines descend. Lord Dafydd was one of the ten great barons in Glamorgan and also the seneschal of Llandaff Cathedral.

As the grand standard bearer to a central figure, King Edward II, he was at the battle of Towton Palm on Sunday, the 29th March, 1461, during the war of the Roses. Although now a much older gentleman in his sixties, he saved the life of the eighteen year-old King Edward IV, also known as the Earl of March.

A grand standard bearer was once an important office to hold within the army when monarchs fought on the battlefield.

The Battle of Towton was one of the biggest, bloodiest battles of Britain, and took place during a snowstorm on a windy, bitterly cold day; with some 70 thousand men. The average age of the fighting men was mid-twenties to late thirties. The 28 thousand casualties that day left a bridge of bodies which the Lancastrians fled over at the end of the battle.

King Edward IV was grateful and showed his appreciation by awarding Dafydd the title of Knight Banneret and granted him the use of the word Towton as an augmentation over the Matthews' family crest following the Towton battle. He became known as one of the most distinguished men of his age.

Lord Dafydd's younger brother, Sir William, was knighted by King Henry VII after the Battle of Bosworth.

His other brother Robert's 7th great granddaughter, Cecilia Matthews, married 1st Baron Charles Talbot of Hensol. Cecilia became the heir to the Hensol estates; the titles went first to their son William, and then to their granddaughter 2nd Baroness Cecil Rice of Dynevor. Their descendants also include the current 10th Baron Hugo Griffith Rice of Dyvenor.

It is said Lord Dafydd was the fourth great-grandson of King Louis VI of France – a line we are still researching.

When the use of surnames came about, the Welsh commonly took the first name of their fathers and added 'S' to create a surname.

Dafydd was one of the first Welsh barons to adopt the English system of surnames. The Welsh used 'AP' (*originally map*) 'AB' 'FERCH' followed by the father's first name, and even sometimes including the grandfather's name.

Lord Dafydd Llandaff took his father's first name Matthew and made it into the adopted surname 'Matthews'. His descendent line in the mid-seventeenth century to modern day, including our grandfather. used the surname spelt Matthews.

There are other alternative spellings of this surname which are Mathew and the French alternative Mathieu. The 's' indicates the 'son of' The Matthew name is derived from the Hebrew given name 'Mattathiah' which translated means 'the gift of the Lord' – a given name to Christ's ancestors, although our research does not evidently prove or disprove this.

Within Llandaff Cathedral, they once had their own family Matthews chapel at the far end of the north aisle. Nowadays, it is renamed The Dyfrig Chapel and contains further effigies, along with tombs and a stained-glass window showing the Welsh King Arthur and King Tewdric, his grandfather. Nearby lies Lord Dafydd's effigy near the high altar, measuring 6ft and 7 inches, representing his true-life size in full battle armour.

His younger brother Sir William Matthews and his wife Jeanette Stradling lie in a large, early Tudor tomb, decorated with shields of the Matthews' family and effigies of him and his wife. The tomb also bares the Cardiff arms: Gules with three chevrons argent, also a variant of the last King Iestyn ap Gwrgan of Glamorgan, and the arms of Iestyn (also linking to the family of Penhurst Place), reverse of the last King of Glamorgan arms.

The Mathew/Matthews clearly showed them being descendants of the Kings of Glamorgan.

Near Llandaff Castle there once stood the ancient mansion of the family of Matthew of Llandaff; it was once called Bryn-y-gynen, but later become Llandaff Court.

In 1578, Lord Dafydd's son Rymborn Matthew was in possession of Bryn-y-gynnen, which was built in the fifteenth century; it was very similar in size to St Fagan's Castle that stands today.

In the year 1849, the Bishop of Llandaff made it his home. Bishop's Palace became Bishop's Court and later Llandaff Court; it stands a short distance away to the south of Llandaff Cathedral *(Church of the Taff)*. According to the mediaeval heritage for Wales, in the 16th century the castle was leased by the Bishops of Llandaff to the family of Mathew of Radyr. In 1596 the building was taken by Edmond Mathew, the High Sheriff of Glamorgan 1592.

The castle was sold at the beginning of the 17th century when Edmond had debts and other troubles. Unfortunately, the site of the ancient manor house is now occupied by The Cathedral School.

The senior Matthews' branch was seated at Llandaff, whilst the junior branch was at the Radyr seat. Lord Dafydd's brother Robert founded the Castell y Mynach branch, leading to the Talbot line.

One of Dafydd's eldest sons, Reinborn, held Llandaff Court, this stayed the family seat and within the line of descendants, including Admiral Thomas Matthew. Llandaff Court and estate were ruined by the time it reached Thomas Matthew (1741-182), and later Llandaff Court was left to his wife's nephew.

Lord Dafydd's other son, Thomas, was the custodian of St Telios relics, and founder of the Radyr branch. He passed his lands to his son Sir William Matthews, who was knighted at the Battle of Bosworth by King Henry VII. Sir William also accompanied the King to the field of Cloth of Gold. Sir William's descendant and successor was George Matthew (d.1636), who sold the Radyr estate and then emigrated to Thurles, Tipperary in Ireland.

This branch ended with George Matthew (a common name) who died in 1760. George left both his Irish and Welsh estates to kinsman The First Viscount, Thomas Matthew of Llandaff (d.1777) of Anne field House.

His son and heir, Francis Matthew I (1738-1806) of Thurles Castle, was created Baron Llandaff in 1797. His son and heir was Francis James Matthew II (1768-1833), but on his death the titles became extinct. During his life, he sold the Glamorgan estates in 1818. Most of the estates were brought by Sir Samuel Romilly, and part was conveyed to Anthony Matthew of Ty Mawr, Cardiff (d.1825), an agent of the Llandaff estate and kinsman of the Earl who died without issue and named his niece Elizabeth *(nee John)* his heir.

The Record Tower at Dublin, Vol VII P18, under funeral entries, names the founder of the Irish branch of the family as George Matthewes, Oct 1670.

Admiral Thomas Mathew, a descendant of George, of Llandaff Court.

Later, this branch of the family then changed the spelling of their surname to Matthew. This change took place between the 2nd Earl of Llandaff and his descendants, due to the title of Llandaff being denied to the Reverend Arnold Harris Ochterlony Mathew (AKA 4th Earl), as the surname they had been using was not spelt Matthews.

COAT OF ARMS: There are two different coats of arms that are recorded as being used by the Matthews' family. Both consist of lion rampant argent, but with differing tinctures. Adopted in honour of the white rose.

CREST: A blackcock proper, field cock (grouse family) or known as a heath cock, Moorcock (a partridge of the pheasant family).

SUPPORTERS: These are two unicorns, collared and chained. The original armorial bearing of the old sable lion of Gwaithvoed.

MOTTO: *Y Fyn Duw A Fydd*. The translation – 'What God willeth will be.'

CHIEF SEAT: Llandaff Court.

HEIRLOOM: Before the Battle of Hastings in 1066, the Matthews' family became guardians of Saint Teilo Skull. The skull was handed down for seven generations, carrying with it a tradition going back to the early church and practices. The body or any part of a saint was a high-status important object back in that era.

Saints were members of the ruling class. Married men with families of the regional dynasties. The church's 'clasau' was more like a college where the children of nobility could attend for an education. They were founded by family-run businesses and therefore classed as processions, and when a founder died the ownership passed to the next heir. Welsh inheritance was passed equally between children, illegitimate or not. Unlike the English system, where the oldest son would inherit. Llandaff Cathedral was founded by King Lucius (Lleirwg) but rebuilt by Saint Teilo.

Saint Teilo was born in Penalun around the year 500, but may have been later. He was one of the first bishops associated with the founding of the original diocese of Llandaff in Wales. In the late twelfth century he was recognised as a patron of Llandaff, and during his lifetime he may have been known (in old Welsh) as Eilliau. He lived in Brittany for several years during the time of the yellow plague, which lasted over 25 years. The disease was called this due to the jaundiced appearance it caused within its host.

When he returned, he lived in Dumnonia, now known as Devon, and planted fruit groves which became known as the groves of Teilo. Throughout his lifetime he became one of the most venerated men in Wales, and died around the 9th February, 560 or later, according to records in Llandaff Fawr. Upon his death, Teilo's body was said to miraculously become three identical bodies.

During these times, Saints served as the landlords of a community and guaranteed rights including property and privileges of territories and of bishops. Upon their death, these were passed to the holder of the relics (relics being body parts). However, there was confusion and competition from other foundations to claim the body of its founder. With St Teilo's body, it was claimed by three different foundations; They were Llandaff Cathedral; Llandeilo Fawr; and Penally Abbey. It was therefore very important for Llandaff to acquire the relics of Teilo.

The new tomb of St Teilo would have flanked the high altar on the south side, but the new church that had begun construction in April 1120 was not yet ready to receive the relics, so they had to be placed in an old church.

St Teilo's relics within the cathedral were said to have been accompanied by many miracles. The relics were tested by placing them in water before the altar where water began to boil, assuring their validity. The possession of relics was important for the esteem and power of the clergy to be shown. Whoever possessed the relics was most likely to receive St Teilo's favours. The vitae of St Teilo were probably the result of the struggle between him and St David and Llandaff in the eleventh century.

In 1480, Lord Dafydd restored the shrine of Saint Teilo, which had been pillaged and desecrated by a gang of pirates from Biston. Dafydd was presented the Teilo Skull by Bishop Marshall as a reward for his service. Set in a costly reliquary, it became the Matthews' family heirloom, and it was carefully preserved for over 200 years until the death of William Matthews in Llandeilo in 1658. William, in his will, left the skull to the Melchoir family – St Teilo's well was part of their farm land in Llandeilo – where it remained for many years. The water was said to treat chest complaints and more, if drunk out of the skull. An elderly Melchoir woman at the time the family acquired the skull was thought to say a curse came with the Saint Teilo skull, in which she repeated:

'Misfortune will fall on the house of Matthew for over 200 years and then the skull of St Teilo will be restored to the last male of the line, and their luck will turn again, and those that kept the skull will get a double blessing. He who restores the skull to the Matthews will see St Teilo's, the bishop, riding on a pure white stag. St Teilo will bless their apple trees so their next bearing will be very vast.'

A branch of the family had emigrated to South Wales, Australia, and they had the skull restored to them in 1927.

They were the eighth-generation descendants of Lord Dafydd's brother, Robert of Castell Y Mynych, who had emigrated to County Antrim Ireland in 1599.

Sir Arthur Keith, a Fellow of the Royal College of Surgeons, examined the skull and stated it was of Welsh origin, and of a small man of between 50 and 60 years of age. The Bishop of Rochester archive holds a collection of papers relating to St Teilo's Skull.

On the 9th February, 1994, during Sung Eucharist on St Teilo's Day, the Dean of Llandaff the Very Reverend John Rogers presented the skull to the cathedral from Capt. Robert Matthews – the hereditary keeper – where it was placed in a reliquary in St Teilo's Chapel.

We did wonder why the skull was a hereditary heirloom to our Matthews' family, so after further research we came across a shared ancestor to both St Teilo and our Matthews' family, The Over High (Gwledig) King Cunedda of Cardigan was our 39th great-grandfather, but he was also St Teilo's sixth great-grandfather, making St Teilo a distant cousin.

King Cunedda was the progenitor of the royal dynasty of Gwynedd. It is also believed his grandfather was one of the greatest Roman historians and politicians, Saint Padarn Beisrudd, 'Tacitus' of the Scarlet Robe. Tacitus wrote many major works such as The Annals, along with The Histories.

This dynasty's descendants include King Henry VII's great-granddaughter Katheryn Tudor of Berain and her descendants, the notable Salusbury family; it was using this hereditary fact that King Henry VIII made his claim to the throne. The British Library holds a large number of Welsh genealogy records, including this information.

When a noble family, the Gammage-Turbervilles of Coity Castle, Neath (Catell-Nedd), became embroiled in a land quarrel causing a riot in 1484, Lord Dafydd– now in his eighties but still a vigorous knight – rode to Neath to aid in straightening out the matter. Browne Willis states in *A Survey of the Cathedral-Church of Llandaff*' that Lord Dafydd was murdered by the Turberville family during the altercation.

Lord Dafydd's effigy was ornamented with his full-length figure in alabaster, and lies in St Mary's Chapel in the Cathedral of Llandaff. The Matthews' Chapel was once part of the Llandaff Cathedral due to its links, and today it is known as St. Dyfrig Chapel and still contains various monuments and two tombs of the family that can be found within the building.

The Radyr branch of the Matthews' family comes through the descendant of Lord Dafydd's fourth son Thomas, who was politically and at times actively Roman Catholic. It is this branch that emigrated to Thomastown Castle, Ireland, and is also where the infamous second curse and witchcraft come into play.

Thomastown Castle had been the property of the Augustinian Abbey of Athassel until 1558. It was then granted to Earl Thomas of Ormond by Mary Tudor.

George Matthew, 1670, built a two-storey classical mansion of pink brick on the Thomastown property in 1786, which was described as an ancient but handsome edifice, whilst further additions were made. The heir of Lady Elizabeth Matthew, Viscount Chabot Major Louis Charles Guillaume De Rohan-Chabot, Comte De Jarnac (1780-1875), was recorded living there in the mid-19th century, and by then it was a gothic castle, designed by Richard Morrison. The property was held in fee, and the buildings at that time were valued at £100.

Thomas was born on the 10th October, 1790, at Thomastown Castle, near Golden, County Tipperary. He and his brother, James, were great-great-grandchildren of ESQ. George Matthews and Lady Elizabeth Poyntz-Butler of Thurles. Lady Elizabeth was also the mother to the great 1st Duke James Butler of Ormonde, from her first marriage. We have seen portrait paintings of Thomas Matthews displaying a chin dimple, which seems to be a Matthews' trait and something shared with us and other living descendants. It also includes, from the past, Admiral Thomas Matthews who we will speak about further in this book.

Father Theobald's grandmother was the niece of the celebrated General Matthews, who is mentioned in *The Life of Swift* by Sheridan. They lost their parents at a young age, leaving them to be adopted by distant relatives, and he was then tutored by the parish priest Reverend Dennis O'Donnell of Tallagh in Waterford. When he reached the age of 13, he then attended the lay school, St Canice's Academy at Kilkenny, until the age of 20, continuing his ecclesiastical studies at Maynooth College, and later joined the Capuchin Order in Dublin and was ordained on Easter Sunday 1814 in Dublin by Archbishop Murray. A rescript sent by Pope Gregory XVI, he received the degree of Doctor in Divinity along with a dispensation to possess property. To the poor, he became their counsellor, friend, treasurer, and executor.

Where no Catholic education system existed, he organised schools, industrial classes, a library, and benefit societies. He was appointed Provincial of the Capuchin Order in 1828 for the next 23 years.

One day, Father Theobald met a neighbour on the road, and whilst they were speaking two men passed them by in a trap. One of the men was wearing torn clothing and the other a suit full of patches. 'Who do you think is the poorest?' Father Theobold asked the neighbour.

The answer was the man with a suit full of patches. Draw your own conclusion as to what you think is the reasoning behind his answer.

Theobald gave the poor all that he owned, and he was able to obtain a long lease of the Botanic Gardens for a cemetery for the thousands of the poor who died of cholera in 1832.

He also provided relief and consolation for the poor in their last, dying hours. Reverend Theobald's family were extensively connected to the wine and spirit trade, did not complain, yet founded Father Mathew with large sums. Rev Theobald started the total Abstinence Association, and within five months there were over 130,000 signed names in Cork. Theobald was not only an Irish Catholic priest and teetotalism reformer, but was also known as the Apostle of Temperance. His fame travelled to Kerry and Limerick and many other towns, where crowds in their thousands attended his sermons just to touch his garment. He visited Lancashire, Yorkshire, London, Liverpool, Manchester, and Glasgow, where his fame became synonymous with over 600,000 people. Father Matthew viewed both Catholics and Protestants as equals, where religion did divide them.

During the Irish potato famine of 1845, Father Mathew tried to warn the government of what was impending. He organised societies for collecting and distributing food, spending £600 (which is over £36,000 in today's money) a month. Over two thousand people died in Ireland in just two years. During 1849, he went to America, travelling to New York, Boston, Washington, and New Orleans – just some of the 25 states he visited, reaching more than 7,000,000 with his pledge.

Queen Victoria's admitted that while she admired Father Mathew's crusade, she did not wish to be the patron of anyone who relied upon 'superstition'.

Father Mathew suffered a stroke in 1852, and after suffering from ill health, died four years later.

His eternal resting place is in his own cemetery, beneath the cross in Queenstown, Ireland.

Bronze and marble statues of Father Mathew were erected in his honour – in St Patrick's Street in Cork, and O'Connell Street, Dublin. although this statue is being moved to a new

14

location to facilitate alignment for transport. There is also a Father Matthew's Bridge in Limerick City. In Cork there is a memorial hall, and a Holy Trinity Church stands on Father Matthew's Quay – all commissioned by him. Today, Dublin publishes a monthly magazine 'The Father Mathew Record'.

CHAPTER TWO

THE EARLS OF LLANDAFF WITH TWO CURSES AND WITCHCRAFT

THE CURSE AND WITCHCRAFT

There are three stories that we have come across in our research, involving a young child drowning at Thomastown Castle. The first story involved witchcraft and a second curse on the Matthews' family.

Having extensively researched the curse and witchcraft involved, we surmise that three separate incidents/stories have been intertwined into one. The first account is the most likely, with some details that may include extracts from the second account. The years go by, and things can be misconstrued, which would include the death of the little girl in the first story being misremembered.

The First Tale:

The Matthew family accused a young English nanny they employed of witchcraft in the death of their young family member. It is believed the child belonged to Reverend Theobald Matthew's brother James and his wife Charity Cherry Pennefather. They at the time were living at the nearby Rathcloheen. That evening, the nanny was not in charge to look after the two-year-old little girl, leaving the child in the sole care of her mother. The family stated a sleeping spell was cast upon the mother to make her fall asleep.

The little girl, who must have wandered, was found drowned in one of the very fancy fountains on the grounds of Thomastown Castle. A judge, who happened to also be a family friend, was fetched from Cork and found the nanny guilty and condemned her to be burnt at the stake, on the estate grounds, in 1831.

This was the curse she said as she burned, according to Burgess Bartlett's book:

Eye of newt and tongue of thieves

To throw to burn, we have none of these.

Just a frenzy of rage and ire.

With these alone, we conspire

First, the family Mathews beguiled

Not one of them to raise a child.

The second curse on their golden health,

And is to never realise their family wealth.

There have been other tragedies that are believed to have taken place at Thomastown Castle –including one involving Charity's sister, Hortense, who died falling out of the castle ballroom window in 1881.

The Second Tale with two accounts:

Both tales involve a small boy within their stories.

The first account is from the Dublin Society, that was sent to us upon request. It is recorded that an elderly lady gave an account regarding a small boy called Johnnie O'Hara, an heir to an estate. Part of Johnnie's daily routine was for his nurse to take him out for a morning walk. The story unfolded that this one particular morning she took him out by the lake, where she threw a ball into the water and the child followed it and drowned.

The nurse then went back to the castle and told the mother, who rushed down the steps of the castle and knelt with her bare knees on the gravel, raising her hands to heaven, and cursed Thomastown Castle that there would never be an heir to the castle. The reason given for such a despicable act was that the nurse was bribed to drown him in a lake near the castle; which we can only assume was for money.

The second account:

We came across a book called *Father Theobald Mathew, The Apostle of Temperance,* and inside there was an account written on page 140. It described the grandson of George Mathew, who was heir to Thomastown Castle and all the estates. The year was 1738, and at the tender age of five years, he drowned in the lake on Thomastown estate. With his death came the end of the Thomastown branch. His uncle, George of Thurles Castle, succeeded him in the inheritance, uniting all properties and estates of Thurles, Thomastown, Radyr, and Llandaff. This in turn made the Thurles' descendent line the senior line of the Mathews' family.

Our 9th cousin, the 1st Earl Francis Matthews of Llandaff, under the Peerage of Ireland, was heir to his father, 1st Viscount Thomas Matthews of Llandaff, MP of Tipperary. Francis was one of six children, which included his sister, Lady Elizabeth – the last direct heir within this branch. His father Thomas had inherited the properties through the death of his five-year-old nephew George.

The estates were worth £40,000 a year, which in today's money approximately £1,762,916,000.

Upon his death in 1833, he devolved everything to his only surviving sibling Lady Elizabeth Matthew, an eccentric individual.

In turn, according to the Landed Estates, in her will she bequeathed her inheritance to her cousin – a French nobleman, Viscount De Chabot in 1842 – despite having a son, Capt. William Matthews, Elizabeth died in the same year the Morpeth Roll was presented to George Howard, leaving her only near relative not only provided for, but appointing him the executor of her will of the ancestral property. You could say due to the extensive debts owed, it may have been more helpful to him.

Lady Elizabeth had inherited from her brother, the 2nd Earl Francis James Matthews, as his only living sibling. James is also recorded to have had ownership of townlands in the parish of Kilfeacle and Barony of Clan William.

In the *Ordnance Survey Name Books of 1840*, the daughter of the 1st Earl Francis Matthews of Llandaff, Lady Elizabeth, had an illegitimate son – Captain William Fitzwilliam Matthews – by the Prince Regent and the future King George IV of the United Kingdom. We can estimate his birth was about 1816, following the Prince's trip to Ireland. Unfortunately, William died before he was 40, and no records are found for any children.

This is on the record for Lord Viscount's testimonial roll of 1841 relating to Thurles, Ireland, and the birth of Capt. William Matthews.

There were substantial mortgages on all the estates amounting to £104,200. (In today's money a value of £10,875,870.26.)

On the Thurles estate, there was a mortgage of £36,200 with approx. 1,713 acres of land, and on the Thomastown estate of 2,378 acres a mortgage of £38,000 alone.

The total annual rents expected only amounted to a small annual amount of £4,500.

Viscount De Chabot stayed for 17 years and eventually sold the estates later to the Daly family in 1859. The Daly's are relations of Lady Elizabeth Matthews through her maternal side, and

Thomastown Castle was then later bought by the Rt. Reverend V. Mathew, then came into possession of another branch of the family, the Dawsons.

SISTER HANORA 'NANO' NAGLE (1718-1784)

Sister Hanora was our distant eighth cousin and the great-great granddaughter of Captain George Matthew and his wife, Lady Elizabeth Poyntz-Butler of Thurles. Lady Elizabeth Poyntz-Butler was the 9th great-grandmother of Queen Elizabeth II, through her mother's ancestral line, and also Princess Diana's eleventh great-grandmother through Princess Diana's grandmother's Hamilton ancestral line. Lady Elizabeth held properties of over 4,000 acres, including Thurles Castle, which were seized under the new penal laws of Cromwell. When King Charles II came to the throne, all properties were restored back to Lady Elizabeth.

At the time, Catholics were forcibly suppressed by lack of education and travelling for education under the Penal Laws, and breaking these laws would result in a prison sentence.

Hanora had a privileged childhood but witnessed severe poverty around her. After the deaths of her parents and sister, Hanora made the needs of the poor her 'life's work', joining a convent in Paris, but found she had hardly any communication with the poor. Hanora felt her mission was to enrich the Catholic poor's lives for the better by giving them access to education to enable them to have better lives. She felt returning home to live with her brother Joseph was where she could make a difference.

Hanora opened a secret school in the 1750s that taught girls the basic subjects of education,

And within ten years she had founded seven schools for all children across Cork, Ireland.

In the poorly lit evenings after the school day, Hanora would visit the city's poor where the crime was rife.

In 1771, from an inheritance from her uncle, Hanora was able to build the Ursuline Sisters' convent, which you can visit today, along with the museum and tomb of Hanora in the beautiful bustling city of Cork. It tells Hanora's story, celebrating her life, work, and vision.

ADMIRAL THOMAS MATTHEWS (1676-1751)

Thomas was the eldest son of ESQ Edward Matthews and his wife Jane Armstrong, born in Llandaff Court, Wales, in October 1676. Llandaff Court was the family seat for many generations. Thomas was a distant fifth cousin of ours and led a very interesting life, but let's first start with his grandfather, MP Sir Thomas Armstrong. He had quite the reputation, having been part of a plot to seize Chester Castle in 1655, and at first a great supporter of King Charles II. In August 1675, he was reported to have killed the son of a lady-in-waiting of Queen Catherine at a London theatre; his plea to this was that his opponent drew first, to which he was given a pardon.

Sir Thomas was a great supporter of King Charles II and would carry funds on behalf of 20th Earl Aubrey De Vere of Oxford to deliver to King Charles in exile.

Thomas Armstrong was found guilty for high treason and imprisoned for a year, before later being hung, drawn, and quartered on Friday, 20th June, 1684, at Tyburn, being a partaker in the Rye House plot of 1683 against King Charles II and his brother James, Duke of York. It was quite a gruesome death being hung for at least half an hour; then he was cut down, emasculated, and his head cut off to be held up to the people to be shown as a traitor. His heart and bowels were then removed from his body and thrown into the flames. His body was further quartered into four. His head was destined for Newgate to be disposed according to His Majesty's wishes. It was affixed at Westminster Hall, whilst his remaining bodily parts went to other places, including Stafford. Further information on Sir Thomas Armstrong's execution can be found from *The Curiosities of Street Literature*, p168, by Charles Hindley.

Thomas started his naval carer in 1690 under his uncle Sir Francis Whelern on board the HMS *Abemarle* ship. The seafarer's life was extremely harsh, with poor pay, very cramped conditions, disease, and poor food in the form of a ship-style biscuit and consisting of salt beef, pork, cheese, fish, and ale. Vermin such as rats were present on board, and punishments included being tarred and feathered, which was being tied to a rope, swung overboard, ducked into the water, and then dragged underneath the ship. Another form of punishment was being flogged by the cat o' nine tails in front of all the crew, but the most extreme punishment was being hung from the yard arm.

We found it interesting that Sir Francis Wheler was Thomas's uncle. Sir Francis had several children, including a daughter married to the 2nd Viscount Henry Hood. One of their children was Samuel Hood, who we will explain more in depth later with our 4th great-grandfather ESQ. Admiral William Butterfield.

We do wonder if Thomas crossed paths or even knew our 4th great-grandfather, Admiral William Butterfield, being such close connections. William, like Thomas, spent time at Chatham dockyard in Kent.

Thomas rose to become Captain of his own ship by 1703, seeing service by racing to Scotland to prevent Claude de

Forbin-Gardanne's Dunkirk fleet landing a Franco-Jacobite invasion. This was an attempt to get James Stuart – 'The Old Pretender' – back on the throne, to take part in the conquest of Nova Scotia, and capture the Port Royal. His conflicts included the Battle of Cape Passaro in August 1718, where he captured *San Carlos* and its Admiral. Other missions included the ridding of the pirates in the East Indies, who harnessed the East India Company. Upon his arrival in the Port of Bombay, he quarrelled over who he should salute first: the ship or the fort.

Other services included the nine years of war and Spanish succession, including Toulon.

Thomas faced a court martial in 1724, being deprived of four months' pay for charges of disallowed merchandise on a Navy ship, and he retired to Llandaff Court where he continued shore-based civilian employment as commissioner at Chatham dockyard from 1736 to 1742.

Part of Thomas's fleet was the HMS *Stirling Castle,* of which Admiral William Butterfield had also taken command in a different year.

Thomas then returned to active Naval service after the outbreak of war with Spain. His promotion on return was to Vice Admiral of the Red on the 13th March, 1741, when he took command of a fleet of 38, while on HMS *Namur* in the Mediterranean in 1742.

Thomas was also given an appointment as a plenipotentiary to King Charles to visit Emmanuel III of Sardinia and other Italian states. His appointed second in command was Rear Admiral Richard Lestock. The two men had served together at Chatham dockyard where Richard had commanded the guard ships. This was not a good idea, as Thomas and Richard had not been on good terms at the dockyard. Part of Thomas's role was to rely upon Richard in managing the fleet, but working together exacerbated tensions, and performing delicate diplomatic duties was difficult.

One such example of this was at the Battle of Toulon with a Franco-Spanish fleet. Between the evenings of 22nd-23rd February, light winds had caused the ships to spread out. Thomas had given a signal to the fleet to form a line northwest but the circumstances were fraught with confusion, with poor communications along with a breakdown of the chain of command.

Richard instead commanded the rear obeyed to halt by turning in the wind southwest without forming the line, which separated the fleet considerably in distance. Thomas, with his ships not organised, was reluctant to start an attack until Richard was in the line, but Richard was slow to respond to Thomas's further signal to make more sail, giving the Franco-Spanish the opportunity to escape. The two signals caused further confusion, causing some vessels to follow Thomas's instructions and some not. It allegedly pleased Richard to see Thomas in great difficulty, and he refused to obey further orders and stated he could not understand them.

The French came to aid the Spanish fleet and with Thomas giving no clear instructions or any more orders, the line broke which resulted in several of the fleet sustaining damage, along with the loss of one vessel and the enemies escaping. Thomas tried to give chase after the Spanish but was unsuccessful, and so his fleet returned to Hyeres.

Thomas's fleet retreating left the Mediterranean Sea temporarily under Spanish control, giving the Spanish the advantage in the war. Shortly after returning from this mission, Thomas resigned and went back to the country life of Llandaff Court, building a new house to replace the old one he had instructed to be pulled down during his absence.

The victory escaping them resulted in a court-martial and the House of Commons petitioning King George II for a public inquiry in 1746, lasting over a year. The charges were of having taken the fleet into action in a disorganised manner, then fleeing the enemy and not taking advantage of the conditions.

Thomas was being described in terms as choleric – in other words easily angered and ill-tempered. This is a trait the Matthews' family are known for.

Whig man 4th Earl Horace Walpole of Orford, speaking in a House of Commons debate during Horace Walpole's inquiry in 1745 stated: 'Matthews remains in the light of a hot, brave, imperious, dull, and confused fellow.'

A John Bull-type character, in fact. In a letter to Sir Horace Mann, by 4th Earl Horace Walpole of Orford, wrote 'Matthews believes that providence lives upon beef and pudding, loves prize fighting and bull baiting, and drinks fog to the health of old England.'

Others described him as being warm-hearted, kind and affectionate, a keen sportsman and capable farmer, and just as importantly, a clear-sighted magistrate.

Sir Horace Mann wrote: 'Tis wonderful how void Matthews is of common sense, good manners, or knowledge of the world. He understands nothing but yes or no, and knows no medium. Matthews has sent me a ridiculous note written by the claw of a great lobster, by way of thanks for a present I sent him of some Cedrati and Marzolini cheeses, which are more delicate than our cream cheeses in England.'

To which Thomas replied, 'I am much obliged to you for yr kinde present. The sweetmeats are good; so, says sume of my gentimn is the cheeses, but it's good for me. I love nothing after the French fashion.' Most naval officers and some squires had poor writing, where Thomas's writing was better than most of the day.

Other friends and supporters that stood by Thomas included the Commissioner of the Navy George Marsh, who at some length writes in his diary that he considered him a worthy friend.

Twelve captains were tried for court-martial; one of seven officers was cashiered for not engaging the enemy or providing support to fellow vessels, as required in the Articles of War. Thomas was being blamed for poor planning and ill-temper by Richard and his government supporters. When Richard was tried and acquitted, Thomas was shown to be brave in battle but was convicted and dismissed from the Navy. The public, however, did not agree with Richard's acquittal, thus leading to the amendments to the Articles of War.

JOHN PIERPOINT MORGAN (1837-1913)

John was our eighth, three times removed cousin through both our direct Matthews and Matthews-Cheney lines. The shared ancestor recorded was Hyfaidd ap Bleddri; the Morgan family also originated from Llandaff in Wales.

Hyfaidd was the third son of Bledri ap Cydifor, a Welsh chieftain of Dyfed, and through his sister there are family connections with the Prince of Powys.

The Morgan's are one of the oldest Welsh surnames dating back to the King Arthur legends. John's direct Morgan descendant was Miles Morgan, born in 1616 in Llandaff, Wales, son of William Morgan II and another Morgan, Elizabeth; William II was a Merchant of Dderw (Thurrow). Miles and his brothers, James and John, decided to search for a better life and sailed for Boston, in the Americas, in April 1636. During that voyage, Miles met his wife. Miles was an intrepid fighter, farmer, and town leader, and he operated a boat which he used to trade with other colonists and Indians.

A life-size statue stands in Court Square in Springfield, Massachusetts, celebrating Miles successfully defending an attack on Springfield. His parents, William Morgan II and Elizabeth, were the ancestors of many infamous and interesting descendants. This branch produced not only the famous

Morgan we know in the banking industry, but also Princess Diana and her sons.

Other descendants include the 13th USA President Millard Fillmore; film star Humphrey Bogart; American poets John Robinson Jeffers and Archibald Macleish; and American playwright and screenwriter Thomas Lanier Williams III, 'aka Tennessee Williams'. Some of his plays include 'Cat On a Hot Tin Roof' and 'A Streetcar Named Desire', shortlisted for the finest American plays of the twentieth century.

John's father, Junius Spencer Morgan, was the patriarch of the Morgan family. He was the only son of his father Joseph, and inherited $3,000,000 in 1847 (in today's sterling that's £727,896,63.86). Junius founded the bank J.S. Morgan and Company with George Peabody in London, England. George is known as the father of modern philanthropy, and the bank's head office relocated to New York in the 1800s. Interestingly, Junius researched his genealogy, as he believed his mother Sally Spencer was a distant cousin to the Fifth Duchess Georgiana Spencer.

Junius became obsessed for over 25 years with rightful ownership of Thomas Gainsborough's portrait of the Duchess, and in later years his son was able to purchase it for $150,000 in 1901. It was then sold in 1994.

Junius left an inheritance of $10,000,000 (£255,127,642.37) to his eldest son John, who changed the bank's name to J.P. Morgan. Today it is known as J.P. Morgan Chase. Famous for founding the bank and also a Republican, he started his working life as an accountant before partnering with Anthony Drexel in 1871, forming the Drexel Morgan Company. The company created a national capital market for industrial companies to operate, and also bailed out the U.S government during the economic crisis of 1895 and rescued the New York Stock Exchange during the economic crisis of 1907.

At the beginning of the USA railroad system, he bought failing railroad companies to enhance their potential, and assisted in the merger of Edison General Electric and Thomson-Houston Electric to become General Electric Corporation (GEC), as well as forming the first billion-dollar corporation, United States Steel Corporation. He went on to found a trust called the International Mercantile Marine Holding Company. The trust included companies such as the Red Star Line and White Star Line shipping companies, and he attended the christening of the ship *Titanic*.

John was an educated, bilingual man, able to speak both French and German like a native, and was also an avid art and book collector. The majority of his art collection was donated to the Metropolitan Museum of Art in New York, while his book collection became part of the Morgan Library and Museum. Upon his death, his son J.P Morgan II inherited more than $50,000,000 in 1913.

John's son, John Pierpont Morgan II, was taught both by his father and grandfather in the family firm. At the beginning of World War I, he became the purchasing agent for three years on behalf of both the French and British governments, and purchased $3,000,000,000 of military supplies from American firms, giving him one per cent of the total spent by both governments.

He rallied over 2,000 banks to make the largest foreign loan in the history of Wall Street, totalling $1,500,000,000. Through this side of the business, J.P. was targeted by a terrorist ex-Harvard professor Erich Muenter, aka Frank Holt, who broke into J.P.'s Long Island summer home in July 1915. Under his coat was hidden two revolvers and a stick of dynamite. When the butler, Physick, answered the door, the intruder presented a business card and demanded to speak to J.P. pushing past the servant. Both the butler and intruder reached the library, with Physick calling out for the Morgan's to hide. Upon reaching the second floor, the intruder and J.P. exchanged words. The intruder, with a revolver in each hand, shot J.P. – one bullet went through his groin, exiting at his hip. J.P. fell forward onto the intruder, which enabled his wife to get hold of one of the guns.

The second shot missed J.P. whilst the third failed to be fired. J.P. fought the intruder. with his butler striking the man on the right temple with a lump of coal. It later came to light that the same man had planted a package containing three sticks of dynamite with a timer, at a telephone switchboard within the Capital Building in Washington D.C. on the evening of 2nd July. The timer was set for midnight, before Holt took the night train to New York. Holt's reasoning was to convince J.P. to use his 'great influence' to halt the USA's exports of arms and ammunition to Europe.

It is believed Muenter was a spy within the US, but he refused to state who he was to the police and it was through a tip that his identity was confirmed. Found in his pocket were the names of J.P.'s four children, along with a cartoon clip of Lady Liberty pointing to a firework crate, telling Uncle Sam that they were dangerous fireworks.

Muenter's original intention was to take J.P.'s wife and children hostage, although he also admitted to intending to murder J.P. A truck was tracked down in storage in New York that contained 134 sticks of dynamite; blasting caps; coils of fuses; batteries; nitric acid; windproof matches; smokeless explosive powder; mercury fulminate; and three explosive tin can bombs that were complete.

He used an alias name after deliberately going missing on suspicion of his pregnant wife, Leona's murder from arsenic poisoning in April 1906. Muenter attempted to commit suicide by cutting his wrists the day before he was found dead. It was concluded he had run out of an open door, and jumped out of the building 20 feet below.

A study conducted by the British Treasury in 1916 found that the UK was dependent on the US for its financial ability to conduct war; Britain would have exhausted its reserves of gold and securities by 1917 without the US.

J.P.'s company went on to float loans up to $10,000,000,000 for the reconstruction of Europe. The Banking Act of 1933 resulted in J.P. having to separate investment banking from commercial banking deposit activities. Today we know the investment part as Morgan Stanley and Company. His son Henry co-managed with Harold Stanley, while commercial banking became J.P. Morgan and Company. which J.P. managed. Forbes listed J.P. as being the richest man in the US in 1918, with $70 million.

Another of J.P.'s companies was the Pullman Company, which was included in President Lincoln's funeral train. After the death of George Pullman, President Lincoln's son and our cousin Robert Todd Lincoln assumed the presidency of the Pullman Palace Car Company.

Other properties of J.P.'s included his summer home, but it no longer exists after being demolished in 1989. However, his London home was later donated to become the American Embassy.

Another renowned descendant was Sir John Morgan of the Holy Sepulchre of Tredegar, supporter to King Henry VII. Sir John was Sheriff of Wentloog and Newport, and he commissioned Tredegar House to be built; part of this house still stands.

Through Sir John Morgan, we have another family connection. Sir John married Jenet Verch Matthew, who was the daughter of John and granddaughter of our direct ancestor Sir Dafydd Matthews. They had nine children, including son Sir Thomas Morgan, the squire to King Henry VII.

CHARLES BARNES TOWNS (1862-1947)

Charles was a direct descendant and our eleventh cousin twice removed through the Matthews, via his grandmother Louisa Pope Matthews. Charles started life on a small farm in Georgia and spent his teenage years working on the farm before eventually becoming successful in life insurance.

He decided to move to New York to start a partnership with a brokerage firm that later folded. At that time, an unknown person approached him regarding curing drugs and alcohol addictions, which led him to educating himself on the subject and advertising for clients wanting to be cured. During this time, he met Dr Alexander Lambert, a professor from Cornell University Medical College who also participated. Dr Alexander was also a physician to President Theodore Roosevelt, and the cure they created was known as the Towns-Lambert cure.

Their formula involved using the deadly nightshade (Atropa belladonna) with deliriant and prickly ash. All this caused hallucinations, diarrhoea, and confusion, but was believed to purge the body clean.

The US government appointed Charles a drug treatment ambassador to assist the Chinese with the recovery of some 160 million addicts, where he perfected the only world-known opium cure. Charles published his work in the *Journal of the American Medical Association,* and by 1915 he sponsored and aided with both the Boylan Bill and the Harrison Act.

Charles also founded a 50-patient Manhattan hospital for alcoholism first in 119 West 81st then 293 Central Park West, and in the roaring twenties it became very successful. Strangely, with worlds colliding, it was developer Judson Scott Todd – our distant tenth cousin – who became involved. He engaged the architectural firm Neville and Bagge to design the buildings in Manhattan, which included Charles's hospital, made up of regular rooms and suites equipped with ensuites and telephones. Individual nurses and meals were supplied, with a rooftop garden looking over Central Park. Prices started at $200 and were expected to be paid in advance. Charles opened his facilities more than 70 years before the Betty Ford Clinic.

Charles treated clients such as American actress and singer Lillian Russell, and actor John Barrymore, alongside others such as bankers and clergymen. Other clients included Cokey Flo Brown and Mildred Harris, both involved in the trial of Italian gangster Lucky Luciano.

Charles lobbied for hypodermic needles to be prescription only, and for people to be educated on drink and drugs. He believed addicts and alcoholics were sick and not deprived, and his campaign was to shine a light on addiction, stating: 'The real cost is not to the drug taker but to the world. The loss of what a person might have given to the world.'

Henry Ford also sent addicts within his Detroit workforce to the hospital when needed for treatment. And Alcoholics Anonymous (AA) co-founder Bill Wilson used the services of Charles's hospital himself several times, under the care of one of the directors William Duncan Silkworth. William believed both physical and mental health go hand-in-hand, and this gave Bill Wilson the enlightenment to co-found AA, to which Charles was both a supporter and creditor.

When the Stock Market crashed in 1929, business started to decline, due to costs of treatment and falling admissions.

Charles wrote many books on the subject of both addiction and alcoholism. And his son Edward continued his father's work, living with his family at the hospital on the fifth floor.

In 1961, their daughter Caroline moved in with them, with her two daughters. Caroline had left her husband Thomas Lewis, but on October 17th in the early evening, he came to their apartment and their eight-year-old daughter Linda was requested to ask her mother to join her father in the lounge.

An aggressive argument followed, and Caroline's mother ran from the room whilst gunshots rang out. Some 15 shots were fired by Thomas before he turned his 45 automatic onto the police officers attending. Edward's wife and Thomas were both killed and Caroline wounded. The hospital finally closed in 1965, becoming residential apartments.

Other Matthews' descendants and cousins include the Viscount of Galway, who is also related to our Coningsby line. A lovely painting of the Mathew family at Kelvedon Hall, Essex, was on loan by the Mathew descendants to Clandon Park. It was painted by Johann Zoffany, but unfortunately was destroyed in a fire in 2015. The Viscounts of Galway include Daniel Dering Mathew, who was later put on trial for the attempted murder of his brother-in-law over ownership of a property. In 1819, Daniel – a timber getter, merchant, magistrate, as well as Australia's first architect – acquired a grant of 400 acres named Clanville Estate. He sold the land in 1830 to Richard Archbold. His cottage 'Roseville' gave its name to the suburb that stands today.

Some other descendants include Jane Anna Elizabeth Austin, the great-niece of the great author Jane Austin, and Olympic bronze medal winning Canadian rower, 13th Viscount John Philip Monckton-Arundell of Galway.

CHAPTER THREE

HISTORY OF HAMPTON COURT CASTLE, HEREFORDSHIRE

Hampton was originally formed by merging the manors of Hampton Richard and Hampton Mappennor.

In the Domesday Book, the lands were listed as 'Hantone' because of the two rivers, the Lugg and the Humber Brook.

Hampton Court Castle stands on the Welsh borders in a pretty village named Hope-Under-Demore, four miles from Leominster in Hertfordshire. A very beautiful and imposing castle, it dates from 1427, when King Henry VI of England owned the lands.

King Henry VI started construction in the early 15th century, then gave it to his courtier and Master Yeoman of the Robes, Sir Roland Lenthall, to build a house upon the marriage to his cousin Lady Margaret Fitzalan, the daughter of the wealthy 13th Earl Richard of Arundel. Lady Margaret inherited one-third share of her brother's wealth (the 15th Earl of Arundel), their grandfather being one of the richest men of the millennium.

Sir Rowland Lenthall built the original house in stunning pink Herefordshire sandstone in a quadrangular courtyard style, and today it still retains its basic form. He was also granted a licence to crenellate by King Henry VI; an abstract of a document relates to this in the patent rolls for 6th November, 1434. Only a small part of the 15th-century building remains standing, with the oldest part being the family chapel, dating back to 1428. Some of the chapel's stained-glass windows now reside in the Victoria and Albert Museum.

It is said in *A Genealogical and Heraldic History of the Commoners of Great Britain and Ireland*, written by John Burke, that King Henry VI laid the first stone at Hampton and had a picture within it.

Being related through marriage to King Henry VI, Sir Roland was given the maintenance of a thousand pounds a year, part of which included a grant for the town of Ludlow.

Some years later when the son and heir of Roland Lenthall, Edmund Lenthall, had died, the estate then devolved into female heirs – his cousins. The Lenthalls went on to sell Hampton (its name at the time) with 10,000 acres to Sir Thomas Cornwall of Burford.

Sir Thomas Cornwall was the grandson of Sir Rowland Lenthall, and later sold it to fellow courtier Sir Humphrey Coningsby in 1510.

In the 1700s, Hampton was renamed Hampton Court Castle in support of King William and Queen Mary.

In the previous history, the gardens were very grand, with formal avenues and canals. A painting called 'Oil on Canvas' by Leonard Knyff in 1699, shows the gardens in a similar style to those of the Palace of Versailles.

1st Earl Thomas Coningsby and King William III were good friends, and the inspiration for the gardens may have been the influence of that friendship.

Hampton remained in the Coningsby family for four centuries, until 1781, with the last family member to hold the estate being the 5th Earl Sir George Capel-Coningsby of Essex (grandson of Countess Frances Hanbury-Williams *nee Coningsby*).

In 1810, the estate was purchased by the son of Sir Richard Arkwright I, Richard Arkwright II (1755-1843).

In 1912, the estate was sold to Major William M. Burrell and his wife, and during the First World War they established a military convalescent hospital at Hampton Court Castle.

In 1924, the estate was sold again, with most of the land falling into separate ownership. During the period of the 1960s, the estate deteriorated, including the collapse of the Paxton Conservatory roof, and from there continued to have several owners.

In 1972, Hampton Court itself and the remaining 1,936 acres of land, were purchased by Viscountess Hereford. This led to some of the contents of Hampton Court being sold by the 18th Viscount Devereux.

The Van Kampens, who became the owners in 1994, restored the house and grounds before it was sold again in 2008. The gardens changed with each owner throughout time, but they are still incredibly breath-taking, with many different species of plants, and awe-inspiring water features, including the hidden passage and caves under the waterfall which can only be reached on completion of the large maze.

CONINGSBY COAT OF ARMS: The Coningsby coat of arms is represented by three conies (hares) of Arundel.

This represents the visual canting charge.

The red represents warrior, military strength, and magnanimity.

CREST: Out of a ducal corone, topaz, a plume of five ostrich feathers there on a cony sejant all argent. All pearl.

SUPPORTERS: Two lions' ruby, each charged on the shoulder with three billets, and ducally crowned, topaz.

MOTTO: *Vestigia Nulla Retrosum, Justi Terram Incolant*

When translated into English, it means: No retreat, no steps backwards, may they just inhabit the land.

CHIEF SEAT: Hampton Court Castle near Hereford.

There is also a very large coat of arms that hangs in the Coningsby Museum, quartered into eleven individual sections. One of these quarters is an Or, Gules Lion Rampant (red lion on a gold background). The particular section of the coat of arms represented the Prince Madog of Powys, the Royal dynasty of Powys going back to the Welsh Kings in the ninth century. They played a very important part in history, going back to the first King Bleddyn, who was a powerful and outstanding Welsh ruler who reigned over most of the eleventh century. Bleddyn's mother was the widowed Queen Angharad, daughter of King Maredudd of Dyfed. One of Wales's primary and very important historical documents is called 'Brut Y Tywysogion' or 'Chronicle of the Princes'. The document describes Bleddyn as a benevolent ruler; the most loveable and most merciful of all kings; civil to his relatives; generous to the poor; merciful to pilgrims and orphans and widows; and a defender of the weak. The mildest and most clement of kings, he did injury to none, save when insulted. Open-handed to all; terrible in war, but beloved in peace. Bleddyn changed the legal composition of the homestead in Gwynedd's Venedotian Code for inheritance purposes, along with a revision of the Welsh law.

Researching further on this, there is a link to this particular section of the coat of arms. We do know this line is also on the Matthews's direct branch of the family, which also shows up in our DNA genealogy.

The other, a silver lion wearing a gold crown, was the coat of arms that links back to King Vladislaus II of Bohemia, but we have not yet researched any further regarding this. However, we do wonder how John Coningsby of Morton Bagot researched this line back in 1700, all the way back to the Prince of Powys.

CHAPTER FOUR

THE CONINGSBY FAMILY

The Coningsby's were a great noble and political family, and can trace their roots back to 1180, to Sir Roger Coningsby (our 30th great grandfather). Believed to have originated from Brittany, France, they came to live in Coningsby, Lincolnshire, to which the Coningsby's may have taken their name. They also held an ancient seat in the county of Salop (Shropshire), where it is believed to come from Coningsby, near Sleaford in Lincolnshire.

Soalebar Coningsby was a benefactor to the Kirkfield Abbey in Lincolnshire during the reign of King Henry II.

It is believed that Baron John Coningsby of Coningsby was killed fighting in the battle at Chesterfield on 15 May, 1266. He supported the cause of Earl Simon de Montfort of Leicester in the Baron's War, opposing King Henry III in 1264 over money and power, believing he had too much and exercised it poorly. King Henry needed money for wars against France and Wales, amongst other things.

It seems that quite a few of our ancestors were involved on either side of this war.

The first Baron War in 1215 paved the way for the Magna Carta. Four are known to have survived today – one is on display at Salisbury Cathedral; two are held at the British Library; and the last is in Lincoln.

In the White Tower of the Tower of London hangs a portrait of 1st Earl Thomas Coningsby with both his daughters, Margaret and Frances. It was painted by Sir Godfrey Kneller in 1722.

In the background stands the Tower of London, and on the table bears his full quarters with the following inscription in the left-hand corner of the painting: 'This first coat of arms was in the manner born by John Lord Coningsby, Baron of Coningsby, in Lincolnshire, who was slain in the Battle of Chesterfield, in Barons' Wars in the reign of King John, the which town and castle of Coningsby being then confiscated, is now in the possession of Lord Sheffield, and this is approved by the heralds upon perusal of the evidence of Humphrey Coningsby of Neen Sollars, who is lineally descended from the said John.'

The family have held many important positions throughout time, including MPs, Speakers of the House, vice treasurers, diplomats, and judges, one of whom, Sir Ralph, attended Sir Walter Raleigh's trial at Winchester. The Coningsby's also had a rich history with the court system, whether taking people to court – including the Crown – or being taken to court, with the majority of cases being won due to their strong sense of justice.

Our line of descent comes through Lady Elizabeth Coningsby, daughter of Sir Ralph Coningsby, descending down through the Bentleys and Bunyan's, including the Reverend John Bunyan, author of *The Pilgrim's Way*, and son of our ancestor Margaret Bentley, down to our great-grandmother Maria Butterfield, and to our grandfather George Matthews.

Researching our family tree brought us to the day when our family was able to visit one of our ancestral homes.

Hampton Court Castle, Gate entrance, 2019.

It was the most beautiful summer day in August 2019 when we stood at the arched gatehouse entrance. Before us lay the longest and grandest drive we had ever seen, at the end of which stood the most magnificent yet imposing castle one had ever viewed. And instantly we felt a connection of home. The grounds seemed to be vast, and beyond were trees and mountains of various heights and colours. As we walked down the drive, on the left was a huge lake with white swans and ducks. To gain entrance to the castle, there was a small bridge which led to imposing arched doors made of wood and iron.

We wondered if our ancestors could sense our presence and imagined them looking out through the large grand window facing us – the first Coningsby blood to step foot on the grounds for centuries. We later sat with our picnic under a tree, overlooking the very large pond, all wondering what it would have been like for our ancestors, including Sir Humphrey Coningsby.

1ST BARON JOHN CONINGSBY OF CONINGSBY (1200-1266)

Our 30th great grandfather was 1st Baron John Coningsby; John was the son of Sir Roger Coningsby and a De Badlesmere in 1200.

After King John signed the Magna Carta on the 15th June, 1215, in Runnymede, his heir King Henry III was trying to rule with an iron fist without his people's agreement, resulting in what we know as the Baron's War in the rebellion against the King. King Henry wanted more finance, implementing a method of government his people didn't agree with. Crops were failing, which led to famine, and the King was not listening to his Barons who were there to advise and aid in running England. The Barons chose Simon De Montford to aid their quest in reasserting the Magna Carta. The King, however, was displeased with Simon, being the marriage choice of his sister Eleanor without his permission. The castle and town of Coningsby were confiscated and came into the possession of Lord Sheffield. In the will of Edmundus Sheffield, dated 20th May, 1544, held at the National Archives, the Coningsby possessions such as furniture were mentioned and were used for his son and heir John Sheffield.

Baron John Coningsby was killed in one of the battles that took place in Chesterfield in 1266.

SIR THOMAS CONINGSBY OF MORTON BAGOT (1415-1498)

Following research, Sir Thomas was able to prove his descent and how the title came into the Coningsby family. This in turn enabled him to recover the title of Morton Bagot, by proving he was a direct descendent of Sir Roger Coningsby in a court of law.

The Morton Bagot title came from his 4th great-grandmother and heiress Lady Joan Bagot of Morton.

The history of the Bagot family shows that they were a notable noble family that held the manor until 1296.

William Bagot the Younger conveyed it for the sum of 130 marks to Roger De Coningsby and his wife Joan. Roger De Coningsby was granted free warren in his demesne lands of Morton Bagot in 1303. Morton Bagot and other hamlets of Spernall, Offord, along with other hamlets, were held by Roger Coningsby, William Trussell, and Thomas Durvassall in 1316.

Joan Bagot was the eldest daughter and heiress of her father Lord Roger Bagot of Morton Bagot. Roger Coningsby's son John disputed, with the prior consent of Kenilworth, the patronage of Morton Bagot church in 1333.

John's son William Coningsby was recorded in 1365 as having connections with land in Ullenhall. William had no children, so the manor passed through his sister and on to her granddaughter Alice.

Alice married Richard Archer in 1436, and made a settlement for the manor and advowson for herself and her future heirs. But in 1461, Alice died young without any children, leaving her cousin Thomas Coningsby claiming the manor as an heir.

The trustees of Alice's estate claimed at the request of Alice they had released the manor to Richard Archer to be sold.

The money was to be used for masses for the souls of Richard and Alice and their ancestors.

They also claimed Thomas was no cousin of Alice, due to his great-grandfather being the illegitimate son of William and had no brother called John, Alice's great-grandfather.

Thomas Coningsby evidently established his claim, and his descendent William sued the Archers over the detention of deeds to the manor in the early 16th century.

The manor in 1536 was conveyed from Humphrey Coningsby to Richard Coningsby for life. Richard's heir was his eldest son Humphrey, with reversion to the sons of the elder Humphrey.

The latter Humphrey Coningsby's son John died in 1567, and his son and heir Humphrey conveyed the manor to Nicholas Coningsby in 1593.

The last Coningsby to hold the manor was Thomas Coningsby, who sold it in 1629 to Richard Butler and William Gibbons.

The last mention of the Manor of Morton Bagot was in 1903, when the Earl of Warwick trustees purchased Studley Castle Estate. His son was Sir Humphrey Coningsby.

SIR HUMPHREY CONINGSBY (1459-1529)

Our 21st great-grandfather Sir Humphrey Coningsby was born in 1459 within the family seat at Rock, near Kidderminster.

He was the grandson of Judge Sir Thomas Coningsby of Neen Sollars and Morton Bagot and Lady Elizabeth Whettall, and the Son of Thomas Coningsby and Lady Katherine Waldyff.

Thomas Coningsby inherited and held the manor and family seat of Bower, Rock Warwickshire in 1509. In the area stands Rock Church, built by the standard-bearer to William the Conqueror in 1150. At the church, he then built the South Chapel, south aisle, along with the West Tower. Within the south aisle there was once a beautiful stained-glass window, where Sir Humphrey was portrayed in a scarlet gown with his sons behind him and his wife and daughters opposite.

In St Peter, St Paul's Church in Rock, there was once an inscription:

'Here lieth Thomas Coningsby ESQ. who deceased A.D. 1498, father to Sir Humphrey Coningsby, knight and one of the lord justices of the king's bench, who built this aisle and steeple of the church, A.D 1510 at his charges. He died in Aldnam, in the county of Hertford.'

Other Coningsby's, including Lord John Coningsby, descendant of another Sir Humphrey Coningsby are interred.

King Henry VIII knighted Sir Humphrey in 1509, after he became a justice of the King's bench on the 21st May, 1509. Sir Humphrey Coningsby was one of the four named serjeants-at-law named in a recital of King Henry VII's will, dated 31st March, 1509.

The following 21st May, and within a month of the accession of King Henry VIII, Sir Humphrey was made a sole puisne judge. He was a great judge of his time, and his future clients also included Queen Elizabeth I and the Duke of Buckingham.

Sir Humphrey Coningsby was present at the Coronation of Ann Boleyn in 1533, and during some of the formal receptions held. Humphrey also took an interest in his genealogy regarding 1st Baron John Coningsby of Coningsby and the confiscation of the town and castle. Humphrey's lineage was approved upon perusal of evidence by the heralds.

Hampton passed down to a younger son and our ancestors, Sir John Coningsby of

North Mimms, born in 1512. He married Lady Elizabeth Frowick and together they had several children, including our 18th great-grandfather Sir Henry Coningsby.

Sir Henry married Lady Elizabeth Boteler; their son was Sir Ralph Coningsby.

SIR HENRY CONINGSBY (1546-1593)

Sir Henry Coningsby was the son of Sir John Coningsby, and married Lady Elizabeth Frowick. Elizabeth was the daughter of the Lord Mayor of London, Sir Henry Frowick and his wife Lady Joan Lewknor. The Lewknors were descendants from the Plantagenet line. Upon his death, Sir Henry left his wife the entire estate.

SIR RALPH CONINGSBURY JUDGE AND MP (1555-1645)

Our eighteenth great-grandfather Sir Ralph Coningsby was born in 1555 in Hertfordshire, the first son of Sir Henry Coningsby and Lady Elizabeth Boteler.

Sir Ralph was educated at Oxford and was mainly dependent on his mother for maintenance for much of his adult life. He first married our ancestor, Margaret Whethill, daughter of a merchant tailor of London. By this marriage he gained eleven messuages in London. His second wife was Jane Lambe of Coulston in Wiltshire, and the widow of William Button of Alton Priors.

The offices he held included Governor for Queen Elizabeth I, Justice of the Peace, and Sheriff for Hertfordshire between the years 1591-1597.

Sir Ralph was a Middlesex freeholder who served on the jury that condemned Sir Walter Rayleigh for complicity in the main plot of July 1603. Ralph served on the King's Bench. The indictment for Sir Walter Rayleigh was issued on the 21st of August at Staines in Middlesex. The trial itself took place on the 17th of November, 1603, at the Great Hall in Winchester. The reason it was held at the Great Hall was due to the great plague raging in London at the time. The common law was named as being common to all the King's courts across England. This followed after the Norman Conquest in 1066, and consisted of three central courts: the King's Bench, the Court of Common Pleas, and the Exchequer.

Sir Ralph also served as a ranger of Enfield Chase, and he looked after the limited sporting interests of the 1st Earl Robert Cecil of Salisbury; he was granted the benefit of Recusancy in 1608.

In 1611, Sir Ralph led the Hertfordshire delegation – appointed by magistrates at quarters sessions in consultation with freeholders and yeomen of the county – that presented Salisbury with demand without any leverage of compromise on the 1st April, 1611. This was for the abolition of purveyance which included carriages for the royal stables.

In 1614, Sir Ralph was elected to represent Hertfordshire in Parliament, leading onto the 1st April 1614, where he was named to the Privileges Committee, where he was to consider the extension, revival, or repeal of statutes.

Amongst his duties, on the 13th of April, included being ordered to prepare a protest against 'undertakers' to consider a bill against false bail to restrain the removal of cases from local courts to Westminster Hall.

Ralph, along with his two brothers John and Henry, sold various outlying estates and property that included property in Surrey.

On the 14th of March, 1616, he made his will whilst he was ill. He left his principal estate to his second wife. The eldest son Francis Coningsby would receive an annual allowance of 150 pounds, only if he married with the wishes and approval of six trustees, which included Sir John Boteler.

His death nine days later left Herefordshire without three good deputy lieutenants and patriots.

Coincidentally, Sir Ralph's great-great grandson Sir William Coningsby (1488-1540) was also a Judge and MP. This said, William – a distant uncle to us – was also appointed to hear causes in Chancery in the relief of Cardinal Worsley.

His granddaughter, Lady Elizabeth Coningsby (1530-1608) of Wallington and Eston Halls, Norfolk, married Sir Francis Gawdy. Sir Francis Gawdy served on the trial of Queen Mary of Scotland.

THOMAS CONINGSBY (1591-1654)

The son and heir of Sir Ralph and Margaret Whethill, Thomas, was the High Sheriff of Hertfordshire in 1638 for several years, being appointed by King Charles 1st. It was later declared that any sheriff appointed by King Charles 1st was not legal.

Thomas married Martha Button, and they had six sons and 12 daughters. Soon after this, Thomas became a prisoner of Cromwell. His house was soon plundered, and he was carried to the Tower where he was imprisoned for several years until his death.

HUMPHREY CONINGSBY (1516-1558)

Grandson of Sir Humphrey Coningsby, Humphrey Coningsby married Lady Anne Englefield, who was a descendant of the Throckmorton line, from which Guy Fawkes descends.

Humphrey was the eldest son of 1st Earl Thomas Coningsby and his wife Cecilia Salwey.

They had three daughters and two sons; Humphrey also had an illegitimate son.

At the age of 19, Humphrey succeeded to the Judge's lands in both Herefordshire and Worcestershire, as stated in the History of Parliament. He sued out of livery of the inheritance in May 1537.

The following year, Humphrey became the gentleman treasurer to Queen Elizabeth 1st, including the office of Steward and Lordship of the manor of Leominster. He also fought in the French War with the King, as well as in Scotland, being a pensioner to Queen Elizabeth 1st as he was before to her father and brother.

He was granted a passport to go overseas to deal with their affairs, but shortly before this was granted, Humphrey had been prosecuted in the Star Chamber for an assault on Edmund Foxe in November 1541 near Temple Bar. There had been a previous incident at Ludlow with Edmund Foxe, and the Foxe brothers had also made accusations against the President of the Council.

Humphrey was the brother-in-law to Sir Francis Englefield (in high favour with Queen Mary I) and sat in all except one of her Parliaments for Berkshire. He stood for the 'true religion', and voted against the restoration of Catholicism'.

In 1553, he purchased monastic lands in both Leicestershire and Northamptonshire for 700 pounds. He also further acquired lands in Bodenham and had a part in developing local industry. Being licensed in 1557 for 40 looms and making and weaving all kinds of woollen clothes, he sustained losses and charges in erecting two woollen mills in Hope under Dinmore in Herefordshire.

Humphrey was re-elected to Parliament in 1559, but died on April 4th, shortly after making his will. His widow and sole executrix then married John's husband. The eldest son of Humphrey, Edward, died the following year in the wardship of Sir Edward Rogers, therefore the inheritance was passed to the second son, Thomas Coningsby.

This branch of the family is interred at St Mary's in Hope under Dinmore, a short distance from Hampton Court Castle. The church was built by the Coningsby's, and it is an everlasting testimony to them.

It is a pretty church but difficult to get to, being on a main dual carriageway but it is definitely worth the visit. The day we visited, the church was locked, but luckily for us one of the church wardens had come along to wind the clock and he kindly let us in to see the beautiful marble monument. At the very top, the coat of arms is displayed with pride, showing their resting place. Built for the late Earl Thomas Coningsby, whose remains – along with those of his wife Lady Philippa Coningsby and infant son – are deposited in a vault under a chance. The remains of their son Fitzwilliam and grandson, Sir Thomas Coningsby and his wife Philippa Fitzwilliam, rest there, too.

1ST EARL SIR THOMAS CONINGSBY (1551-1625)

Sir Thomas was born on the 9th of October, 1551, at Hampton Court Castle, to Humphrey and Anne, and married his friend Sir Philip Sidney's (The Earl of Leicester's nephew) first cousin, Phillipa Fitzwilliam.

There was an issue between these two good friends involving an unfounded accusation of theft. The story is told that their friendship was severely strained whilst in Italy, and an unfounded charge was brought by Sir Philip against Sir Thomas. The party stayed at an inn and was most likely short-changed by the innkeeper – not an uncommon occurrence back then. Sir Philip did not realise this and found he had less money, accusing Sir Thomas of stealing the money. The circumstance of small value shows Sir Philip's temper.

Sir Thomas was also one of the major landowners in the Welsh border county throughout most of Elizabeth I and James I reign. As a boy he inherited extensive estates across Pencome, Bodenham, Hampton, and the site of Blackfriars, as well as lands at Orelton and Leicestershire, Shropshire and Worcestershire. He became enemies with other leading families, including the known Croft family – a dominant family in the history of Herefordshire politics.

He had a strong foothold in Hereford, being a High Steward, MP for Leominster, and Sheriff, and on October 8th, 1591 in Rouen, was knighted by the Earl of Essex.

A portrait of Sir Thomas, in fine Elizabethan costume with his dwarf cricket, hangs in Breamore House, near Fordingbridge, Hampshire. A play in 1606 by Ben Johnson, was based on Sir Thomas, called 'Every Man Out of his Humour'. The main character, Puntarvolo, is a glorious but vain knight who supposedly represents Sir Thomas. It was claimed that the players had purloined a suit of Sir Thomas's own clothes from Hampton Court Castle, and the actor dressed in them to perform his role. Sir Thomas, it is said, saw the play and cried out in confusion, because he could not tell which was the real man: him or the one on stage.

After the death of Queen Elizabeth I, his position was weakened, forcing him to yield control of the county to his rivals, the Croft and Scudamore families.

Sir Thomas founded the Coningsby Hospital for the Red Coats – a distinctive Coningsby uniform with embroidered badges of white conies. It is thought King Charles's mistress, Nell

Gwynne, influenced the King in deciding to clothe his Chelsea Pensioners' uniform in red. After the dissolution of the priory in Hereford, the priory and the hospital came into the ownership of Sir Thomas. The alms houses were later constructed by Sir Thomas out of stone from the priory in 1614, with the chapel, hall, and infirmary repaired by him.

Sir Thomas, according to the *Oxford Dictionary of National Biography*, wrote an extraordinary and bombastic will.

SIR FITZWILLIAM CONINGSBY (1589-1666)

Fitzwilliam, fourth and only surviving son of Sir Thomas and Phillipa, was born at Hampton Court Castle. In 1621, he was a Herefordshire MP for the House of Commons between 1621-1640, and High Steward for Leominster. One of the nine Justices for the Royalist leadership in Herefordshire in the summer of 1642, one of the other eight included John Scudamore, who was an avid supporter of the Royalist cause during the English Civil War.

Fitzwilliam married Cecily Neville from the noble Neville house. Also a descendant of the Throckmorton house, she was considered a great beauty and was often painted by John Hoskins. Together, Fitzwilliam and Cecily had five children.

Fitzwilliam went into exile after 1646 following the Siege of Worcester, where he fought for the King throughout the Civil War. As a result,, he, his wife and children suffered greatly in the sequestration, with the estates being reduced to comparative poverty.

In the *Calendar of the Committee for Compounding* (pages 2064-2071) are his, his wife, and son's petitions, along with counter petitions of his tenants and Sir Thomas Allen, to whom the bulk of estates had been granted.

When King Charles II took the throne, Fitzwilliam was at last able to recover his estates.

Fitzwilliam's grandson described him 'as a man of great extravagance and expense, as well as beyond description negligent in the management of his affairs'.

When his father Sir Thomas made his will in August 1616, his concerns were voiced at the 'disturbance and facility to entangle himself to all detriments. Innocents taste not of his folly', regarding Fitzwilliam. He also added a codicil that instructed Fitzwilliam to continue living at the latter's house in Hampton Wafer for a further three years after his death, and not to spend above 1,000 pounds by the year.

Only on the 2nd July, 1623, did Sir Thomas appoint his son sole executor of his will.

Fitzwilliam was a very active Magistrate and an important figure in Herefordshire County politics, even refusing to support Sir John Scudamore in 1625, which was a major blow to Scudamore's chances of securing re-election for the county.

He gave Leominster a silver mace (1646) like his father who gave two maces (1618), but no evidence was recorded.

In 1629 he commissioned a stained-glass window depicting the removal of Christ from the cross to be installed in his chapel. The window bore a defensive inscription: 'The truth hereof is historical, divine, and not superstitious.' In 1638 he took a loan of £1,300 but did not repay in full £1,600, to which lands in Marden were reprocessed. Sampson Wise married his daughter and, with him, paid off the debts and bought estates.

Fitzwilliam was expelled from the long parliament for the county in October 1641 on the grounds that he was a beneficiary of the soap monopoly. He was exiled at the surrender of Worcester in 1646, after Charles I execution, and he petitioned to compound for his delinquency.

Fitzwilliam's estate was then valued at £1,684 p.a. but most of it was mortgaged or extended for debt. His fine was set at £4,243, but this was subsequently reduced to £1,316 on discovering several miscalculations. It seems that nothing was repaid. He sought election for Leominster in 1661, but this was denied a poll on the grounds that he was a prisoner of debt. In 1652, with depleted family fortunes and loans, he pleaded guilty to the starvation of his family.

He was ordered to pay £2,000 within two weeks, which was not paid. Fitzwilliam was then imprisoned in the year 1654.

A document stated that Fitzwilliam had been betrayed by his steward and was not able to preserve a single acre or any form of records of his possessions from any inquisitors of the times.

Fitzwilliam made his will on the 25th February, 1666, and within two months was buried at the parish church in Hope under Dinmore, dying in the year of the Great Fire of London.

His son died five years later in a debtor's prison, and his grandson, Thomas Coningsby (MP for Leominster) was elevated to the peerage.

1ST EARL LORD THOMAS CONINGSBY (1656-1729)

Through Fitzwilliam's son Humphrey and his wife Lady Lettice Loftus, his grandson Lord Thomas Coningsby and our distant fifth cousin was born on a cold November day in 1656 – a direct descendent of the Earl of Cork, Ireland, through his mother's line. Lettice's brother was a philosopher and founder of modern chemistry and is best known for Boyle's Law – Robert Boyle.

He was born into an era leading into the Georgians, when only 200,000 men at the time were financially comfortable, influential, and able to vote (in a UK population of just over 7 million). The majority of the population were illiterate. These were the times when the poor rented and only the wealthy owned property. Superstition was still an everyday part of life, as were the many diseases such as smallpox and consumption, as well as the notorious highwaymen who robbed travellers along the roads. London had started to go through the redevelopment of its medieval muddy streets to the architecture we recognise today.

Lord Thomas was a very interesting and colourful character; his personality was belligerent and litigious certainly. A passion that Thomas had was that he enjoyed researching the family history and collecting documents – a trait that has carried through the generations of today. Thomas started his genealogy research at the time of the Norman Conquest, and all manors believed that should have been part of the family inheritance.

Thomas used the Domesday Book, deeds, and court records, with everything he researched being stored in his 'Evidence room' (unusual for those times to have one).

He wanted to prove his lineage to royalty, and installed an evidence room to store essential genealogy and deeds. The Coningsby family owned property in the early seventeenth century in Kentchester, with Thomas not wasting any opportunity presented to him. In his evidence room, he adorned the floor with the local Kentchester Roman remains of square bricks he excavated. It is thought the site was a Roman town called Roman Magna.

When a child, Thomas received very little education and had not come from a wealthy background, because his grandfather Fitzwilliam had heavy debts, but Thomas was very determined to get the family fortune back. The estate then valued at £4,000 was heavily mortgaged.

Both his parents died when he was young; his mother, after Thomas's first marriage, leaving him the ward of his future father-in-law, Ferdinando Gorges – a merchant and slaver in Barbados.

Thomas was described as being upright, courageous, high principled but vain, while also impulsive, impatient, and a bit of a ladies' man. He was possibly Autistic and had ADHD, due to an impairment in social communication and obsessions with suits and other counter suites, along with restricted patterns of behaviour and conversations on narrow subjects. Yet he was full of energy and impulsiveness.

Thomas was married twice. The first was to Barbara Gorges at a young age, and from their marriage came four daughters and three sons. This marriage took place after Ferdinando had Lettice imprisoned, so never attended the wedding or agreed to the marriage. It was a marriage he felt he was forced into and where he felt his loss of inheritance began. Thomas felt he was defrauded of his own inheritance and felt the man responsible for this was Ferdinando Gorges, his guardian. The close connection to Ferdinando comes through Ferdinando's brother marrying Sir Thomas's maternal aunt. He disinherited all the children from this marriage.

In 1692, Thomas brought the Duke of Buckingham's manor in Leominster, which King James, I had gifted him. Thomas was further granted the manor of Shuttingdon in lieu of forfeited estates in Ireland. This was part of Margaret's inheritance, passing onto her sister Frances' descendants, 5th Earl George Capel Coningsby of Essex.

He loaned money to the Crown and was well known for often taking his enemies, neighbours, and Leominster Corporation to court, as well as the Crown itself.

Lord Thomas helped in the Treaty of Limerick and gave his support to King William in his war against the Jacobite's at the Battle of Boyle. As Privy Councillor, vice treasurer of Ireland, Thomas rose to be joint Paymaster General of Ireland, then the only Paymaster General.

At the battle, King William suffered an attack when the Irish chiefs observed the then Prince of Orange taking breakfast on the bank of the river. The Prince mounted his horse in line with the target, and the first bounced off his holster, resulting in his horse falling. The King shouted out when he himself was shot, grazing his shoulder. Thomas took out a piece of his coat and put his handkerchief on the wound, and by this act Thomas was given lasting favour by King William, whilst also rising further. Thomas kept the handkerchief in an ebony casket with the lid displaying miniatures of the King and doughty liegeman in the library at Hampton.

Thomas was appointed, through his loyalty, as William and Mary's Commissioner of Appeals, with a salary of £23,966.78 today.

Lord Thomas held several titles including the Baron of Clanbrassil in Ireland, which King William III created in April 1692, and was also a vice treasurer and Paymaster for Ireland. Thomas did expect a viscountcy for the Irish peerage, but instead accepted the barony.

He was a Whig for Leominster and High Steward for Hereford, and was a key supporter of William and Mary's bid for the throne, showing his support by adding a court to Hampton in honour of Hampton Court Palace.

During his lifetime, he became involved in a duel with Lord Chandos over politics, but all was well.

Lord Thomas was the most distinguished member of the family and a well-known Member of Parliament.

There is a story about Lord Thomas Coningsby regarding an incident with a neighbour, however it could possibly be just enemies making up stories. It is said that Lord Thomas rode his horse, with his sword in hand, to his neighbour, Sir John Goode, demanding possession of Burghope House. A furious Sir John challenged Thomas by combat, to which Thomas turned and went home.

Thomas had several grievances, one being a charge that Kyrwood had stolen one of the Coningsby estates and concealed the evidence.

In 1720, he was imprisoned in the Tower of London for six months, following his purchase of manors in Leominster and Marden. Whilst imprisoned, Thomas spent his time further researching records for his rightful claims to property and rights that should be rightfully his. The records at the time were kept in the Tower by archivist Richard Topham.

Thomas indeed brought about a court action over missing deeds in which he lost revenue of £2,000 per year.

Thomas was accused of libel against the Lord Chancellor during the South Sea period and was sent to the Tower of London, where he was imprisoned from 27th February to 29th July, 1721. Before his incarceration, Thomas was under house arrest in Albermarle Street whilst the Tower was being prepared for his imprisonment. He was escorted to the Tower by Black Rod, along with his daughters, Chaplin, and his 14 servants.

Lord Thomas, during his time in the Tower, had commissioned a fowling piece – a Flintlock sporting gun. It was made of the blades of rebel swords from the Battle of Boyne, possibly from captured Jacobite weapons held at the Tower from 1715. It was made by an employed Tower gunmaker, William Mills. (More information can be found in the Royal Armouries collections.)

It has the following inscription engraved on it, showing his loyalty to the Crown:

In seventeen hundred and twenty-two

I in the tower became a gun;

Earl Coningsby a prisoner there

Bespoke and took me to his care,

And fit am I the loyal lords,

Made of the blades of rebel swords;

Fit for the noble Earl whose crime

Was speaking the truth in south-sea time,

Traitors beware when I'm enlarged

When he or I become discharged

For this is my first and true report

Pray to use me well at Hampton Court.

Also, at the Tower of London, and originally hung at Hampton Court Castle, was a portrait by Kneller. It hangs in the white tower on the north wall, and features Lord Thomas Coningsby and both his younger daughters, Countess Margaret and Countess Frances (grandmother to George Coningsby Capel).

On his release, he attacked the government and Lord Chancellor in the House of Lords. He believed he had connection with litigation over the manor of Marden, and thought his rights as Lord had been infringed by the copyhold tenants. The documents he collected on the history of the manor formed part of the writings that he later published.

These terms caused Lord Cowper to observe the following: 'He should have more regard to the chancellor' because he might come some time under his direction, presumably as a lunatic.

Thomas continued to prosecute his feuds, distraining cattle, imprisoning bailiffs, and threatening to hang the Sheriff of Hereford, and some of these accounts can be found in the British Museum.

In April 1667, he received a grant under the privy seal of several crown manors. The Harley family were also included in Thomas's vendettas, due to revenge for his ancestors. King William also indicated he would grant a pardon for his transgressions.

In 1692, he was made Baron of Clanbrassil and given a seat on the Privy Council for England. Thomas was involved in the Treaty of Limerick, signing the civil treaty, being one of the main people in the drafting.

After King William's death, Queen Anne ascended the throne. Thomas was a supporter of Marlborough, and unpublished letters between the Duchess and himself are held at Yale University.

Thomas, not in favour of King William's successor, was dismissed after a heated exchange with Queen Anne regarding Thomas telling the Queen her ministry, in what she could and must not do, and is recorded in the Parliament Archives. Thomas allegedly stated the following in an interview with her: *Thomas is said to Laid before her, the inevitable dangers that must attend her making… change in her ministry (till after the peace of France) to the credit of the nation; to herself, with regard to her civil list; and even to the safety of her person and government, and the whole protestant interest of the world.*

Queen Anne was furious and closed Thomas's prospects for rehabilitation. He spent the rest of Queen Anne's reign improving Hampton Court Castle. A book, *The Life and Times of Thomas, Lord Coningsby. The Whig Man and His Victims*, by Pat Rogers, explains in detail Lord Thomas Coningsby's political life.

Lord Thomas claimed to be the last man in England to employ a jester, and would dress up and re-enact tournaments on the grounds.

There are over 100 court records for cases Thomas had been involved with; some of these are held at the British Library and Parliament Archives. The evidence he formed included everything he could associate with the house, legal papers stretching back a century, family papers, and the portrait of King Henry IV laying the first stone for Hampton Court Castle. This portrait was sold to Cornwall of Burford, who in turn sold it to the ancestors of Lord Thomas. Every item reflected the Coningsby family history, and he put trust in paper and family papers dating back over the centuries. On the wall was a painted board that traced his proud family lineage.

In the 1680s, Lord Thomas modernised Hampton Court Castle to its present standards. It is thought the designs may have been provided by William Talman – the leading country architect best known for such esteemed houses as Chatsworth House.

He refitted rooms to become staterooms, including a beautiful crimson red silk damask-covered room with a magnificent stately four-poster bed fit for King William. Today, the red room still remains, with damask wall coverings, in Hampton Court Castle. The elaborate bed now resides at Het Loo Palace in the Netherlands. And today, in the New York Metropolitan Museum, there is a similar blue silk damask four-posted sculptured wooden bed, which was made for Queen Mary in the style of King William III by architect Daniel Marot. This bed is dated about 1698 and stands over 12ft tall. You can find the photograph of the crimson bed further in the book under the sub-heading: furniture.

Lord Thomas presented Leominster with two silver maces on 23rd October, 1723, and evidence of this is in a receipt for delivery. The maces' description on the Leominster council records was that they were 21 inches in length and divided into three compartments by a raised circular boss. The portion between each was tooled with oak leaves and acorns. The summit of each mace was surmounted by a large imperial crown, and underneath the canopy of the crown were the royal arms of William and Mary in relief. Around the circular margin were the letters W and M interlaced and forming a kind of knot; alternate with the Conyingsby arms (3 conies serjeant on a shield below a baron's coronet) with a Lion Rampant (on a shield) bearing its paws a fleece, with the word's 'Leominster Burgus'. The following words were also engraved on the circle of the crown: *The gift of the Rt Hon Thomas Lord Conyingsby to ye Borough of Leominstre.'*

The maces date by about 30 years before they were given as a gift, given the dates and title. The reason behind the gift was a disagreement between the Coningsby family and the council over land.

Earl Thomas Coningsby made several cases which he wrote about. He called one 'The first part of Earl Coningsby's Case relating to the vicarage of Leominster in Hereford', to include all chapels within the manor, borough (including woods; fields; pastures; waters; mills; fisheries; and rents), and liberty of Leominster.

This was in the time of King James I, who granted the Marquis of Buckinghamshire in 1619 (the seventeenth year of his reign) Leominster and other estates. Thomas points out that Queen Anne had part of the manor granted to her in jointure in 1602. It did not include the liberty, lordship, and manor of the Leominster. The Marquis sold a considerable amount of the estates to different purchasers in 1662, and Thomas was able to reclaim some of the estate by buying it from Major Wildman in 1692 for £3,060.

Thomas felt the Crown had snatched certain manors and lands which rightfully belonged to the Coningsby family, so he campaigned tirelessly to put right what was wronged for him and future descendants, to claim it back from the Crown. He kept the evidence in the ledger book of the Priory of Leominster, in his evidence room at Hampton.

The records held at Parliament are quite damning against Thomas, describing him as being the true picture of a Court Whig: greedy, ill-tempered, unscrupulous, and possibly corrupt. He is described as being accustomed to fawning upon the powerful and bullying the powerless, a 'hot and violent man'. In fact, Thomas, in one of his outbursts, did tell Parliament in a four-letter obscenity where to go.

A local historian's assessment was that he came from a neglected education without early discipline and self-control.

Thomas was upright, courageous, and highly principled, yet impulsive and impatient.

He was borrowing money on the security of the estate to make loans to the Crown, and was accused of treason then given a Royal Pardon in 1694. He also had to defend himself from impeachment. His only recorded speech was on the 18th of December, 1693, for a reintroduced triennial bill.

The impulsive and impatient part is believed to possibly be due to his SEN. Thomas certainly had a trying time, both in his private and political life, and he came from a poor background rather than the comfortable one that our shared ancestors had. It was a time when being different could mean death, yet Thomas fought his way through, claiming back what was lost due to his grandfather. If Thomas had been without determination and eloquence; he might not have succeeded in this.

COUNTESS MARGARET NEWTON-CONINGSBY OF HEREFORD (1709-1761)

The daughter of Lord Thomas Coningsby and Lady Frances Jones, Countess Margaret was born in Lord Thomas's second marriage.

Lord Thomas, due to lack of an heir, changed his title to Lord Coningsby remainder to Margaret and her male issue on the 8th June, 1716 – a singular limitation despite having sons with his first wife. On the 9th of May, 1719, he did the same to the Earl of Coningsby title.

In the reign of George I, on Jan 26, 1716, Margaret became Viscountess and Baroness of Hampton Court, and later in 1729 inherited her father's title with the limitation on the remainder of her heirs male. Countess Margaret was a co-heiress to her father.

On the 11th of April, 1730, Margaret married the 4th Baron Sir Michael Newton, Champion to the Order of Bath. Their only child and son was born on 16th October, 1732, and died as a baby on the 30th January, 1733. The story behind the infant's death is that one day the nurse was carrying the child atop the great stairway in Hampton Court Castle, when a pet ape came out of nowhere, frightening the nurse so badly that she dropped the child. The fall unfortunately killed him.

COUNTESS FRANCES HANBURY-WILLIAMS (1710-1781)

Countess Frances married Sir Charles Hanbury-Williams on the 1st of July, 1732, in St James's Westminster, to which her father provided a marriage dowry of £10,000. Being the younger sister of Countess Margaret of Coningsby, Frances next inherited the titles from her sister.

5TH EARL GEORGE CAPEL-CONINGSBY (1757-1839)

Grandson of Countess Frances Hanbury-Williams, and an English aristocrat and MP for Westminster and High Steward for Leominster in 1802, Earl George became a Fellow of the Society of Antiquaries in 1801 and a major patron of the arts while building a large fine art collection at Cassiobury.

He took the additional name Coningsby when he inherited Hampton Court Castle in 1781 from his grandmother Countess Frances Hanbury-William *(nee Coningsby)*.

He sold Hampton Court Castle in 1810 for the sum of £226,535 (in today's money this is approx. £16,909,893.85), to pay off debts to Hereford MP Sir Richard Arkwright. Sir Richard was the grandson of the inventor and industrialist Richard Arkwright. By this time, only 6,220 acres of the 10,000 remained, Sir John Arkwright later inherited the estate. The 5th Earl George is also related via our Todd line.

HAMPTON COURT CASTLE FAMILY CHAPEL

The earliest part of the original castle, the family chapel is a beautiful section of the house and has wonderful wooden-framed high ceilings that seem to reach into the heavens.

Originally the chapel housed painted glass depicting the arms of the founders, the Lenthalls and others; a beautiful stained-glass window was also installed showing the three coats of arms of the Coningsby's, dating 1613-1614, and was marked with T.R.

The V&A Museum now holds the stained-glass window and further information on it.

BURIAL PLACES OF THE CONINGSBY FAMILY

Humphrey Coningsby of de Neen Sollars (1567-1610) is our distant fourth cousin; our shared ancestor would be Lord Thomas Coningsby of de Neen Sollars and Morton Bagot.

Humphrey is interred at the All-Saints Church in Neen Sollars. The church was built by the Mortimer family of Wigmore Castle and restored, strangely enough, by a Butterfield in 1857.

Humphrey himself has a black marble and alabaster wall-standing monument dating from 1624, with his effigy displayed in full armour in a reclining position, with his head cupped by his hand. A large arch is above, incorporating on either side the two muscular figures of death and time.

Two small, armoured figures stand upon two columns framing the monument, while the tomb's chest displays trophies of armour, and inscriptions tell of Humphrey's world travels and of his death. At the top stands a crest displaying a 12-quarter coat of arms and a hare as the crest.

*The marble family monument in the church of
St Mary's in Hope under Dinmore.*

FURNITURE FROM HAMPTON COURT CASTLE

Much of the original furniture and pieces have since disappeared from the castle; some of them have ended up in private collections or museums, such as this beautiful state bed – one of two.

A gorgeous rich velvet and bright crimson, with a timeless silk damask that flatters and is edged with gold and silver braid, the bed successfully shows the elegance and wealth of the family that had it commissioned.

The bed was made for King William III for when he came to stay, but unfortunately, he never did. It was later sent to him at Het Loo Palace, near Apeldoorn in the Netherlands, where it resides to this day and is on view to the public.

The photograph of scarlet bed was kindly given by
Het Loo Palace, Netherlands.

The blue damask silk bed was gifted by Mr and Mrs Randolph Hearst in 1968, and had been previously stored in the attic of Hampton Court Castle, where H. Avray Tipping, of the *Country Life* magazine found it in a good condition in 1911. The bed was later sold in 1925 to a dealer, Permaine of Bond Street, London. Shortly after, it resold to American newspaper publisher Mr Randolph Hearst.

Often these items were matched with other furnishings, such as chairs, stools, curtains, and wall hangings.

Other pieces of furniture include a sofa which is currently in the Victoria and Albert Museum in London, and a beautiful grandfather clock on display at the Science Museum.

CONINGSBY CARRIAGE

Lord Thomas was keen to show his coat of arms through the colour crimson on his coach.

The carriage itself had an interior of lined crimson velvet – a colour that seems synonymous with the Coningsby family. We can only imagine what the carriage looked like, as there are no further descriptions, so we are unsure as to the style of carriage, but as family we have a very good idea of how it may have looked. Lord Thomas would often travel by his coach to Leominster, which he considered his borough.

In April 1725, the family carriage was sold at auction held by the Earl of Bradford at his house in Soho, alongside items such as a velvet damask bed, a large pier, chimney glasses, India and Japan screens and cabinets, paintings, jewels, China, etc.

We have tried to track down the carriage that our dear cousin Thomas owned, but to date we have been unable to find any information after the auction.

The Coningsby Sofa. Victoria and Albert Museum 2018.

THE CONINGSBY SOFA AND CLOCK

We visited the Victoria and Albert Museum in September 2018, specifically to see our ancestor's sofa, and although the colour was faded it was still in a remarkable condition, thanks to conservation efforts. It was amazing to see a piece of our family history, knowing that our ancestors used this furniture and it was a part of their daily life.

The Coningsby Clock. The Science Museum 2018.

We happened to visit the Science Museum by chance in 2018, where we came across by chance a longcase clock proudly displayed with a small portrait by Thomas Bate, of 1st Earl Thomas Coningsby. Thomas commissioned the clock from Daniel Quare.

CHAPTER FIVE
THE TODDS

The Todd's descend from a very noble line originating from Scotland. There are three branches to this side of our family: one branch stayed in Scotland and down into England; another went to Ireland; and some to America. Our particular branch went to England.

Within the family, we had two Masters of the Mint for Scotland. One is our fourteenth great-uncle, Alexander Todd (1430-1456), the Kings Coiner for King James II. A photograph of one of his coins, a groat, can be found in Australia in the museum's Victoria collection.

The second Archibald Bothwell is related to our Todd-Campbell line, born in 1699, and died in 1756 without issue. Very little is written about Archibald which we can only briefly mention.

JOHN HENRY GUINNESS (1935-1988)

Alexander's descendants include John Henry Guinness, the chairman of Guinness Mahon bank. John Henry, our 15th 1st removed cousin, came from a family of bankers and brewers. John's great-grandmother Jane Tod was directly descended from Alexander Todd.

On the evening of 8th April, 1986, John Henry Guinness's wife Jennifer was kidnapped by three masked men outside the family's Howth mansion in Dublin, Ireland, for the ransom of two million pounds. John Henry was hit over the head with a pistol, and one of his daughters, Gillian, tied up along with her husband and a book dealer. At the time, the bank was a subsidiary of Guinness Peat, valued at over £200 million. When John Henry died in Snowdon from a mountain walking accident, he left £161,622 in his will.

Another of his descendants, and our thirteenth third removed cousin, was an American author and artist Eleanor Frances Lattimore-Andrews, who was born in 1904 in China. Eleanor wrote at least 47 books, featuring characters set across the world, some based on the adventures of her grandchildren to appeal to young readers. Her books included titles such as *The Little Tumbler*, *More About Little Pear*, and *Three Firecrackers*, to name but a few. Both Eleanor's parents were secondary school teachers.

SIR WILLIAM TOD (1470-1545)

Our 13th great-grandfather, Lord William Todd, was the Mayor of York and High Sheriff in 1477. He was an Alderman who exported a considerable amount of lead and wool. As a merchant, William was in a more elevated social position of the times.

Elections were made for Alderman by the Mayor when vacancies arose due to ill health, death, or old age. If this honour was refused, as in William's case, a fine of ten pounds (in today's money £6,857 approx.) was issued.

Aldermen wore robes of scarlet which had to be worn on all civic occasions.

York's loyalty to King Henry VII was put to the test when Lambert Simnel was refused entry into the city and beaten off at Bootham Bar. King Henry VII visited York at the end of July 1487, along with a thousand noblemen, to show his military strength. They executed several men from the opposing side.

William, along with Mayor Richard York, was knighted by King Henry VII in gratitude for providing support against the forces of Yorkist pretender Lambert Simnel.

In celebration, William restored the arch Fishergate bar – a medieval entrance to the city in 1487, and 55 metres of wall. A stone above the archway is on display to this day.

At one time, within the city's walls there were two inscriptions regarding Sir William Todd, at his own cost. This was described by the antiquary John Leland, who was known as the father of English local history, in a book regarding his travels around England and Wales in the 1500s.

The first was near the table under the city's arms, reading 'mair jou-ates sometyme was schyriffe did this cost him-self'. Near this, on a table under the city's arms read a further inscription: 'A Domini M.C. -CCC.L. XXXVII. Sir William Tod, Knight l. Mayre this wal was mayde in his dayes lx yerdys.'

A panel, also described by the antiquary Leland, is held in the Yorkshire Museum and displays two figures. On the canopy are two shields, each displaying a merchant's mark. On the left, a man – possibly a senator in civilian dress – is standing facing outwards. On the right is a kneeling figure, possibly a woman in profile. Inscribed at the level of the figure's shoulders: 'lx yerdis of length'.

The year before King Henry entered York by the royal entrance, Micklegate Bar, crowds cheered and sprinkled rose water over him and his men. However, a few years later in York, King Henry VII raised the taxes to repair and strengthen the walls in York, including the obtaining of guns and powder, resulting in an uprising from its citizens.

During the unrest, the Fishergate Bar was severely damaged. William pleaded poverty to the King and was then granted £98 (In today's money £65,643 approx.), but the guns were not installed until 1511, in the reign of King Henry VIII.

Through a grandmother's genealogy line, William Tod's ancestor Lady Mary Loudon descends from the Lairds of Drummond and Innerpeffray, and also the Lindsey of Crawford lines. These lines go back through the Stewart family branches to King Robert Bruce II of Scotland. It is recorded that the Bruce line goes to the Earls of Orkney; Earl Brusee; Earl Einar; Earl Hunde Welp; Earl Somerled; Earl Thorfinn; an earlier Earl Einar of Orkney; and brother of Duke Rollo of Normandy. It goes further back to Scandinavian origin, from Princes and the great Rollo himself, to Lords and Nobles of Sweden, Norway, and Denmark, to ruling families of Russia and Germany. This genealogy is recorded by the statistical account of the Scotland genealogy of the Bruce family.

THE BRUCE CURSE

The first curse, most likely a Celtic myth, was called the Curse of Annan and refers to blood-drinking spirits. It starts not long after Malachy's Curse, when the plague came to Annan from a Yorkshire man on the run. The Bruce's gave shelter to this man, but he did not change his ways before dying of the plague. After he was buried, locals reported seeing the man's rotting corpse with a horrible crowd of dogs, and the priest was sent to cleanse the town with new prayers they composed. But the plague raged and spread.

One evening, the Bruce's held a banquet for the visiting clergy, during which two brothers held a conversation concerning their father's death from the plague. They volunteered to rid the town of the plague in revenge for their father's death. During the banquet, they left the castle, travelling through the silent streets of Annan to the grave of the Yorkshire man, where they resolved to disinter the cadaver and set it on fire. They both started to dig until they reached the body, finding it swollen with enormous corpulence. The face was red and swollen and the clothes were cut. One brother took his spade and, full of anger, started hitting the chest. Blood burst out, soaking their feet and filling some of the other graves. Both brothers believed they had disinterred a vampire full of the victim's blood, so they hauled the corpse out of the grave, dragged it through the streets to the edge of town, where they placed it on a pyre, before using their spades to remove the heart. They burnt both the corpse and heart separately in the flames.

The second curse was around the year 1148, when a visitor passed through the valley of Annan.

It was recorded by a grey friar of Carlisle, in the Chronicle of Lanercost. The chronicles, *A Northern English History*, covered mainly the years 1201-1346, for the wars of Scottish independence.

The Bruce family was given a charter of lands of Osticroft, Annadale part of Dumfries by King David I in 1124, and today it is known as one of Scotland's great trails. It leads to Hoddom Castle, where a ruined medieval castle can be seen along the route; this castle was built by allies of the Bruce family, the Herries.

Robert Bruce's grandfather was known as The Competitor Lord Robert De Brus of Annandale. Annan Castle was built by King William 'The Lion' in the mid-1100s, and was one of his 13 castles along the rivers. The lands of Annandale were forfeited to the 4th Earl Humphrey De Bohun of Hereford after the murder of John Comyn in a holy place. Through the De Bohuns, the Annandale charters came to form part of the muniments of the Duchy of Lancaster. These included seven undated writs that contained grants by or relating to Robert De Brus – all are assigned to Robert Bruce, Lord of Annadale from 1215-to 1245.

The records are also recorded under the Calendar of Documents preserved at the Public Records for England; several Annadale charters are amongst the papers of the Duchy of Lancaster.

The Archbishop of Armagh and Down Malachi O' Morgair (today known as the Irish Saint Malachy) was born of noble birth and a son of a teacher. When his parents died, he was only seven years old and was sent to join the religious order taught by Saint Malchus. His brother was the Saint Christian O'Morgair of Clogher. Malachi was ordained at the age of 25 and became the Abbot at Bangor, then Bishop of Connor, and instituted celibacy regulations within the Irish clergy. He was known as a warm-hearted humane Irishman, a miracle worker and healer, but also known to place his hands upon people and curse them instantly.

It is said that Malachi's claims were the gift of prophecy. When he visited Rome, he received a vision showing all the popes from his time to the end of time. He wrote a description of each one and presented the manuscript to Pope Innocent II. Malachi's hope was to obtain the promised pall for Ireland from the Pope. He became well known for the Reformation of the Irish Church to align with Rome.

He was greeted by King David on his arrival to Scotland, and travelled through Annadale on his way to Rome. When he came upon the estate of the Bruce's, he sought refreshment from the current Lord, the son of the original grantee, Lord Robert De Bruce of Annadale, who gave a warm welcome to St Malachi.

He was seated at an ornate table on the north side of Bruce's hall and was partaking of food, along with two fellow clerics – his companions – when he heard the servants discussing the fate of a robber who was about to undergo a sentence.

Lord Bruce entered, greeting his guests heartily. The Bishop, however, had thoughts of the poor robber whose doom was near, and he appealed to Lord Bruce who, as Baron, with the jurisdiction of pit and gallows, held the thief's fate in the hollow of his hand.

'I demand as a pilgrim that since the judgement of blood has never yet violated the place of my presence if the man has committed any crime, you will grant me his life.'

The grey friar had recorded that the Bishop's noble host nodded, not in courtesy but in deceit. And acting according to the prudence of this world, which is folly with God, he secretly gave orders to hang the thief. Meanwhile, the Bishop, in happy ignorance and rejoicing that he had saved a human life, finished his repast and prepared to go on his way. Before setting off, he bestowed his solemn blessing on Bruce's house, table, and household. But as he was departing, to his surprise he saw the body of the robber hanging on the gallows near the roadside! The life which he had interceded was not his after all, so he revoked his blessing and turned it into a curse: first to Bruce and his offspring; and then to the town. A great storm raged over the town shortly afterwards, causing flooding which swept away the curtain wall and half the bailey of Annan Castle. The household and administration were forced to relocate to Lochmaben Castle.

The chronicler states the dire effect upon Bruce and his line, stating that the family never prospered again. But the genealogy does not share the same with the chronicles of King Robert the Bruce.

On his coming of manhood, he visited the Saint Malachy resting place, a shrine within the monastery in Clairvaux, on his return from the Holy Land in 1273. Craving his pardon, he then continued to visit the shrine every three years and to make peace he provided a perpetual rent of three silver lamps, with their lights to be maintained on the Saint's tomb. St Malachi had been dead by a century at this time.

4TH PRESIDENT JAMES MADISON

James was our seventh cousin twice removed, born in 1751, and one of 12 children. He became known as the Father of the Constitution after becoming one of the authors writing the Federalist Papers. The Federalist Papers' idea was based on the separation of powers of the national government, forming three branches: legislative, executive, and judiciary.

James represented Virginia as one of the founding fathers of America, and wanted a strong central government. He wanted Americans to have freedom of speech and was against unreasonable searches and seizures, and lining the pockets of the 'wealthy'. James was active in the American Colonization Society, which aimed to return freed slaves to Africa, although he did enslave people himself – something his father detailed in his will.

Strangely enough, his wife Dolley had been married to a quaker lawyer John Todd. We do not know if John was a relation, having not researched his line. After James's death, Dolley sold seven volumes of his Madison papers to Congress, which paid $55,000 for editing and publishing them.

MARY TODD-LINCOLN (1818-1882)

The ancestors of our Todd genealogy line go back to the Lairds of Stirling and Dunbar in Scotland, and even further back to the Orkney islands and Somerled.

There are many remarkable descendants, including Mary Ann Molly Todd-Lincoln, who was born on the 13th December, 1818, in Lexington, Kentucky. Another notable descendant was Queen Elizabeth II, through Queen Victoria's line. Something the family all seem to share in common is migraines, which could be inherited from the Bruce line.

The First Lady of the White House was our distant twelfth cousin through our Todd branch, via our great-grandmother. Having married President Abraham Lincoln (who coincidentally is a cousin on our Butterfield line), they had many children who unfortunately passed, but were survived by one son, Robert Todd Lincoln. Abraham's Confederate Army also has a connection through our 3rd great-uncle, John Condon, on our Irish paternal line. His descendants include the Mayor of Knoxville and businessman Martin Joseph Condon II.

Mary's second great-grandfather, Robert Samuel Todd, emigrated to the USA from Ireland, taking his wife and children with him. Many upstanding senators, including her father and judges, also fall on this particular branch, which we have listed below.

Mary's father, Robert Smith Todd (1791-1849), was the senator for Kentucky USA.

Mary's dress can be seen at the National Museum of American History, where it was donated by a close family member, and believed to be made by Elizabeth Keckly. It is said that Mary haunts her dress by appearing next to it.

HON. THOMAS TODD (1765-1826)

Thomas was a 6th cousin of ours, the common ancestor being Sir John Todd. Thomas was born to local Sheriff Richard Todd and Elizabeth Richards in the early part of 1765, whose wealth was inherited from a wealthy landholding ancestor of the 17th century in Virginia. His father died whilst he was very young, leaving the estate to his older brother William. Thomas and his mother were left to make their own way financially.

His mother, Elizabeth, was very resourceful and opened a boarding house to make a living and to pay for Thomas's education. Unfortunately, Thomas was to lose both his parents at a young age and had to live with a family friend and guardian, and though his education was being paid for, the rest of Thomas's inheritance was squandered. After his education, Thomas left to join the continental army for a short time.

His political career started whilst living with his cousin, Kentucky Supreme Court Judge Harry Innes. Thomas at that time was working as a tutor to Harry's children, having previously taught at Liberty Hall Academy. In exchange for his tutoring and board, Thomas became Harry's clerk. Both Thomas and his cousin Harry joined a campaign to have Kentucky become its own state within the USA.

Thomas was called to the bar in 1786, and within two years he started his practice in land law in Danville. He also had experience in court reporting, and was delegated to the Virginia House of Delegates, once known as the House of Burgesses. The first English representative government and the legislative body for Virginia was first founded in 1642 for passing laws. When this was achieved, Thomas wrote the new state's constitution.

Thomas achieved many firsts, including becoming the first secretary of the legislature and the first clerk of the Kentucky Court of Appeals.

He achieved the position of Judge of the Supreme Court of the United States in 1801, going on to become a Chief Judge – a position for which third President Thomas Jefferson personally nominated Thomas in 1806, after his congressmen of Kentucky suggested him. Thomas served for a full 14 of his 19 years. He was Jefferson's supporter, otherwise known as a 'Jefferson' – a political party founded by Thomas Jefferson.

Thomas was very successful and wealthy through his own private practice, but he also had inherited land from a former Judge who refused his pension and for whom Thomas had taken on the responsibility of taking care. Known to be a kind and a fair Judge, he married twice – firstly to Elizabeth Harris, until her death. Their son, Charles Stewart Todd, chose a career that involved being a US diplomat and ambassador to Russia, before retiring as a writer.

After Elizabeth's death, Thomas went on to marry Lucy, the sister of First Lady Dolley Madison *nee Payne*. Previously, Lucy had been married to the nephew of President George

Washington. Thomas's two marriages brought him eight children, some of whom were notable, such as Charles.

His second wedding was on Sunday, the 29th of March, 1812. Dolley announced the marriage to her father on her sister's behalf by letter. She told him that the forthcoming wedding was unexpected, but that she did like Thomas, describing him as being estimable and amiable, very rich and very handsome.

The wedding was to be recorded in history as the first in the White House, and was held in the blue room on the state floor with the best and most beautiful views. This was before the first White House was burnt down in 1814, during the war with the British. (First Lady Dolly saved the George Washington painting and other treasures, and the stone exterior walls still stand today.)

Lucy was attended by three bridesmaids – her sister, the First Lady; Miss Hamilton; and Miss Hay. Thomas had three groomsmen – the First Lady's son, Payne Todd; Lucy's brother John Payne; and Mr Edward Coles. The couple honeymooned at one of the many properties on Thomas's estate in Kentucky.

Thomas also funded the first public and more improved highways in Kentucky, and was also a shareholder – along with being a charter member – in the first business for the Kentucky waterway navigation.

He died whilst the Supreme Court was in session in 1826. Once his children had inherited over $70,000, he left some of his fortunes to be spent on improving Kentucky. Thomas was interred twice: firstly, in the family cemetery; and then in the State Cemetery in Frankfort. A similar thing happened to Lucy when she was not laid to rest near Thomas, her headstone only mentioning her first husband.

Other descendants include Berry-Oil co-founder, Robert Younger Berry, whose third great-grandmother was Agnes Pace Ware, *nee Todd*.

JOHN BLAIR SMITH TODD (1814-1872)

Governor John Blair Smith Todd was our distant twelfth cousin, and first cousin to First Lady Mary Todd. He had a successful military career, serving in the Florida Indian War, the Mexican War, and the Battle of Blue Water against the Sioux Indians, rising from Second Lieutenant to Captain by 1843. He resigned from the army in 1855, believing he could make his fortune from the frontier boom, becoming a sutler at Fort Randell. John's reason for coming to Dakota from Lexington was due to being part of the Harney Expedition, during which John kept a diary.

The Wild West during this time was full of cowboys, including famous characters such as Jessie James, Wild Bill Hickok, and Calamity Jane. Later to follow was author Laura Ingalls Wilder of the Little House, more commonly known as The Little House on The Prairie. With business partner and fellow West Point Officer, Daniel Marsh Frost, they founded the company, Frost, Todd and Co, that traded with Indians, from selling groceries to building trading posts along the Missouri River. The government wanted extensive Sioux land, but the Indians refused all offers. John, who had good relations with squaw men, was able to successfully negotiate a treaty in 1858, with the aid of Charles F. Picotte (Eta-kecha), which enabled the opening of 14 million acres of Indian Sioux lands to reach the white settlements. Charles was of mixed blood. Not only was he a leader, but he could also translate.

Unfortunately, the government had plans to possibly take the land by force if there was no treaty, and there was a lot of misunderstanding about this. This treaty was known as the 'Treaty of Washington' and also more often known as the 'Treaty with Yankton Sioux'. The treaty involved 16 chiefs to negate, from there the Indians would be left at least 400,000 acres but were encouraged to live like ranchers and to also farm. Many Indians were later to be found starving due to financial corruption.

John was awarded a cheaper buying rate to invest in land for future towns, and founded the capital Yankton. He and his partner further founded the Upper Missouri Land Company, and both companies flourished when new settlements were formed. Part of their enterprise was to make individual plots and market them to attract newcomers from as far away as Germany.

He could not have foreseen the forthcoming trail of tears and the Dakota War in which a lot of innocent lives were to be lost on both sides, before he was called to the Bar in 1861.

John lobbied Washington D.C. for the creation of Dakota Territory, which was then granted in 1861. He became the territory's first congress delegate to the House of Representatives, where he served two terms before resigning in 1861.

John further served as a Brigadier General of volunteers in the Union Army in 1867, which led to him serving as Speaker in the House of Representatives and also Governor of Dakota.

A county was named after him – Todd County, near Fort Randall, which once belonged to the Rosebud Indian Reservation. Years later, this county's boundaries were redrawn and Todd County disappeared.

A cane was presented to John in 1865, by First Attorney General William Gleason and George Pinney, the First Speaker of the House of Dakota territory in 1866-1867. The cane describes three buildings which were important to John – West Point; the Fort Snelling building in Minnesota; and the Dakota territorial Capital Building. Both the cane and a portrait of him with the cane are on display at Dakota Territorial Museum.

On the evening President Abraham Lincoln was murdered, John was at the theatre, sitting in the next booth, and he helped carry Lincoln from the theatre to the Peterson boarding house across the street.

CAPTAIN THOMAS TODD TUNSTALL (1787-1862)

Born to cabinet maker Thomas Tunstall II and his wife, our eleventh cousin Mildred Todd, in Pittsylvania, USA, his great-grandfather had emigrated from Ireland to Kentucky, USA. When Thomas was a young man, he served in Simrall's Calvary regiment of the Light Dragoons during the war of 1812.

During this time, the steamboat was the main form of transport, and Thomas was the pilot of a steamboat named the *Waverly*. This boat was the first steamboat on the White River in January 1831, in a predominantly native Indian territory.

While working as the pilot, he realised the value of the land when he transported his goods such as cotton, timber, livestock, and meat to Jacks Creek, later known as Jackson Port. Thomas brought extensive land below the mouth of the river, as well as other property in Paraquet, Independence. He became known as the founder of Jackson Port, where he owned and operated the steamboats *William Parsons* and *Harp*, along with several others from Jackson Port. Thomas also built the first two-storey hotel there named Tunstall Hotel.

He had a passion for thoroughbred racehorses and would often win. He invested in buying a large farm in Dota Creek in 1834, which was becoming a popular place to visit with the public, and he made one of the early racetracks on the land there. He also bought property along river banks, and in particular Jackson County, where he created a river port.

Thomas led a fulfilling and busy life and his various business ventures made him wealthy. His son William was business-minded like his father, and owned warehouses trading in timber, cotton, and corn, etc. The two planned the layout of Jackson, and at a later date William gave land to the county to build the local Jackson Port courthouse.

Thomas died of pneumonia at the age of 61 in 1862, and was buried at Sulphur Rock. His grave is marked by a tall, thin gravestone, with William and his wife on either side.

JAMES GETTYS (1759-1815)

We felt it was important to include James, because he was married to our tenth cousin, Mary Todd, and is also a relation to Mary Todd-Lincoln. James was the son of both Irish and Scottish immigrants, and the founder of the city of Gettysburg, Pennsylvania. Mary Todd and James had two children – James Gettys II and Robert Todd.

James started his venture by purchasing 116 acres of his father's 386-acre farmland in the Marsh Creek settlement in 1786, in a bankruptcy auction for £790. This land stood at the crossroads of York and Black Gap Roads; today, the land is around the town circle.

James was very business-minded and divided the acres into 220 lots, for which he held an official lottery; the citizens then purchased the rights to buy one or more of the lots. This was the foundation of the Gettys town, which would become renowned for the American Civil War battle in July 1863.

James also became the Sheriff, state legislator, tavern owner, town clerk, and Brigadier General of the local militia. A book entitled *James Gettys and the Founding of Gettysburg*, by Melissa Gettys and Amanda Howlett, is more in-depth regarding the Gettys family which is definitely worth reading.

Having built some of the roads, the first house, shop, tavern, and courthouse stood for one hundred years before the incident happened. The Gettys's house was constructed, before any roads were built, behind the Globe Inn. One day in October 1880, John Gilbert's hay shed caught alight in the early morning. The shed stood close to the Gettys's house and the fire quickly spread to the property; the Doerscm family were living there at the time. The Hancock-Garfield Democratic campaign demonstration had taken place the evening before, with guest speaker McDowell Sharp from Chambersburg.

James was a man who always helped good causes, and he was described as being affectionate, cheerful and a sincere, public-spirited man who lost his mother. He and our cousin Mary died within days of each from typhus fever.

Along with his wife and other family members, James's body was moved and buried at Evergreen Cemetery. Years after his death, President Lincoln gave a speech within the Evergreen Cemetery.

Today a monument still stands to James, erected by his son James II. It displays the medallion head of James Getty. At the front was a large cast iron greyhound, James's favourite dog. The dog wore a collar with the inscription 'I'm James Gettys' dog, whose dog, are you?' and was erected many years after James's death. However, the dog is no longer there and is thought to have been stolen.

JOHN DAVIDSON ROCKEFELLER (1839-1937)

John was born to our distant fifth cousin Dr William Avery Rockefeller and his legal wife, Elizabeth Davison, in New York. One of at least eight children, he spent most of his childhood with his father being absent, before Elizabeth became a single parent when the children reached their teens.

John's destiny was to become America's first billionaire as well as America's richest person, which would still stand today. But let us first go back to his roots and to his father, William. Their genealogy was both of German and English descent.

William used the pseudonym Dr William Levingston for most of his life, but was not an actual medical doctor or any type of qualified doctor. Unfortunately, William was not of good character, unlike his son John. He peddled proprietary medicines, including selling items for non-existent cancer treatment at $25 a time. His other ventures included selling loans to poor farmers at a 12 per cent interest rate, which some were unable to repay. William may have engineered this because it gave him the opportunity to recall the debt and reprocess the farm's in order for the loans to be settled

He met Elizabeth during one of his business trips to New York. At that time he was portrayed to be both deaf and blind – part of his peddling – and would communicate with her by a chalkboard. He used this pretence in order to trade in Indian herbs and remedies, but he was unable to speak Indian so felt this aided him. The Indians were extremely superstitious and admired anyone who was missing any form of sense. They believed these types of people were gifted by the gods to be able to heal others.

William would also trade as a master oil peddler within the American oil medicine Petroleum and Seneca oil business, earning $2 a bottle. This was to serve as a medicine for most ailments someone may have. He would dress the part in both Indian and trapper clothing and work alongside the medicine men of the tribes from the Indian springs. He was also known to mix with unreputable characters that were both unsavoury and dangerous.

By the time he met Elizabeth, he already had two illegitimate children with his housekeeper Nellie. Elizabeth's father, a farmer, greatly disapproved of their forthcoming nuptials, but did give William a dowry of $500 upon their marriage.

A very conscientious and religious woman, Elizabeth taught her child to be good to people, work hard, dress well, save, and be charitable. Throughout his life, the more he earned the more John donated, until it reached $550,000,000.

William also traded in horses, some of which may not have been legally owned, and he taught his children to be meticulous in business. He was a bigamist, and left Elizabeth then illegally married Margaret Allen. Margaret may possibly have started out to be a paramour, but there is no evidence of this. It is said that after William left Elizabeth, her father sued him for bail money regarding an accusation from a woman accusing him of a sexual crime.

John, on the other hand, was very honest, pleasant, hard-working, serious, very diligent, persistent, and patient. When he was 12, he worked on neighbouring farms and raised turkey stock for which he earned $50 that he insisted on giving to his mother. Elizabeth instead guided him to use the money as a loan to a farmer, charging a seven per cent interest rate. Part of the loan agreement was for the money to be repaid within the year, when it would be fully settled.

In 1904, John said of this experience, 'The impression was gaining ground with me that it was a good thing to let money be my servant and not make myself a slave to the money.'

Through his education, John had learnt both single and double bookkeeping, commercial history, and mercantile customs, amongst other forms of finance and business.

John never completed high school, but instead visited every business in his town to apply for a job, eventually being rewarded with the chance to train as an apprentice bookkeeper at Hewitt and Tuttle. He quickly progressed within the company, dealing with complicated and complex deals. He was gifted in arithmetic, which was to serve him in good stead for future businesses.

William gave his son John a coming-of-age present of $1,000 dollars, then loaned him a further $200 dollars at a ten per cent interest rate.

With the money, John went into his first business and partnership with Maurice Clark with a grain commission company named Clark & Rockefeller. John only made calculated risks that would succeed with planning. Their business was to deal in hay, meats, and any other necessary supplies. Within their first business year, the gross amount in 1860 was $450,000, leaving the company in profit of $4,400;

the following year it was making a profit of $17,000. The business flourished during the Civil War.

A Christian and regular church attender, John met Samuel Andrews who had already started investing in oil refining. The business peaked John's interest, and they formed a partnership in 1865 along with John's brother William and a couple of others from the church. John delivered his oil in blue barrels using his horses, as this was the only way during the 1860s that it could be supplied. The company became trusted, and a vast majority of Americans used the oil to give them light within their homes for a cheaper price. As this was a preferable choice to electricity and coal, it made John America's first billionaire. President Lincoln also brought oil during the Civil War, helping raise the price per barrel and making it more profitable. John did the majority of things himself where he was able to, and built kilns, barrels, and his own delivery system. This helped to keep the costs low and helped the company competitive.

To avoid any waste, John sold lubricating oil to be used and to produce such things as Vaseline and paraffin for candles. They could also produce paints, making his oil more affordable than whale and coal oil, as well as electricity.

By 1870, their company became known as Standard Oil, and had become the largest supplier. They continued reinvesting in the company by upgrading equipment and employing chemists. John was a visionary, which led him into taking calculated risks which others in the oil industry would not. He invested millions in buying land in Ohio and held it for two years without doing anything. The area is known as Lima oil reserves and no-one would touch it due to its sulphur base.

He studied foreign markets and even sent spies and agents to foreign countries to be able to sell internationally. John did, however, believe in looking after his workers and their health, and he would authorise full paid leave for sometimes months at a time, and built schools and churches. He also tried to find cures for diseases such as meningitis and yellow fever. He was a fascinating, generous man who, despite his own tribulations, succeeded both in his personal and business life.

John was to be the ancestor to 41st Vice President Nelson Aldrich Rockefeller, 37th Governor Winthrop Rockefeller of Arkansas, along with another famous sibling, David Rockefeller.

STEPHEN LUSHINGTON, MP (1782-1873)

Our fifth distant cousin was the son of 1st Baron Stephen Lushington, MP for Helson, and a director and chairman of the East India Company. Stephen started his political career aged 24, despite having a speech impediment, rhotacism, where he was unable to pronounce the sound 'r'. He did, though, have a clear and shrill tone which attracted attention to his speeches from fellow MPs. During his speeches, he would bare his teeth and fix a gaze over those who were listening, but he was described as good-natured and obliging in demeanour in the Parliamentary Archives.

Starting a law career aged 26, he joined the Inner Temple after being called to the Bar in 1806. Stephen had been involved in a libel case in which the father and an uncle of Charles Dickens were the witnesses and defendants. During his career, he became a legal advisor to Lady Byron in her separation case.

Queen Caroline's counsel included Stephen defending her at a trial before the House of Lords in 1820. The trial stemmed from future King George IV stopping his estranged wife from being queen. Queen Caroline, who intended to become queen at the time, was living in Italy since their separation in 1796, following her alleged infidelity.

Lord Liverpool's Tory government was requested by the future king to bring a Bill of Pains and Penalties before the House of Lords. On the 5th of July, it was entered, and followed by proceedings on the 17th of August. The Bill was to aid in proving Caroline's infidelity while living abroad and to bring an annulment to their marriage.

Prints and curvatures were produced in colour, including one called 'All a Bottle of Smoke' by John Fairburn, which is held in the Parliamentary Archives.

The trial lasted 49 days, ending on the 10th of November. But despite the majority of the public being in support of Caroline, the House of Lords voted in favour of the king and his government. However, the House of Commons did not support the Bill and it was withdrawn, George was crowned a year later, but Caroline was barred, dying a short time later.

Stephen became MP for Ilchester in 1820, but was forced to resign after being opposed to the slave trade. He became a Judge of the Consistory Court of London and progressed further to become a Privy Counsellor and Judge of the High Court of Admiralty. In 1835 he came very close to a duel with Prime Minister Sir Robert Peel, after labelling both Peel and the Duke of Wellington 'convicted swindlers'.

Stephen's final post was Dean of Arches upon retirement. During his political career, he supported the Cotton Mills Regulation Bill, protecting children from excessive working hours within the mill industry. Stephen also supported the Jewish Emancipation Bill, acting as a majority teller.

Throughout Stephen's life, he was an advocate of the anti-slavery cause and became Vice President of the Anti-Slavery Society. He was also a director of the African Institution, and was in fact chiefly responsible for bringing the Act in 1824 which was to abolish the forced transfer of slaves between the British colonies. Stephen also aided in securing the Emancipation Act in August 1833, which gave all slaves in the British Empire their freedom and plantation owners compensation. He was also active in campaigning against the slave trade in other countries. His name is inscribed on the Buxton Memorial Fountain in London, designed by amateur architect MP Charles Buxton. Originally installed in Parliament Square costing £1,200, it was moved in the post-war redesign to Victoria Tower Gardens after several figures went missing and it ceased to work. It was restored to celebrate the 200th anniversary of the Act in 2007.

DEAN ARTHUR STANLEY, OF WESTMINSTER ABBEY (1815-1881)

Upon researching the Todd line further, we came upon Dean Arthur Penrhyn Stanley of Westminster Cathedral. The Dean, our sixth cousin three times removed, was born in 1815. His mother's line descends from both the well-connected and influential Lushingtons and the Leycester family of Toft Hall. Our own connection to the Lushingtons is through Mary Altham, a distant second cousin who married the Reverend Henry Lushington's ancestors to the Dean.

Further research showed how family lines in our various branches entwine, and an example of this is Dean Stanley's wife Lady Augusta Frederica Elizabeth Bruce. Augusta unveiled a statue of John Bunyan, who is a distant great uncle of ours through our Bentley branch.

Lady Augusta was a lady in waiting to HRH the Duchess of Kent, and she was also a resident woman of the bedchamber to Queen Victoria. Interestingly, she is also a descendant of our ancestor Robert the Bruce through her father the 7th Earl Thomas Bruce of Elgin and Kincardine.

Queen Victoria wrote an entry in her diary regarding the event she and her daughter Princess Beatrice attended – Lady Augusta's funeral in 1876, which was unusual. Through his love for his wife, the Dean had a stained-glass window installed to her memory in 1877, which celebrated her ancestry and her life. Unfortunately, in 1940 it was destroyed by a blast, but the inscription remains to this day on the ledge.

The Dean had a very fulfilling career both as a Canon before becoming a Dean, and as an author. He was considered one of the greatest thinkers of his time, having been educated at both Rugby, Warwickshire, and later at Oxford, where he graduated with honours. He later went on to become a Professor in Ecclesiastical History before becoming a Dean.

He was popular with Queen Victoria and the royal family during his illustrious career, and he officiated the wedding of Queen Victoria's son Prince Alfred to The Grand Duchess Marie of Russia in St Petersburg in 1874, although the Queen herself did not approve of his marriage.

Within the Royal Collection Trust is both a colourful miniature of Dean Stanley, displaying the badge of the Order of the Bath, along with a black and white photograph taken in 1877.

During the Victorian era, the accounts kept by Westminster regarding the location of tombs were unclear, so Dean Stanley kept an account of various tombs and memorials within the Abbey.

One of the Dean's missions was to find the tomb of King James I of England, who is also known as James VI of Scotland. The Dean gathered a group of Abbey staff to aid in his quest every night, and one evening in 1868 the historian James Anthony Froude joined them. With flaming torches in hand, he opened each and every vault.

As a result of Dean Stanley's diligent work, he found the king in his wooden lead coffin, with an inscription on a copper plate stating the following:

Depostitum

Augustissimi

Principis Jacobi Primi,

Magnae Britanniae

Franciae et Hiberniae, qui natus apud Scotos Xiii

During our research, we came across a striking newspaper article by the Dean, printed at the time in the *London Atliemcum* in 1870. And although we are unable to state word for word what he wrote, we can summarise it.

Within the article, he describes being among the tombs of both the Tudors and Stuart royalty, and the names he mentioned were William III; George II; Charles II; Queen Anne; and Prince Frederick of Hanover, to name but a few.

His description of Queen Elizabeth the First's coffin was both astonishing and strangely fascinating.

The Dean describes that, with only a dim light to light his way within the vaults of his search, he found the coffins of both Elizabeth and her sister together. Elizabeth's coffin was similar to that of Mary Queen of Scots, and the coffin lid was integrally carved with moulded panelling made of oak and the base of elm. The lid displayed a Tudor badge, with a carved full double rose with ER on either side of it and the date 1604 beneath. It was inlaid with rich red silk velvet and an ornamented silk cover.

King James was found interred within the King Henry VII vault, and in fact with the king himself and his wife Elizabeth of York. In his will, it was clearly stated that the vault was for the sole use of his wife and himself to have eternal peace together, but for some unknown reason the three of them lay side by side. Henry spent £7,000 on his funeral arrangements, which today is approximately £4,639,354, so he might not have been impressed to find a royal third wheel in his eternal resting place. This vault seems to have been very busy, with another account stating that Queen Elizabeth I was interred there after her funeral and before being moved in 1607, at the cost of 46 shillings and 4 pence. The Dean died suddenly at the deanery as the result of erysipelas.

Dean Stanley's Effigy. Westminster Cathedral 2018.

DEAN STANLEY'S TOMB

Upon one of our visits, we met one of the clergymen, a verger, who kindly showed us the south eastern section of King Henry VII'S chapel. Here stood Dean Stanley's monument. Further research through Westminster Abbey shows his monument was paid for by public subscription, designed by J.L Pearson, and unveiled in 1884. From the photograph that the verger kindly allowed us to take, you can see that it is made from alabaster with a marble white effigy and proudly displays four shields on both sides, including the Stanley coat of arms.

Argent, a bend azure, three stag heads cabossed or.

The motto of the Stanley family is '*Sans Changer*'. Translated this means 'without changing' and is shared by the Earls of Derby that are related to the younger Stanley branch.

The engraved inscription on the top reads:

Arthur Penrhyn Stanley second son of Edward Stanley Bishop of Norwich, Dean of this Collegiate Church MDCCCLXIV LXXXI. Born Dec XIII MDCCCXV Died July XVIII MDCCCLXXXI

Below lies his grave, and you can see the inscription by the photograph.

When leaving, the verger allowed us to walk down the main aisle leading down to the throne. This area was closed to the general public, and walking along the aisle we were in awe of the architecture. Suddenly the organ started to play, which was excellent timing and gave us the chance to share a laugh with the verger.

ELIZABETH BARRETT-BROWNING (1806-1861)

Our fifth cousin four times removed was the daughter of Edward Emmanuel Moulton-Barrett and Mary Graham Clarke. She was born 6th March, 1806, in Durham, the eldest of 11 children.

Edward's wealth came from his inheritance from his grandfather Edward Barrett, heir to extensive sugar plantations in Jamaica. His estate in Herefordshire, 'Hopes End', nestled between Ledbury and the Malvern hills and comprised of 500 acres. It had an extensive drive leading through the grounds, lined with magnificent fruit trees, woodland, evergreens, flowers, and a walled garden, and there were also large lawns, waterfalls, gravelled paths, cottages with gardens, and a farmyard with farm buildings.

Elizabeth had an idyllic childhood spent riding and having picnics on the Barrett estate. She started writing poetry at the tender age of 15.

Edward suffered financial losses from the mismanagement and uprising at the plantations, which forced him into selling the Hereford estate at public auction in 1831 to Thomas Heywood. The family then went to live in several rented houses in Devon before moving to London.

Falling from a horse in her adolescent years resulted in a spinal injury, and Elizabeth also suffered a great deal of ill health during her lifetime. She joined the literary society in the 1840s following an introduction from her cousin John Kenyon, a verse-writer and philanthropist.

Her first collection of poems was published in 1838 and showed a much more humane and liberal point of view. Elizabeth became political in 1841, campaigning for the abolition of slavery.

Elizabeth's work helped influence reform in the child labour legislation regarding children working in mines, trades, and mills of England. And she wrote very influential volumes such as *The Cry of the Children* due to the terrible conditions they had to endure.

She became a worthy rival to Tennyson as a possible successor to the Poet Laureateship when Wordsworth died.

Elizabeth become a pen pal of Robert Browning after reading poems he wrote to her, and they married in secret in the autumn of 1846, at St Marylebone Parish Church. Her father did not approve of her husband and disinherited her. The couple left for Italy immediately after their marriage, and she lived in Florence until her death in 1861, leaving a son, Robert Wiedeman Barrett Browning, known as 'Pen'. Robert Junior, who painted much of his life, came to live in London with his father after his mother's death.

Elizabeth became independently wealthy through inheritances from both her grandmother and her uncle.

ALFRED MAY TODD (1850-1931)

A distant ninth cousin, Alfred May Todd, was the founder of A.M Todd's company at the tender age of 19, along with his brother Oliver.

Born in 1850, in Michigan USA, Alfred was the youngest of ten children, and his parents were farmers who had moved from New York. Albert went on to study chemistry and received a Master's with honours in the subject in 1922, continuing his studies on a particular mint in Europe.

Albert borrowed $100 and rented five acres from his father. But when Oliver came away from the business, leaving his brother to run it alone, Albert got into debt. He had bought 1400 acres of swampy land for $25,000 to further his company, but the land was not ideal due to it needing to be cleared of wood and other organic items, and the horses had difficulty working due to the boggy land.

Albert was a world leader in peppermint oil, along with other botanical extracts, and he patented his crystal white double distilled peppermint in 1875. As a result, he became known as the Peppermint King. He had two large plantations named Mentha at 1,640 acres and Campaignia at 2,000 acres.

Campaignia was the world's largest plantation in 1894, and Albert constructed houses, barns, libraries, distilleries, warehouses, ice houses, and windmills, amongst other things, to build a small village for himself and his workers.

Albert purchased a further 7000-acre farm named Sylvania Range and bought 500 shorthorn cows, which he fed with mint hay during the winter months. In all, he owned nearly 11,000 acres making peppermint for his company. He had brought Black Mitcham rootstock from England in 1883, and this variety yielded more oil than the other varieties.

The company was bought in 2011 by a Swiss flavouring company called Wild Flowers GMBH, who then sold the company for $3 billion to Archer Daniels Midland.

Albert tried running for Governor under the Prohibition Party banner in 1895, and the following year he tried to run for Congress. He won the third Michigan Congressional District seat but was later defeated in 1898. He went on to found an organisation, The Public Ownership League of America, in 1916, through his interests in public ownership of railways and utilities, and he wrote several articles on the subject. He served as a President of the organisation until he died in 1931.

Albert also had a love of art and rare books, which he collected, and he made donations to help fund the Kalamazoo Public Museum in 1927. At Kalamazoo College, he established the A.M. Todd rare book room.

His sons Albert and Paul both served as Mayors and City Commissioners of Kalamazoo, and Paul Todd, his grandson, continued carrying the political torch when he entered the House of Representatives.

Paul II was the first Kalamazoo Democrat to stand for Congress in 67 years, and he was also the founder of the international Kalamazoo Spice Extraction Company in 1958. This company, now called Kalsac, uses herbs and spices along with other natural ingredients. It is still within the family, and run by Paul's granddaughter Martha.

His company quote was: 'We hold nature in awesome respect.'

Paul was described as being a great, genuine, and sincere person, who viewed public service as a high honour; Paul wanted a better world, and made his contributions privately.

He became Chief Executive Officer of Planned Parenthood in 1967, and was appointed in 1972 to the Governor's Commission on Ethics.

PRIME MINISTER SIR WINSTON CHURCHILL (1874-1965)

We were researching a DNA match when we came upon Lydia Miller-Stow, born in Connecticut in 1711. Lydia was the daughter of Governor Benjamin Miller of Middlefield, and her maternal grandfather Christopher William Todd, from Yorkshire, emigrated to the USA.

We researched first the DNA match through Lydia's daughter, also Lydia, reaching the said match using records. We then turned our attention to one of Lydia Miller's other daughters, Thankful, and in turn her daughter, Elizabeth. Elizabeth married Jerome, and their son Leonard was Vanderbilt's business partner. Leonard was an American financier and maternal grandfather to Winston Churchill, our Prime Minister and our twelfth cousin first removed.

Leonard was not of calm temperament, and was very flamboyant, yet witty and charming. He had his hand in most things, whether it was as a diplomat, an investor, or a sportsman. He took gambles to see if they failed or were successful, and became known as the 'King of Wall Street'. Leonard, like most in his era, worked at a young age to learn the ropes and how to haggle. Interestingly, he struggled with maths but went on to study law and later open a practice.

Leonard went on to found a newspaper and printing business before he and his brother invested in and managed a telegraph enterprise. They sold it for a large sum and Leonard went into Wall Street stocks, where he lost a vast amount of money, making him bankrupt. However, he did become one of the wealthiest, most influential men in New York, and would also partner with Cornelius Vanderbilt in business.

His daughter, Jennie, was said to love another, but her marriage to Lord Randolph would assist both families. Leonard gave a wedding dowry for her of $50,000, plus a yearly allowance of $1,000. Within seven months of the wedding, the future Prime Minister Winston was born.

Also descended from Lydia was the author Anne Theodosia 'Anita' Leslie-King and her younger brother Desmond. Anne wrote various novels regarding her family, including *The Marlborough House Set*, *Madame Tussaud*, and *Waxworker Extraordinary*, amongst others.

Desmond was not only an author but also a film director, and he produced 'Stranger at My Door' as well as other BBC productions.

CHAPTER SIX

THE BUTTERFIELDS

The Butterfields are related through our great-grandmother Maria Butterfield, and this part of our family was also mentioned in the Domesday Book. Both ancestors and descendants include many interesting characters that led fascinating lives.

We decided to begin with our ancestor John Butterfield of Oakworth Hall, who was born in 1676, in Keighley in Yorkshire. His many descendants include not only the famous Mr William Gates, but also our seventh cousin Sidney Albert Goff.

During his lifetime, Sidney was part of the cycle speedway team in 1958, while his daughter is successful and passionate about the hairdressing industry. She is Chair of one of the largest independent training providers in Wales, having received an MBE for her services in 2015.

WILLIAM MASTERMAN, ESQ. (1722-1786)

William was a distant great uncle of ours, and was born in 1722 to Thomas and Catherine. Masterman was a solicitor and a political agent of Restormel Park, Lostwithiel in Cornwall, and MP for Bodmin.

Our great-grandfather was also under his patronage, and entered the Naval service as a Midshipman on his first Buffalo, under the command of Captain William Truscott, on the 20th February, 1781. Here William partook in the battle of Dogger Bank against the Dutch, where casualties were high on both sides. His great-niece Elizabeth Harrison married Edward Butterfield and was to become the mother of William Butterfield, ESQ.

WILLIAM BUTTERFIELD, ESQ. AND ADMIRAL (1766-1842)

Our fourth great-grandfather William Butterfield, was both an ESQ. and an Admiral, and was born in Durham in 1766 to Edward and Elizabeth. His maternal grandmother was a Masterman and a cousin to William Masterman. (See previous regarding Masterman.) William married a few times, resulting in him having a very large family.

During William's career, an unfortunate situation occurred in a well-known tavern, 'The Star and Garter Inn' in Portsmouth Point in 1790, involving the crew on board the *Melampus* that William was serving on, and in particular a gentleman called Mr Richard Hancorn.

Hancorn was a petty tyrant, who was quick to hand out harsh and unfair punishments for transgressions that were mostly minor. He handed out one particular punishment to our great-grandfather, then aged 24. William had come on deck, fully rigged to embark ashore for the evening. He had not advised Richard that he was doing so, but had already received permission from the First Lieutenant. This Lieutenant was already now ashore, so unable to confirm the story, so William was lashed to a grating and then hauled up to the mizzen peak, in full view of the assembled vessels in the anchorage.

When Lieutenant Richard Hancorn entered the Inn, followed not long after by William and four other midshipmen – Hannam, Hamlin, Parkinson, and Trollop – William told Richard just what he thought of him. The other midshipmen also decided to join in, challenging him to fight, but Richard refused, reminding them of his rank. In turn, Richard was then called a coward and labelled a rascal and scoundrel. Richard left the Inn and, upon returning to the ship, reported the incident to Captain Pole, who in turn reported it to the Port Admiral, Vice Admiral Robert Roddam. Although Robert reported it to the Admiralty, it was decided that the incident happened ashore so they had no jurisdiction, and they referred it to the Attorney General. This led to a trial at Winchester Court, when all five were brought before the Winchester Assizes at the beginning of June 1791.

Mr Richard Hancorn won his case, and it was decided by the Judge that the Admiralty would decide the punishment. The Admiralty took into consideration the bullying of my great-grandfather by Richard and decided to take no further action. William left the Navy soon after and joined the Merchant Service. At the start of the French Revolutionary War three years later, he was recruited back into the Navy as Quarterdeck on the American ship *Anna*, docked on the Thames, under the command of Sir Charles Cotton. He was then appointed Junior Lieutenant of the *Anna* on the eleventh of April 1794.

Most of the Merchant Seamen under William's care were heavy sailors and weakly manned, so William needed to be persistent and patient to keep them on the right path. William made many voyages including to the Cape, but did not receive any prize money, like the Commanders and Mates of the East Indian Company.

In August 1812, William's court martial was held in Madras. After arriving in India, he found himself the senior officer there, because Vice Admiral Drury had recently died and the Commodore Broughton was absent. William decided to continue to Calcutta and then sent the *Minden* to England at the urgent request of the Merchants, but without the proper authority. This led to William's dismissal from that frigate.

The following April 1782, he was involved on HMS *Nonsuch* in the Battle of the Saintes that took place in the Caribbean, between the British and the French.

William went on to pass his exam for Lieutenant in 1788, and his position was aboard the HMS *Majestic* – a 74-gun ship built at Deptford Dockyard and launched in 1785. It was a third-rate ship and the largest type at the time, costing £31,543,16s,4d. The further fitting out came to an additional £4,867, which in today's money would be over £3,060,482. The ship at the time was part of the Lord Howe fleet and under the charge of Captain Charles Cotton.

In later years, The *Majestic* joined Nelson's force in the Battle of the Nile, where it fought a bloody battle in 1798. After coming under heavy French fire, Captain Westcott was shot and killed upon its decks, and there were over 50 dead and 143 wounded. Admiral Brueys was struck in the midriff by a cannonball that virtually cut him in half, which shows the brutality of the battles taking place.

William went on to serve aboard the HMS *Mars*, a large class 74-gun warship under the command of Captain Alexander Hood. HMS *Mars* was built at Chatham Dockyard between 1788-1794 and carried 24-pound guns instead of 18-pound guns on the upper deck.

Captain Hood first entered the Navy in 1767, under the famous Captain James Cook. His second voyage of exploration was to be in 1772 and lasted for several years. The Hood family mostly served in the Navy, including Alexander's brother, 1st Baron Vice Admiral Sir Samuel Hood (which is possibly where our 3rd great-grandfather's name came from).

On the evening of 21st April, 1798, in the Battle of Raz de Sein off the coast of Brittany, they fought the famous French 74-gun ship, *L'Hercule*. *L'Hercule* attempted to escape, but due to the tide running in the wrong direction, it was forced to anchor. The anchors became entwined, leading to both vessels touching. The guns were fired inboard due to not being able to run out on *L'Hercule*, leaving Captain Alexander Hood to attack at close quarters.

After nearly two hours of bloody battle, *L'Hercule* lost over three hundred men. On the *Mars*, 31 men were killed including Captain Hood, who was mortally wounded in his thigh. His femoral artery had been cut after being hit by a musket bullet, and he was carried below deck where the sword belonging to L'Heriter, the Captain of *L'Hercule*, was placed in his hand.

The *Mars* went on to partake in the Battle of Trafalgar in 1805, before being decommissioned and taken apart for scrap in 1823.

William received a very elegant 50 guinea sword from the *Mars* crew for his part, which his son Edward Harris Butterfield inherited. We presume it then went to his sister Elizabeth Semple, along with all his personal effects upon Edwards's death. The trail goes cold here.

William became a Commander in July 1798, on the warship *The Hazard,* a 16-gun built in Frinsbury, Kent, and launched in 1794. On the 7th August, 1798, William captured an American snow vessel that two brothers, one a French Privateer, had taken possession off a few days earlier. William was able to gather information regarding the French Privateers from the Master of the *Snow*, and then decided to try and find them. It took five days before William encountered a 24-gun French Privateer vessel, and gave chase for a further two days. The French Privateer vessel readied the guns and then escaped from *The Hazard*'s clutches.

Not long after, William's ship spotted the French 20-gun warship *Neptune* with over 300 on board, and a fight ensued. *Neptune* was only carrying ten guns at the time and used muskets to help fight *Hazard* before surrendering. William rescued the ship *Triton* (East India man), which was one of the East Indian Company ships from the dangerous coast of

Ireland, and he conducted her safely to Portsmouth. The house of David Scott, and the company of London, presented him with a piece of plate valued at 150 guineas.

He also rescued a transport vessel without masts carrying military supplies for the Army. The ship itself went on to fight in the Napoleonic Wars, and it was sold eventually in Portsmouth, at the end of October 1817, to Mr Sprately for £1,010.

William was eventually posted Captain in 1802, and advanced to Rear Admiral of the Red on 10th January, 1837 – a senior position in the Royal Navy only outranked by the Vice Admiral of the Blue. The Navy was divided into three squadron colours of Red, White, and Blue from the time of Queen Elizabeth I, due to fleets increasing in size. An Admiral of the Red is the highest rank one could achieve, and only one person at a time could hold this rank, which lasted a lifetime. This rank was abolished in the late twentieth century, and in 1864, the coloured squadrons were disregarded.

William's Navy career spanned 61 years, and during this time he never lost a single ship in his charge. He was appointed to succeed Admiral Sir Home Riggs Popham, for the command of HMS *Stirling Castle* in June 1814. The only opportunity he had was to perform a service of bringing the guards from Bordeaux to England, due to peace in France, and in return William received a letter from the Officers of the Corps, acknowledging the attention he paid to their comforts.

William made donations from September 1803 to the Havant Volunteer Corps to help pay for costs and expenses for clothing.

HON. JOHN WARREN BUTTERFIELD (1801-1869)

Hon. John Warren Butterfield I, a distant 9th cousin, was born in 1801 in New York, and spent much of his childhood on his family farm. At the age of 19, he became a stagecoach driver and then later the owner of a large network of 40 stage lines in New York, along with other companies including steamboats operating on Lake Ontario.

During his lifetime he became the President of the Overland Rail Mail, which became the largest stage company in America. John lost stock and equipment to the Confederates, so he moved the company north due to the Civil War in 1861. When the war finished, John then became a director of the Wells Fargo company, which took mail from the East to the West coast using various companies. This gave John the idea of making a company infrastructure that could bid for a contract from the government. The directors that he chose came from National Express, Adams Express, Wells Fargo and Co Express, and American Express, who all had their own stage lines and experience.

He built the longest stage line in the world at that time, which would become the Butterfield Trail. And he had a rule for his Mail Road: 'Nothing on God's earth must stop the U.S mail.'

This enabled him to meet the Government requirements to secure the contract with a bank loan of $162,000. Unfortunately, due to circumstances beyond his control, this loan led to John being voted out in 1860 when the money was not repaid.

John did not take this lightly and left the meeting extremely disgruntled. It then had to be rescheduled with John present so that a compromise could be reached, with John having a lesser vote.

The company, which also took passengers – essential for the new frontier settlers and other businesses – was fortunate never to have been attacked by outlaws. But it was once attacked by Indians in early 1861 in the Apache Pass, when the conductor received a shot in the leg.

There is a museum in Pott's Inn in Pottsville, Arkansas, which once formed part of the Butterfield Trail.

John became the Mayor of Utica from 1865 until 1869, and he was planning to rerun, but unfortunately died after suffering a stroke in 1969.

Interestingly, his daughter Sophia married a director of the American Express Company, Alexander Holland.

SAMUEL H. COLT (1814-1862)

Another notable Butterfield family member was industrialist and inventor, Samuel H Colt, who was the founder of the Colt Patent Firearms Manufacturing Company. Born one of at least nine children, he lost his mother at a young age to tuberculosis. Samuel started his early working life in textiles, and for a brief time his father sent him away to sea. It was during this time that he came up with the idea of the Colt and its rotating cylinder by use of cocking a hammer and an attached pawl to turn the cylinder, which firmly locked in alignment with one of the barrels.

His father financed both designs of a rifle and a pistol, with the rifle being the more workable of the two. With a lack of further finance from his father, Samuel made a portable lab which he took on his travels to earn a living, performing a demonstration with laughing gas.

Samuel found a gunsmith, John Pearson, to construct his revolver design which, in 1835, he patented. One of the first to use an assembly line, he thought himself a man of science, but he was actually a pioneer of advertising. During one of the visits to John, he became partners with Hiram Powers, and together they combined their skills: Hiram in wax sculptures, and Samuel in fireworks, to produce shows depicting demons, centaurs, etc.

Samuel's brother John Caldwell Colt (1810-1842), a bookkeeper, wrote a few textbooks regarding double-bookkeeping. John went on to kill a creditor he owed in New York, after disagreeing on the amount. He was convicted of his murder, but on the day of his execution held in the Tombs Jail, he committed suicide.

During the American-Mexico War, the Texas Rangers ordered 1,000 revolvers. Samuel's firearms then went on to be used in the Western frontier during the Pioneer era; the other available firearm at that time was the Pepperbox gun. Samuel demonstrated his gun to President Andrew Jackson and received an approval letter that led to a bill being approved by Congress. Samuel died from complications of gout, leaving his wife and three-year-old son Caldwell his wealth of $15,000,000 (around $407,000,000 in today's money).

The Colt family also included both US Senator LeBaron Colt and his brother Samuel Pomeroy Colt, or Pom for short, born in 1852. They come from a large family of six children. Pom started his career in law, but his passion was politics, having attended both the Massachusetts Institute of Technology and the Columbia Law School. Pom first began law in 1877, along with his brother LeBaron, but his passion for politics led him to the position as a Military Aide-de-Camp that was part of the Republican Governor Henry Lippitt's staff. He then became Colonel, which Pom used throughout the rest of his career. His marriage to Elizabeth Bullock in 1881 brought him three sons, including Russel Griswold who married the actress Ethel Barrymore. Ethel, known as the first lady of the theatre, was part of the famous acting family and related to current actress Drew Barrymore. It is said Sir Winston Churchill was smitten with her and asked her to marry him in 1900. Russell and Ethel's three children continued within the family acting profession.

During Pom's career, he became only the Assistant Attorney General then eventually the State Attorney General in 1885.

His political career waned by 1886 after a failed bid to be a US Senator, but by then his business empire had started to become successful.

Pom became the founder of Industrial Trust Company, one of the largest financial institutions, serving as the Bank's President until 1908. Pom then went on to be appointed the receiver of the bankrupt National Rubber Company of Bristol in 1887. He not only took over the company but also reorganised and reopening it as The National India Rubber Company. The company later merged with several other companies to become the United States Rubber Company, which became the largest supplier of rubber goods to the world. Having become very wealthy through his business, Pom helped his local town by financially aiding civic projects and giving access to his farm, now called 'Colt State Park'. Sadly, Pom suffered a stroke that led to his death in August 1921, at Linden Place.

Another seventh-removed cousin in this particular branch was Lewis Henry Lapham, who founded the Texaco Oil company. Lewis shares a common Smith ancestor with the Colt family, who all descend from our Butterfield line.

MAYOR SAMSON FOX OF HARROGATE (1838-1903)

Samson is related to us through his great-grandmother Mary Butterfield. He was one of at least five children to her grandson and our cousin Jonas, a loom overlooker.

He left school aged eight to work in the cloth mill, where his father was employed, but showed an aptitude for engineering and design. Later on, with one of his brothers, he started a tool-making business at the Silver Cross Works, based in Dewsbury Road, Hunlet. He then later started as an apprentice for railway locomotive builders in Leeds – Smith,

Beacock, and Tannett – as a travelling representative at the Victoria Foundry. During his time there as an apprentice, he came across Scotts Shipbuilding and Engineering Company, and they invested a major amount into Samson's founded Leeds Forge company in 1874. After borrowing money for 18 acres of land that formed part of the Castleton Lodge estate in Armley, Samson issued his first patent in 1861, for improvements to machinery which he issued yearly.

Part of Samson's business was that he patented a corrugated furnace, with which he was able to employ over 2000 men; he further issued a patent for the 'Corrugated Boiler Flue' which was to improve the steam boilers. Although there were a few setbacks, the products became very successful and Samson became rich and made his name. This tube was later used by both the Americans and the Germans.

Samson was able to move into the grand Grove House which he altered and where he employed servants, grooms, and gardeners. His home was the first to have gas lighting and heating in Yorkshire. A newspaper called *Today* accused Samson of being a swindler by floating a company with vastly inflated prices that thousands of small investors were eager to be a part of. Unfortunately, the bubble burst and the small investors lost their money. Samson himself had hugely invested in water gas, which led to him suing Today owner, Jerome K Jerome for libel; he won his case, but by then the newspaper had gone bankrupt.

Samson founded a further company, named 'Fox', which produced solid pressed steel railway bogies in Joliet, Illinois, in 1889. Samson gave Harrogate their first steam fire engine, being the main benefactor of the town. Through Samson's wealth, he was able to pay for the Royal College of Music building, costing £45,000, which the Prince of Wales officially opened with Samson being the guest of honour. During this time, Samson became Mayor of Harrogate, standing for three years. He provided affordable social housing, and his agents distributed coal and meat to the less wealthy. Harrogate benefited from Samson's engineering through his water gas plant that provided the main street lighting. In 1891, the College of Arms granted him a coat of arms, the motto being 'To the brave, nothing is difficult'.

He married actress Hilda Hanbury and they had nine children, but only four survived. Their son Arthur William Fox was the ancestor of the Fox acting family, which includes Edward and James Fox OBE, along with Emilia Fox.

When Samson died, newspapers carried headlines such as 'Mill-boy to Millionaire', and King Edward VII sent Harrogate a telegram of condolence.

SIR ERNEST SHACKLETON, OBE (1874-1922)

Our shared ancestor with Sir Ernest was our 5th great-grandfather Edward. One of Edward's sons, Rodger, was also the ancestor of Sir Ernest Shackleton OBE. Ernest was one of ten children born in 1874, in Kilkea, Kildare, Ireland. Sir Ernest also had some very interesting siblings, though they are not as well-known as him.

He was one of the main players in the heroic age of Antarctic exploration – something that was both very brave and required courage to undertake the unknown in those times. Recently Sir Ernest's ship the *Endurance* has been discovered. A museum in Athy can be visited to find out more about Shackleton's fascinating history.

Son of Henry Shackleton ESQ and his wife Henrietta Letitia Sophia Gavan, ESQ Henry Shackleton is related to our Butterfield line, whilst Henrietta is related to our Sole line.

Both these lines make Sir Ernest our seventh removed cousin. He was born one of 11 children, some of whom also made a name for themselves in their chosen fields, including his sister, the artist and MBE Kathleen., and another sister the writer Helen Brietzcke.

Sir Ernest's younger brother was Francis Richard Shackleton-Mellor, also an interesting character. Francis was born in 1876 at the Kilkea House, Ireland and, like his family, was educated at Dulwich College.

During his career. Francis was appointed Assistant Secretary for the Office of Arms at Dublin Castle, and he also fought in the Boer War, as well as succeeding to full Lieutenant in the Royal Irish Fusiliers.

During King Edward VII'S visit, Francis served as the Gold Staff Officer, and mixed with the social circles of the Duke of Argyll, brother-in-law of King Edward VII and Lord Sutherland-Gower.

Francis's character has been described as flamboyant and dapper, but later could be described as dubious, due to business dealings which resulted in him eventually being convicted and sentenced.

On July 5th, 1907, the Irish Crown Jewels and collars of five Knights of the Order were found to be missing from the new safe within Dublin Castle, before a visit by King Edward VII to Dublin. The collars, valued today at £110,000, belonged to the Marquess of Ormonde, Earls of Howth, Enniskillen, and Mayo, and the 9th Earl of Cork. The Irish Crown Jewels were the regalia of the Order of St Patrick. St Patrick's was one of the four orders of chivalry that included the Orders of the Bath, Thistle, and Garter, founded in 1783.

Created by the 394 precious stones, including diamonds of Queen Charlotte's English Crown Jewels, the creation was produced by London-based business Rundell, Bridge and Company. Appointed goldsmiths and jewellers to the throne, they held a Royal Warrant and served George III, George VIV, William IV, and Victoria.

It also consisted of the Order of the Bath Star of George III – a diamond badge of the Grand Master of Saint Patrick's sky-blue enamel circle, comprising the motto of the order 'Quis Separabit MDCCLXXXIII' in rose pink diamonds, surrounded by a wreath of trefoils in green shamrock emeralds. It then had encrustation of large single Brazilian diamonds of the first water (meaning highest quality), surmounted by a crowned harp in diamonds and loop, and included a red Saint Patrick's saltire of rubies with a beautiful silver mount.

The value of the jewels would be over £1,730,000 in today's money.

The Office of Arms had been moved to Bedford Tower due to restructuring, therefore the jewels also had to move from where they were kept to Bedford Tower. There, a newly constructed strongroom was to hold a new square safe, but it was too large to fit through the two-ton steel doorway. Sir Arthur Vicars, the then Ulster King of Arms, tried to secure funds to have the doorway modified, but without success. So, the safe was placed in the library, where it stayed for four years. However, the library also served as a public waiting area.

Sir Arthur was described as having negative qualities and being unpleasant, fussy, and irritating. His nephew was the Cork herald, whilst Francis was the Dublin herald. The Athlone Pursuivant was Arthur Bennet Goldney; Arthur applied for this position to aid his profile in the elections in Canterbury, Kent.

Francis and Sir Arthur met through their heraldic and genealogy work, and they shared a house as tenants, although Francis spent little time in Ireland.

Three days before the theft, the cleaning lady reported that Bedford Tower was unlocked, the library and strongroom doors unlocked, and the Office of Arms office front door unlocked.

Sir Arthur's keys had gone missing a short time before the jewels went missing, but were found at his Dublin home just days after the theft. He was the nephew of the Ulster King of Arms, and one of the seven keyholders of the Office of Arms; Sir Arthur also held one of two keys to the safe, and named Francis as the thief in his will. Sir Arthur's own family jewels, valued at £160,000 in today's money, were also stolen.

With the aid of spiritualists and mediums, Sir Arthur conducted a seance and was told the jewels were buried in the graveyard of a church in Clancilla. This was once the home of the Shackleton family and, using this information and with the help of Sir Arthur, a police investigation of the graveyard was conducted but nothing was found.

The police also received a telegram from Great Malvern, containing an address; it stated the jewels were at 9 Hadley Street, Dublin, but this address did not exist.

Both Detective Inspector John Kane, of Scotland Yard, and Sir Arthur were convinced it was Shackleton's handwriting, so the telegram must be from him.

Sir Arthur was also a great friend and distant cousin to Sir Arthur Conan Doyle, who wrote the book within the Sherlock Holmes series *The Adventure of Bruce-Partington Plans*. It is suggested that the book's fictional character Valentine Walters was based on Francis Shackleton.

It has to be said that 22 individuals gave evidence in the investigation, including one stating that 'Sir Arthur was not a stranger or as careful in showing off the jewels to a variety of people on more than one occasion'.

The reason possibly behind the theft may have been a failed Unionist plot, and the jewels may have been returned to the Crown. A file written by DI Kane is said to name the offender, but this is yet to be released by the Home Office.

Certainly, John Kane believed the theft to have been committed by someone familiar with the surroundings, and pointed out that they had taken their time to remove a ribbon from one of the items and left it behind.

Francis was one of the final witnesses to give evidence, and appeared both composed and extremely helpful.

The key findings of The Viceregal Commission report in January 1908 were: 'Having fully investigated all the circumstances connected with the loss of the Regalia of the Order of St Patrick, and having examined and considered carefully the arrangements of the Office of Arms, in which the Regalia were deposited, and the provisions made by Sir Arthur Vicars, or under his direction, for their safe keeping, and having regard especially to the inactivity of Sir Arthur Vicars on occasions immediately preceding the disappearance of the Jewels, when he knew that the office and the strong room had been opened at night by unauthorised persons, we feel bound to report to your Excellency that in our opinion, Sir Arthur did not exercise due vigilance or proper care as the custodian of the Regalia.'

Due to the report, Sir Arthur Vicars' appointment as the Ulster King of Arms was terminated. In his anger, he refused to give back the keys to the strongroom, causing the newly appointed Ulster King of Arms to have to break in to gain entry.

The other Heralds, along with the Athlone Pursuivant, were also dismissed from their positions by order of King Edward VII.

The Dublin Metropolitan Police moved the safe to Kevin Street Station where it stayed for over one hundred years, before being moved to Garda Museum at the record office in Dublin Castle to be put on display. A reward of £1,000 for the return of the Irish Crown Jewels still remains unclaimed today.

There are lots of theories about what happened to the Irish Crown Jewels, which include that they were sold to a Dutch pawnbroker or a private collector. According to an official document, they were offered for sale to the Irish Free State in 1927. Another possibility was that they were hidden in the crypt walls in Chichester, although we were unable to find further information on this theory.

In 1910, Francis had debts of over £85,000 and had to be officially declared bankrupt. He emigrated to West Africa where he became a plantation manager for a few years. In 1912, he was arrested for fraud and his trial took place in London. This followed a business dealing in which Miss Mary Brown's funds of £6,000 had been used for fraudulent conversion. Francis was sentenced in October 1913 to 15 months of hard labour, and was also charged with defrauding Lord Ronald Gower in the same year. When Francis was released, he changed his surname to Mellor.

In 1920, Francis moved to Sydenham, and lived with his sister Amy, opening an antique shop under the name Frank Mellor. He also became a genealogist.

CHAPTER SEVEN

THE BUTTERFIELDS OF CLIFFE CASTLE

ISAAC BUTTERFIELD I (1766-1831)

This branch of the family starts with our 2nd cousin Isaac Butterfield I. He was born one of at least five children in Keighley, Yorkshire in 1766, and his descendants lead down to our seventh cousins, the French Bourbon line. But for now we are going to describe the life of his children.

Isaac I had married Hannah Sugden in 1781, and they had at least five children including their eldest son, John. John grew up to be very business-minded and became a wool stapler, flourishing in this venture.

John regularly went to East Riding and Lincolnshire to buy his wool directly from farmers. The wool was then brought back on lowlander boats by the Ouse, the Aire, and the Leeds and Liverpool Canal to Keighley and Stocksbridge, where he had a warehouse.

John, unfortunately, died young in 1817, leaving his brother Isaac II a large sum of 30,000 (approx. £15,600,738 in today's money) in his will. This enabled Isaac II to become a local cotton manufacturer. The remainder, it was stated in his will, went to his illegitimate son John Butterfield Hodgson, and set the foundation of wealth for this branch of the family.

Isaac II went on to be described in the Directory of Yorkshire for 1821 as an Esquire.

The family at the time lived at Spring Gardens, a charming old house not far from Cliff Castle.

ISAAC BUTTERFIELD II (1784-1832)

Isaac II married Sarah Shackleton, a daughter of a gentleman farmer of Green Top, and they became parents of five sons and one daughter.

Unfortunately, Isaac III died as a small baby, leaving the other sons to go into the family business, becoming the Butterfield Brothers worsted woollen manufacturers and stuff merchants for over 40 years.

RICHARD SHACKLETON BUTTERFIELD (1806-1869)

One of Isaac II's sons, Richard Shackleton Butterfield, saw the potential to expand the businesses by exporting to America. The brothers started branches in both Philadelphia and in New York, and became merchants for other manufacturers, while their shipping business took British goods to Europe and China.

Younger brothers Henry Isaac and Frederick set off for New York to expand the business and manage the export side. But as travelling between the two countries could take between six to 17 days back then, the two moved to live in America.

Richard Shackleton Butterfield's part was to manage one of the mills near his home in The Woodlands. He married Jane Wright Barlow, and had a daughter Jane (Jennie) in 1850. Later, after the deaths of both Richard and his wife, Jane became the ward of his younger brother Henry Isaac.

Richard was described as being almost a capture of a wicked Victorian industrialist, and he was immensely wealthy. In his will he left £180,000, which in today's money is £11,269,620.00, but he paid his workers the lowest wage possible. He vehemently opposed any steps to improving his workers' quality of life, and they were paid the bare minimum that Richard could get away with. He made his workers use two looms each at a time, which was a very dangerous practice.

On the 18th of May, 1852, all his workers downed tools and protested by a way of a strike. Richard, also a magistrate, had eight ringleaders arrested when his workers refused to return to work. Two of them were sentenced to two months' hard labour, but one of the men – Robert Redman – declared in court that he was in the possession of evidence that proved the Butterfield brothers' malpractice and law-breaking.

It's known that Richard walked with Charlotte Bronte, from Keighley to Haworth, and during their conversation he persuaded her not to write about the chartists or that subject. Both Reverend Patrick Bronte and his daughter Charlotte, the famous author of *Jane Eyre*, were pleased with Richard's defeat in court regarding his striking workforce.

Richard had his own access to the clean water supply and did not want to pay a higher rate which would allow the poor to also access clean water, so he started a petition, which was signed by leading property owners and inhabitants, alleging malpractice in the elections to the Board of Health.

The Board of Health had made recommendations to improve the water supply after many people had died from a waterborne disease. Richard opposed Reverend Bronte several times over his clean water scheme to bring piped water and a sewage system to the village, yet this would carry on for another six years with people dying of disease.

After Richard's management practices at the mill were exposed in 1852, Charlotte Bronte made a comment: 'I cannot help enjoying Mr Butterfield's defeat.'

The brothers had one of the most successful wool textile mills in Haworth, Keighley, and

Stanbury in Yorkshire, and the census of 1851 shows the number that they employed was 1,413,243 – some being children.

After renting it from Christopher Netherwood for £3,999, the Butterfields bought Cliffe Hall from the Craven Bank in 1848. It was described at the time as an Elizabethan-style residence, with gables and pinnacles, and this purchase showed how the family was progressing in status. It was just below Spring Gardens, the then-family home.

They extended the estate from 20 to 300 acres – reported in the *Keighley News* in 1878 – and employed a large staff of housemaids, cooks, chambermaids, butlers, footmen, grooms, coachmen, and gardeners.

Sarah, an unmarried sister to Henry, was in charge of the children within the family and also managed the house. Upon brother John's death in 1865, it was stated in the *Keighley News,* he was described as being 'the leading member of one of the largest and most important commercial establishments in the district'.

Younger brother William continued running Prospect and Lumb Foot Mills, until his death in 1874.

Frederick was now living with his wife and family in America, and upon Sarah's death in 1870, Cliffe Hall was left in the hands of brother Henry Isaac.

ESQ. HENRY ISAAC BUTTERFIELD (1819-1910)

Henry Isaac was an extrovert compared to his siblings. Whilst living in America, he had met Miss Mary Roosevelt Burke, daughter of Hon. M. Burke and niece of Judge James John Roosevelt of New York. Judge Roosevelt and his wife Cornelia Van Ness were powerful within the social scene and hosted the French Emperor when he visited.

Mary was also the first cousin to President Theodore Roosevelt of the USA. They shared, through her mother, a great-grandfather James Jacobus Roosevelt (1759-1840), second great-grandson of the first Roosevelt in America. An Alderman and businessman in refined sugar and a banker, he amassed a vast fortune which included an inheritance. James Jacobus Roosevelt's other family members included President Franklin Delano Roosevelt. A description of Mary can be found in the *Queens of American Society* by Charles Scribner & Co of New York.

The couple were married when she turned 16, and they bought a home in France, where they welcomed distinguished visitors and diplomats. They also bought a villa in Nice, and attended the French Imperial Court where they were presented to Queen Victoria's Court. Mary attracted much attention in the drawing room of the English Court, as she was a truly elegant, charming, and sincere woman.

They had two children, but their young daughter Eugenie Dora died aged only a few months. Their son was named due to family connections: Frederick William (named after Henry's brothers) Louis (named after the French Emperor) d'Hilliers (named after friend, Marshal Baraguay d'Hilliers) and Roosevelt Theodore Butterfield. He was born in 1858.

Mary sadly died young, at the age of 29, so Henry sent four-year-old Frederick to live at Cliffe Hall with his aunt, uncle, and cousin Jane, during a cholera outbreak, whilst he travelled.

Henry Isaac renamed Cliffe Hall to Cliffe Castle in early 1878, and he hosted lavish social gatherings where he invited friends from both America and Europe, along with local dignitaries and manufacturers. He printed visiting cards and installed communications at Cliffe Castle, where he also held an impressive white ball in 1884, at which the guests wore white (according to the *Keighley Herald*).

Henry extended Cliffe Castle, adding a music room with a high vaulted ceiling, and other rooms were given bay windows whilst a conservatory, towers, and a medieval-inspired entrance with a grand staircase and marble columns were added. An extravagant centrepiece was a vast stained-glass window that was also installed as part of the staircase.

He had to negotiate with the council to expand Cliffe Castle, such as donating money towards the Eastwood House and Park. A footpath in Dark Lane ran across Cliffe Castle lawns that were closed as part of the contribution.

The beautiful stained-glass window was designed to show Henry Isaac Butterfield, his wife and his son, all in Elizabethan clothing. Above them, Madonna and the child represent Mary's Catholic faith, surrounded by armorial glass showing her descent from the Earls of Mayo.

When Henry Isaac commissioned the Powell brothers in Leeds to design the window, his vision of his Butterfield dynasty was with his connection to his French imperial family. The description of the window was written in an article in the *Bradford Weekly Telegraph* in 1883. And the window is still in place, and can be seen at Cliffe Castle today, which is run by the Bradford Museum.

In the Winter Gardens were beautiful marble fountains, greenhouses, and further conservatories, and Henry was an avid collector of items such as furniture and fittings.

He built the Victoria Jubilee Tower in 1887, at Steenton, to commemorate Queen Victoria's Jubilee. And ten years later, Henry Isaac became Honorary Freeman of the Borough.

When his son Frederick become older, he was left to oversee and manage Cliffe Castle, and gave the impression in his autobiography that he didn't at times approve of his father's extravagance.

When he wrote his book, he quoted himself with:

'My best years for the study were employed in representing my absent father and generally watching over his enormous expenditure at Cliffe Hall 1875-1880 when he turned the

comparatively modest Cliffe Hall into the present elaborate Cliffe Castle and proceeded to fill the new building with every costly detail his Parisian experience could suggest.'

Henry Isaac had spent approximately £130,000 on items to furnish Cliffe Castle, which included a large ornate crystal mirror owned by King Louis XIV, cut-glass chandeliers, tapestries, goblets, bronzes, pictures, and French furniture. A special lot was a large green Malachite fireplace with gold fittings, which was installed in the drawing room, and is still there today.

It was claimed that Henry Isaac won it in a gambling match, however this was not true. Prince Anatole Demidoff had it commissioned in the 1840s; his family owned the Russian malachite deposits in the Urals, and in the Crystal Palace official catalogue of 1851, this chimneypiece was illustrated as part of the Russian exhibit.

The fireplace was moved to Palazzo San Donato in Florence, for the salon of Prince Louis 18th, but after the death of the prince and his brother, the contents of the castle were sold at an art auction. The auction was attended by the Rothschilds, Vanderbilts, and the Butterfields, amongst others. Henry Isaac bought from this auction not only the fireplace but also tapestries and busts; his granddaughter Countess Manvers, an artist in her own right, painted the drawing room showing the fireplace within the room.

His great-granddaughter moved it to Thoresby Hall after inheriting it; Frederica then moved the fireplace to her sitting room at Butterfield's Cottage on the Thoresby Hall estate. Frederica stated in her will that it was to be given to Cliffe Castle upon her death.

Henry Isaac was presented with a ceremonial key on the 8th of July, 1893, by the Mayor of Keighley Alderman Ickeringill, to commemorate the opening of Victoria Park, to which Henry Isaac donated £5,250. His great-granddaughter Lady Frederica left the key in her will to Cliffe Castle.

The Mayoress's chain for Keighley was presented to Henry Isaac, displaying in the centre a form of the royal coat of arms, supporters, and a motto with heraldic colours. Decorated with diamonds and rubies at intervals around the framework, on either side is displayed an enamelled English rose, surmounted by the imperial crown. One rose with the initial E is set in diamonds with VII in blue enamel, the other is with the Queen's initial A set in diamonds. It dons an enamelled ribbon which gives the date 1902, and on the front is a series of festoons that connect three important badges – one is placed between the badge and the centre link of the chain. It is a craved wrought link with the arms, crest, helmet, and motto of Henry Isaac the donor.

The inscription on the chain reads:

'Presented by H I Butterfield of Cliffe Castle Esquire, to the corporation of Keighley on the coronation of Edward VII, 9 August, 1902 to be worn by the mayoress and successors Annie Longsdon, Mayoress George Burr, Town Clerk, Vivate Rex.'

When Jane's mother, Jane Wright, died, Henry took Jane under his wing and she became his charge. She was introduced to French society and to the Court of Napoleon the 3rd. Sir Henry Isaac travelled with his son and his French manservant Constant, booking rooms in a London hotel, to attend the funeral of the Prince Imperial at Chislehurst. Henry introduced Jane to his friend Comte De Palikao, a General at the time who had been appointed by Empress Eugenie to be her Minister of War. The General was awarded his title after the Battle of Paliko in China in 1860, and he was reported to have carried off millions from the sacking of the summer palace at Peking. This indeed proved to be untrue.

He had only one son, Vicomte Charles De Montauban, then a Colonel of Hussars. Jane married Vicomte De Montauban in 1873, and on her marriage became Viscountess of Palikao. The Vicomte went on to become the 25th Prime Minister of France. Jane's large inheritance from her father helped the couple, and they went on to have two daughters. Unfortunately, Jane died when the girls were small, in 1878.

Her daughter, Marie Pie Charlotte Elizabeth Jeanne Cousin-D'Montauban, was born in 1874 in Paris, France. She went on to marry the Marquis Anne Henri De Rochechouart. The House of Rochechouart is the oldest French noble family after the royal family, and they were supporters of Charles the Bald.

Jane's older daughter, Marie Pie had six children; one was the Marchioness Jeanne Elizabeth Charlotte Cousin Marie Edwige Virginie Renee Victurnienne Yvonne De Rochechouart, born in 1911.

Jeanne went on to marry the Comte Fortune Rene d'Andigne Marie De Bourbon-Bussett. The Comte d'Andigne was the Municipal Councillor of Paris. He descended from Duke Charles I of Bourbon, who was the 5th cousin to King Charles VII of France. The Bourbon-Bassett line is an illegitimate line descending from the agnatic descendants of the Capetian dynasty, but they may be canonically legitimate, making them the senior male branch and thus senior to the Bourbons that reign in Spain.

Jane's youngest daughter married the Marquis de Mortemart, from the same family as her brother-in-law. The Mortemart noble family was one of the oldest in France and had a part in history during Queen Isabella and Edward II's time. One infamous member of the Mortemart family was Madame de Montespan, mistress and mother of seven children to King Louis XIV during the 1600s.

Henry Isaac bought land and built the family mausoleum at Utley in 1895. It is a very ornate building, with a pitched roof and a tall pinnacle flanked in the centre, while at the rear there is a stained-glass window.

The building was designed in a gothic style, and the family crest over the door and underneath displayed the motto: 'VIS UNITA FORTIOR'. When he died in 1910, the flags in Keighley were flown at half-mast.

The estate then passed to his son Sir Frederick, who lived there after selling his home in Paris.

SIR FREDERICK WILLIAM LOUIS D'HILLERS THEODORE ROOSEVELT BUTTERFIELD (1858-1943)

Frederick married American Jessie Kennedy Ridgeway in 1888, after meeting her at Cliffe Castle's summer party the year before. Their marriage produced a daughter, Maria Louise Roosevelt in 1889. Sir Frederick moved his family to Ingle Dene House in Banbury Road, Oxford. He had enrolled as a member at Balliol College, where he stayed for ten years and was awarded a MA.

Maria was just six years old when they moved to Oxford, and there she met, spent time and took tea with Alice Liddell, a woman in her forties, and the inspiration for Alice in Lewis Carroll's book.

Frederick was well educated and achieved degrees from Oxford for law and Leipzig for music. But he considered himself to be American, like his mother. In 1906 the family were invited to the White House for the wedding of Alice Roosevelt. He did have American citizenship and became a member of the Diplomatic Service for the US Consul at Ghent. However, he renounced his citizenship in 1912 to enable him to enter politics in England.

He became Mayor of Keighley from 1916 until 1918. During his term Frederick was given two days' notice for a royal visit, when the town was to play host to King George V and Queen Mary, who would be visiting Keighley on the 29th of May, 1918. Their visit was to boost morale for the textiles industry as the war effort required 16 million blankets, for which Keighley's industrial industry was well known. The town took up the challenge with excitement and rose to the occasion.

Frederick also held office as a Justice of the Peace for West Riding, in 1922, and he was then appointed Knight Bachelor.

Three years after his wife's death, he married the very glamorous and extremely wealthy Hilda Johnson-Waters, who he met on a liner travelling to New York.

Maria became a Countess when she married the 6th Earl Gervas Pierrepont of Manvers. But tragedy struck Maria and her husband after they had their three children. Their son and heir Rt. Hon. Evelyn Louis Butterfield Pierrepont, died aged four in a road accident. And just two years later, their eldest child Lady Mary Helen Venetia Pierrepont died, aged ten, of cholera.

This left their only surviving child, Lady Frederica Rozelle Ridgeway.

LADY FREDERICA ROZELLE RIDGEWAY PIERREPONT (1925-2015)

Being a female, Frederica did not inherit the title of Manvers, but she did inherit the estate of Thoresby Hall and Cliffe Castle. She auctioned off many of the fittings over a four-day sale – nearly one thousand lots – including Bryon's wine glasses. She further sold Cliffe Castle to Sir Bracewell Smith, the Lord Mayor of London, in 1950, who in turn gave it to the people of Keighley.

During the war, Frederica Rozelle worked as a Wren and became a successful author when she went on to write *The Sea Bird* in 1979, regarding her career at sea. A further book she wrote was *A Boat Called Martha* in 2001, about her adventures with Martha McGilda, who sailed single-handedly from Dover to Finland. Frederica's second husband worked as Deputy Medical Director of Health for the London borough of Newham.

She founded a scheme to help rehabilitate east-end boys who were in care in the borough of Newham, that were in care. They took the boys out on the Thames in a canal boat called the *Martha,* and called them the Tuesday boys, teaching them how to sail. This scheme became known as the Martha McGilda charity in 1980.

Other books she wrote included *Limehouse Lil,* which was about the area of Limehouse and the redevelopment of Canary Wharf, and *Maid Matelot.* Frederica used the author's name Rozelle Raynes.

She and her husband moved from Thoresby Hall after a fall in 2010, and built a bungalow named 'Butterfields' on the Thoresby Hall estate. They sold Thoresby Hall to the National Coal Board in 1984, and today it is a hotel, while Cliffe Castle is now a museum which is open to the public.

Frederica died in her sleep in 2015. Although she had been married twice, she had no children, making her cousins her heirs on her father's side.

TOM CLIFTON BUTTERFIELD (1856-1937)

Another of our notable cousins was Tom Clifton Butterfield, who was born into a working-class family in Keighley and a son of a wool sorter. Tom was a quiet, reserved, and unassuming character, who had a great talent for drawing, and joined the Keighley Mechanics Institute art class at the age of ten.

From this, Tom excelled, and by his early teenage years he started winning prizes for his art.

He went on to gain an Art Master's certificate, which enabled him to be employed as an assistant art teacher at the Keighley School of Art.

From 1889-1919 he became the head of Keighley School of Art, during which time Tom introduced subjects that included woodcraft, stone carving, cabinet making, bookbinding, and other new subjects like decorating to be taught. This helped play a part in the rehabilitation of wounded World War I soldiers who needed new skills to help them both financially and mentally.

Tom had a great love of painting, and would often paint the local landscape in both watercolour and oil. He had a very good understanding of the trees and plants through his experience in gardening, and exhibited his artwork several times at the Glasgow Institute, as well as in other places.

One such painting is called 'The Lily Pool', believed to be inspired by the pond at Cliffe Castle. Today, Bradford Museums and Galleries hold examples of his great work such as, 'The Aire Valley'.

In his later years Tom became blind and was forced to retire as his eyesight failed.

His great-nephew was the famous Scottish landscape artist, Edward Atkinson Hornel, from Broughton House in Kirkcudbright, where he lived until his death.

SIR HERBERT BUTTERFIELD (1900-1979)

This branch of our family also included our 7th cousin, Sir Herbert Butterfield, who was born three months before Queen Victoria's death and named after his uncle. He had a bright future ahead of him.

The Butterfields, by the time Herbert was born, had a very remarkable history and were famous locally. Yet this Oxenhope branch was leading a very different and humble life compared to their Cliffe Castle relations. Both Herbert's father and grandfather worked in the mills as wool sorters, while his father Albert helped run a book shop in which Albert brought back a three-penny edition book, *Alice in Wonderland*. Ironically, it was Sir Frederick Butterfield's daughter taking tea with the lady that inspired the story.

Albert would also often help the blind son of the local mill owner. Through helping the son, Albert met his wife. She was from Leominster and would visit the village to help care for the blind boy. Through this set of circumstances, Albert was also able to advance his position within the mill to become the clerk.

By the time Herbert was eight, he wanted to become a writer, having become a great admirer of Robert Burns, and he would often read the Bronte novels and Walter Scott. Herbert's own writings would include stories of distant lands and boyhood fantasies.

Whilst Herbert attended primary school, he took the 'pledge'. We like to think our cousin the Reverend Theobald Matthews had an influence on his thinking, along with Herbert's father at the time.

He then attended a grammar school before winning a scholarship to attend Cambridge, where he gained the nickname 'Boottercoop' within the junior common room, due to his accent. Herbert's appearance was described as being five feet and seven inches tall, with a slim build, and a strong Yorkshire accent.

Herbert graduated with first class honours in 1922, and then went on to become a Master of Peterhouse, a Regius Professor of Modern History, the Vice-Chancellor of the University of Cambridge, as well as a well-established author. He wrote over 20 books, including *The Whig Interpretation of History* and *The Peace Tactics of Napoleon*.

He also had many quotes attributed to him, one being the following: 'If history can do anything, it is to remind us that all our judgements are merely relative to time and circumstance.'

Herbert was one of the leading historians of the twentieth century with his books on politics, and he accomplished much within his career, with 13 honorary degrees. He was knighted in 1968. From such humble beginnings, he achieved much within his lifetime.

CHAPTER EIGHT
MAKING HISTORY, COVID TIMES

When we started this book, the world was its usual bustling, busy self, aeroplanes flying overhead off to far exotic and distant places. Life and people were going about their usual busy pace in their everyday life, like us in our usual routine of school, college, and work – normal everyday family life that we all take for granted.

We will be honest with you. When back in January 2020 the news was full of people in China who were suddenly dying in the streets, and that China had then taken to welding people into their homes, we did not – along with the rest of the world – think it would have any impact on our lives here. It was the other side of the world, after all.

Whilst it seemed like another illness on the scale of the Plague or the Spanish Flu, it hit us all worldwide.

But today, we all feel like extras in a blockbuster film that none of us asked to be part of. All over the world, planes have stopped flying, public transport is running at a minimum, and educational institutes have closed.

The government, and current Prime Minister Boris Johnson, is pleading for all to self-isolate, and for no-one to mix with other households, including family. No journeys, whether by car or on foot, to be made unless essential.

Italy, Iran, and Spain are the worst hit, with Italy far more than China, where this infection possibly originated at a wet market. Conspiracies fill the air, one of which is that Covid is biological weapon and originated from a Wuhan laboratory.

American President Donald Trump was calling it the 'Chinese Virus', which upset China, whilst Russia blamed the UK.

It is very surreal, and the only communication to the outside world is via technology; the only places now open are the supermarkets and local food shops. Schools are distributing home learning packs, whilst the colleges are switching to online learning for exams.

It is a beautiful sunny day in March, spring has started, but we are all on our fourth day in our own self-isolation; the world has come to an eerie standstill.

The numbers currently infected stands at 4,000 in the UK alone, but the true number is believed to be 180,000. The death toll stands at 177, with London being the UK's epicentre; Italy stands at over 4,000 deaths and over 109,000 infected.

Today is the first day of the official lockdown in the UK, and our day started with a text from a family member.

'It is a different world we wake up to this morning, now the government have put us in lockdown for the next three weeks to help control the spread of the virus Covid 19.

Please stay at home with your children, if you aren't already, this is very serious. Don't go out unless it is for actual shopping or the pharmacy.'

This virus is caught through contact with each other; it is deadly and will take anyone's life.

We are now reaching the end of March 2020, and so far in the UK the number of deaths stands at over 800.

The Duchess Maria-Theresa Bourbon-Palma died from it a couple of days ago, the Prince of Wales has also been diagnosed with Covid-19, and now the Prime Minister has caught the virus and is seriously ill, along with former French Prime Minister Patrick Devedjain.

It is now the beginning of April, and the virus has come close to home, with regard to a close cousin's mother who died two days ago of the virus.

The days merge into one another, except for a Thursday at 8pm when the nation claps for the NHS.

It is affecting a lot of the government's main officials: the Prime Minister is now in hospital, and some close royal connections, including the Marquis of Bath, have died of the virus.

We are now into mid-May, and Prime Minister Boris is almost back to full health, but our death toll stands at nearly 33,000 people. Education is still closed, but those who cannot work from home – except in non-essential retail stores – are allowed to go back to work.

Halloween is now upon us, and we are currently waiting for the government to announce a second lockdown until December 2nd as death rates for all ages are up and local lockdowns haven't fully curved the infection rate.

We have reached the Christmas time of 2020. Kent, the area in which we live, is classed as the UK's worst area affected since Covid-19 began, and a new variant now named after Kent has evolved.

We live in hope that we stay uninfected, whilst we hear news of others who have tested positive. With the news reporting over 51,000 people per day testing positive nationwide, our area is classed currently as being tier 4; this means the third lockdown locally in our area.

April 2021, it was announced at midday that the Duke of Edinburgh has passed away. He had been ill for two weeks in hospital, and had received heart surgery. We are still fighting

Covid-19, and his grandson Prince Harry, didn't make anything easy for his grandfather leading up to his death, with possibly false tell-all interviews and newspaper articles. Along with Prince Andrew's forthcoming court case, it has been a very stressful reign for The Queen.

Summer brought the lifting of some restrictions and possibly a form of normality.

And we are now just passed Christmas 2021, and the virus has evolved into the variant Omicron – a more contagious strain – with a new pandemic high of over 183,000 for the week. The majority of the UK has had several vaccinations against the variant.

We wonder how our ancestors felt in the Great Plague – Sir Ralph Coningsby, Sir William Todd, The Mayor of York, and also William Bentley who nursed his younger sister until her death from the Black Death. What were their thoughts at the time, and how did they cope?

CHAPTER NINE

END OF AN ERA,
OUR BELOVED QUEEN

A lot of historic things happened during the time of writing this book, which we felt were important to include.

We end our story with a famous, ground-breaking royal cousin of ours – Queen Elizabeth II (Elizabeth I of Scotland) – who shares one of many ancestral lines to us that include Robert the Bruce. Queen Elizabeth was well-known for her favoured dogs, her corgis – a Welsh word, meaning small dog.

It was a grey, heavy, rainy midday on the 8th September, 2022, when the Royal Household issued the first of grave concerns over the health of our Queen, the nation's grandmother and only monarch that most of her subjects have ever known.

This was the day that no-one expected to end in the way that it did. By early afternoon, HRH Prince Charles and his sister Anne, the Princess Royal, attended the Queen's bedside at Balmoral. By late afternoon, other senior members of the royal family hurried to Scotland after being informed that the Queen's health had declined.

Our Queen had reigned over most people's lives, and in some cases, all of their lives. She was the second longest reigning monarch in history after King Louis XIV of France, and the United Kingdom's longest reigning for 70 glorious, and sometimes turbulent, years.

Queen Elizabeth II ascended the throne in 1953, at the tender age of 25, after her father King George VI died from cancer on the 6th February, 1952. In a world dominated by men, she was never expected to be on the throne like her father, and it was a time when Stalin was still in power in Russia and Winston Churchill was her first Prime Minster.

In her 21st birthday speech on April 21, 1947, the then Princess Elizabeth said: *'I declare before you all that my whole life, whether it be long or short, shall be devoted to your service and the service of our great imperial family to which we all belong.'*

She was a remarkable woman who would shine brightly for many decades to come, and as a nation we celebrated her Silver, Golden, Diamond, and Platinum jubilees.

The Queen was born in the roaring twenties era, in 1926 – a time that brought jazz music, a new uninhibited lifestyle, and the start of the consumer age – and lived through the Great Depression of 1929, which lasted for the next ten years.

In one of the earliest television broadcasts, her grandparents, King George VI and Queen Mary, were shown at the opening of the BBC television service.

The Second World War, that started in 1939 and finally finished in 1945, saw Princess Elizabeth take her place in the war effort, from stripping down motor engines to serving in the Auxiliary Territorial service. She became the first royal female of standing to serve within the military. The war saw the start of women being able to go to work, unlike previous generations of single women working in domestic settings. The number of women in the workforce rose to half, and many others were taking further education.

Elizabeth married her first love, Prince Philip Mountbatten, in 1947, and their first child Charles, heir to the throne, was born in November 1948.

The rock and roll years of the fifties and the start of television then arrived, while the world was still recovering from the war, and the Queen was to ascend to the throne and become our Head of State. A world first was marked when the Coronation was televised, against many negative protests from Churchill, the Cabinet, and the Duke of Norfolk, amongst others. The Queen then made British history in another first by making her mother, the dowager, a Counsellor of State. Together, they lived in Buckingham Palace – the Queen, her beloved husband, the Dowager Queen, and for a time, Princess Margaret.

From the time the world started to change and Elizabeth took her role, she began her lifetime work on behalf of the Commonwealth – a cause that she held close to her heart. And she was able to travel around the world, thanks to the growth and development of air travel.

The great smog in London in 1952 was a yellow tinge in colour, with a sulphur odour to it. It was caused by severe air pollution from coal plants, diesel powered transport, electricity, heat, and an anticyclone during a very cold weather spell that lasted nearly a week and resulted in thousands of deaths.

Queen Elizabeth was involved in the regeneration after World War II, and this included housing and the welfare state, to help the nation recover from the war.

In the Queen's speech of 1957, she wanted to include the new cultures moving to the United Kingdom from across the globe.

The swinging sixties arrived with the progression of women's civil rights, along with miniskirts and the Beatles – a global sensation of the time, who were presented with MBEs at Buckingham Palace. It also saw the start of the Northern Ireland troubles which was to last for the next 30 years.

This time also marked the start of the space race, nuclear power, and the assassination of President John Kennedy, his brother Robert, and Martin Luther King, as well as the horrific Aberfan mining disaster in Wales with great loss of lives, many of them children.

As we entered the hippie seventies and the year of the Silver Jubilee, it came with soaring inflation; it also brought a three-day working week, due to the oil crisis – something the Queen wanted to address but was advised against.

Disco music, pocket calculators, the first commercial computer, microwaves, and the first email– sent by the Queen in 1976 whilst visiting the Royal Signals and Radar Establishment in Malvern.

It was around this time that the Queen began to introduce her famous 'walkabouts' to greet the public in the waiting crowds.

The first assassination attempt – 'The Lithgow Plot' – occurred while she was on tour in Australia. There was an attempt to derail the train, where a log was placed on the railway track, but fortunately her train was travelling at too slow a pace for any damage to occur.

This was followed by the attempted kidnapping of Princess Anne, on the Mall, where the man involved stopped her car with his white Ford Escort. Brandishing two handguns, he shot at the royal driver, who was injured along with the policeman who tried to shield Princess Anne and her new husband within the car. The gunman then tried to pull Princess Anne out of the car, ripping her clothing in the process, but she kept remarkably calm, and refused. A police car patrolling nearby heard the struggle and confronted the gunman, but one officer was shot in the stomach. Other people nearby came to the Princess's rescue and tried to hold the offender, but he fought back and was able to escape briefly before being recaptured.

The man involved was finally foiled by the security guard assigned to the Princess, and later police searching his car found two pairs of handcuffs, Valium tranquillizers, and a ransom note addressed to the Queen demanding £2million.

The eighties arrived, and the Queen by this time had seen seven prime ministers during her reign before we were introduced to the Iron Lady Margaret Thatcher, and her attempted assassination.

It also brought the advancement of the digital age, with global internet and video gaming.

The first Buckingham Palace intruder broke in during the early hours of one morning, wandering around before breaking an ashtray – he took a piece – then entered the Queen's bedroom. The Queen woke up when she felt someone sit on her bed, but she remained calm whilst the intruder bled. She left the room briefly to fetch help, then stayed calm until a footman arrived to escort the intruder away.

An assassination attempt was made during the annual Trooping the Colour event, when a teenager fired six blank shots towards the Queen on horseback, scaring her horse. Nevertheless, the Queen remained calm and carried on.

The last attempt on her life took place on a tour in Australia, involving a concealed gunman. He fired a shot as the Queen exited the car, but luckily the bullet was nowhere near her.

The eighties also brought a royal marriage for the future heir to the throne, Prince Charles. This took place at St Paul's Cathedral and seemed like a real-life fairy tale and a happy future for the United Kingdom.

The nineties brought the end of the Cold War and the start of the global war on terrorism. Cell phones made an appearance, though they were not very mobile due to their size. Email was starting to become popular along with instant messaging, whilst there was also growing use of CD roms, portable CD players, and MP3s. The music had now moved to rave and grunge, along with hip hop, and there was growing popularity for cable TV and 24-hour news. Science had evolved to cloning and gene therapy, and companies like Apple, Amazon, and eBay were also growing.

1992 was not only the Queen's Ruby Jubilee, but it was the year which she herself described as her 'annus horribilis'.

Two of her sons – Charles and Andrew – and her daughter Anne all ended their marriages, and a great fire took place at Windsor Castle destroying over 100 rooms and with the loss of some irreplaceable history. Buckingham Palace was opened to the public to finance the cost of repairing Windsor Castle, and it was an idea the Queen had created.

Happier events saw the opening of the Channel Tunnel, making the world an easier place to access. But towards the end of the decade, the world was stunned with the death of Princess Diana in a terrible car crash in Paris. This attracted controversy when the Queen remained at Balmoral in Scotland, did not fly the flag at half-mast over Buckingham Place, and did not make a national speech. On taking advice, the flag was lowered and the Queen returned to London to make a national speech whilst also greeting the public who were mourning.

The Queen's personality always shone through in her smile, and in the way she made people feel at ease. Many people have funny stories to tell. Prince William, when he was small, was unable to say 'Granny'. One day, when he fell over whilst playing at Buckingham Palace, he called for help, crying out, 'Gary! Gary!' For a brief time everyone was confused, until one guest asked who Gary was (thinking it was one of the household staff). The Queen responded, 'I'm Gary,' scooping William up, and added, 'He hasn't learned to say Granny yet.'

The Queen's nicknames included Lilibet – lovingly given to her by her family whilst a child, because she could not pronounce her own name – and 'Cabbage' by her beloved husband, meaning 'Sweetie' in French: *'Mon petit chou'*.

On one occasion the Queen took her corgis for a walk in the gardens of Buckingham Palace while the Romanian Dictator Nicolae Ceausescu was visiting in 1978. She could see them coming the other way, but decided she couldn't face talking to them, so she hid in the nearest bush to avoid interaction with her visiting houseguests. Other visiting dignitaries, such as President Trump, broke protocol by walking in front of her at Windsor Castle during his visit in 2018. It was an ill-timed walk whilst going to inspect the Guard of Honour, but diplomatically the Queen sidestepped him and allowed him to walk first.

The 2000s brought the Golden Jubilee – the first Monarch since Queen Victoria to reach this milestone. It also brought the sad loss of her younger sister Margaret and, shortly after, the death of her mother Elizabeth. There were, though, marriages of grandchildren and births of great-grandchildren to celebrate, as well as the wedding of her eldest son and heir to Camilla Parker-Bowles.

In 2002, the Queen hosted the Party at the Palace, which was a pop/rock music concert for the Golden Jubilee. Those taking part included Ozzy Osborne, Phil Collins, S Club 7, Annie Lennox, and Tom Jones to name a few great artists, and Brian May was on the roof of Buckingham Palace, playing *God Save The Queen* with his electric guitar.

Another funny story told, which illustrated The Queen's sense of humour, involved two American tourists. Hiking in her tweeds and headscarf near Balmoral Castle with one of her protection officers Richard Griffin, they came upon the tourists. Failing to recognize the Queen, the tourists asked if she lived nearby, to which she replied that she did. They then went on and ask if she had met the Queen, to which she said, 'No, but he has.' The tourists then requested a photo to be taken of them with the protection officer by Her Majesty, before they then had a photo taken of themselves with her. After waving goodbye, the Queen remarked, 'I'd love to be a fly on the wall when they show that to their friends.'

When the Olympic Games were hosted by London in 2012, the Queen herself was to be part of the sketch jumping out of a helicopter into the stadium. During a meeting to enquire about the stunt double who would represent her and what the Queen would be wearing that evening; it was revealed by her dresser that Queen wanted to appear in person within the sketch. The Queen then further enquired if she could have a line to speak.

She was also the first to send a tweet in 2014, at the Science Museum. It read, 'It is a pleasure to open the information age exhibition today at the @scienceMuseum and I hope people will enjoy visiting. Elizabeth R.'

In April 2018, the Queen and Sir David Attenborough appeared in a TV documentary 'The Queen's Green Planet'. Whilst walking in Buckingham Palace gardens, they passed the trees planted in honour of the births of her children. Above the noise of helicopters that could be heard, The Queen stopped and listened before remarking, 'Why do they go round and round when you want to talk? It sounds like President Trump or Obama.' President Trump's helicopters had been responsible for damaging the Palace lawns previously.

Also in the programme, the Queen remarked on a sundial being placed neatly in the shade, stating, 'Isn't it good?' then noting the placement before laughing.

The Queen was known to drive herself in her car, at times with no detectives or bodyguards, bouncing at alarming speed over the beautiful landscape at Balmoral, which amazed ramblers and tourists within the area. The Queen last drove herself at the grand age of 95, around the Windsor grounds.

After the outbreak of Covid-19, the Queen made a televised speech to the nation on April 5, 2020, which was a very powerful one:

'While we have faced challenges before, this one is different. This time we join with all nations across the globe in a common endeavour, using the great advances of science and our instinctive compassion to heal. We will succeed - and that success will belong to every one of us.

'We should take comfort that while we may have more still to endure, better days will return; we will be with our friends again; we will be with our families again; we will meet again.'

One of Queen Elizabeth's iconic moments was at the funeral of the Duke of Edinburgh on the 9th of April, 2021. It took place during the Covid restrictions, so a smaller funeral of only 30 was held at St George's Chapel, Windsor. Household bubbles were still in place for stopping the spread of the virus. The Queen's bubble was Philip and her small selection of picked household staff.

At the funeral, the Queen – dressed in black, wearing a black and white face mask – sat alone in her moment of grief for the man that had stood by her side for 73 years. It was a perfect example of leadership, whilst some in Parliament – unbeknown to the public – were partying, including on the day of the funeral and against the Covid restrictions policy.

In June, the Queen attended an event for volunteers working on the Platinum Jubilee, and a very large cake was presented for her to cut. However,, the Queen insisted on using a ceremonial sword. When someone did remind her there was a knife, she replied, 'I know there is. This is something that is more unusual.'

During the Queen's Platinum Jubilee, she made an appearance on the famous Buckingham Palace balcony on June 2nd to observe 1,400 troops, musicians, and a royal flyover, while a gun salute echoed out in honour. Paddington Bear came to tea at Buckingham Palace, during which the Queen pulled a marmalade sandwich from her handbag. To give a grand finale, the Queen then tapped out a tune from a teaspoon onto a China cup in time to the song, *We Will Rock You.*

On her death, former Prime Minister Boris Johnson made a poignant speech in Parliament, describing The Queen as 'timeless, wonderful, naturally wise, and understanding' and commented that we all believed she would go on and on. 'With a great sense of duty, Elizabeth the Great is the longest serving, and in many ways the finest Monarch in our history.'

His predecessor Theresa May recounted a story regarding a picnic in one of the bothies at Balmoral Castle, which she attended at the request of the Queen. It was expected that everyone helped, regardless of who attended. After taking a plate and cheese from a hamper to take it to the table, a cheese fell onto the ground. Having a split second to consider what to do, and using the three-second rule, Theresa picked it up and put it back onto the plate, then placed the plate onto the table with the other food.

Turning round, Theresa found Her Majesty had observed her every move. Looking at each other, the Queen just smiled, and the cheese remained on the table.

The Queen's cortege and coffin left Balmoral Castle on 11th September, just after ten in the morning. The hearse, draped in the Scottish flag, was closely followed by her daughter Princess Anne to Holyrood House where the coffin remained until the following afternoon. The Princess Royal followed her mother to first lie in state in St Giles Cathedral in Edinburgh, before travelling to Buckingham Palace. St Giles had the honour to hold the first national lying-in state for 24 hours.

The Queen's procession was followed on foot by her children from Holyrood House to St Giles Cathedral, and crowds lined the roads from Balmoral and for days afterwards to pay their respects. The Scots Guard and Grenadier Guards played compositions during the Queen's processions within Scotland.

The hearse left St Giles for the airport, to be flown to Northolt, London on a military plane. As the plane took off from Edinburgh, the Band of the Royal Regiment of Scotland played the national anthem. The cortege then travelled to

Buckingham Palace where her family would welcome her. On the journey into London, the roads again were lined with the public, with some cheering, clapping, and throwing flowers in front of the hearse as it drove through the darkness.

Across the world, buildings such as the Empire State Building were lit up in purple, while the Sydney Opera House displayed the Queen's picture. A Swiss artist projected into the sky photos of the Queen with Prince Philip, holding hands on the way to heaven, as his tribute.

Our own bridges, such as Tower Bridge, were lit up in purple to honour Britain's longest reigning queen, and Dover lit up the cliffs, displaying a photograph of the Queen with dates of her birth and death. The Eiffel Tower, too, was dimmed, and the European Commission & Parliament flew their flags at half-mast. Denmark's Queen Margrethe II curtailed her own Jubilee celebrations as a mark of respect. Berlin's Brandenburg Gate showed its respects by illuminating the colours of the Union Jack on the 9th of September, and thousands of flowers were left at the gates of the various royal palaces and castles across the UK.

Nature itself displayed rainbows over both Windsor Castle and a double rainbow over Buckingham Palace when the Queen's death was announced.

On Wednesday, 14th of September, the Queen's children started their 38-minute walk behind the gun carriage down the Mall, their timing in the beat of the drum with every step they all took. Along the Mall, the United Kingdom's flags moved gently in the wind with pride.

The procession moved towards Horse Guard's Parade, where the Commonwealth flags were hung in pride, and all routes were packed with thousands of people silently standing and watching with tears and heavy hearts.

Through Whitehall and onto Westminster Palace, where the Queen would lie in state for the thousands of public to pay their respects, both day and throughout the nights for four days. She lay where her mother, father, and ancestors had lain before, on a rich purple catafalque with gold edging. A gold five-foot cross and a ring of white flowers at her head, sitting proudly on the Crown of England on a purple pillow with gold woven ribbon, along with the golden Sceptre and Orb screwed to the roof of the coffin.

There were four flickering yellow candles, each with a Queen's Guard, four Beefeaters, and four police personnel, at the four quarters on the wide scarlet platform. Two cavalierly men stood at her head with their heads bowed, alongside the Scots Guards and the Beefeaters from the Tower, whilst MPs, vicars, priests, nuns, and the public – young and old, fit and disabled – filed past, paying their own respects by bowing at the Queen's coffin in silence. The only noise was signalled by the Commander's cane, tapping twice on the stone floor for the change of guards, boots echoing in the Great Hall every half hour before the tap of the capped sword to position themselves. Over the course of the national mourning period, several Guards, including one on vigil at Westminster Palace, fainted, as did some members of the public and even a royal cousin.

On the late Friday evening of 16th September, when the Queen's children had attended the Vigil of the Princes at Westminster, another incident occurred. A 28-year-old man, Muhammad Khan, rushed out of the queue, pushing a seven-year-old girl out of the way, and managed to lift the draped Royal Standard and touch her Majesty's coffin. His behaviour had appeared strange to other mourners in the 14-hour queue leading up to the paying of respects, but he was tackled to the floor by police officers and arrested. The reason he gave was that he wanted to check if the Queen was dead.

The following evening, all eight of the Queen's grandchildren held a vigil beside her coffin. This was another first, and a modern twist to tradition.

We ourselves went and paid our respects to Her Majesty, and the TV does not give a true representation of the Elizabethan Walk. We joined the very long queue at London Bridge at about half past eight in the evening, and after walking for ten or so minutes we were given yellow wristbands. We continuously moved until reaching Lambeth Bridge, snaking round along the Thames riverside where you can view the lights of the Shard, St Paul's, the Oxo building, and the London Eye. There was lots of encouragement along the way from stewards and the Army.

We past Big Ben and the Houses of Parliament on the opposite side, and by the time we reached Lambeth Bridge, it was now about midnight and a little chilly. Our wristbands were checked and hot drinks were on offer, then we were shown across the bridge where there was a bag check on the other side.

We continued down the steps and into Parliament Gardens, joining the first part of a 19-row snake queue, manned by stewards, St John's Ambulance and armed police. When we finally reached the green barriers, we thought we were nearly there, then realised there were another 52 rows we had to join. By this time, it was the early hours of the morning and the queue slowed once more, due to Westminster being closed for the funeral rehearsals. Most people had sat either on the rigid, bumpy walking mats covering the grass, or on the cold pavement, and blankets and water were given out while volunteers were checking everyone were alright. We were aching all over and freezing cold, and wondered how the elderly were coping.

Finally, at 3am, the queue was moving again, and as we moved closer, we could see the reporters and cameras filming and interviewing people within the queue. We finally reached the last airport-style security check, handled by the Irish Army, and followed the path round to be welcomed by Parliament staff. The road was empty, with bollards blocking the way for any traffic, and we could see different types of soldiers practising in the distance.

We walked up the stone steps, which were carpeted and felt soft underfoot, and upon reaching the top we were directed to the left queue. We stood waiting in single file, and were able to see across into the extremely large and grand hall. Below was the scarlet platform holding the Queen's Royal Standard-draped coffin, with the lights bouncing off the glittering Crown Jewels that glisten upon the top. The Scouts, all in line, were paying their own respects in turn.

We slowly made our way down the carpeted steps to the bottom, where we were stopped due to the change of guard. Not a whisper could you hear, only the boots of the orchestrated movements and the taps of the cane and sword upon the floor.

We moved into a position to pay our respects by bowing and making the sign of the cross, and were struck by how high the coffin was and how small the Crown Jewels looked. It was all over so quickly. After queuing for nearly nine hours, we walked away, looking back for one final glace of the coffin as we reached the doors.

Outside, the sailors were practising bringing in the gun carriage which would be accompanied by 148 sailors. At the gates, a coach of Guardia guards had arrived, and most of the area had been closed to both traffic, and in some areas for pedestrians.

The lying-in state closed at six thirty, and the last mourner was a woman from the military.

This was to be the first Westminster State Funeral since Winston Churchill's in January 1965, and the first royal funeral in two hundred years since King George II in 1760.

The Dean of Canterbury, Most Reverend Justin Welby, in his sermon read: 'Leaders of loving service would be remembered when others are long forgotten. People of loving service are rare in any walk of life, and leaders of loving service are still rarer. But in all cases, those who serve will be loved and remembered when those who cling to power and privileges are long forgotten.'

The Queen's coffin was made of English oak, lined with lead weighing at least 500 plus lbs. Her English pallbearers' party from the Queens 1st Battalion Grenadier Guards lifted the heavy coffin and the fixed Crown Jewels no less than ten times on Her Majesty's journey from Westminster Hall to St George's Chapel, Windsor. The Grenadier Guards date back to 1656, and it is the most senior regular army regiment. In total, the number of armed forces deployed for Operation London Bridge (the Queen's funeral) was at least 5,948, without counting other services such as the police.

The funeral service was attended by 2,000 guests that included not only her family, but members of European, African, and Asian royalty, USA President Joe Biden and his wife, New Zealand Prime Minister Jacinda Ardern, French Prime Minister Emmanuel Macron, Italian President Sergio Mattarella, Emperor Naruhito and his wife from Japan, Australian Prime Minster Anthony Albanese, and Ukraine's First Lady Olena Zelenska. It also included our own Prime Minster Liz Truss, Scottish First Minister Nicola Sturgeon, First Minister of Wales Mark Drakeford, Ireland's President Micheál Martin, and Presidents from India and Kenya. There were some dignitaries who were invited but missed the service due to rail transport issues.

Once the funeral service at Westminster Cathedral was completed, the Queen was driven by the Royal Hearse to Windsor Castle, escorted by the death march down the long walk. The Crown, Orb, and Sceptre were removed and placed upon the altar.

This left only the wreath – chosen by King Charles III, and comprising flowers from Buckingham Palace, Clarence

House, and Highgrove House gardens – remaining on the coffin. In the shades of deep burgundy, pinks, whites and golds, nestled amongst moss and oak branches, the sustainable arrangement displayed strength and love. Rosemary for remembrance; Myrtle a symbol of a happy marriage (this was taken from a plant grown from a sprig from the Queen's wedding bouquet).

A note was adorned next to the wreath simply saying,

'In loving and devoted memory Charles R.'

The Wand of Office was broken by the Lord Chamberlain Andrew Parker, Parker of Minsmere, which is a symbolic gesture to signify the end of service to the Queen, and he placed the two halves onto the coffin. This was to show the Queen would ascend to God as a mere mortal and not as a monarch. King Charles II respectfully placed a royal flag over his mother's coffin, in an act of knowledge of the Queen's affiliation with The Queen's Company, Camp Colour of the Grenadier Guards.

The BBC reported that over 5.1 billion watched the service, which is roughly over 60 per cent of the world's population.

Later that evening there was a private ceremony for the royal family to attend, then Prince Philip's coffin was brought up from the Royal Vault before the couple would be laid to rest, interred together with her parents and sister in the King George VI Memorial Chapel, on the 17th September 2022. Until that time, the Prince's coffin had been waiting on a plinth in the Royal Vault until The Queen died.

Queen Elizabeth was a mother, grandmother, and great-grandmother, both to her children and the nation. The Head of State shared her values of public service, wisdom and, later in her life, her experience, an inexhaustible limitless understanding, and immeasurable dedication for her sovereign role from the time she was anointed as queen up until the moment that death came to take her hand.

Her son, now King Charles III, is the oldest heir to ascend to the throne.

'Grief is the price we pay for love.' The Queen in 2001 after the 9/11 attacks in New York.

'May flights of Angels sing thee to thy rest.' Quoted by King Charles III, at his mother's funeral, 2022, taken from Shakespeare's *Hamlet*.

We sadly say goodbye to the Elizabethan era, during which so much has happened, and we welcome the Carenlean era.

DEDICATION:

We dedicated this book to all that have passed, whether centuries ago or of recent times.

RESEARCH RESOURCES

MATTHEWS

Limbus Patrum Morganiae et Glamorganiae, The Genealogies of the Older Families of the Lordships of Morgan and Glamorgan
Llandaff Pound
Nanonagleplace.ie
Chatham Dockyard Historical Society
Naval History archive
The Llandaff Society
Glamorgan Archives
Morgannwg Archives
History of Parliament
Discovery National Archives
British-history
History Ireland
Naval History archive
Artuk
Chatham Dockyard Historical Society
Admirals of the World: A Biographical Dictionary, 1500 to the Present by William Stewart
The Letters of Horace Walpole Earl of Oxford, Volume 1 by Peter Cunningham
Diary of George Marsh 1722-1800 Commissioner of the Navy
The Court-Martials of Mathews and Lestock
Royal Navy, Mathews, Thomas, Admiral
A Narrative of the Proceedings of His Majesty's Fleet in the Mediterranean, and the Combined Fleets of France and Spain, from the year 1741 to March 1744... by a sea officer.
History of the Mediterranean Fleet 1741-1744

Historical Biographies by JJHC
Hause Genealogy
History of Health New York
King Charles of New York City
Wikipedia
Nano Nagle Place
History Ireland
landedestates.ie
lordbelmontinnorthernireland
The Earldom of Llandaff
Thurles Information
Ireland, Valuation Records, 1824-1856
theirishaesthete
househistree
The Peerage of the British Empire as at Present Existing by Edmund Lodge
Collection List no 94 Papers of Dr Martin Callanan
American and English Genealogies in the Library of Congress by M.A. Gilkey
Dictionary of Irish Biography
UK, Foreign and Overseas Registers of British Subjects, 1628-1969
Who's Who in the World, 1910-1911
UK Registers of Employees of the East India Company and the India Office, 1746-1939
buildingsofireland.ie
tipperarystudies.ie
Ireland, Marriages in Walker's Hibernian Magazine, 1771-1812
Ireland, Casey Collection Indexes, 1545-1960
ancientwalesstudies
earlybritishkingdoms
biography.wales
Genealogy of the Royal House Polanie-Patrikios
gutorglyn

mathewsfamilyhistory by David Mathews
Kings College, London
A General Armory of England, Scotland, and Ireland by John
Burke, Bernard Burke
pravoslavie.ru
Death and Commemoration in Late Medieval Wales by
D. Hale
insearchofholywellsandhealingsprings
Towton Battlefield Society
College of Arms.
Parish Records –Various for baptism, birth, marriage, death

EARLS OF LLANDAFF

Genealogy of the Earls of Llandaff
Orca.Cardiff.ac.UK
Ancient Wales Studies
Early British Kingdoms
Matthews of Wales
The Gentleman's Magazine, volume 202
Pure.south wales.ac.uk
Pravoslavie
Gutorglyn
The Blood of Avalon by Adrian G. Gilbert
The Curse of Thomastown Castle: Irish History by Bartlett
Burgess
Twixt Chain and Gorge. A history of Radyr and Morganstown
Cardiff History
Genealogical And Heraldic Dictionary of the Landed Gentry
by John Burke
Antigua and the Antiguans
Househistree.com/louis-William-de-Rohan-Chabot
American and English Genealogies in the library of Congress
Tipperary Studies. i.e.

thurles.info
Landed estates.ie
Jstor
Kilkenny castle.ie/the-Ormonde-picture-collection

THE CONINGSBY FAMILY

Victoria and Albert Museum
Science Museum
British-history.ac.uk
Worcester Branch of the Birmingham & Midland Society for genealogy and heraldry
The Peerage of England; containing a genealogical and historical account of all persons of England, viii.
Lordship, knighthood, and locality: A study in English society.
digital.NLS.uk
The Historical Antiquities of Hertfordshire.
Stemmata Robertson et Durdin by Her Robertson
The Peerage
Criminal Trials, supplying Copious Illustrations of the important periods of English History during the reign of Queen Elizabeth and James I, by David Jardine
arenbergfoundation.eu/en/armorial-Belgian-nobility
History of Parliament
Cracrofts Peerage
The Case of The Lord Coningsby's two infant daughters, with respect to the Bill passing the Honourable House of Commons, for sale of the estate of the late Earl of Ranelagh at Chelsea and Cranborne by Richard Jones, Viscount and Earl of Ranelagh.
library.villanova.edu
The Georgian Group
The Life and Times of Thomas, Lord Coningsby: The Whig Hangman and His Victims by Pat Rogers
Tours Through the Whole Island of Great Britain, Volume 3

Genealogical and Heraldic Dictionary of the Peerage and Baronetage… Volume 3
greatenglishchurches
Lordship, Knighthood and Locality: A Study in English Society, C.1180-1280 by Peter R. Coss
electricscotland
Plantagenet Ancestry: A Study in Colonial and Medieval Families, 2nd Edition
The Peerage of England; containing a genealogical and historical…, Volume 3, by Arthur Collins
Stemmata Robertson et Durdin
Dictionary of National Biography, Volumes 1-22
The Gentleman's Magazine, and Historical Chronicle, for the Year, Volume 95
College of Arms
Parish Records –Various for baptism, birth, marriage, death
British Chancery Records, 1386-1558

BUTTERFIELDS

Bradford museums
www.lenbutterfield.co.uk
bradfordunconsideredtrifles
keighleynews.co.uk
bradfordunconsideredtrifles
industrialrevolutionspod
www.annebronte.org
www.bradford.gov.uk
www.gutenberg.org
www.dc.ewu.edu
The Cambridge Companion to the Brontes by Heather Glen
Strange World of the Brontes
China Bound by John Swire and sons
In the Footsteps of the Brontes by Ellis H Chadwick

The Brontes by Juliet Barker
historic England
stgeorgeswoolwich
memorialsinportsmouth
southsealifestyle
newforestexplorersguide
British Library
Portsmouth-guide
The Gentleman's Magazine, Volume 19; Volume 173
three decks
welcometoportsmouth
NavalChronicleVol6-1799-1818
The Navy List, Great Britain. Admiralty
H.M. Stationery Office, 1843
Great Britain. Admiralty
H.M. Stationery Office, 1843
Royal Naval Biography: Or, Memoirs of the Services of All the Flag-officers by John Marshall
morethannelson
sailsofglory
Greenwich Museum
Shackleton Foundation
The Texas Frontier and the Butterfield Overland Mail by Glen Sample Ely
legendsofamerica
encyclopediaofarkansas
goldbergauctions
killing society
lindsaymurals
Pullman Company Archives
Appleton's Cyclopaedia of American Biography
Colonial Families of the USA
Royalhallrestorationtrust
metcam

Harrogate club
graces guide
icevirtuallibrary
Leeds engine
memorialdrinkingfountains
Britain-magazine
notjusthockney
The life and Thoughts of Herbert Butterfield by Michael Bentley
A History of Keighley by Ian Dewhirst
Ibbetson's Directory for the Borough of Bradford
Country Life magazine
The National Archives
Keighley & District Local History Society
Nottingham.ac.uk
holmepierreponthall
isleofdogslife
University of Nottingham Manuscripts
Thoresby. Blogspot
Antique Collecting magazine
Oxford Dictionary of National Biography
Gifford lectures
Herbert Butterfield. Historian as Dissenter by C. T. Mcintyre
archives.history.ac.uk

TODD

The Ancestors of John Harper and Christine Robinson of Bath Co., KY by Diana J. Muir
Red Tower York
North Craven Heritage
Medieval York: 600-1540 by D. M. Palliser
etheses.white rose.ac.uk
Henry Tudor Society

York Walls
Merchants' Hall York
Western Michigan University
A Description of York: Containing Some Account of Its Antiquities by George W. Todd
Mansion House York
History of York
Heraldry in Scotland - J. H. Stevenson by Bruce Durie
White House History
founders.archives.gov
Dumbarton House
ushistory.org
Lincoln Collection
mtlhouse.org
First Ladies' Library
American Civil War
knox.edu
Abraham Lincoln Association
Complete Book of Historic Presidential Firsts: With Fascinating Details by Michael Duvalle
constitutionfacts.com
Washburn University School of Law
Supreme Court Resources
rte.ie.archives.collections
Los Angeles Times
hd.housedivided.dickinson.edu
Shovel Of Stars: The Making of the American West 1800 to the Present by Ted Morgan
Nebraska State Historical Society
Abraham Lincoln and the Western Territories, edited by Ralph Y. McGinnis, Calvin N. Smith
vol-18-no-4-Dakota-images-j-b-s-todd.
Civilwartalk

It Happened in South Dakota: Remarkable Events that Shaped History by Patrick Straub
A rare find: The Treaty of Washington, 1858/Patrick Coleman
University of South Dakota
Jackson History
Encyclopaedia of Arkansas
Steamboats and Ferries on the White River: A Heritage Revisited by Duane Huddleston, Sammie Rose, Pat Wood
Gettysburg Daily
Getty Museum Collection
James Gettys and the Founding of Gettysburg: Second Edition by Melissa Gettys, Amanda Howlet
Descendants of Samuel Gettys
PBS. ORG
En-academic
heritage-history
Westminster-abbey.org
Royal Collection Trust
UCR
Poetry Foundation
Our Campaigns
Political Graveyard
www.kpl.gov
The Family Kalamazoo
oilwellessentials4health

COVID TIMES/QUEEN ELIZABETH II

Media Outlets
Royal History Research
Own experience

www.ingramcontent.com/pod-product-compliance
Lightning Source LLC
Chambersburg PA
CBHW051219150426
42812CB00053BA/2524

ב״ה

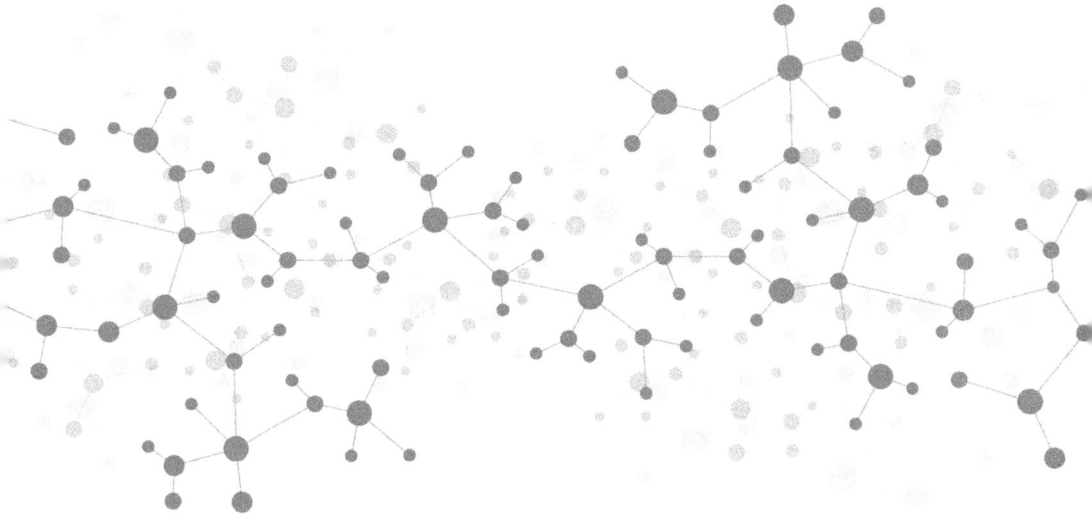

CONTEMPLATING

—— AND ——

TRANSCENDING
MIND

HISBONENUS:
THE MEDITATIVE PATH OF CHABAD

RAV DOVBER PINSON

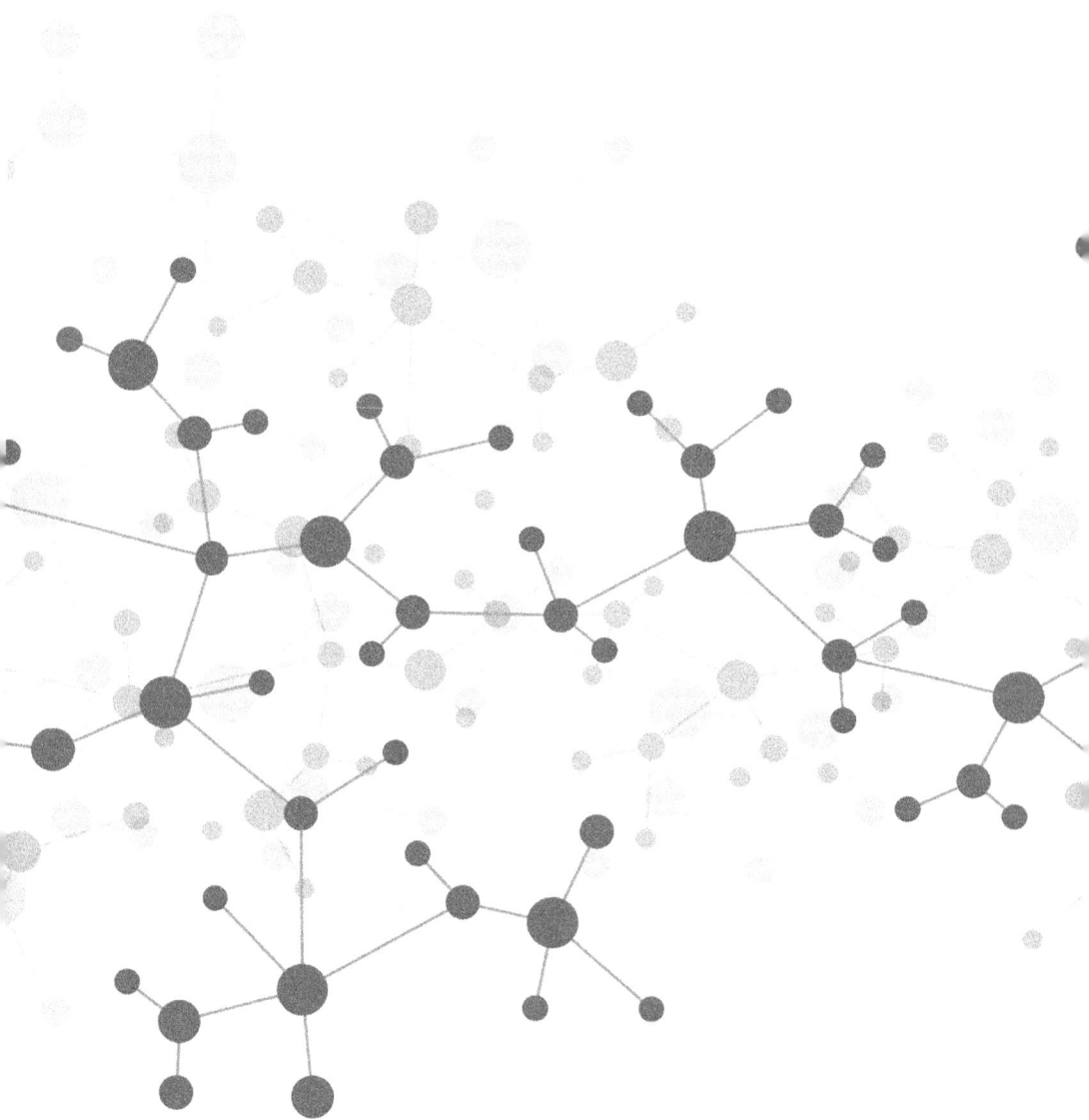

RAV DOVBER PINSON

CONTEMPLATING
— AND —
TRANSCENDING
MIND

HISBONENUS:
THE MEDITATIVE PATH OF CHABAD

THE JEWISH MEDITATION SERIES

THE EXPERIENCE & PRACTICE OF KABBALAH

IYYUN PUBLISHING

IN HONOR OF

**ELISHEVA BAS NAVAH
FENSTER**שתחי'

SPECIAL THANKS TO

REB URI LABER
שיחי'

OLEG AND ESTHER
LANGBORT
שיחי'

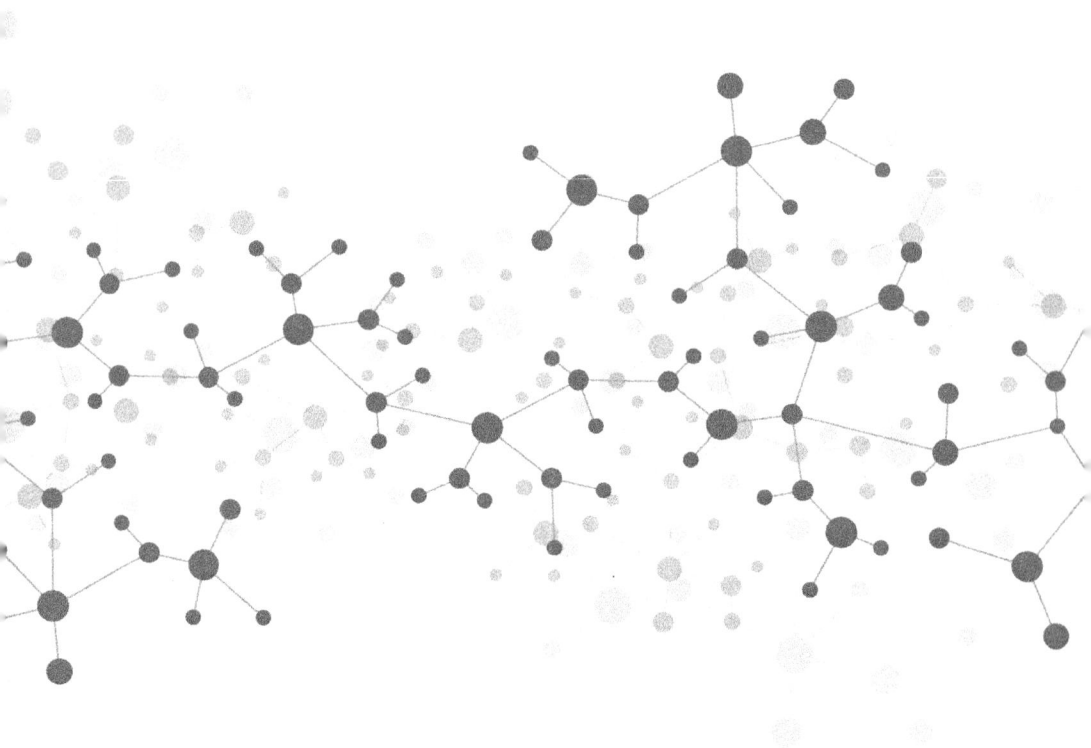

T A B L E   O F   C O N T E N T S

PART ONE

APPENDIX

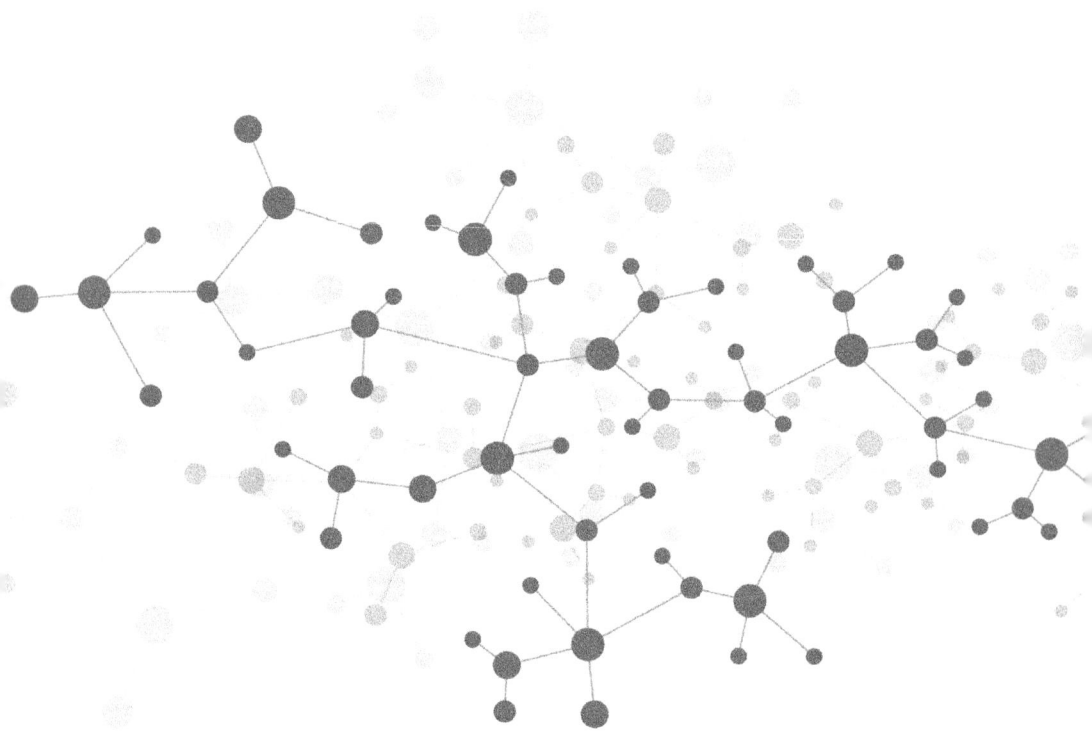

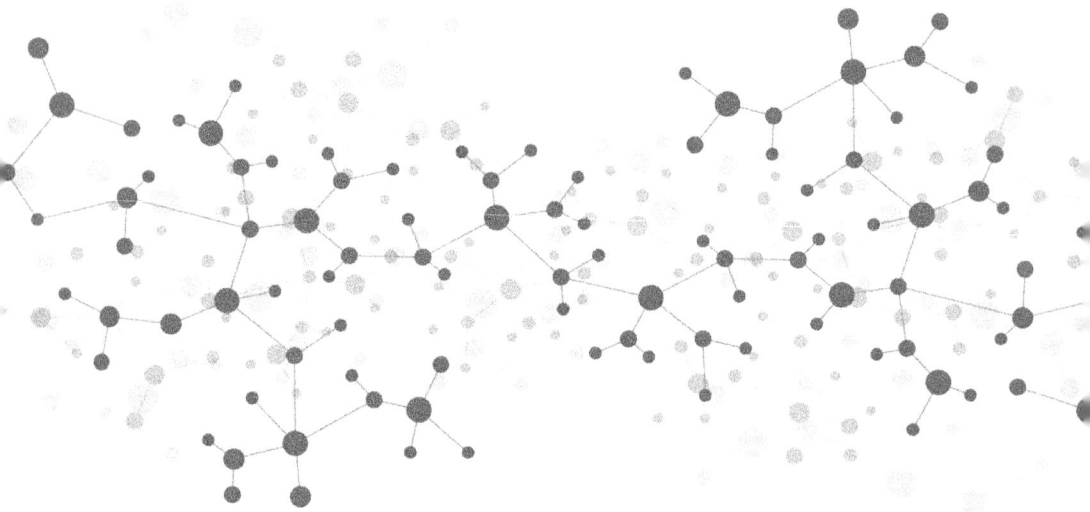

OPENING

....

A WORLD DISTRACTED:

GAINING CONTROL OVER THOUGHTS

OVER THE LAST TWO CENTURIES, TREMENDOUS BREAKTHROUGHS IN SCIENCE, MEDICINE, TECHNOLOGY, GOVERNANCE, AND VIRTUALLY ALL OTHER AREAS OF LIFE HAVE BECOME MORE AND MORE REVEALED. More of the physical nature of this world and its basic properties have been uncovered in the last century than in thousands of years prior, and new understandings continue to develop with exponential acceleration every year. Yet, for all the information produced and all the technical problems solved, most human beings feel more and more distracted, directionless, and confused than ever before.

Even a few minutes spent in the supermarket brings a deluge of decisions and uncertainties. Or, for that matter, just a few seconds of observing the news inundates the brain with a stream of images, concepts, and a complex subtext. Everything around us seems to be pulling our attention one way and then the other until we feel as if our mental coherency is all but lost.

As a result of this over-stimulation, almost nothing plagues our generation, certainly the youth, more than distraction and "attention deficiency." A lack of an ability to sustain focus for even short periods, a continuously interrupted and fractured attention, is a form of suffering that some people actively choose, while others simply cannot find a way to escape it. Sadly, a growing percentage of the population spends nearly all day, every day, fixated on their phone or laptop, texting, leaving voice notes, taking pictures and videos, watching news and entertainment, and using apps for every possible task.

Wonderful human capacities such as 'paying attention', encountering people face to face — even the basic ability to look into another person's eyes — have been hijacked. These powerful human capacities have been diverted into activities such as obsessively reviewing unneeded products and meaningless entertainment, arguing pointlessly on someone else's political agenda, openly displaying their 'private' life on social media in order to get 'likes', and browsing truly unhealthy and even damaging imagery.

People have such weak attention that, while seated at a wedding celebration, they can find themselves paying their bills online, and while 'playing with their children', they are shopping for clothing. People eat in front of their computer instead of in front of their family; their mind is on the news headlines instead of their family or their food.

Sadly, it does not appear that this trend is getting any better. With the onslaught of new devices allowing people to live in a virtual world, and to multitask at all moments of the day, people's *Da'as* / 'aware presence' is going deeper and deeper into exile. The compulsive need to be stimulated by information and images does not allow for proper settledness of mind, heart, and soul.

Even while not occupied with a screen, when one's mind has become habituated to frenetic stimulation, one begins to fidget when nothing 'exciting' is happening. With no externally induced stimulation, one begins to fall into anxious thoughts about the future or daydreams about the past. Even while acknowledging the research which shows that multitasking leads to less productivity and accomplishment, many people are still helplessly driven to scatter themselves in attempting everything at once or interrupting themselves over and over with new ideas or tasks.

Living in the present moment becomes a forgotten way of life.

When a person's mind is addicted to external stimulation, they often develop a habit of procrastination and *Bitul Zeman* / wasting precious time on trivialities. Such people avoid the effort of focusing on their work or duties since these demand their generating motivation from within. Making decisions requires focused thinking, and this effort can seem painful after years of gradually sinking into mental passivity. One begins to consume more and more media, videos, and podcasts, all in an attempt to push away the inevitable discomfort of really using the mind.

As people become accustomed to accepting the manipulative messages and imagery in the media they consume, they insidiously lose authority and control over the content of their consciousness and even over their preferences, emotions, words, and actions. The mind becomes plagued with self-doubt, subliminally comparing oneself to photoshopped images of friends with 'perfect' lives, comparing one's surroundings with fantastic landscapes and digitally exaggerated colors, and comparing one's life with the superhuman personas and extreme dramas depicted by the entertainment industry.

People have lost the art of just being present with themselves.

HORSE THOUGHTS

Even those who recognize this malady and wish to improve their focus are haunted by its elusiveness: after a few minutes or seconds of trying to stay focused, the mind simply wanders away and runs wherever it will. Suppose you decide to think over a particular thought on your walk from home to work. As you step out of your home, you conjure up the thought, but immediately, the first thing you see, hear, smell, or touch pops into your mind. Let's say you hear a siren going off in the distance, and your mind instantly wonders about it. Then you notice clouds overhead and begin to wonder if it is going to rain. This sets off a whole chain of thoughts: 'Where's my umbrella? Good umbrellas are so expensive. I should really make more money. I have a bad job. I don't even like my boss. He is always angry at me. Maybe he is right that I am not such a good worker. Or maybe I am not even such a good person…'

Your focus quickly unravels, and random thoughts take over the driver's seat. In a short period of time, your mind has traveled on a wild ride of loosely connected destinations. The only unifying point among them was that not one of them was chosen. Not one of them was the original thought you decided to think on your way to work.

This phenomenon of scattered consciousness is called having 'horse thoughts'. From what we imagine, a horse is always thinking only about what is right in front of him at that moment: the basin of water or the pile of hay. This phenomenon can be called 'monkey mind' or 'kangaroo thoughts'; in Eastern Europe, the common animal was the horse, so the idea was projected onto horses, hence, horse thoughts.

Just as an animal's attention might be dictated by whatever is in front of it, our attention can be dictated by outer circumstances and events. One thought leads to another in endless free association. In fact, most people do not choose their thoughts at all; thoughts choose them.

How many times do people make a statement only to say a moment later, "I am so sorry! I didn't really mean what I said." It seems as if their mouth has a mind of its own. Many people even act without consciousness and do something only to immediately regret it. In the words of our sages, "The wicked [those not living an integrated life] are full of regret" (*Tanya*, 11. *Reishis Chochmah*, Sha'ar HaYirah, 3. *Sheivet Mussar*, 25).

Again and again, thoughts impose themselves upon the mind, one upstaging the other. And who is thinking these thoughts? In a sense, *nobody* is thinking them. They are just happening on their own, with no conscious guidance or control, dictated by external conditions, memories, and impressions.

Yet, our minds are our most powerful tool. It is our minds through which we appreciate and interpret reality. Our perception of reality is completely dependent on the prism of our mind. In other words, we overlay the impartial, objective reality of what is with our subjective narratives and prisms. In a sense, there is no distinction between an experience in itself and the way we observe, think about, and interact with that experience. The way something appears may seem to be objectively true, but it is actually subjective — filtered through our mind. Therefore, if the mind is often at the mercy of unbridled horse thoughts, our primary objective in life should be to take back the reins and learn to consciously guide the mind.

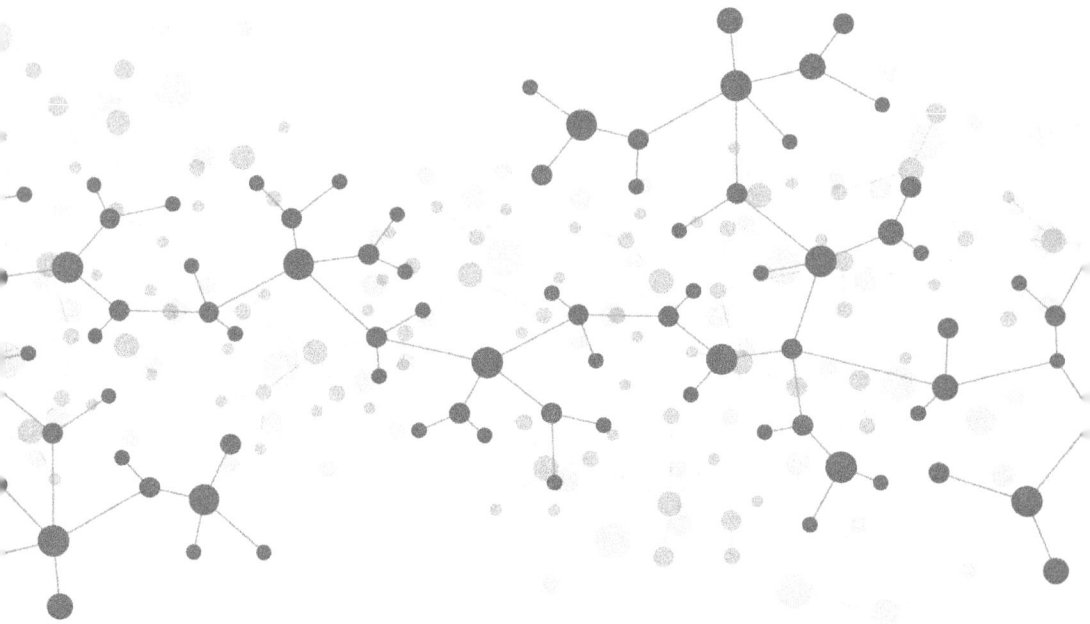

CHAPTER 1

THE NATURE OF THOUGHTS

TO BETTER UNDERSTAND HOW WE CAN CONSCIOUS-
LY CHOOSE AND GUIDE OUR THOUGHTS, AND DIRECT
THEM RATHER THAN LETTING THEM CONTROL US, IT IS
IMPORTANT TO RECOGNIZE THAT THOUGHTS ARE CON-
TINUOUS. Even if we aren't deliberately selecting what to
think about, thoughts will naturally arise.

Whereas we sometimes speak and sometimes we do not
speak, *Machshavah* / thought is continuously active: מחשבה
משוטטת תמיד / "By its nature, Machshavah is restless" (This
phrase first appears in *Avodas HaKodesh*, 2:7: אבל תהיה המחשבה משוטטת
תמיד למעלה בייחוד השם הגדול. In Chasidus, this is used to express the idea

that our thoughts are continuous. For example, in the Rebbe's Ma'amar *Hinei Yaskil Avdi*, 5717: וזהו ג"כ ההפרש בין דיבור למחשבה, דבדיבור הרי עת לדבר ועת לחשות משא"כ מחשבה משוטטת תמיד, דגם כאשר אינו מרגיש שהוא חושב הנה באמת. חושב הוא).

Without consciously choosing your thoughts, what you wish to think about, your mind will relentlessly jump from one thought to the next but will never sit idle, as 'Machsha-vah is never idle' (*Tal Oros*, Chelek 1, Perek 2, p. 9a. שהמחשבה אינה נחה ושוקטת ונמשכת תמיד: *Likutei Torah*, Tzav, 17a. "Thought...when not assigned a task by the mind...remains active" *Hayom Yom*, 16th Chesh-van. See also, Rambam, *Hilchos Isurei Bi'ah*, 22:21. שאין מחשבת עריות מתגברת אלא בלב פנוי מן החכמה).

Keep in mind that whatever you desire, fear, or fixate upon, whether consciously or subconsciously, that is where your thoughts will naturally gravitate. In this way, by consciously choosing a specific subject of thought, you will be able to push away any other intruding, wandering, or unconscious thoughts.

Many contemporary so-called 'spiritual teachers' advise that in order to live in a state of selfless happiness, you need to let go of all concepts and identities, empty the mind, and give up intellectual pursuits and rigid thinking. Honestly, this 'anti-intellectualism' itself amounts to a rigid intellectu-al position. It is a conceptual assertion that misunderstands the nature of thought. Even if one succeeds in quieting dis-cursive thought to the point where it is not noticeable, one's subconscious identity, thoughts, and suppressed yearnings still direct a person's behaviors. This is, perhaps, one reason why so many of those 'teachers' become embroiled in controversies and damaging relationships with their students. They think they are completely free, but they are merely *dissociated* from their minds.

Attempting to discard the mind does not work because the Creator gave us a mind for a purpose. This is why we should train ourselves to choose the thoughts that we will entertain and develop the capacity for focus. In fact, if we learn to use our mind as the Creator intended, in the end, we will transcend it. This is because the human mind is designed with a capacity for self-transcendence — *through the power of deliberate focus.*

NO TWO SIMULTANEOUS THOUGHTS

A person cannot focus his mind on two issues simultaneously, as many *Rishonim* / early Rabbinic teachers write (*Hasagas HaRavad*, Rambam, *Hilchos Parah*, 7:3: א"א בכל אלו לא דעתי משום מלאכה הוא נפסל אלא מפני היסח הדעת וכללו של דבר אין אדם יכול לכוין דעתו לב' דברים כאחד או לשני בני אדם כא' נפרדים במעשיהם וא"א בלא היסח הדעת. See also *Meiri*, Gittin, 53a. See, however, *Kuntres Acharon*, Alter Rebbe's Shulchan Aruch, 73:3. See Shu't, *Afrakasta D'Aniya,* 1, Siman 87, where these opinions are reconciled). Although this fact places a very significant limit on the performance of the mind, it has one outstanding advantage. Since there is always a sequence of single thoughts streaming through our mind, if we can deliberately choose and assert one thought, all the other thoughts in the stream will evaporate for as long as we sustain that chosen thought. Thus, in order to gain temporary hegemony over our mind and stop the onrush of unwanted thoughts, all we need to do is focus our attention on a thought of our choice.

First, choose a simple, uncomplicated idea, such as 'nothing is random in the universe,' and begin thinking about it. If another foreign, unwanted thought enters your mind, just pause and do not engage with it. The less you pay attention to the intruding thought, the less energy it will gain. Just objectively observe it as an 'intruding' thought, keep a distance from it, and let it dissipate. Then, as soon as you can, bring your mind back to your original chosen thought. If the intruding thought was compelling and you found yourself engaging it slightly, simply stop again, keep your objective distance, and let it expire. Then, simply return again to your chosen thought. Try this exercise now.

This simple act of controlling your thinking should produce a subtle mental quietness; with repetition, it should sharpen your ability to gain extended periods of focus. Before we explore the mechanics and significance of this phenomenon, let us delve deeper into the nature of *Machshavah / thought* and the issue of scattered thinking.

MACHSHAVAH NEEDS HIS'CHADSHUS / RENEWAL

When asked, many people state that they can sustain a thought for at least a few minutes when they try. Actually, a person who has not practiced prolonged periods of conscious thought can, at best, hold a single thought for just a few seconds, maybe 5 to 7.

As another exercise, snap a mental picture of the cover of the book that you are now reading, then close your eyes and time yourself how long you can keep *only* the image of this cover in your mind. It is reasonable to predict that within five seconds, your Machshavah will begin to visit a few other book covers, or muse about the contents of the book, perhaps about who wrote it, what it reminds you of, or how much it costs. Perhaps the mind will begin to wander into whether you're doing this exercise 'right' or not, or how you're feeling. After a short time, the mind may not be focusing on picturing the cover of the book at all but rather entertaining itself with all kinds of free associations.

Try this now and see how long you can avoid mental wandering.

Your Machshavah wanders into other thoughts for two primary reasons: A) There is a lack of *Razton* / will and *Cheishek* / desire to stay fastened to the image of this book cover. You probably do not care very deeply or have a compelling emotional attachment or desire towards it, and so you lose interest quickly. This corresponds to a teaching of the Baal Shem Tov: when a person is *Davening* / praying and a thought comes to interrupt him, it shows that there is currently more Cheishek and Ratzon for the subject matter of the interrupting thought than there is for the activity of Davening. B) Machshavah feeds off *His'chadshus* / renewal because renewal creates Cheishek and Ratzon. Our attention is drawn to novelty, animation, and qualitative changes, and these are relatively lacking in a static image (note, *Ma'amarei Admur HaZaken* 5663, p. 671).

Try the same exercise with a short film or video. Even those who cannot hold a single thought for more than 2-3 seconds can probably remain absorbed and engaged in a short film. This is because a) the images in the film are constantly new every split second, and b) the screenplay is probably designed to stimulate your interest, Cheishek, and Ratzon. Now try looking at the same screen while it is turned off. With no media playing, your mind probably wanders and explores 'higher priorities', such as the meal that awaits you, and so forth. With the film playing on the screen, your mind is absorbed, and when the screen is blank, your mind seeks absorption elsewhere.

Finally, use the same technique when trying to hold your attention on the text of the *Davening* / prayers, for example on the *Amidah* / silent standing prayer. Think and pronounce the words with Cheishek and Ratzon, will and desire. Focus on one phrase at a time and keep progressing. If you wish to dwell on a word or phrase that you find especially meaningful, do so for several seconds before moving on.

Here is a more advanced version of the exercise as applied to the Amidah prayer. As you begin, gaze at the word *Baruch* / "Bless." Focus on one of the following options for about four seconds: what that word means, what its letters themselves suggest, how the word sounds when pronounced slowly, the emotional energy of the word, or simply listen to the silence after the sound. Now look at the next word and do the same, e.g., the word *Atah* / You; focus on one of the above attributes of the word for four seconds each. You can also focus on more than one of these attributes, one at a time, each for four seconds. This way, even a slow, contemplative approach to the Davening is experienced like a film. You can easily hold your attention on each word of the text for at least four seconds since each word is deliberately seen, sensed, contemplated, and felt with novelty, will, and interest. A new word or quality is always arriving and being revealed, renewing and re-enlivening your focus every few seconds.

In general, we need inner Cheishek and Ratzon to push us to remain focused on something, but external pressure can also force us to pay sustained attention. For example, if you get a small splinter in your finger, you will notice that the pain holds your attention for much longer than the five seconds that a still image will. However, without His'chadshus or change in the experience, even your attention to the pain will fade somewhat.

In order to choose the thoughts we think, we need to employ the phenomenon of His'chadshus, and generate Cheishek and Ratzon for those thoughts. First, we awaken a desire for a certain subject of thought, and then soon after we begin contemplating it, we introduce His'chadshus, bringing to mind new applications and details of the subject, one after the other.

CONTRAST BETWEEN THOUGHTS & EMOTIONS

While attention on Machshavah needs constant His'chadshus, emotions seem to grip a person's attention even without much His'chadshus. In fact, most gross emotions do not need the power of His'chadshus at all for us to fix our attention on them. For instance, when a person is angry, they can obsess on their extremely negative emotion for hours on end. They might review the image of the other person, who triggered their anger, over and over. Rather than weakening over time, the energy of the anger can keep increasing. If you step back and look at such an experience, you will see that your mind and heart were engaged and absorbed, and they hardly wandered from the emotion at all.

Regarding the extremely positive emotion of love for Hashem, the Rambam writes:* "What is the proper degree of love? A person loves Hashem with a very great and exceeding love until his soul is bound up in Divine love. He becomes obsessed with this love as if he is lovesick, [like one whose] thoughts are never diverted from the love of his human beloved. He is obsessed with her when he sits down, when he gets up, and when he eats and drinks. With an even greater love than that, the love for Hashem is [implanted] in the very hearts of those who love Him, and they are obsessed with Him at all times" (*Hilchos Teshuvah*, 10:3).

Unlike gross emotion, Machshavah is rooted in *Seichel* / intellect. Seichel, in turn, is rooted in *Chochmah* / 'intuitive wisdom', the innermost spark of intellectual perception, and Chochmah is rooted in Divine *Ayin* / no-thing-ness, formless, unmanifest potential (for this reason, the word *Seichel* / שכל can be seen as הס כל / 'the quieting of everything': *Sefer HaSh'rashim*. See the Rebbe's Ma'amar, *VeAta B'Rachamecha*, 5717). In order for a *Yesh* / thing — for example, the form of a concrete thought — to emerge from Ayin, there needs to be a continuous process of His'chadshus to create and recreate its form. Think about this in terms of throwing a ball in the air. The natural state of a ball is to be pulled to the ground by gravity. In order for the ball to fly, it needed to be lifted at every instant by

---

* וכיצד היא האהבה הראויה. הוא שיאהב את ה' אהבה גדולה יתרה עזה מאד עד שתהא נפשו קשורה באהבת ה' ונמצא שוגה בה תמיד כאלו חולה חלי האהבה שאין דעתו פנויה מאהבת אותה אשה והוא שוגה בה תמיד בין בשבתו בין בקומו בין בשעה שהוא אוכל ושותה. יתר מזה תהיה אהבת ה' בלב אוהביו שוגים בה תמיד כמו שצונו בכל לבבך ובכל נפשך. והוא ששלמה אמר דרך משל (שיר השירים ב ה) כי חולת אהבה אני. וכל שיר השירים משל הוא לענין זה.

the momentum imbued in it when you threw it. Once the energy in the throw dissipated, the ball fell to the ground.

Similarly, for the Yesh of a thought to exist, it requires the continuous renewal of the Creator's *Koach His'chadshus /* power of renewal within Creation. In fact, it needs a different grade of renewal and sustenance within each stage of manifestation. Chochmah is the first stage of manifestation to emerge from the threshold of Ayin, and crossing this threshold requires the Koach His'chadshus. For a subtle thought to be identified and drawn from the undifferentiated field of Chochmah into Seichel, it needs another level of His'chadshus. For the thought to become concrete and defined, it needs yet another level of renewal. To sustain this defined thought through a period of time, all of these levels of His'chadshus must be continuously activated over the duration.

As a reflection of the Divine Koach His'chadshus, we need to develop an inner power of His'chadshus to sustain our focus on a given thought form. The world of *Midos /* emotions and personal traits already exists in the world of Yesh, and therefore, they require less power of His'chadshus in order to be sustained over time.

To understand this phenomenon a little better, let us go back to our earlier exercise. You are asked to focus your attention for the next 20 seconds on a book cover. If you are a seasoned meditator, you may try to focus on it by vocalizing inwardly, "Cover…cover…cover…." The problem is that the lifeforce of Machshavah requires being enclothed in multiple *Levushim* / garments. It is as if the mind wants to be 'clothed' in different experiences. In addition to lacking inherent His'chadshus, the image of the cover is only one 'garment'. This is not enough for Machshavah; the inanimate book cover alone cannot enclothe the mind, so the mind will almost immediately start to wander in search of more garments. It will begin asking questions such as, "What weight of paper is this?" or make comments such as, "I've never seen that font before!" Such thoughts will branch out into different subjects, jumping about from one association to the next, as if the mind is trying on clothes, until a 'super-ego' voice within you finally shouts, 'Hey! Focus your attention on the cover!'

THE MECHANICS OF HISBONENUS / CONTEMPLATION

To summarize, we have explored three basic scenarios. While attempting to focus on a static object such as a book cover, the mind quickly begins to wander away in search of stimulation. Here, there was no Cheishek or Ratzon for the object.

While experiencing a gross emotion, such as anger or powerful love, your mind is naturally riveted to it, but its interest will fade in time. There is an abundance of Cheishek and

Ratzon, but there is a lack of His'chadshus, so the mind loses interest. While focusing on a short film, the ever-chang-
ing imagery and stimulation allows the mind to settle into a
focused state for the entire duration of the film. Here, there
is Cheishek, Ratzon, and His'chadshus, so the mind stays
engaged.

Similar to the film, *Hisbonenus* / contemplation uses the
combined powers of Cheishek, Ratzon, and His'chadshus
to produce very profound and sustainable states of transformative consciousness. This is also a method employed
in many Chasidic discourses and texts. A theme, novelty, or answer to a question is presented, which excites the
mind of the student and creates initial momentum. Then,
the frame changes from one scenario to another, each one
illuminating the greater theme from many different angles.
This renews the student's interest and Seichel again and
again until the mind is led through the Chochmah of the
idea into the Ayin beyond it, as will be explored.*

A basic prerequisite to reaching deeper states of consciousness through the practice of Hisbonenus (and of studying
Chasidus as above) is gaining some level of hegemony over
your thoughts. You need to be able to choose your thoughts,
as opposed to thoughts choosing you. You must be able
to remain mindful, present, and focused for an extended
length of time.

---

* This style of the *Hemsheichim* begins with the Alter Rebbe, after his
arrest and liberation, and is expanded upon by the Mitteler Rebbe and
the subsequent Rebbes.

Generally speaking, there are two paths to achieve this prerequisite.

TWO PATHS TO CONTROLLED OR MINDFUL THINKING

There are two paths outlined by the early Chasidic Rebbes, as outlined by the Baal Shem Tov and the Baal Shem Tov's disciple's disciple, the Alter Rebbe, Rebbe Schneur Zalman, the founder of Chabad.

The Baal Shem Tov speaks about *Machshavah Achas* / one thought, entertaining one thought at a time to keep the mind steady (*Ohr HaGanuz*, Likutei Baal Shem Tov, 86). This is a type of meditation called *Hisbonenus K'lalis* / general contemplation. A person should always have one default thought that can be easily summoned to the forefront of the mind whenever needed. Rebbe Mendel of Premishlan, a student of the Baal Shem Tov, taught: "You should always have only one thought in the service of Hashem...because when a person has many thoughts, he becomes confused. This one thought," says Reb Mendel, "is that everything that exists in this world is filled with the Creator" (*Hanhagos Tzadikim* 1, p. 238).

This teaching can be understood and implemented on multiple levels. On one level, you can choose a positive and holy thought, such as the one recommended by Reb Mendel of

Premishlan, and bring it to mind frequently throughout your Davening and also your daily life. If at any time you wish to quiet an onrush of 'horse thoughts' or negative ideation, keep coming back again and again to this focal point. Let it steady the mind and heart, and open you to greater inspiration and guidance.

On another level, one can use this in a dedicated meditative practice, such as sitting quietly for some time before Davening. For example, before starting to recite from the Siddur, sit quietly, close your eyes, and begin to focus on your 'one thought'. To the best of your ability, let your mind become deeply absorbed in the thought. Come back to it again and again whenever your mind wanders. Gently open your eyes when the prayer service begins, staying rooted in the silence. Of course, the challenge with this approach, as demonstrated above, is that the mind becomes quickly bored with a single Machshavah, and after 5-7 seconds, one often wishes to move on to another thought. To mitigate this challenge, you could allow yourself to think about issues immediately and directly connected to the 'one thought."* This will mitigate the mind's demand for *His'chadshus* / renewal, but perhaps not eliminate it.

A more detailed-oriented path is presented by the Alter Rebbe. He calls for the contemplator to delve deeply into a subject matter, exploring it 'in depth, width and breadth', into its deeper meanings, fine details, and a broad range of

---

* This first approach is explored in more detail in a previous book, *Breathing and Quieting the Mind*.

its possible applications. This is referred to as *Hisbonenus P'ratis* / detailed contemplation. One keeps the free flow of Machshavah lively and interesting by moving from one level, detail, or application to the next, within the general topic.

The path of the Alter Rebbe, later elaborated by his son, the Mitteler Rebbe, Rebbe DovBer, and later by the following five Rebbes, follows this path of Hisbonenus P'ratis (Later on, a full *Ma'amar* / discourse by the Alter Rebbe on this very topic will be translated and explored. See also Rebbe Rashab, *Kuntres HaTefillah*, 2, p. 12, with regard to arousing emotions). Keep in mind that the root of the word Hisbonenus is the word *Binah* / understanding, comprehension, and contemplation. Hisbonenus P'ratis means to delve more and more deeply and unearth the finest *P'ratim* / details of 'Binah' possible. This involves a very deep mode of thinking, although it eventually leads to a stage of consciousness that is 'beyond thinking' (Beyond Machshavah — seeing, being: See *Likutei Torah*, Tzav, 17a-b).

מעניין לעניין באותו עניין
FROM ONE TOPIC TO ANOTHER TOPIC WITHIN THE SAME SUBJECT MATTER

Due to its effectiveness, the method of Hisbonenus P'ratis emphasized by the Alter Rebbe became a central characteristic of the teachings of the subsequent Chabad Rebbes. It especially influenced the genre of teaching called *Ma'amarim* / fully expanded mystical discourses with advanced elaborations and many interrelated points — in contrast to the short, inspiring insights favored by some other Chasidic lineages.

Ma'amarim are constructed in a pattern of מעניין לעניין באותו עניין / 'flowing from one topic to another topic within the same subject matter', which allows our Machshavah to be repeatedly rejuvenated, supporting long periods of focused study. The Ma'amarim of the Alter Rebbe's son, Rebbe DovBer, the Mitteler Rebbe, developed this style, and it finds its fullest expression in the Ma'amarim referred to as *Hemsheichim* / 'continuations' of Chasidic discourses, often periodic talks given on the same theme over many years. In a Hemshech, a topic that is only briefly mentioned in one discourse may be expounded upon at length in a later discourse. Hemsheichim were first transmitted by the Rebbe Maharash, Rebbe Shemuel, and then brought to their fullest expression in the Ma'amarim of his son, the Rebbe Rashab, Rebbe Shalom DovBer, the fifth Rebbe of Chabad. Ma'amarim are orally transmitted, springing from a Rebbe's free-associative holy stream of consciousness, as it were, and sometimes with eyes closed, in a deep selfless trance. At the same time, these discourses explore in tremendous detail novel ideas from a wide range of textual sources, building on the wording of previous Ma'amarim. This allows one to engage with these texts for hours on end, immersed in sacred study without distraction, and ultimately allowing one to open to *Deveikus* / conscious unity with the living Presence of the Giver of the Torah.

When we contemplate a Ma'amar, the mind is repeatedly fed new associations and insights into transcendent wisdom until a state of intellectual rapture dawns, our 'thinking self' implodes, as it were, and we gain a direct glimpse of Divine *Ohr* / light and Deveikus, as will be further explored.

CHOOSING OUR INTERFACE WITH REALITY

Practicing the art of Hisbonenus not only helps a person remain in meditative contemplation for extended periods, but it also gives one a general mastery over thoughts. One learns how to apply the same methods to any area in life that requires mental focus.

Thoughts are an overlay on reality. The raw data of experience, the actual stimuli or impressions, are selected, processed, filtered, defined, and represented by the mind by means of subjective interpretations, associations with memories, and meanings in relation to one's established identity. For example, if an artist and a musician walk down the street together, they may both take in the same field of imagery, sights, and sounds, but the artist's mind may select and register more visual stimuli while the musician may select and register more auditory stimuli.

On a deeper level, as mentioned earlier, before any interpretation happens, 'walking down the street' is just neutral sensations and perceptions. Only when thought begins to interpret those data does a narrative appear, for example: 'I am walking to meet a friend... This route is slightly longer than expected... I'll be late if I don't walk quickly, and I don't want it to appear as if I don't care... I am at least getting good exercise by walking the longer route more quickly... The discomfort in my ankles means I need new shoes....' Thought can all but conceal the objective reality of what is happening in the present moment.

Any event or phenomenon that we experience has an objective reality, plus our subjective perspective imposed on top of that, and the subjective perspectives of others as well. For example, the overgrown empty lot near your home looks like a refreshing green garden to one observer, an embarrassing eyesore to another, and a potential real estate opportunity to another. In its objective reality, without subjective thoughts, it is simply an area of a certain size with certain plants growing through the gravel.

Life just happens, but we interact with it through our filters, our mindset and thought processes. Additionally, most people's worldview is not actually theirs. People just adopt a *zeitgeist*, a cultural or countercultural way of seeing things, and that becomes their prism and perspective on reality. In this way, the world around them chooses their thoughts, even while they claim their thoughts as their own. It is impossible for a human being to view phenomena without any lens, perspective, or subjective thinking whatsoever.

But to master our life, we need to learn how to master our thinking and our perspectives; we need to be able to choose them rather than passively let them choose us.

Establish for yourself how you want to experience and interact with the world. Set up lenses for positive, life-affirming, forward-looking, holy, and noble vision. Nourish and strengthen your mind to interpret your external reality in a way that uplifts yourself and others. Your mind is the interactive screen separating your 'internal' subjective experience from the 'external' objective world. How you will use this screen is in your hands and no one else's.

We are bombarded with stimuli, images, sounds, and sensations. It is estimated that the unconscious mind needs to process something like ten billion bits of information per second. If not for the 'reduction valve' of the conscious mind, simply opening your front door would be completely overwhelming. The mind reduces the vast deluge of stimuli to perhaps twenty to thirty bits of information that it deems contextually relevant, makes these a priority, and then chooses how to respond.

Among all the sensations, sights, and sounds, the unconscious mind chooses what to submit to conscious awareness based on past experiences, narratives, and guiding principles. Due to this power to filter out what it does not deem important and allow other stimuli in, it is extremely important that we give our minds the proper categories and prisms in which to observe, confirm, and relate to reality. To the extent that it is possible, we need to be able to see the truth as true and the false as false.

As suggested earlier, we do not see the world the way *it* is but rather the way *we* are. If we think the world is chaotic or orderly, Divinely orchestrated or random, kind or cruel, that is how we experience the world. Whether we experience exile or redemption, constricted states or expansive states, perception of illusion or truth, all depend on our state of *Da'as* / awareness. The world around us is a mirror reflection of our thoughts. The prism through which we see ourselves and the outside world affects how we apprehend them, and this, in turn, further confirms and consolidates our prism and point of view (See Ramban, *Bereishis*, 19:17: לכן היתה אשתו של לוט נציב מלח כי באתה המכה במחשבתה כאשר ראתה גפרית ומלח היורד עליהן מן השמים ודבקה בה / "Therefore the wife of Lot transformed into a pillar of salt, because she attached her thoughts to the idea of salt when she saw the land scorched with brimstone and salt, and thus became salt").

If this prism is clouded by egoism, chaos, fear, greed, despondency, and so forth, then that is what we see in the world and react to. But when we allow our Da'as to be sensitive to holiness, virtue, nobility, life-affirming positivity, and expansive joy, we see the world in this way.

Furthermore, the more optimistic, hopeful, and life-affirming our mindset is, and the more we see those qualities in the world, the more we project that frequency into the world. When we choose to see positivity, we respond with positivity and strengthen the power of positivity in the world. Through our capacity to choose the thoughts that we dwell on, the entire world around us begins to change for the better.

As the basic objective of Hisbonenus is the contemplation of the oneness of Hashem, it is essential to choose positive and holy thoughts and fill the mind with them.*

In the process, we learn how to choose thoughts instead of letting thoughts choose us. Our mind becomes less scattered, unfocused, and reactive, and we begin to add to the positivity and holiness in the world. The world then begins to resonate with joy, goodness, and redemption for other people as well. In this way, the practice of Hisbonenus helps us move the entire world toward redemption.

EXERCISING THE BRAIN

Like everything in life, the more we practice Hisbonenus, the better we become at it. To experience less scattered-

---

* The Alter Rebbe teaches in a Ma'amar that there are two *Ikar Inyanim* / main concepts in Chasidic thought. One is to explain the Mitzvos, such as the Mishkan. Another is to reveal and explain *Achdus Hashem* / the Divine Oneness of all reality. The Alter Rebbe tells us that the latter is the purpose of his teachings and, thus, by extension, all of the subsequent teachings of Chabad.

ness and horse thoughts and to cultivate the power of free choice, we need to exercise the muscle of attention, and in particular, to keep a focus while moving from one issue or context to the next. Attention is like a muscle; the more you work it, the stronger it becomes. The idea of neuroplasticity suggests that we can exercise the brain, deconditioning it from ineffective thought patterns and strengthening effective ones. The more we practice deliberate thinking, the easier it becomes.

In "Chinuch Katan" (Hakdamah, *Sha'ar HaYichud veHaEmunah*), the Alter Rebbe's introduction to his first extensive treatise on the teachings of Chabad Chasidus, he defines the ultimate intention of Hisbonenus: to attain love of Hashem and *Deveikus* / union with the Living Presence of *HaKadosh Baruch Hu* / the Holy Blessed One. By contemplating the Oneness of Hashem intellectually, with developed meditative attention, we can actually transform the prism of our mind to the extent that we become aware of the One in everything, including within ourselves.

In the words of "Chinuch Katan" itself, there are two levels of spiritual experience: A) "...[The first level is] the natural yearning of the soul to its Creator... [one that] will flare up and blaze with a flame which ascends of its own accord, and [the soul] will rejoice and exult in Hashem its Maker and delight in Him with wondrous bliss." B) As not everyone is privileged to attain this state..., the second level is a love that every person can attain when he will engage in profound contemplation in the depths of his heart on matters that arouse the love of Hashem which is in the heart of every Jew. [One can thus contemplate] in a *general way* — that He is our very life. Just as one loves his own soul and life, so he will love Hashem when he meditates and reflects in his heart on the fact that Hashem is his true Soul and actual Life, as *The Zohar* comments on the *Pasuk* / verse, "[You are] my Soul; I desire You!" One can also contemplate in דרך פרט / a *detailed way* — to understand and comprehend the greatness of the King of Kings, the Holy One, Blessed is He, in detail, to the extent that his intellect can grasp, and even beyond"…[The person will then reach a level where he will come to] love Hashem with intense love and cleave to Him, with his heart and soul."*

This ultimate experience of *Ahavah* / love and Deveikus will be explored in depth further on. The other benefit of prac-

---

* In the original Hebrew and precise words of the Alter Rebbe: האחת, היא כלות הנפש בטבעה אל בוראה, כאשר תתגבר נפש השכלית על החומר ותשפילהו ותכניעהו תחתיה, אזי תתלהב ותתלהט בשלהבת העולה מאליה, ותגל ותשמח בה' עושה, ותתענג על ה' תענוג נפלא... אך לא כל אדם זוכה לזה, כי לזה צריך זיכוך החומר במאד מאד...והשנית, היא אהבה שכל אדם יוכל להגיע אליה, כשיתבונן היטב בעומקא דלבא בדברים המעוררים את האהבה לה' בלב כל ישראל. הן דרך כלל – כי הוא חיינו ממש, וכאשר האדם אוהב את נפשו וחייו – כן יאהב את ה', כאשר יתבונן וישים אל לבו כי ה' הוא נפשו האמיתית וחייו ממש, כמו שכתוב בזהר על פסוק: "נפשי אויתיך וגו'". והן דרך פרט – שכשיבין וישכיל בגדולתו של מלך מלכי המלכים הקדוש-ברוך-הוא דרך פרטית, כאשר יוכל שאת בשכלו ומה שלמעלה משכלו...לאהוב את ה' אהבה עזה, ולדבקה בו בלב ונפש...והנה, ראשית הדברים המעוררים האהבה והיראה ויסודן – היא האמונה הטהורה ונאמנה ביחודו ואחדותו יתברך ויתעלה.

ticing Hisbonenus, especially "in a detailed way," is creating a strong mind with the ability to be deeply mindful and present.

BEING PRESENT

In addition to making our prism on life more positive, fanning the flames of Divine love in our heart, and cultivating oneness with our Source, the practice of Hisbonenus allows us to be present and conscious no matter what is happening internally or externally. You learn to become mindful of the thoughts that arise in your conscious mind, and to observe accurately what is really happening around you.

In the Torah, Moshe, our liberator and the receiver of the Torah, represents and embodies the quality of rectified *Da'as* / open awareness and focused mind.* As such, Moshe is the one who has the presence of mind to stop and take notice of the Burning Bush, and witness the revelation of Hashem's desire to liberate His People from slavery. "No slave had ever escaped from *Mitzrayim* / Egypt." According to the logic and experiential prism of the Jewish slaves, there was no possibility of becoming free. One couldn't even entertain a dream of a better life.

Speaking about Moshe's first encounter with the Divine, the Torah says, "A messenger of Hashem appeared to him

---

* As explored at length in *The Haggadah: Pathways to Pesach.*

(Moshe) in a blazing fire out of a bush. He (Moshe) gazed, and there was a bush all aflame, yet the bush was not consumed. Moshe said, "I must turn aside to look at this marvelous sight; why doesn't the bush burn up?" וירא ה' כי סר לראות / "When Hashem saw that *he had turned aside to look,* Hashem called to him..." (*Shemos,* 3:2-4). Moshe had the Da'as and strength of mind to turn aside from the stifling narrative of slavery and simply pause for a moment, observe, be present, and be mindful. As a result, he was able to hear Hashem's words and perceive His Presence.

On a deeper level, this is not merely a description of what happened to Moshe as an individual but to the reality of Da'as itself. When Moshe was summoned to lead Klal Yisrael out of Egypt, he was to take them out of a mental, emotional, and spiritual enslavement — more precisely, a lack of Da'as. *Mitzrayim* means *Meitzarim* / constrictions; their awareness itself was constricted and in a deep exile.

All of this is also an allegory for our own spiritual journey. In a variety of circumstances in life, our Da'as can be in exile, making us unaware of Hashem's Presence. Yet, there is actually a 'Burning Bush', a wondrous Heavenly fire displayed in our world beckoning our attention. It is just that we are not present enough to take notice, stop, listen, and contemplate.

But then, by Divine Providence, Moshe — meaning our own deepest level of Da'as — appears, and miraculously, we have the clarity and presence to stop and take notice. When Hashem sees us pausing and becoming mindful of His Presence in our life, that in itself is enough cause for Hashem to 'call us', and give us the proper understanding that we need in order to become free.

Moshe is chosen to receive the revelation because he is the one who has the *Yishuv HaDa'as* / settled mind to focus, notice, and be present. He is then 'called' to be the agent through whom Hashem takes the entire People out of Mitzrayim.

We are always, in fact, beckoned to behold the majesty and beauty of Hashem's Creation. There is a beautiful sunset or the marvelous wonder of a simple blade of grass before us, if we would only stop and look. The world is so exquisite — "How wonderful is Your work, Hashem" (Tehilim, 104:24), yet we have become jaded and unappreciative, distracted and tuned out. Even when faced with revelatory wonder, we just move on. We have to keep to our schedule; we have to check our mail; we have to get something to eat; we can't afford to stop and contemplate the Source of Life peeking through the changing color of the leaves or the clear eyes of our children. Even if, on the other side of the street, there was a bush on fire yet not consumed,* we sadly just walk on by, perhaps engrossed in a silly distraction on the phone or just simply too worried or unfocused to pause and look.

---

* On a deep level, there is always a "bush on fire": a world aflame with Divine Light, yet miraculously not consumed into no-thing-ness.

Our sages enacted that when we see something beautiful or unusual, we are to stop what we are doing and recite a blessing (*Berachos,* 9:1-2). When we hear thunder, see lightning, or a rainbow, there are blessings to say which force us to stop, pay attention and be grateful, grounding us in the present unfolding moment and notice the Divine Presence.

When we are eating, drinking, coming out of the bathroom, or going to sleep, we are beckoned to do so with presence of mind, so we can fully be there with the experience with intention and focus rather than haphazardly or unconsciously.

The more we learn to control or choose our thoughts, the more present we can be with life, and the more our Da'as can be redeemed. The more we redeem and clarify our Da'as, the more prepared we are to help redeem all of humanity, with the coming of Moshiach: "The first redeemer (Moshe / Da'as) will also be the final redeemer" (*Medrash Rabbah,* Shemos, 2:6. *Zohar* 1, 253a. Arizal, *Sha'ar HaPesukim,* Vayechi. *Torah Ohr,* Mishpatim, 75b), may it be His Will, speedily, in our days.

GOING BEYOND MIND:
THE SPACE OF AYIN / NO-THING-NESS

'Level one' Hisbonenus is gaining the ability to focus and guide your Machshavah for extended periods of time. This should be done with continuous *His'chadshus* / renewal of these thoughts, which will energize your *Ratzon* / will and

Cheishek / desire. As a result, you will be able to engage the entire spectrum and capabilities of your mind, your entire ChaBaD: *Chochmah* / 'wisdom' or spark of intuition, *Binah* / analysis and 'understanding', and *Da'as* / 'knowledge' and integration.

'Level two' of this process is to allow your heart to be aroused by your thoughts. As you progress, these emotions will become more and more subtle and the mind will become more and more *Eidel* / refined. At a certain point, you will reach a level of *Ayin* / transparency of self. Even the forms of your thoughts and senses will become 'transparent' to the Divine Light. This is a measure of *Deveikus* / union with the Source of All Life.

When our mind is occupied with lofty concepts, such as the Unity of the Creator with all of Creation, the natural emotions that will arise will be emotions of awesome love of the Creator. Profound wonder will also arise; wonder in the universe itself, and for the real nature of our bodies, minds, and experience.

As the mind is fully engaged and expanded, approaching its maximum potential for concentration and contemplation, the mind 'implodes' from exhaustion, so to speak — leaving in its wake a state of Ayin. This phenomenon proves that we don't have to circumvent the mind or invalidate the intellect in order to transcend it. Rather, we can transcend the mind using the mechanism of the mind itself. *The mind is a bridge to the Beyond.*

Achieving 'intellectual exhaustion' actually allows us to transition into a state of Ayin-consciousness and mystical union more easily than attempting to leap over the mind or 'amputate' thinking. This stage of Hisbonenus involves a movement from *Binah* / understanding back up into *Chochmah* / supra-rational, and then beyond Chochmah as well, which will be explored in greater length further on.

Some psycho-spiritual approaches to transcendence are designed to jolt a person into the present moment, causing superficial thoughts to evaporate long enough to grasp a deeper insight. Hisbonenus, by contrast, allows the mind to be nourished by finer and finer levels of thought, until thought itself becomes a portal for revelation.

As explained earlier, the word *Hisbonenus* comes from the word *Binah* / understanding and in-detail comprehension. Yet, although Hisbonenus practice involves deeply analyzing a subject matter, the objective is not to become a smug 'walking encyclopedia' of mystical concepts but rather to experience Divinity, which is by definition inconceivable. Thus, Hisbonenus is actually aimed at passing through Binah and rising above all conceptual understanding.

Generally speaking, we cannot transcend our mind, our perception of self, our ego, willfully or directly (although that sometimes happens through a radical shock or trauma). The self does not willingly allow its own destruction — it would be like a person trying to hide from himself. However, the mind or ego will allow itself to be employed and harnessed to the point that it discovers its own transparency and folds in upon itself.

Being 'beyond the mind', experiencing Ayin, often includes a sense of 'oceanic' vastness, spacelessness, or lightness of being. Yet, to be accurate, this is not the essence of Ayin-consciousness itself; rather, it is the sensation of Ayin within the vessel of our *Yeshus* / individual and egoic existence.

Ayin is 'no-thing' — not a 'thing' that can be experienced. It is the formlessness beyond all *Tzurah* / form, the unmanifest *Nekudah* / point beyond the *Hispashtus* / expanse of manifest existence. And yet, it is paradoxically the absolute *Ohr* / Light shining within the *Kelim* / vessels of relative experience, and it is the intangible aliveness deep within the life-force of living creatures.

CHAPTER 2

AYIN AS THE ESSENTIAL TEACHING OF CHASIDUS

FOLLOWING THE PASSING OF THE BAAL SHEM TOV, FOUNDER OF THE ENTIRE CHASIDIC MOVEMENT, one of his students in particular began to water the roots of the movement and became the Rebbe / master teacher of all the others who went on to become leaders and establish their own 'brands' of Chasidus. This was the Maggid of Mezritch, Rebbe DovBer. From the fountain of the Maggid, many rivers flowed, from Chabad, the contemplative "intellectual" branch of Chasidus, founded by the Alter Rebbe, to the more 'ecstatic' branch of Kalisk; from the sharp Torah-study oriented path of Peshischa, Kotzk, and Ger, to the intensely emotional prayer of Karlin; and from the *Hisbodedus /* solitary, inner personal prayer of Breslov, to the more outward *Gemilus Chasadim /* acts of kindness and charity of the Hungarian-based Chasidim.

Sometimes, these divergent paths have seemed so dissimilar as to be in conflict, and yet they were all drawn from the same spiritual fountain. What, then, unites them on a philosophical or 'theological' level? The answer is *Ayin*, the sense of 'nothingness' that lies beyond the *Tzurah /* form of whatever is perceived. Ayin is the self-emptiness of phenomena that is paradoxically full of *Ohr /* Divine Light. It is the 'absence' within everything and everyone that mysteriously shines with infinite Living Presence. Experiential knowledge of Ayin is what the Maggid transmitted to his diversely varied students.

To live with an acute sense of Hashem's Light and Presence within immediate experience, to be in touch and in dialogue with that ineffable Open Space beyond the facade of material and corporeal Tzurah, is also to experience a foretaste of *Geulah /* redemption, perfection, and wholeness, here and now. The light of this future redemption of humanity, hidden for millenia within the darkness of *Galus /* exile, alienation, and brokenness, has been revealed in the present. The different practices and philosophical approaches developed by different Chasidic streams are all ways of revealing this light of redemption more and more, gradually uncovering the Divine Presence within every area of human life and every dimension of the world.

To have the awe-inspiring direct experience of 'Divine Ayin', as it were, we need to realize to some extent the Ayin of our own mind, heart, or body. Ayin can be sensed and experienced beyond one's own intellectual *Tzurah* / form via Chabad contemplation* as insight pierces beyond all intellectual constructs. Ayin can be sensed in the ecstatic release of the Tzurah of one's body, as in the somersaulting of the Kalisk tradition. Ayin can be sensed by releasing attachment to your money and comfort, by giving it away in acts of kindness to others, or by releasing your egoic defenses,

---

* The Maggid of Mezritch frequently used the word *Ayin* in his writings. Besides the 'practices' of Ayin of the students of the Maggid mentioned here, there is also a general 'mindfulness' practice of contemplating the creation of things — their 'evolution' from Ayin to Yesh. Among the students of the Maggid, the way this was transcribed is that one is to harnesses and activate his power of imagination, imagining the Yesh of existence emerging from the Ayin, and returning back into the Ayin (See, for example, regarding using the power of creative imagination in general: *Noam Elimelech*, Tzetel Katan. *Be'er Mayim Chayim*, Parshas Tetzaveh. *Maor VaShemesh*, Parshas Miketz). In general, the Alter Rebbe speaks more of the contemplative, mental practice, although he does suggest that we garner our intellectual creative imagination (ויצייר בדעתו), as it were. For instance, in *Tanya* (Igeres HaKodesh, 11) the Alter Rebbe writes: שהבריאה "יש" מ"אין"... הבריאה הזאת, היא בכל עת ורגע, שמתהווים כל הברואים "יש" מ"אין" מחכמתו יתברך המחיה את הכל, וכשיתבונן האדם בעומק הבנתו, ויצייר בדעתו הוויתו מ"אין" בכל רגע ורגע ממש.

becoming deeply vulnerable and spilling out your heart to HaKadosh Baruch Hu in *Hisbodedus* / informal prayer. You can also transcend your form by losing yourself in unbridled holy emotions within prayer, or by pushing yourself beyond your capacity in Torah study and connecting to the Giver of the Torah, the Ohr within the Torah, with great humility.*

AYIN IN AVODAH

In general, the spiritual posture and *Avodah* / spiritual work of Chasidus is to step beyond your personal Tzurah, and to serve with radical humility. In this way, your life and practice is not ultimately about personal growth, becoming extremely knowledgeable, having sublime, expansive feelings,

---

* The more Torah one learns the more humble they become. The grandchild of the Baal Shem Tov writes that he heard from the Toldos that people used to say, "The Misnagdim / opponents of Chasidus learn, and the Chasidim do not learn." This, he says, is indeed true, as Chasidim learn not, i.e., they learn Ayin, 'what is not'. Some scholars become more arrogant as they learn Torah, whereas Chasidim become more 'not', more humble, as they learn: ע"ד ששמעתי אומרים בשם ר' יוסף מ"מ דק"ק פולנא זללה"ה שאמר על מה שאומרים העולם שהלומדים לערנן והחסידים לערנין ניט, שהאמת שהלומדים כל מה שלומדי' יותר הם גדולים בעיניהם ויוחשב בעיניהם שכבר למדו הרבה כל הצורך, והחסידים כל מה שלומדים יותר הם יותר קטנים בעצמם — *Degel Machaneh Ephrayim, Vayikra*. The Tzemach Tzedek writes that the true objective of Chasidus is to make from the Ani / 'i', ego, into Ayin — ולא לומר אני אלא לעשות מאני אין (עש איז ניטא קיין איך) כמ"ש יעקב קטנתי כו' ואומר לא מרובכם מכל העמים כו' כדפירש"י וזהו התולדה היוצאת ממצוה זו שבהאמנת היחוד שאין עוד מלבדו כנ"ל א"כ צ"ל האדם אין כמו שהוא באמת וזהו אמיתית החסידות: *Derech Mitzvosecha, Mitzvas Achdus Hashem, 2*.

or even experiencing revelations of Divine Light, as high and deep as these achievements may be. Rather, your life is about serving Hashem and, by extension, serving others 'selflessly'. You do what is righteous, ethical, and spiritually transformative, not in order to 'get' something, but simply because it is the will of your Creator.

At the end of *Kiddushin* (82b), the Gemara quotes an earlier teaching of the sages: אני נבראתי לשמש את קוני / "I (as a human being) am created to serve my Creator." This is one version of this quote; another version is אני לא נבראתי אלא לשמש את קוני / "I am *only* created to serve my Creator" (See *Osef Kisvei Yad Shel Talmud HaBavli* (Yerushalayim, 1964). *Meleches Shelomo*, on this Mishnah. *Yalkut Shimoni*, Yirmiyahu, Remez, 276).

There is a subtle but essential difference between these two quotes. The first says, 'I exist to serve my Source' — I have a *Tzurah* / form in order to serve. This service is folded within my 'I', my existence. As such, my service is affirming and strengthening my 'selfhood'. The second quote says, אני לא נבראתי אלא לשמש / "I am not created except to serve," hinting at the sense that my 'I' does not exist, אלא / "rather", לשמש את קוני / "to serve my Creator" exists. Serving my Source is not about me, it's not something I do; I *am* Divine service (See the Rebbe, *Sichos Leil Simchas Torah*, 5752).

In this 'non-self' Ayin path of Avodah, all I seek and all my ambition is simply to be a conduit and instrument of Hashem's Presence in the world, and to give myself completely to this. Whatever is demanded of me, whatever Hashem desires for me to do right now, *Hineini* / 'I am ready and open.'

Lightheartedly speaking, the Hebrew word הנני / *Hineini*, stands for four words in English: ה / 'here', נ / 'now', נ / 'newness', י / 'you'. The most important place is here, the most important time is now, the most important mode of consciousness is viewing everything with new eyes, and the most important person is you. To live by the statement of הנני / *Hineini* means, I am alert and ready to begin anew and to serve my Creator, right here, right now.

This is the overall posture of a person living the living teachings of Chasidus. By being small or 'nothing', we are paradoxically great or 'everything', as in the words of the Zohar: "One who makes himself small, is in fact big" (מאן דאיהו זעיר איהו רב: *Zohar* 1, 122b). There is also a more inner, contemplative practice of Ayin in which the meditator attains a point beyond the *Tzurah* / form of logical or 'linear' thoughts, and reaches a point of pure *Deveikus* / unity with the Divine.

The more we are Ayin in our humble action and in our contemplative transparency of self, the more open we become to the deeper levels of the infinite Ayin, the *Ohr* / Light of the Unmanifest. The Ayin state is also called *Hispashtus haGashmiyus* / divestment from entanglement with physicality, ego and Tzurah (even holy or noble Tzurah), which is the ideal state we need to access in order to immerse ourselves in prayer (*Berachos*, 32b. Tur and *Shulchan Aruch*, Orach Chayim, 98. Shaloh HaKadosh, *Asarah Hilulim*, p. 319), and serve our Creator.[*]

THE ALTER REBBE ON THE POINT OF CHABAD CHASIDUS

The first text by the Alter Rebbe on the topic of Chasidus in general and on the contemplative method (Hisbonenus) of Chabad in particular, is *Sha'ar HaYichud VaHaEmunah* / "The Gate of Unity and Faith." In it, the Alter Rebbe elaborates at length and in detail, on the Oneness of Hashem and all Creation, despite the seemingly separate, physical, natural world.

As a means of introduction, the Alter Rebbe writes, as mentioned earlier, that "There are two kinds of love of Hashem. One is the natural yearning of the soul to its Creator. When the rational soul prevails over the coarseness [of the body], subdues and subjugates it, then (the love) will flare and blaze with a flame which ascends of its own accord, and will rejoice and exult in Hashem its Maker, and will delight in the Divine Presence with wondrous bliss.... The second is a

---

* What the Alter Rebbe did was take the essence of the *Klal* / principle of Chasidus, the teachings of the Baal Shem Tov — the 'general' awareness of living in the living Presence of HaKadosh Baruch Hu, and living in total settled presence because of that — and draw it all the way down into the *P'ratim* / details of human consciousness and understanding, into the world of process: see *Sichos Kodesh*, Chai Elul, 5742, Sichah 4.

love that every man can attain when he will engage in profound contemplation in the depths of his heart on matters
that arouse the love of G-d which is in the heart of every
Jew. Whether [he contemplates] in a general way — that
He is our very life...or in a detailed way — when he will
understand and comprehend the greatness of the King of
kings, the Holy One, blessed is He, in detail, to the extent
that his intellect can grasp and even beyond."

The Alter Rebbe addresses the person who has not yet
reached the first level of love, spiritual bliss, and connection to the Light of Hashem, and who needs to engage
in contemplation to arouse Divine love: והנה, ראשית הדברים
המעוררים האהבה והיראה ויסודן היא האמונה הטהורה ונאמנה ביחודו
ואחדותו יתברך ויתעלה / "...And the first thing which arouses
love and fear, and their foundation, is the pure and faithful
belief in His Unity and Oneness, may He be blessed and
exalted." In other words, the treatise was basically written
in order to help people arouse love and faith in the Oneness
of Hashem, which is the point of intellectual Hisbonenus.
Light, Love, and Deveikus with Hashem comes about via
this contemplation of "what his intellect can grasp and even
beyond." Thus, even בטרם שהגיע למדרגת צדיק / "before one
reaches the level of a Tzadik," and before they are able to
"delight in the Divine Presence with wondrous bliss," they
can get a glimpse and glimmer, a *Katnus* / 'small' version
of the *Gadlus* / the expansive, mature state of pure Divine
bliss.*
_____

* As explained above, to perform the Avodah of Chasidus is to live in
the mode of אני לא נבראתי אלא לשמש את קוני, and thus the goal of Avodah

Allowing ourselves to be consciously connected to, and even identified, as it were, with Ayin,* our lives become suffused with *Ohr* / Light. We ourselves become *Lichtikeh* / luminous, dispelling the darkness of *Yeshus* / egoism, narrowness, and pettiness in and around us. We become free of attachment to specific 'forms' of experience, and hence, equanimous, expansive, and filled with elation and ease.

FROM INTELLECTUAL AYIN TO DIVINE AYIN

In the deeper levels of Hisbonenus, after harnessing and engaging the entire spectrum of our intellect — Chochmah, Binah, and Da'as — we then move up into the subtlety of

---

is not merely to feel bliss, not even the great bliss of a Tzadik. It follows that the idea that בטרם שהגיע למדרגת צדיק / 'before one reaches the level of *Tzadik*, one is able, in a minor way, to delight in the bliss of the Divine Presence,' refers to *Derech Agav* / a side effect or by-product of Avodah. If bliss manifests, however, it should be welcomed and relished, not rejected or ignored, because it is a gift given to you to encourage and strengthen you in your Avodah and Emunah, and eventually to reach the level of Tzadik, at least in some measures.

* This level of Ayin is not transcendent of all Yesh; it is rather Ayin as it includes Yesh. In fact, in *Nefesh HaShefeilah* and *Igeres HaKodesh*, Siman Chaf, which were written shortly before the Alter Rebbe passed on from this world of Yesh, he wrote about the *Ma'alah D'Gashmiyus* / the advantage of physicality and the world of Yesh. See *Likutei Sichos*, 16, 24th of Teves. Indeed, the *Tachlis* / purpose of life is to live the spirituality of Ayin *within* the conventional context of Yesh.

the Ayin of Chochmah *within* thought. From there, we release and transcend all thoughts and conceptualization, as will be explored.

Most thoughts of most people are based upon sense perception. Even when we think abstractly, we tend to garner imagined *Tzurah* / forms, whether these are mental images, symbols, or letters. These are finite constructs that define and limit the thought so that we can access the thought's abstract, formless content. In truth, the essence of the thought, prior to being enclothed and limited in a Tzurah, is limitless; it is the pure content of the thought 'immersed in Ayin', before becoming enclothed in the Tzurah of images, symbols, and letters.

Once we connect with the Chochmah or Ayin within and beyond the thought, the mental Tzurah that we relied on falls away. Our mind and heart are then purified, and we experience a nullification of sense perception. Attaining this state, we eventually slip into a state of total immersion within the 'Ayin' of the *Ohr Ein Sof* / the Infinite Light.

IS THE EXPERIENCE OF AYIN PRODUCED OR EXPERIENCED BY THE BRAIN?

Ultimately, Hisbonenus practice is not intended merely to fill the mind with chosen and deliberate thoughts, nor even to create proper, holy, wholesome prisms through which to view the world and interact with it. Rather, the goal is to use the brain to go beyond the brain; not just to conceptually understand the Unity of Reality, but rather to experience it directly. Indeed, Oneness is not known through gaining information but rather through undergoing a thorough self-transformation.

Since the direct experience of Unity affects the entire soul, mind, and body, it behooves us to touch upon the 'mechanics of mystical experience'. What is happening objectively, so to speak, to a person when deeply absorbed in unitive consciousness or having subtle sensations of spacelessness, an infinite expanse of Light, oceanic love, or a sense of transcendence of the separate self?

On the one hand, it can be argued that these states of consciousness are not really 'spiritual' in nature; rather, they are natural phenomena corresponding to physical shifts in the behaviors of neurotransmitters. Perhaps it can be posited that meditators who have extraordinary experiences have merely learned to release endogenous opioids, dopamine, serotonin, norepinephrine, and so on.

Mapping the activity of the brain with computer-generated scans before and during peak moments of meditation, contemplation, and relaxed focusing shows striking color changes in a certain part of the brain. On the left side of the cerebrum, behind the crown of the skull, there is a region called the posterior superior parietal lobe. When a person is in a normative state of consciousness, this part of the brain shows up on the computer as red, showing higher levels of activity. However, during peak moments of meditation or contemplation, this area becomes azure, showing a substantial decline in that region's activity.

The parietal lobe helps us orient ourselves in time and space and gives the body a sense of physical limits. It helps us locate ourselves in space and, for example, not walk into closed doors. When there is a substantial decrease in that region's activity, there is no longer a vital sensory stimulus to clearly define the borders between the person and the surrounding world. The brain senses and concludes that the self is transparent or interwoven with everyone and everything, or that existence is a limitless expanse of Divine peace and Unity.

While neurophysiological explanations for states of transcendent consciousness arguably confirm that there can be physical representations of spiritual phenomena, such explanations do not reveal whether the neurophysiological events are the cause or the effect of the states of consciousness. Are the phenomena in the brain physical symptoms of spiritual attainments, or are these physical phenomena merely interpreted by seasoned practitioners according to their worldview?

Actually, this is not a difficult question. If we map a person's brain activity while they are looking at a particular object, the brain activity does not deny the fact that there is an external object that is being observed; all we have done is show what happens in this person's brain when looking at the object. The same can be said with someone who is observing an inner experience of 'Ayin'. An empirical observation can show us what is happening in the brain during the person's experience, but it does not offer any proof that the brain activity is the *cause* of the experience.

SUMMARY

The nature of the mind is to wander about, to jump from one thought to the next, never resting and always seeking freshness. To counter the randomness and mindlessness of thoughts, the deluge of unwanted thoughts, we ought to consciously choose a thought and begin to be able to sustain focus and be mindful.

The quieting of the mind from the onrush of thoughts is a desirable mechanism to gain some measure of control over your life by controlling the prism through which you see life. The choosing of thoughts allows you to take control of the context that creates the content of life. Indeed, when you choose holy, noble, transcendent, positive, life-affirming thoughts, you will get to observe the world as holy, noble, transcendent, and life-affirming.

The next step in contemplative practice is to fill your mind with Divine thoughts, and harness your entire spectrum and capacity to think, your Chochmah, Binah, and Da'as. The objective is not merely a bombardment of intellectual information but, at first, to arouse the heart and then, ultimately, to attain some measure of ecstatic emptiness or ecstasy, a state beyond all thoughts. An overload of Divine thoughts implodes the system, and one slips into a state of Ayin, motionless ecstasy, and connects with the Ayin.

This state of Ayin is also called the *Bitul* / nullification of the *Yesh* / existence of the small 'i', the ego. Let us now delve more deeply into this subject.

NOTE:
As this text explores and explains the Chabad Method of Hisbonenus, the primary sources are from the Chabad, and more specifically, Chabad-Lubavitch *Rebbes* / masters. There are seven Chabad - Lubavitch Rebbes (corresponding to the seven lower Sefiros), beginning with Rebbe Schneur Zalman of Liadi and culminating with the Rebbe, זצוק״ל זי״ע. The following are the seven Rebbes' names, dates, and sobriquets:

Rebbe Schneur Zalman of Liadi, "the Alter Rebbe" (1745-1812)
Rebbe DovBer, "the Mitteler Rebbe" (1773-1827)
Rebbe Menachem Mendel, "the Tzemach Tzedek" (1789-1866)
Rebbe Shmuel, "the Rebbe Maharash" (1834-1882)
Rebbe Sholom DovBer, "the Rebbe Rashab" (1860-1920)
Rebbe Yoseph Yitzchak, "the Rebbe Rayatz" (1880-1950)
Rebbe Menachem Mendel, "the Lubavitcher Rebbe," or simply "Rebbe" (1902-1994)

CHAPTER 3

THE NULLIFICATION OF THE 'SEPARATE' I & THE TRANSPARENCY OF THE EGO

WHEREAS OTHER SCHOOLS OF THOUGHT TEACH METH-ODS TO DIRECTLY OVERCOME EGOIC QUALITIES SUCH AS ANGER AND INSATIABILITY, and to increase qualities such as patience and generosity, the principle Avodah in Chasidus is Bitul HaYesh / rendering the ego 'nullified' to the soul. When the ego itself is nullified, so are its negative qualities and expressions.

TRANSPARENCY OF THE EGO

To be clear, Bitul HaYesh does not mean to kill the ego, to break or humiliate yourself, or to become a nihilist. As noted earlier, the ego is the seat of instincts of survival and self-perpetuation, so it is not possible to get rid of it; attempting to eliminate it would be like a criminal dressing up as a policeman and arresting himself. If one declares, 'I have killed my ego,' not only does his ego still exist, but now it is even bigger, giving itself credit for supposedly removing itself.

"Breaking yourself," said the great Chasidic master, Rebbe Mendel of Kotzk, "does nothing, and now instead of one negative trait, you have two: the original trait, plus the arrogance of thinking you have broken it." Rather than trying to fully surrender, extinguish, relinquish, or crush our ego, we should actually work to render it more *transparent*. In fact, 'transparency of the self' is a more accurate definition of Bitul, implying embracing and including the self within a context of transcendence and also noble behavior. When this is achieved, its opacity, its self-aggrandizement, self-centered greed, and anxious self-concern are indeed 'removed'; however, the main characteristic of Bitul is that the self becomes a medium that reveals the light of the soul.

As mentioned earlier, the natural egoic 'i' is the dimension in each of us that seeks physical survival, perpetuation, and thriving. These pursuits are not intrinsically 'selfish'. In fact, it is none other than our soul's trait of *Chesed* / giving that drives us to perpetuate ourselves through having children, and our soul's trait of *Gevurah* / restriction is reflected in the drive to survive. A healthy, transparent ego is one that reveals these soul qualities without an overlay of selfishness. The natural 'ego' within a tree causes it to bend toward sunlight for survival, and the 'ego' of a lion causes it to hunt for sustenance. A healthy human ego reveals the soul more clearly than that of other beings because it will also seek the survival, protection, fulfillment, thriving, and achievements of other people. At the peak of transparency, a person can authentically recognize themselves, and all individuals, as expressions of the 'I' of HaKadosh Baruch Hu. This is the fullness of 'self-nullification' — total transparency to the all-pervasive Ultimate Self, the Anochi or Atzmus of Hashem.

Rendering the ego transparent does require purging and uprooting its inclination to negativity; however, this can only be accomplished by harnessing its drive and vitality for positive and constructive purposes. The fact is, without the vitality of the *Yetzer* / drive for survival and self-perpetuation — the two essential qualities of the universe, Chesed / giving / perpetuating and Gevurah / drawing in / surviving — the body itself would cease to be.

The cessation of self and body is not the desire of the Creator, but rather that we cease from negativity, do what is truly good, and experience eternity. This means elevating our survival instincts into the realm of *Olam HaBa* / the world of eternal harmony and spiritual bliss, which will one day be revealed to all humanity. Every activity that was once used for temporary, self-oriented gains will be elevated and become a channel for the ultimate, eternal benefit of all creatures.

THE ETERNITY OF SELF, NOT ITS EXTINCTION

Whereas the extinction of the individual self would be contrary to this path of elevating self, our hard *Avodah* / spiritual, mental, and emotional work will eventually cause, in this lifetime or the next, the extinction of the selfishness and cruelty of the ego but not of the (healthy) ego itself. Our individuality, our unique way of thinking, feeling, and experiencing, is Divinely orchestrated and part of our eternal soul signature. Our unique soul is an expression of the Infinite, Unique One expressed in the multiplicity of the finite world. Every individual is rooted in the Indivisible. As such, when we are liberated from our narrow, separate sense of self through *Bitul HaYesh* / transparency of ego, our narcissistic self-concern vanishes, but not our self or vitality. In fact, the fullness of life is attained, and our soul's purpose in being embodied is reached, when our unique individuality is maximally expressed. When we are imprinting our unique positive gifts of self into the very fabric of the world and human consciousness, we are fulfilling the Creator's intent in giving us these specific gifts.

A soul is not meant to lose its unique place within the universe but rather to find its depths, and its unity with Source, even while embodied. Parenthetically, it is for this reason that once we leave corporeal form, we do not disappear as a drop of water into the ocean of Oneness, as it were. Rather, we live on as a defined 'entity', an extension of the life we lived on earth, a unique and eternal soul within the Eternal.

When, in our journey through life, we reach points of Bitul, we create openings to *Deveikus* / unification with HaKadosh Baruch Hu, conscious union with Infinity. *Deveikus* literally means cleaving or 'adhesion'— being 'glued' to Hashem, so-to-speak. Just as a drop of dew cleaves to a leaf by 'giving itself over' to the leaf, Deveikus requires giving ourselves over to Hashem in Bitul, in a state of Ayin. The attainment of Bitul can be accomplished in various ways, such as through constant deeds of kindness and devotion, or through deep, subtle states of Hisbonenus.

BEYOND THINKING & THOUGHT — AND EVEN BEYOND THAT

Ayin can be glimpsed through various perceptual avenues and levels. On an emotional level, Ayin can be revealed in a temporary absence of emotion, culminating in a perceptual transparency of the 'self' that feels emotions. On the level of sensation, there can be a gap or cessation in sensing, culminating in a 'cessation' of the seeming separate perceiver of sensations. On a visual level, one may cease visualizing or constructing internal images and forms and gaze into vast emptiness. The fullest expression of this is a sense of 'seeing without a separate seer'.

On a cognitive level, one can empty the mind of all thoughts through Hisbonenus and dwell in an 'intellectual Ayin'. The maturation of this state is to realize the absence of a separate 'thinking self' as it becomes absorbed within the Divine Ayin.

Experiences of these forms of no-thing-ness are attained when we are able to still the mind, thereby undergoing a complete withdrawal from all perceptions, both internal and external. In these initial states of Ayin, our mind is unmoving and free of thoughts, perceptions, and sensations, whether they are 'physical' or 'spiritual'. The only sense perception is of still emptiness; the only cognition is of silent no-thing-ness.

Sensation begets associative cognition; there is, for the most part, no thought without the presence of, or memory of, an object impressed upon our senses. But the converse is also true. Even when we are thinking abstract thoughts, they are associated with or intermingled with subtle objects — whether mental images or symbols, imagined words ('the letters of thought'), and imagined sensations. Without connection with such subtle forms, an abstract thought is almost impossible to access or grasp. Yet, in deeper states of

Hisbonenus, that is exactly what is achieved; we are able to connect with the formlessness and inner light of the chosen thoughts while the mind and heart are emptied of all sense perceptions.

Finally, when Chochmah, the emptiness of thought, is reached, the *Ani* / 'i', the 'thinker' will be nullified as well. In other words, when there is no thinking, there will be no thinker present. When there is no perception, there will be no perceiver. This is because the Ani is, in fact, composed of thinking and perceiving; it is a collection of instinctual functions and activities of perception and cognition.

Once, however, this exclusive transcendent state of Ayin is attained, we are invited to go beyond it to a point of inclusive transcendence, a state beyond the Ayin, where Ayin and Yesh seemingly collapse into one. Here, there is a reemergence of self, a healthy and holy self, as will be explored.

HISBONENUS DURING DAVENING

Historically speaking, the practice of Hisbonenus has been tied to *Davening* / *Tefillah* / prayer, either before or during the prayers.* Hisbonenus while Davening has served as a

---

* Reb Eizik Homiler writes in a letter that all Chasidim, and especially students of the Alter Rebbe, have *Emunah* / faith while praying the Amidah that אלץ איז גאט / everything — the entire world — is essentially one with the Divine: *Chanah Ariel*, 3, pp. 1,199. See also *Migdal Oz*, p. 352. Interestingly, he ends the letter saying that although this perception was true to him, he was not able to fully integrate this idea into ac-

gateway for deeper states of Deveikus, or as assistance in making the activity of Davening itself more meaningful. In times of complete absorption within the practice, a person may enter into a trance-like state of inner stillness and bodily immobility, even while Davening.

Hisbonenus can be practiced by studying a particular *Ma'amar* / Chasidic discourse before Davening, contemplating a central theme revealed in it, and then maintaining that idea as a focal point in the Davening itself. Or we may choose a particular passage or phrase within the *Siddur* / prayer book and focus on the deeper meaning of this passage for extended periods of time. Each day, you can choose

---

tual life, and he begged the Mitteler Rebbe to help and advise him, but was rebuffed time and time again, until one time the Mitteler Rebbe agreed and told him that he would reveal a new teaching of Chasidus for him. Reb Eizik writes that when the Rebbe began to teach, he was induced into an altered state: "I did not know if it was day or night!" When the Rebbe finished teaching, "like an arrow of light piercing my innards was the strength and power of this Emunah." In other words, until he 'experienced' Chasidus, as transmitted to him from his Rebbe, he merely 'understood' it intellectually and conceptually. From that moment forward, however, the Emunah that אלץ איז גאט / 'Everything is (one with) Hashem' was no longer just a concept but a lived truth.

* Hisbonenus assists us in engaging in a more contemplative form of Davening. Still, the Rebbes add, such Davening needs to be done in a settled way, not running about and to and fro (meaning not ecstatically moving about, dancing, or gesticulating, as many early Chasidim did during their formal Davening): *Igros Kodesh*, Mitteler Rebbe (5773), p. 196. Rebbe Rashab, *Kuntres HaAvodah*, Chap. 11.

another theme or phrase to focus on and Daven the entire Davening with this one thought, or you can use the same idea for many days or even years and deepen the contemplation indefinitely.

If you are having difficulty focusing for an hour at a time, you could begin with five minutes at a time. Build upon a successful five minutes of contemplation by advancing to ten minutes. Appreciate and build on your achievements; even a small success breeds greater successes. Gradually, you will be able to focus for longer spans of time with very little internal distraction. With practice, you should be able to suffuse your entire Davening with a Hisbonenus mindset, and then all of your Davening will resonate more profoundly and deeply.

Many great Chabad Chasidim, my illustrious grandparents among them, would spend five to six hours a day in deep meditative states of Hisbonenus during Davening.

A violinist might focus every day on practicing just one segment of a larger musical composition. Over time, the particular segment becomes ingrained in them until they are, in a sense, *Batel* / nullified to and unified with the music. Now, instead of the violinist playing it, the music plays through them. At this point, they might choose to move on to the next segment of the composition, until they have mastered the entire piece. This is a helpful analogy for building the 'muscles' of Hisbonenus within Davening. We can begin by focusing on mastering one segment of the Davening at a time, until the entire Davening is infused with contemplative consciousness. Finally, instead of 'doing' the Davening, it will happen through you, as you have become an 'instrument' of prayer.

In this stage of Davening, your mind is not 'emptied' of thoughts; to the contrary, it is deeply focused in contemplating thoughts, but as the practice progresses, you become lost in the Davening and it flows 'through' you rather than 'from' you. This is the initial stage of Bitul or Ayin-consciousness.

CHAPTER 4

PREPARING FOR THE EXPERIENCE

HISBONENUS WAS ORIGINALLY DEVELOPED BY THE ALTER REBBE, and after his passing, it was further articulated by the successive Chabad and Lubavitch Rebbes and their Chasidim. Their holy writings are the primary sources gathered, adapted, and presented throughout the following chapters.

It is interesting to note that among all the *Ma'amarim* / discourses, *Sichos* / lectures, and *Igros* / letters on the topic of

Hisbonenus, there is not one single discourse that sets forth an explicit outline or set of instructions for the method, from preparation until post-practice assimilation. The illustrious son of the Alter Rebbe, the Mitteler Rebbe, Rebbe DovBer did produce *Kuntres HaHispa'alus* / "Tract on Ecstasy" and *Kuntres Hisbonenus* / "Tract on Contemplation," however, both texts are extremely deep and dense, and quite difficult for the average novice reader to decipher and put into practice. *Kuntres HaHispa'alus* is an exploration of the feelings, or more accurately, the 'non-feelings', that the practitioner experiences in deeper meditative states. *Kuntres Hisbonenus* is an in-depth analysis of the various modalities of intellect utilized in deep contemplation. Drawing from these sacred texts, among countless others, an attempt will be made to construct a manual with step-by-step suggestions for developing the art and practice of Hisbonenus.

STEPS TO PREPARE

As with any discipline or art, the better prepared we are, the more deeply we can engage, digest, and learn from the Hisbonenus. The preparatory steps place the individual in the optimal state of readiness. These steps optimize our coordinates and align our *Olam* / space, *Shanah* / time, and *Nefesh* / state of consciousness to empower the most transformative practice.

The three are as follows:

1) Space: Make sure that your surroundings allow for a turning inward, without external distractions.

2) Time: Set aside a time period that will be conducive for uninterrupted focus.

3) State of consciousness: Take notice of your mindset, and ask yourself if you are settled enough and willing to undertake an intense contemplative exercise.

SPACE

Securing a suitable location in which to practice Hisbonenus is essential for the success of the practice. Since Hisbonenus is most often practiced within Davening, traditionally, this was done in a *Shul* / synagogue or within a special dedicated space within a Shul designated for contemplative Davening. Whether it is practiced within a Shul or another space and not even during Davening, the designated space must contain the minimum distraction possible. Simplicity helps. A room filled with exquisite furniture may be good for entertaining guests, but that same furniture can become a distraction. Clearly, there should be no phones or devices connected to the outside world in the room; even if all screens, media, ringtones, alerts, notifications, and vibrations are turned off, these devices will subliminally command attention just through their presence. There should be no distractions, whether from objects or from people.

Throughout history, the most spiritually evolved people found the silence and peace that supported their prayer, study, and contemplation in the open fields and meadows away from the cities and urban settings. The *Avos* / Patriarchs, the twelve sons of Ya'akov, Moshe, and King Dovid were all shepherds by profession. This allowed them to dwell apart from the distractions and pettiness of the world and remain enveloped in spaces conducive to reflection and inner contemplation (Rebbe Avraham ben HaRambam, *Sefer HaMaspik LeOvdei Hashem*, Hisbodedus. The Tashbatz, *Magen Avos* 2, Chap. 2, p. 16a. *Kli Yakar*, Bereishis, 4:3. The Rebbe Rayatz, *Sefer HaMa'amarim, 5699* (5746), p. 183. The Rebbe, *Likutei Sichos*, 1, p. 229. And to receive prophecy: *Rabbeinu Bachya*, Bereishis, 46:32. Shemos, 3:1. *Panim Yafos*, ad loc. The life of a shepherd also cultivates compassion: *Derashos Rebbe Yehoshua Ibn Shuaiv* (student of the Rashba), Shemos, 21:1. *Shach*, Torah, Bereishis, 46:31).

While the open meadows are not readily available for most urban dwellers today, we can certainly find ways to carve out spaces where we can be alone with ourselves, or at least quieter and more settled, spaces where the moment we enter into it we feel more at ease and primed for contemplation and introspection.

If we are practicing Hisbonenus in the Shul, that carved-out space usually means our Makom Kavua / designated space where we Daven, as familiarity with the space allows us to drop into deeper states of inwardness immediately. If Hisbonenus is undertaken in our home or office space, for example, we can set aside a room or a corner within a room as a designated quiet space that is 'ours', our Makom Kavua.*

Having carved out a space for yourself to focus and be alone and then using that space over and over again to do just that will ensure that when you enter into the space, there will be an almost visceral positive reaction, and you begin to feel at ease with self and where the rest of the world will automatically melt away. Just by entering into the familiar, safe space associated with contemplation and inner work, your internal world comes to the foreground of awareness, and everything else recedes.

It is for this reason that the prototypical Chabad Shul in the old country included a *Cheider Sheini* / secondary room adjoining the main sanctuary, where those who Davened with Hisbonenus, *b'Kavanah v'Arichus* / with deeper intention and at great length, could remain undisturbed.

In general, every action leaves an imprint. Every action taken, every word uttered, and, in fact, even every thought

---

* "One who sets aside a designated place for prayer, the G-d of Avraham will help him" *Berachos*, 6b. For the purpose of Davening, a Makom Kavua should also be selected at home: *Yerushalmi, Berachos* 4:4. *Shulchan Aruch*, Orach Chayim, 90:19, as the *Alter Rebbe* (90:18) and the *Mishnah Berurah* (90:59) write. Besides the reason that one is not bothered by other people at home, a person concentrates better in a familiar place: *Menoras HaMaor*, Ner 3, Klal 3:10. In addition, Davening in a designated place makes that space more refined and sacred than others: *Beis Elokim*, Sha'ar HaTefillah, 5.

entertained releases a frequency into our immediate environment. A place in which people speak idle words fills the atmosphere with hollow frequencies, as it were. In a room where people share words of Torah or even just think about Torah, the atmosphere of that room is imbued and permeated with holiness and purity. Considering this, it is clear why certain locations, environments, or even lands naturally induce feelings of ease and peacefulness, whereas other places produce more aggressive sentiments.

Indeed, there are spaces where we naturally feel an inner sense of relaxation, and the space itself stimulates inward movement, whereas other spaces feel haggard and chaotic. Certain places and climates feel particularly favorable for more cerebral activities, whereas certain places feel very much action-infused. Certain environments are more conducive for inner work, reflection, contemplation, and meditation, and certain spaces less so.*

---

* Rebbe Rashab, *Sefer HaMa'amarim, 5669*, p. 42. In Chasidus, there is an expression, יש ארץ שמגדלת חכמים ויש ארץ שמגדלת טפשים / "There are lands that give rise to wise people and lands that give rise to fools": Alter Rebbe, *Ma'amarei Admur HaZaken, 5568*, 1, p. 117. 2, p. 618. Mitteler Rebbe, *Toras Chayim*, Shemos, 55a. See also *Sefer HaIkarim*: ומזה הצד ימצאו אנשים בעיר אחת או במחוז אחד יותר חריפים ויותר פקחים מאנשי ארץ אחרת / "For this reason, there are certain people found in one city or town, who are intellectually sharper than people in another land": *Sefer HaIkarim*, Ma'amar 1:25. The Zohar speaks of the waters in different places having different types of properties, hence, people drinking certain waters are wise, whereas other types of water produce the opposite effect. *Zohar* 1, 125a. 2, 30b. *Ma'amarei Admur HaZaken*, Ma'amarei Razal, p. 204. *Imrei Binah*, Keriyas Shema, 4. 17b. יש ארץ שמגדלת גבורים, ויש ארץ מגדלת חלשים: *Medrash Rabbah*, Bamidbar, 16:12. A major trope

Isolation from distracting objects and other people serves to quiet all external noise; however, you still must create some level of internal isolation and a cessation of involvement with sense perception.

Try to create inner calm and quiet, since prior to practicing Hisbonenus, you need to settle the mind as much as possible (Rebbe Rayatz, *Sefer HaMa'amarim*, Kuntreisim, 2 (5746) p. 300. See also *HaMaspik LeOvedei Hashem*, Hisbodedus, in the beginning. Ralbag, *Milchemes Hashem*, Ma'amar 2:6, p. 19).

in Medieval *Chakirah* / philosophy is that there are various spiritual climates across the earth, with *Eretz Yisrael* / the Land of Israel at the center point, being the climate that is most conducive to prophecy and *Chochmah* / wisdom. Chazal tell us, אוירא דארץ ישראל מחכים / "The air of Eretz Yisrael makes a person wise": *Baba Basra*, 158b. The Seforno writes that Eretz Yisrael is a perfect place for Hisbonenus and serving Hashem — שהיתה מפורסמת אצלם לארץ מוכנת להתבוננות ולעבודת האל ית' / "(Eretz Yisrael) was famous as a land that is primed for Hisbonenus and Avodas Hashem": *Seforno*, Bereishis, 12:5. The Mabit writes, כי בהיות א"י מעולה מארץ מצרים כ"ש שהיא מעולה משאר הארצות כמו שכתבתי, ושבחיה הכוללים הם שנים, מעלתה בדברים השכליים, ומעלתה בדברים הגשמיים. ומעלתה בדברים השכליים הוא, כען מה שאמרו אוירא דארעא ישראל מחכים / "Eretz Yisrael is superior above all other lands, as I have written, and her praise includes different aspects: her superiority for intellectual (achievements) and also material things. But the essential superiority is in intellect, as it is said, 'The air of the Land of Israel makes one wise'": *Beis Elokim*, Sha'ar HaTefillah, 5. The Kuzari speaks at length about how *Neuvah* / prophecy is *only* available in Eretz Yisrael, as it is the perfectly measured midpoint of the earth. The Radak writes that Yerushalayim has the perfectly balanced weather and temperature to breed good physical health, wisdom and intelligence — כי בישוב נחלק לשבעה חלקים ובחלק האמצעי היא ירושלים והיא באמצע היישוב לפיכך אוירה טוב וממוסך מכל האוירים לבריאות הגוף ולחכמה: Radak on *Tehilim*, 87:3.

Due to the need for an absence of distractions, the practice of Hisbonenus is often performed in private. The Baal Shem Tov, however, suggests that all deeper spiritual study and contemplative practices should be performed alongside another person, or at least with another person in the room. This is because if done completely alone, some practices may be disturbing or even dangerous. A person can transcend 'too high', as it were, and lose touch with reality, have a mental or emotional breakdown, or even enter a state of blissful transcendence from which it is impossible to return to human functioning and responsibility.

Once, the Alter Rebbe and Rebbe Avraham *HaMalach* / 'the Angel', the son of the Maggid of Mezritch, were engaged in deep mystical contemplation in the same room. The Alter Rebbe noticed that Reb Avraham was beginning to drift off and become swallowed in the ecstasy of his experience. He rushed to the kitchen, returned with a delicious bagel with butter, and forced Reb Avraham to have a bite. Reb Avraham was thereby able to return to the world and rejoin his soul and his body.

TIME

Not only is location integral to the success of the practice, but so is timing. In the early morning or very late at night (*Eiruvin*, 65a), when the world is still sleeping, there is less spiritual 'pollution' in the air, as it were. As a cacophony of negative and ego-driven thoughts, words and actions have not yet been released into the atmosphere in those hours of the day, and so many people find those times of day more appropriate for introspection, study, or Hisbonenus.

Of course, all of these environmental conditions of space, noise, stimuli, and negativity are external, and if you have the internal willpower and desire, you can choose to overcome these environmental influences and practice at any time in any place. Yet, instead of dispensing energy to overcome external conditions, it could be helpful to choose a time and space that are more conducive.

The level of your alertness plays a vital role in the success of the practice. Throughout the day, if you are attentive to your states of mind, you will recognize that there are times when you feel more alert, awake, and present and times when you feel more fatigued, lethargic, or 'shut down'. There are times when it is easier to think and be inspired and to engage in intellectual contemplation. Some of our mood changes throughout the day are related to our sleep and exertion patterns, as well as to when and what we eat.

A person becomes more sluggish following a heavy meal. On Shabbos, our sages tell us, we should not try to teach children new concepts in Torah. One reason is that משום דבשבתא אכלין ושתין ויקיר עליהון עלמא / "On Shabbos children eat and drink more than they are accustomed to eating, and their world is heavy upon them. Their heads and even their limbs are sluggish, and they are incapable of concentrating and studying well" (*Nedarim*, 37b).

Following a large meal, the mind tends to cloud over and become foggy. One becomes less able to concentrate. Certainly, this is true if one eats coarse or heavy foods that create physical fatigue, heaviness, and a foggy mind (Since the physical brain is the receptacle for intellect, it is important to watch what we eat, for what we consume will ultimately become part of our brains and heavy, coarse foods will cloud the mind: Rebbe Rayatz, *Sefer HaMa'amarim*, Kuntreisim, 2 (5746) p. 918. See also *Sefer HaMa'amarim, 5703*, p. 21. In general, coarse foods cause drowsiness. Rabbeinu Gershon ben Shelomo, *Sha'ar HaShamayim* (1968), Ma'amar 10, p. 68. *Reishis Chochmah*, Sha'ar HaKedushah 7. Generally, excessive eating causes tiredness: *Yuma*, 18a. לא היו מניחין אותו לאכול הרבה, מפני שהמאכל מביא את השינה: Medrash *Tana D'vei Eliyahu*, 13).

For this reason, it is advisable to refrain from large meals prior to practicing Hisbonenus. Early mornings and late nights can be more fitting, also since they are some distance from meals (Although, eating a meal also creates a joyous mood, and joy is a prerequisite to reaching higher states of consciousness and even literal prophecy: *Derashos HaRan*, Derush 5. *Rabbeinu Bachya*, Shemos, 18:12. *Me'am Loez*, and *Tiferes Yonosan*, ad loc. Rabbeinu Bachya, *Kad Kemach*, Rosh Hashanah 2, p. 379).

Conversely, an empty stomach or hunger pangs can also cause considerable distraction. Prior to eating, say *Chazal* / our sages, a person has two hearts (*Baba Basra*, 12b). This means that his heart is unsettled and split into two, as no matter what his intention is, he will be distracted by his hunger. 'Heart' in Hebrew is לב / *Lev*. When a person has 'a לב and (ו) another לב', two hearts, as it were, he experiences בלבול / confusion (*Ben Yehoyada*, ad loc).

Rebbetzin Rivka, the daughter-in-law of the Tzemach Tzedek, was but a young woman when she fell gravely ill and was ordered by her doctors to eat immediately upon waking. She refused to do so, however, for she did not wish to eat before Davening, as is the *Halachah* / law. When the Tzemach Tzedek heard of her refusal to eat, he said, "It is better to eat in order to Daven, then to Daven in order to eat" (*Hayom Yom*, 10th of Shevat).

When a person is very hungry, the subconscious mind will wage a mighty battle to get the person to think about food and not what they desire to focus on. Some people, even when just mildly hungry, have a difficult time concentrating on anything other than food. If you are hungry while you are practicing Hisbonenus, your attention may shift about or be pulled away from your focal point — at least when your body and mind have not yet been transcended. Once you are in deeper levels of Hisbonenus, the need for food, as well as the sensations of discomfort, might be suspended for as long as you remain absorbed.

CONSCIOUSNESS

As the state of our body affects our consciousness, bodily aches and discomforts can also disturb our concentration and collectedness. The Maggid of Mezritch once said, "A small hole in the body is a large hole in the soul" (*Maggid Devarav LeYa'akov*, 191. See also the Rebbe, *B'Tzeil HaChochmah*, p. 28). If your body is failing or ailing, injured, or irritated, try to the best of your ability to relieve the physical discomfort and mend the 'hole' in the body so that your mind and your soul can be united and whole.

The Baal Shem Tov talks about how sometimes a person wants to Daven, and his mind, heart, and spirit are up to it, yet he cannot focus because "his limbs are heavy" (*Amud HaTefillah*, 66. *Ohr Torah*, Ekev). We need to check in and ensure that our limbs are not 'heavy' and acquire the 'consent' of our body so that we can enter fully into the experience with lightness and strength.

For most people, not feeling physically well or comfortable will present significant difficulties. We need to tend to the body in whatever manner necessary. While a seasoned master of contemplation may be able to overcome such external obstacles and physical limitations, they can still make the Hisbonenus more challenging. In the long run, it is better if we have our body's consent to engage in Hisbonenus with all the effort, focus, alertness, and openness that it requires.

Although there are no clear sources in Chasidus for the position of the body when practicing Hisbonenus, logic dictates that whatever comes naturally and opens the way into a deeper state of consciousness is a good approach to explore. The position that will induce the minimum amount of distractions possible is optimal. Most people find that sitting in a chair is the most comfortable posture, although a very relaxing position may cause one to be drowsy, clouding their collectedness and unification.

At any given moment, most people are functioning in one of two fluctuating states of consciousness: *Mochin D'Gadlus* / mature, expansive mind or *Mochin D'Katnus* / immature, contracted mind. These are temporary states of consciousness, not persistent stages, although there is occasionally a person who can enter a stage of consciousness that persists for years. Usually, within a single day, there are times of expansion and times of constriction, times of feeling elated and times of feeling low.

When one is 'having a good day', they may feel empowered, energetic, and able, whereas when they are 'having a bad day', they may feel lonely, lethargic, and incompetent. In a constricted state of consciousness, you may feel as if your intellect has been reduced to that of an incognizant and immature child, where you cannot think straight and see beyond the immediate (*Ma'amarei Admur HaZaken*, Inyanim, p. 201).

In higher states of consciousness, one recognizes with wonder the Divine abundance they are being given, and are grateful, happy, collected, aware and alert. In lower states, one is small-minded, impatient, petty, lost in narratives of disempowerment, conflict, craving or anxiety, complaining of scarcity, and so on.

All such states should be taken into consideration before undertaking the practice of Hisbonenus. As you prepare, become aware of the mood and state you are currently in, so you can own it, and confirm that now is the right time to practice. You do not have to already be in an expanded state to enter Hisbonenus, but if you are in a contracted state, you may need to remedy it. If possible, settle your heart or even manufacture a feeling of well-being, so that you can begin to collect and unify your mind.*

---

* Yet, there is also a value in performing Hisbonenus, and other forms of Avodah, even when tired. For example, in the Mitzvah to read the *Shema*, the paragraph of *VeAhavta* / "and you shall love Hashem," is the Hisbonenus, the contemplation of the Oneness of Hashem which eventually arouses the heart to love: *Torah Ohr*, Ki Sisa, 86d. Here, the *Mitzvah* is the Hisbonenus, as the Baal Shem Tov teaches: *Shnei HaMeoros* (Homiler), 2:2. See also The Tzemach Tzedek, *Derech Mitzvosecha*, L'Havin Mitzvas Ahavah, in the Tziyunim VaHa'aros on this Mitzvah, p. 408. And see Rambam, *Hilchos Yesodei HaTorah*, 2:1. *Peleh Yoetz*, Ahavah. With regards to the Mitzvah of Shema, the Torah tells us that the Mitzvah is בשכבך ובקומך / "when lying down" (the time when people do so) and upon awakening, "when you stand up." On a deeper level, all of this means that Hisbonenus is connected with a state of clarity, expansiveness, day, 'standing up', but also with times when one is 'lying down', tired, lethargic, and lacking clarity. In fact, as the Mitteler Rebbe writes, there is a type of 'Avodah of tiredness' that helps elevate

If you are emotionally deflated or disturbed, or feeling sullied or weighed down by mistakes, you should practice *Teshuvah* / 'returning to yourself and to Hashem's Presence' before attempting Hisbonenus. Supportive practices can include immersing in a *Mikvah* / ritual pool (which also helps with intruding thoughts and the ability for focused concentration, The Rebbe, *Igros Kodesh*, 13, p. 245. 15, p. 375), reciting *Tehillim* / Psalms, and making a *Cheshbon HaNefesh* / self-reflection and accounting along with *Hachlatos* / resolutions to change and transform yourself. There are times, as the Alter Rebbe writes (*Ma'amarei Admur HaZaken*, Inyanim, p. 130), when honest self-reflection gets a person nowhere, as arrogance and a conceit will not allow any light to penetrate. And there are times when even the slightest thought of remorse, for example, awakens powerful feelings of Teshuvah, opening into inspiration and self-empowerment.

Your choice of a Torah subject to study or contemplate will also modulate your state of consciousness. Our sages teach us that we should choose subjects that *Libo Chafetz* / our heart finds appealing (*Avodah Zarah*, 19a). Although one is in general encouraged to study Torah quantitatively and cover as much ground as possible, when we wish to use a thought as a focal point in Hisbonenus, it is most effective to use one that piques our interest and holds our attention, a thought that arouses *Cheishek* / desire, as explored earlier. The idea

---

that reality of 'night' and unclarity: *Toras Chayim*, Tetzaveh, p. 319.

should speak to us, resonate within, or grip our imagination. Fanning the flames of this Cheishek will lead the mind into a more expansive state.

If you are already in an expansive state when you begin, you may wish to focus your Hisbonenus on the more subtle teachings of Hashem's Unity, whereas, in more constricted states, your focus could be on teachings related to joy. Joy is a master key and antidote to break yourself out of constriction and open your capacity for clear contemplation and Hisbonenus.

CHAPTER 5

THE OBJECTIVE OF THE PRACTICE

AS EXPLORED EARLIER, MOST PEOPLE BELIEVE THAT THEY CHOOSE THEIR THOUGHTS, WHILE SADLY, THEIR THOUGHTS ACTUALLY CHOOSE THEM; they are not at all premeditated; rather, they are 'random' occurrences. They are dictated by their external or internal environment. If this describes your current experience, however, there is no reason to feel dejected or deterred from engaging in Hisbonenus practice. From a more positive perspective, if your mind is open to being filled by the external objects, narratives, and emotions that happen to arise, then it has the power to be filled by a chosen focus, as well. That chosen focus just needs to be interesting and compelling enough. If a person is taking a stroll and sees a beautiful home, and thoughts of homes automatically occupy their mind, that is only because beautiful homes pique their interest.

If one's mind is fully controlled by the world and events happening around him, it would do him well to gain authority over his thoughts and liberate himself from this subtle state of enslavement. It is important to note that the tendency to be absorbed in trivialities is the same tendency that we can utilize to become deeply absorbed in meaningful thoughts. A horse might have a tendency to run wildly about, or to subserviently follow a carrot dangled in front of its nose. Yet this same raw energy and desire for satisfaction can be used to shape that animal into a disciplined and elegant racehorse.

Hisbonenus is the means by which we can shape our mind into a powerful instrument of spirituality. Through this training, our 'operating system' can be gradually tuned to the frequency of true light and joy. On the most basic level, this involves harnessing the raw energy of the mind and giving it some semblance of control. On a higher level, however, we begin to recover our human faculty of free choice, to make conscious decisions regarding what we would like to be thinking about (Through proper preparation, we can control our thoughts, as the Rishonim write. גם בחירת המחשבה מסורה בידו אחר ההכנות: *Rabbeinu Bachya,* Devarim, 29:18. See also the fascinating letter by the Tzemach Tzedek printed in *Meah Shearim,* 17a).

There will be challenges, as explained. Simply telling yourself to think a particular thought can be a futile endeavor; within a few seconds, the mind will be wandering elsewhere, as the subconscious mind tends to regurgitate ideas that are unrelated to the matter at hand. Beyond the conscious mind, there are layers upon layers of inner experience that cannot be easily controlled or manipulated. The subconscious mind can seem to have a life of its own. It can seem to invade our consciousness in the most inopportune moments with erratic or chaotic thoughts.

An ability to focus and remain focused liberates the conscious mind from the tyranny of habitual and random thoughts, and even from subconscious or subtle interferences. The power to freely choose clarity and coherence may at first be available for just a few short moments at a time, but with practice and patience, the duration increases until it becomes the very baseline of our life.

In truth, meditation, contemplation, and prolonged states of focus are not foreign activities for the human mind: in fact, we are always 'meditating' on something or another and focusing on what pleases us. For example, if we are faced with a pressing issue such as how to pay a certain bill, when to close on a home or a business deal, or how to resolve a conflict with our boss or employee, we will find that we can stay laser-focused on these challenging tasks for longer, uninterrupted periods of time with unwavering and intense concentration. The issue is what we are meditating on and how much power of choice we can activate in relation to what we are focusing on, whether we are choosing to think about these thoughts or these are thoughts to choose us.

Right now, look at the last twenty-four hours of your life and ask yourself: how much of that time were you exercising control over your thoughts, and how much time did your thoughts simply run amok? If and when you did choose your thoughts, were they thoughts about your materialistic or selfish desires, thoughts about your self-aggrandizement, self-preservation, or self-perpetuation? Or were they more transcendent thoughts, ideas on how to meet other people's needs and be in service to others, or how to live more deeply and connect with the Source of all Life?

Once you are able to see your thought patterns in this way, you will have some distance from them, and you can begin to replace mindless chatter with loftier, more noble thoughts. This will help you prepare for the practice of Hisbonenus. Now, let us begin to explore its basic practical instructions.

REPLACING MINDLESS CHATTER WITH LOFTY THOUGHTS

In the first stages of formal Hisbonenus, one selects an idea or *Ma'amar* / Chasidic discourse to focus on, and one contemplates an idea or theme in this Ma'amar for extended periods of time. Due to the beautiful and elevated insights, novel thoughts, and Divine revelations woven into the fabric of the Ma'amar, plus the Hischadshus that continually enlivens the discussion, the mind is drawn into contemplation. Whenever the mind wanders, one draws it back to the Ma'amar, and this strengthens the 'muscles' of focus and choice. All of this trains the mind to naturally gravitate deeper and deeper into these G-dly thoughts. In time, these thoughts will seep in and transform our inner life and our state of consciousness.

The loftiest of all thoughts, and the classic focus of Hisbonenus, is the truth of אין עוד מלבדו / *Ein Od Milvado* / "There is nothing besides Him." Later on, a full exploration of this contemplation will be explored, but in the simplest description, it means there are no independent forces in the universe; there is only Hashem. This is the core of absolute monotheism: *nothing at all exists but Hashem.*

Hisbonenus is tied to the practice of Davening, historically speaking. It is both a preparation for deeper, more contemplative levels of Davening and a companion that comes along into the process of Davening itself. In fact, there are three 'types' of Hisbonenus.

THE THREE STAGES OF HISBONENUS

The Rebbe Rayatz writes that there are three ascending 'stages' of Hisbonenus.[*] The first stage is 'intellectual Hisbonenus'. After studying and understanding a chosen concept correctly, we meditate on its depth until it becomes utterly illuminated and it 'shines' within our mind. The second stage is the Hisbonenus practiced before Davening. Here, the point is to experience the 'vitality', the aliveness of the idea that we are contemplating, not only its intellectual properties. The third stage is the Hisbonenus practiced

---

[*] שלשה מיני התבוננות הם: א) התבוננות למודית, אחר שמבין הענין על בוריו, הוא מתבונן בעומק הענין ההוא, עד שהשכלי מאיר אצלו. ב) שקודם התפלה, ענינה הרגש חיות הענין שלמד ולא הרגש השכלי כמו בהתבוננות למודית. ג) שבתפלה, ענינה הרגש האלקות שבהענין שלמד. And the Rebbe adds, שלש אלה הם שליבות סולם ההרגשה ורק בחסדי השי"ת עמנו מרגישים לפעמים — דערהערט מען ג־טליכקייט בלי שום עבודה כלל, והוא מפני מעלת העצמות שיש בנשמה, אבל מצד העבודה שבכח עצמו מוכרחים שלש הנ"ל / "These are three rungs on the ladder of spiritual sensitivity. At times, due to Hashem's kindness from Above, one truly hears and senses Divinity without any form of hard and inner work. This is because of the essential quality of the soul. However, with regard to Divine service that stems from our own initiative, the above three steps are necessary": the Rebbe Rayatz, *Igros Kodesh* 3, p. 525-526. *Hayom Yom*, 20th of Tammuz.

within Davening. Here, the purpose is to sense, beyond just the 'vitality' of the idea, the *Elokus* / Divinity within the idea.

Hisbonenus can evolve through these three stages in a single practice session. For example, before Davening, one begins studying and pondering an idea, such as the idea of Ein Od Milvado, until the insight becomes fully secured in the mind and illuminates the mind. Then, one sits with the idea until one begins to feel the vitality, the life force, or the inner energy that enlivens the subject matter. Finally, when Davening, one senses the *Elokus* / Divinity within the idea and, by extension, the Elokus within everything.*

Following this progression of Hisbonenus in Davening, one is left with a solid, anchored sense that all of physicality and the entire world of sense stimuli is imaginary and devoid of any true or substantial content — all that exists is Hashem Alone.

The custom of my grandfather, the great Chasid and *Mashpia* / spiritual mentor, Reb Zalman Moshe HaYitzchaki (ז״ל) was to Daven for 5-6 hours each morning. His *Tefill-*

---

* If one did not contemplate before Davening, he can practice Hisbonenus on the first level even just by thinking about Chasidus while Davening: Rebbe Rayatz, *Igros Kodesh*, 10, p. 379. Note also the practice of the Tzemach Tzedek to write (or even verbally expound) Chasidus during Davening: *Beis Rebbe*, 2, p. 8.

ah / prayer was an act of deep Hisbonenus and inner reflection, full of *Ga'aguim* / longing and yearning for Deveikus
and to sense the living Presence of HaKadosh Baruch Hu.

Once, in his later years, when he was living in Tel Aviv,
after finishing Davening, he looked out the window of the
Shul and saw a young man called Mottel Dubinsky walking by. He waved his hand, beckoning him into the Shul.
When Mottel entered, Reb Zalman Moshe told him, "We
are going to say a *LeChayim*. I will fill up two little cups of
schnapps, but only I will drink." He filled two little cups,
said *LeChayim*, and declared, ‏אין עוד מלבדו! ס׳איז ניטא גארניט,‏
‏גארניט‏ / "There is nothing besides Him; literally, nothing,
nothing!" He said the Berachah and drank. He then turned
to the young lad and said, "Now Mottel, you too, say 'There
is nothing besides Him; nothing, nothing!' Mottel did so.
Then they sat together for fifteen or twenty minutes before
parting ways (*MeShulchano Shel Reb Yoel,* p. 378).

Reb Zalman Moshe Davened while absorbed in the truth
that ‏אין עוד מלבדו‏ / *Ein Od Milvado* / 'There is nothing besides Him,' but apparently, when he finished Davening, he
felt that this absolute truth had not yet — on his level —
transformed him. Only when he had another person declare it and reflect the truth back to him did he feel somewhat satisfied and able to leave the Shul for the 'outside
world' while maintaining a deeper awareness of this truth.
Apparently, he felt that his contemplation of Ein Od Milvado on that day needed this additional step in order to

solidify his nondual state of consciousness. This shows that Hisbonenus can be deepened indefinitely; there is no end to unifying with the Infinite. While Reb Zalman Moshe was on an indescribably high level of achievement, he was still growing every day.

Hisbonenus is not just for the great *Ovdim* / spiritual laborers like Reb Zalman Moshe. If anyone sincerely enters the path of Hisbonenus and continues day after day, with longer and longer periods of uninterrupted absorption in the concept of Ein Od Milvado, tremendous changes will begin to occur. Our mind will be more and more transformed from egocentric to Divine-centric, from self-conscious to G-d-conscious. Slowly, we begin to focus on, feel, and experience the Divinity within all of Creation, within all of life situations and encounters, and within our heart.

EXPANDING THE MIND

We can operate, understand, and engage with reality from two almost diametrically opposed perspectives. We can access reality through the ego-driven perspective of the external self, what the Alter Rebbe calls the *Nefesh HaBehamis* / 'animal soul', or from the perspective of our internal self, our *Nefesh HaElokis* / Divine Soul.

The Nefesh HaBehamis is the part of us that can direct us to act instinctively in relation to threats or benefits, similar to the behavior of an animal. This level of self seeks survival, perpetuation, and aggrandizement, and it views the outside world as distinct and separate from itself. It lives in a world of fragmentation and disunity, scarcity and aggression — a world separate from the Infinite Creator.

Our Nefesh HaElokis, by contrast, sees a world of endless abundance and holistic unity. All of Creation is at one within itself and with its Infinite Creator. It sees the 'outside' as part of the 'inside' and its apparent multiplicity and duality as part of the total Oneness of Hashem.

As the Alter Rebbe describes at length in Sefer HaTanya, the animal soul and the Divine soul are full 'selves', as it were, each containing their own intelligence, emotions, and abilities to actualize thoughts and feelings. Their main difference lies in the way they function and accomplish what they set out to do.

With regard to intelligence, the animal soul operates within the laws of nature, within the set patterns and confines of the time-space continuum. Its thought process is restrained to logical, sequential, and dimensional thinking; one plus one is two, and so on. It gathers only the kind of data that fits with its agendas, and it processes this data in a linear, deductive mode of thinking.

The Divine soul, however, is "a part of Hashem, literally"; it is not a separate creation, as is the animal self. As an inseparable extension of the Creator, the Nefesh HaElokis operates and functions on a transcendent level, and its mode of processing and understanding information is beyond all linear and conventional ways of thinking, beyond the laws of nature and logic. It has an ability to 'grasp' the ungraspable, to sense the ineffable, to touch the Divine.

Due to these contrasting natures, one of the objectives of Hisbonenus is to direct the rational intellect of our Nefesh HaBehamis to appreciate more and more transcendent thoughts, expanding the capacity of the 'animal soul' to appreciate higher levels of existence and ultimately to become aware of HaKadosh Baruch Hu. Broadening and expanding our natural mind strengthens the neurological links between the right and left hemispheres of the brain and opens it to new vistas. Ultimately, the natural mind can be released from its habitual confines of perception and cognition and become capable of apprehending the truth of Ein Od Milvado.

THE TOTAL TRANSFORMATION OF SELF

A thought of Ein Od Milvado is gradually extended into periods of contemplation until, eventually, it deconditions the conventional mind and changes its mode of functioning. In due time, instead of your 'animal instincts' automatically scheming and directing you toward fight or flight reactions, insatiable desires, self-aggrandizement, and self-denigration, the Nefesh HaBehamis 'onboards' deeper thoughts and finally settles into on-demand 'Divine-centricity'.

Gradually, this transformation of the mind becomes all-encompassing, including our core identity and our very surroundings. Not only is our new status quo to naturally think this way, but all of our thoughts, feelings, words, and actions 'inhabit' the domain of *Elokus* / Divinity. No part of ourselves remains outside this holy realm of aliveness and being. Our character traits become more G-dly, as it were; just as Hashem is Compassionate, so are we compassionate. We experience Divinity within all of life, all objects, and all our personal situations and encounters.

FROM THOUGHT. TO EMOTION TO TRANSCENDENCE

As mentioned, the word Hisbonenus stems from the word *Binah* / understanding. It actually employs the entire spectrum of the mind's capacities — Chochmah, Binah, and Da'as — to develop a chosen thought, understand it, and contemplate it for extended periods of time. And the aim of all this deep thinking and contemplation is to instill the light, aliveness, and Elokus of the chosen thought into your heart. In this way, the quest of Hisbonenus is to perceive and *feel* Divinity, not just to 'know' it. Through exercising your mind, your emotions are eventually aroused until your heart physically aches in longing and desire for Elokus. Such *Hishtokekus* / longing will draw you directly into *Deveikus* / unity with the Source.

BEYOND FEELINGS AND SELF

Emotions of longing aroused through Hisbonenus can become so intense that they are difficult to contain within the
heart. They can feel like they will burst forth with a fiery,
unbridled holy passion for the Ineffable, Infinite One, and
this intensity leads the individual to an ecstatic state of *Bitul* / self-transcendence and Deveikus.

In intimate relationships, emotions of longing can find an
outlet and a means of diffusion through physical contact.
Such diffusion of desire is experienced when the two individuals collapse into one. In Divine love, however, the
yearning desire for contact with the Infinite has no physical
or tangible outlet, and thus, the desire itself must self-im-
plode, revealing a state beyond desire, beyond the duality
of lover and Beloved. This is a collapse of the separate 'i',
the ego, within the Ultimate I of HaKadosh Baruch Hu,
and there is no longer a feeling of longing, as there is no
longer a separate individual to feel. There is no 'me' and no
'You'; there is just total Deveikus in the Oneness of Hashem, without anyone there to experience it.

USING INTELLECT TO
TRANSCEND ITSELF

In general, in the practice of Hisbonenus, we garner all the
faculties of the intellect in order to transcend the intellect.

Yet, for this transcendence to occur, it needs to happen gradually and incrementally, one step at a time. In the earlier stages of Hisbonenus, the activity is quite cerebral and heady, as we are still trying to make sense of the idea that will become the focus of our deeper contemplation, and we are using the rational mind's linear mode of thinking. This is done intentionally so that when we have progressed beyond the rational mind, and we enter the deeper levels of Deveikus (by means of Bitul or Ayin, as explored), our system will have a solid foundation to ground the experience and ensure that the transcendent experience can be later integrated and assimilated properly. We do not want to 'fly away' into transcendence or 'kick away the ladder' back into the world, as it were, because it is vital to avoid a mental breakdown or total dissolution of identity. Authentic Hisbonenus creates tangible positive effects on our daily life. Also, when we have a good anchoring mechanism, including the capacity to return to rational thinking at any given moment, our subconscious mind is more secure and will allow us to leap higher than it would if it were afraid of disappearing and never coming back.

The Avodah of transcendence functions in a paradigm of *Ratzo V'Shov* / 'running' to higher, selfless states of being and 'returning' back into a basically normative state of consciousness and sense of self.

CHAPTER 6

CHABAD: CHOCHMAH, BINAH, DA'AS

HISBONENUS ENGAGES THE ENTIRE SPECTRUM OF A HUMAN BEING'S INTELLECTUAL FACULTIES. There are three essential dimensions of intellect, collectively called ChaBaD, an acronym for *Chochmah* / wisdom, intuition, or conception, *Binah* / understanding and comprehension, and *Da'as* / knowledge, perception, or intellectual awareness (These three categories do not include capacities of the mind such as fine motor skills, nor do they include the more instinctual forms of 'knowing' such as instincts of self-preservation, which we share with other living beings — *Baba Kama*, 52b. 54b: פקח ומהלך ביום, פטור, nor the instinct to self-perpetuate — אתתא דידי פקיחא היא, ולא מבעיא חיה: *Baba Kama*, 59a, as these are not proactive, conscious thinking processes).

When the Torah recounts the qualifications of Betzalel, the chief architect of the *Mishkan* / temporary 'Temple' in the desert, the Torah says, "I have filled him with the spirit of Hashem, with Chochmah, with *Tevunah* (Binah) and with Da'as" (*Shemos*, 31:3. The juxtaposition of these three forms of intellect is found throughout *Mishlei* — 3:5-7. 8:12-14. 24: 3-4. 30:2-3. See also *Yeshayahu*, 11:2). These three basic three properties of the mind allowed Betzalel to draw the knowledge of how to build the Mishkan through abstract 'kernels' of ideas, down into detailed understandings, and finally down into fully developed practical know-how. In order for us to build our own inner Mishkan, a space where the Divine Presence is manifest, we need to garner these three intellectual potentialities. Our faculties of ChaBaD are the proper prisms through which we apprehend the world around us and act with inspiration and practical wisdom.

Chochmah is an initial creative insight before it is understood. Binah is understanding and comprehension, where germinating ideas of Chochmah become fleshed out and developed, and Da'as is where information becomes action and where intelligent choices can be made (In Hebrew, and in the Yiddish vernacular, *Seichel* / שכל means the wisdom, understanding, and wits to know how to choose what to do and how to act. Regarding the word השכל / 'the *Seichel*' (*Yirmeyahu*, 9:23), Rashi explains that it means אנטיליינ״ט בלע״ז / "*intellect* in Old French." The word 'intelligence' in English and French is derived from the Latin word, *intelligere*. This is a composite of two words: *inter*, which means 'in between', and *legere*, meaning 'to pick out', to choose. Rashi is saying that *Seichel* means the cognitive ability to choose between things).

CHOCHMAH & BINAH

Chochmah is where new thoughts come to mind and begin to germinate. The kernel of an idea first exists within the world of Chochmah, and from there, it can begin to sprout and flower outwards. The word *Chochmah* is composed of two words *Cho'ach Mah*, literally, 'the potential of *what*' (*Zohar* 3, pp. 28a, 34a, 235b. *Tikkunei Zohar*, Hakdamah, Tikkun 65, Tikkun 69. The Chayit, *Ma'areches Elokus*, Chap. 4, p. 71b. *Pardes Rimonim*, Sha'ar 23:8. Mahara deFano, *Sefas Emes*, Erech, Chochmah, p. 18b. *Shefa Tal*, Sha'ar 2:3, p. 40a. *Tanya*, Chap. 3). Chochmah is the raw potential of articulated thoughts. In the realm of Chochmah, thoughts are still elusive, ungraspable, and not fully comprehensible. They are like premonitions or intuitions, indefinable and intellectually incomprehensible, evading clear and logical explanation. Because of this elusiveness, we are unsure 'what' exactly the thought is about, hence the syllable *Mah* / 'What (is it)?'

While Chochmah's first flash of intuitive perception cannot yet be elaborated in rational terminology, Binah takes this raw 'potential of what' into a state of cogitation. The seminal point of an idea is elaborated in fine detail.

Binah is the cognitive ability that absorbs the abstract or ambiguous seed of Chochmah (also called *Abba* / 'father'), and articulates it through the process of associative analysis (Rebbe Rayatz, *Sefer HaMa'amarim Kuntreisim* 2, p. 576. *Sefer HaMa'amarim, 5701,* p. 107). The kernel of Chochmah is given form and nurtured into maturity in the womb of Binah (also called *Ima* / 'mother').

With the power of Binah, we are able to ponder the totality of a thought in its length and breadth. Examining a thought in its 'length' involves taking the thought from a purely abstract state and transforming it into something more understandable, bringing it down into the world, as it were. 'Broadening' a thought means giving the thought greater implications once it has been brought down into the world. The thought is dressed in comprehensible and rational connotations and applications. In Binah, thoughts become comprehensive and filled out.

In general, Chochmah is a masculine quality and Binah is a feminine quality. In order to bring a new life into this world, the male supplies the seed, and when the female's eggs are fertilized, the embryo is nurtured in the womb and gradually develops into a fetus and eventually into a fully formed baby in the womb of the mother. Similarly, in the world of Binah, the initial sprout of creativity, the kernel of

Chochmah, incubates until the created thought can be externalized and articulated in comprehensible language. As such, Chochmah is the non-contextual creative force, which can only be brought into fruition when enclosed within the womb of Binah.*

Chochmah is likened to a dot, a seminal point (*Zohar* 1. 6a. *Tikkunei Zohar*, Tikkun 5. *Tanya*, Igeres HaKodesh, 5. *Likutei Torah*, Re'eh, p. 18b) that comes to a person in the form of a concentrated, illuminating lightning bolt (*Torah Ohr*, p. 74b. *Sefer HaMa'amarim, 5703*, p. 54). The thought flashes in front of your eyes as a fleeting image. It is as if you have 'seen' the thought

---

** According to the Arizal, the father gives to his child the *Ohr Makif* / surrounding light, whereas the mother gives the child the *Ohr Penimi* / inner light. Makif is more 'general' and Penimi is more 'specific' — כי בהיות האיש מזדווג עם אשתו להוליד בנים, הנה מכח האב נמשך בחי' אור מקיף בבן, ומכח האם נמשך מבן ג"כ בחי' אור פנימי: *Sha'ar HaGilgulim*, Hakdamah 10. The Arizal also continues: והנה אם תרצה לידע, מי גובר בו, כח האב או האם, תוכל להכיר זה כפי קלותו של הבן או כבדותו, לפי כי האור הפנימי מוגבל, ואינו יכול להתנועע. אבל האור המקיף מבחוץ, מתנועע, ומניע את האדם למקום שהוא חפץ. ונמצא כי אם תראה איזה אדם קל כנשר ורץ כצבי בכל מעשיו, ומהיר במלאכתו, נמצא שגבר עליו אור המקיף אשר מכח אביו. ואם הוא עצל וכבד התנועה, יורה תגבורת אור הפנימי בו מצד האם / "Indeed, if you wish to know, who prevails within a person — whether it is the strength of the father or the mother — you can recognize it by the ease of movement of the child or by their heaviness. For the *Ohr Penimi* / inner light is confined and unmovable. However, the *Ohr Makif* / surrounding light moves about and moves the person toward their desired place. Thus, when you encounter an individual who moves gracefully like an eagle and swiftly like a deer in all their actions, diligently pursuing their work, it signifies that the surrounding light, derived from their father, prevails and dominates. Conversely, if they exhibit laziness and sluggishness in movement, it suggests that the inner light, originating from their mother, holds greater sway."

and are absolutely certain of its value and insight, but you cannot yet explain it to others or even to yourself.

Chochmah is the state of the thought prior to words. Binah takes that theoretical sense and enclothes it in rational language. Chochmah is comparable to 'seeing' a solution to a problem, whereas Binah is 'hearing' and assimilating it (*Torah Ohr*, Mishpatim, p. 75a. *Ma'amarei Admur HaZaken*, HaK'tzarim, p. 555. The Mitteler Rebbe, *Sha'arei Orah*, Sha'ar HaChanukah, p. 40. *Toras Chayim*, Bereishis, p. 48a. Rebbe Rayatz, *Sefer HaMa'amarim, 5701*, p. 132. *Sefer HaMa'amarim, 5709*, pp. 59-60).

Binah is likened to fire, whereas Chochmah is likened to water (*Eitz Chayim*, Sha'ar 50. *Tanya* Chap. 3. See also *Sefer HaBahir*, 119. היינו חכמה ה, ומאי ניהו מים של הקב"ה: *Zohar* 1, 32b). The nature of fire is to deconstruct and break materials apart into small particles. In Binah, a person deciphers and breaks down the thought into finer details through analysis, comparison, scrutiny, and development (*Sefer HaMa'amarim*, Kuntreisim, 1, p. 201). Water is pure and undifferentiated. A thought within the world of Chochmah is undifferentiated, fluid, and difficult to grasp, and it needs to be channeled in order to become contextualized and grasped (*Derech Chayim*, Sha'ar HaTeshuvah, p. 61. *Sefer HaMa'amarim, 5708*, p. 24).

Pre-linguistic thoughts are like images or symbols, such as a mental picture of the entirety of a solution. Let's say you are trying to figure out a difficult issue at hand, and you are concentrating your focus, locked on the issue, with no resolution. Suddenly, out of the blue, a lightning bolt of a solution flashes in front of you, and you experience an 'aha' moment. You 'see' the solution to your dilemma, and it is crystal clear to you, yet you cannot explain it. An explanation can only form later when this flash is drawn into a conventional framework and the realm of language.

The Rambam (Rebbe Moshe ben Maimon, 1335-1204), in his foreword to his monumental philosophical work, the *Moreh Nevuchim* / "Guide to the Perplexed" (see p. 7), writes that the mysteries and secrets of Creation are never fully revealed to man, although, at times there are flashes of truth which illuminate the darkness for short moments. What differentiates a prophet from a layman are these isolated moments of illumination. The prophet, while walking in darkness, experiences a sudden flash of light, a vision that radiates their path. Only to Moshe, the greatest of all prophets, were these flashes of illumination continuous. Chochmah is similar to this form of illumination. At times, we feel as though we have been walking in darkness, feeling things but not knowing what it is we feel or the way around them, and suddenly a flash of insight appears and everything becomes illuminated (Rebbe Avraham Abulafia writes that wisdom, for the most part, comes to a person as an illuminating light: *Ohr HaSechel*, Hakdamah, pp. 2-3).

CHOCHMAH AS SEEING THE FUTURE AND MEMORY OF THE PAST

"Who is *Chocham* / wise? He who perceives the future" (*Tamid*, 32a). In the modality of Binah, we comprehend and understand the details, the trees within the forest, as it were; in the world of Chochmah, we sense the entire forest with all its details as one unified whole, one image. To see individual trees, one needs to be there, presently, in the forest; Binah happens in the 'now'. To see an image of the entire forest, one needs to still be a distance from the forest, not having arrived there yet; Chochmah is a vision of the future. Perceiving the future means to project an unfolding of the present into its eventual development. Consequently, "a wise man is one who can observe within the beginning, the end" (Yerushalmi, *Sotah*, 8:10).

In a manner of speaking, a wise person's viewpoint and comprehension transcends the limitations of time, and for this reason, Chochmah is also associated with memories of the past (Alter Rebbe, *Likutei Torah*, Tetzaveh, 81c and Shir HaShirim, p. 33a. See also *Ma'amarei Admur HaZaken, 5564*, p. 142. The Mitteler Rebbe, *Toras Chayim*, Shemos, p. 33a).

All memory is stored in the brain in a nonverbal form as a totality of an idea or experience, in the mode of Chochmah. Only when the memory is triggered and it surfaces in the conscious mind does it acquire the context in which it can be formulated in language.

Binah is the world of sequential thinking; one event follows another, 1 plus 1 equals 2, and one idea is analyzed in comparison to another idea. We can delve deeper into a concept and break it down until it is fully understood. We can deduce deeper understandings from the teachings we have already learned ("*Tevunah* (Binah) is understanding a matter by one's own intelligence deducing it from the things one has already learned": Rashi, *Shemos*, 31:3). The root of the word *Binah* is *Bein* / in between (גם בינה מגזרת בין: Ibid, *Even Ezra*, although the Even Ezra uses this idea differently). Ideas as they exist within the consciousness of Binah are broken down into distinct bites of information and then individually deciphered by distinguishing them 'in between' one another, perhaps until they are reconciled (Rebbe Rashab, *Sefer HaMa'amarim, RaNaT* (5659), p. 57). As such, Binah breaks down creative ideas into finer and finer particles like fire, as opposed to Chochmah, which is the water-like, unified state of an idea.

MASCULINE AND FEMININE MODES OF KNOWING

In general, Chochmah is a masculine quality and Binah is a more feminine quality; the former is the 'giver' of the idea, and the latter is the one who develops the idea. Within the womb of Binah, the initial creative kernel of an idea incubates, matures, and then can be 'born' into language.

The microcosm mirrors the macrocosm; "As Above, so below." Indeed, the 'below' is a physical representation of the Above; all that exists on a physical plane parallels its spiritual counterpart, it is a manifestation of an 'image' in its Source. In this context, a male person is generally more inclined to think about his metaphysical Source and to deal in the power of Chochmah, disembodied, abstract issues and inventive ideas. A female person is, in general, more inclined toward Binah, thinking about practical, present, and immediate issues. In the language of Chazal, "An extra measure of Binah was given to women" (*Niddah*, 45b).

Women and men approach thoughts differently.* Faced with a problem that needs to be solved, a male will frequently seek to find solutions, while the female will frequently focus on further articulating the problem in finer detail. Women desire to speak about their problems, and only then perhaps find a solution. Often, though, the problem is reduced or mitigated just by speaking of it. The first instinct of a man is often to resolve a problem as fast as possible without speaking at length about it, if not to totally ignore the problem.

These root distinctions are manifest in the world of thought, and on the physical plane as well. Men, on average, are more imposing than women; on average 10% taller, 20% heavier, and 30% stronger (especially in their upper bodies) than women. Nevertheless, women are generally more resistant

---

* Note: This paragraph does not represent an original Chasidic text; rather, it is an implication derived from original sources.

to fatigue. In comparing men and women who were equally in shape, in short-distance running races, for example, men are generally faster than women, yet the longer the distance of the race, the smaller the gap is between men's and women's results. Endurance and persistence are thus more common traits in women than in men. This is similar to the fact that Chochmah is the sudden flash of creative insight that lacks permanence, and Binah contributes stability, practical focus, and endurance.

THE REGIONS WITHIN THE BRAIN

Chochmah, Binah, and Da'as are housed in different parts of the human brain. Within the brain, says the Zohar (*Zohar* 3, pp. 136a, 146a, 262a), there are three basic compartments that house the three modalities of intellect (הנה תלת חללין

דגלגלתא הן תלת מוחין חב״ה. ועל כל חלק מוח גשמי שורה אור השכל השייך למוח ההוא:

Alter Rebbe, *Torah Ohr*, Tetzaveh, p. 83d. See also Ramak, *Pardes Rimonim*, Sha'ar 31:8, regarding the shape of the body paralleling the inner and higher workings of Creation. See also Rebbe Shem Tov Ben Shem Tov, *Sefer HaEmunos*, Sha'ar 4:10. Rebbe Rashab, *Sefer HaMa'amarim, 5678*, p. 146. Rebbe Rayatz, *Sefer HaMa'amarim, 5710*, p. 257. *Sefer HaMa'amarim, 5704*, p. 163. *Sefer HaMa'amarim*, Kuntreisim 1, p. 401. *Sefer HaMa'amarim, 5700*, p. 164. Note also *Even Ezra*, Shemos, 31:3. Rebbe Gershon Ben Shlomo, *Sha'ar HaShamayim*, Ma'amar 9, p. 52).

Today, we know that there are multiple 'compartments' in the brain associated with various types of intelligence. Certain regions of the brain are connected with memory, and others are connected with language. There are parts of the brain connected with balance and coordination, and parts connected with vision and color perception. The division of the brain into three is a more general map of Chochmah, Binah, and Da'as.

Once, the findings of a scientific periodical that explored the various compartments of the brain were told over, with great excitement, to the Rebbe Rashab. The journal claimed to discover a new "vein" in the brain associated with memory and deep thinking. A short while later, the Rebbe walked over to his bookshelves, removed a handwritten text by the Mitteler Rebbe, opened it, and showed them that this very same "vein" was explained years earlier by the Mitteler Rebbe. The text noted that if a person desires to recall something, to bring something up to memory, he tilts his head backward, facing up, bringing this "vein" closer to the compartment of Chochmah (and Binah. See Note 7, *Likutei Sichos*, 2, p. 364). Conversely, when the need arises for contemplation, the head falls forward, facing down, bringing this vein closer to the compartment of Da'as (See, *Sefer HaSichos*, 5704, p. 68. *Reshimos*, 69, p. 8. This idea has also been explored in many earlier sources, such as Rebbe Meir Ibn Aldavi (a grandson of the Rosh), *Shivilei Emunah*, Nasiv 4, p. 151. Rebbe Meir Paprush, *Torah Ohr*, Bo, p. 86. *Segulos Yisrael*, Ma'areches Zayin, 28).

A Medieval text called *Shushan Sodos*, attributed to a student of the Ramban, speaks of using the physical movement of the head to create a shift in consciousness. He writes that if one wants to elevate his Binah, his lower level of consciousness, and connect it with his Chochmah and Keser, his higher levels of consciousness, "he should lift his head and tilt it a little backward" (*Shushan Sodos*, Os 76). The physical movement of the head, upwards and backward, can thus propel an inward shift from a lower to a higher state of consciousness (note, *Tzava'as HaRivash*, 80). Indeed, tilting the head backward slightly connects a person to memory. Memory, as explained, is connected to Chochmah.

THE RIGHT & LEFT HEMISPHERES OF THE BRAIN

In a very general way, the brain is divided into left and right hemispheres. The left side of the brain controls the functions and movements of the right side of the body, and the right side of the brain controls the left side of the body. In addition to controlling the body, these hemispheres also differ in their intellectual functions.

Visual constructs seem to be more connected with the right part of the brain, while language is more connected with the left. People with a severed left hemisphere, whether through a stroke or an accident, G-d forbid, suffer disabilities on the right side of their body. Additionally, they may lose their ability to communicate verbally, as the left hemisphere of the brain appears to control speech. Furthermore, the left hemisphere seems to specialize in fine analysis and processing data in a sequential, linear fashion.

By contrast, the right hemisphere, in addition to controlling the left side of the body, is understood as the more creative aspect of the brain. It helps us grasp holistic and abstract notions, see comprehensive patterns, and transform these 'pictures' into ideas. The right hemisphere controls the capacity to process spatial and visual concepts, as well as grasp shapes and pictures. People without a functioning right hemisphere tend not to comprehend well-known sayings, such as 'You are what you eat.' A phrase of this kind sounds meaningless if assimilated one word at a time and is only comprehensible as a full statement or 'image'.

People who have dysfunction in the right part of the brain tend to lack the ability to view ideas as a whole. Those who suffer from a stroke in the right hemisphere of the brain tend not to recognize objects or people 'at a glance'; they will look at someone and not know who that person is. Only if there is a marked distinction, such as a distinct nose or crooked teeth, can they recognize the person. This is because a right brain impaired person recognizes other people by focusing on specifics; they will observe individual parts or features, and from there, deduce who that person is 'as a whole'.

Chochmah is associated with the nonverbal right hemisphere of the brain, as Chochmah-type processing is above
and beyond any contextualization and verbalization. Binah-
type processing is associated with speech, the capacity of
the left part of the brain.* Yet, functioning at an optimum
level, both creatively and analytically, requires coordination of both hemispheres and healthy neurological linkage
between the two regions. Being creative and being able to
bring creativity to fruition is largely contingent on an individual's ability to operate with both hemispheres of the
brain in concert with one another. Talented musicians, for
example, whose creativity is translated into instrumenta-
tion, composition, and improvisation, possess larger masses
of nerve fibers connecting the hemispheres.

As explored, Chochmah is masculine, and Binah is feminine. Being more connected with Binah, women are naturally more skilled in verbal expression and master the skill
of language more easily than men. Women enjoy speaking
more and are better communicators than men (*Berachos*, 48b.

---

* Although when the Zohar speaks of the תלת חללין דגלגלתא, it is unclear
what part of the brain the Zohar is describing. Yet, the Alter Rebbe
(quoted above) teaches, והמצח הוא כנגד מוח הדעת כי מוח הדעת הוא באמצע
שמוח חכמה ומוח בינה הם מלפנים ומוח הדעת באחוריים באמצע ב' המוחין חו"ב. ולכן הוא
נגד המצח / "And the forehead is against the brain of Da'as; for Da'as is in
the middle, whereas the brain of Chochmah and the brain of Binah are
in front and the brain of Da'as is in the back, in the middle of the two,
Chochmah and Binah. Therefore, Da'as corresponds to the forehead."
In other words, the lobe of Da'as sits between the right and left hemispheres, seemingly as the frontal lobes behind the forehead. Further on,
the connection between the frontal lobes and Da'as will be explored.

"Ten measurements of speech given to mankind, nine were taken by women, and one was left for men": *Kiddushin*, 49b).

When a difficult situation arises in life, a male desires to be left alone in his own space, aloof like Chochmah, either trying to figure out a solution or ignoring the situation. A female often wishes to chat about the situation with others and feel the comfort of this shared Binah. In these, there are obviously no absolutes, and some males have strong feminine Binah and enjoy more verbally communicating than other men ('Women are more connected to Binah than men': Mitteler Rebbe, *Derech Chayim*, Sha'ar HaTefillah, p. 121. Binah is rooted in Keser, the ultimate 'womb', Circular Light, that contains all of life, and Keser is the meta-source of language: Rebbe Rashab, *Sefer HaMa'amarim*, RaNaT, pp. 3-9).

CHOCHMAH & BINAH GIVE BIRTH TO EMOTIONS

Another way of thinking about Chochmah and Binah is 'father' and 'mother' since together, and when in harmonious unison, they give birth to healthy emotions (Chochmah and Binah are *Abba* / Father and *Ima* / Mother: *Zohar* 3, p. 290a. Ramak, *Pardes Rimonim*, Sha'ar 8:17 and Sha'ar 9:5. והן הם אב ואם המולידות אהבת ה' ויראתו ופחדו / "These [*Chochmah* and *Binah*] are the very 'father' and 'mother' which give birth to the love of Hashem, and the awe and trepidation of Him": *Tanya*, Chap. 3).

Every person has both masculine and feminine qualities, and the harmony between them can produce healthy 'offspring'. We need to engage and harmonize the 'seed' of the masculine mode of knowing and the 'womb' of the feminine mode of knowing in order to attain our potential in serving our true self, others, and *HaKadosh Baruch Hu* / the Holy One (on a deeper level, these three services are one and the same).

Hisbonenus requires using our Chochmah and Binah to contemplate and meditate on the omnipresence of the Creator. Through this process, our emotions of love and awe of HaKadosh Baruch Hu will be born. From another perspective, the 'natural' love deep within our soul will be 'revealed'.

There is a Mitzvah to love and fear Hashem (higher fear is actually 'awe'). "What is the path [to arouse] love and fear of Him? When a person contemplates His wondrous and great deeds and creations and appreciates His infinite wisdom that surpasses all comparison, he will immediately love, praise, and glorify (Hashem), yearning with tremendous desire to know Hashem's great name" (Rambam, *Hilchos Yesodei HaTorah*, 2:2: והיאך היא הדרך לאהבתו ויראתו. בשעה שיתבונן האדם במעשיו וברואיו הנפלאים הגדולים ויראה מהן חכמתו שאין לה ערך ולא קץ מיד הוא אוהב ומשבח ומפאר ומתאוה תאוה גדולה לידע השם הגדול. Note that according to the Rambam, it seems that 'love' is expressed as a desire to 'know', not as a standing emotion on its own).

In fact, in order for there to be a comprehensive under-standing of any thought, harmony between Chochmah and Binah is crucial. When there is deeper unity between these capacities, the thoughts that are produced are healthier, and in turn, the emotions that come forth are also more positive and long-lasting. If we want to have enduring positive emotions and thoughts that are creative, articulate, and ground-ed, we first need to ascertain that Chochmah and Binah are united in producing these emotions, and that these 'parents' have a healthy relationship.

Another metaphor for Chochmah and Binah is 'inseparable friends' (*Zohar* 1, p. 123a). Deep friendships and intimate rela-tionships are forged when each partner can find within him or herself aspects of the other. This allows intimacy because they share a part of themselves with the other, and they hold an inseparable part of the other within themselves. In the friendship and union between Chochmah and Binah, they הבן בחכמה וחכם בבינה / "understand (Binah) within Choch-mah, and perceive wisdom (Chochmah) within Binah" (*Sefer Yetzirah*, 1:4). They reveal that traces of Chochmah are within the womb of Binah and traces of Binah are within the creative element of Chochmah.

An interinclusion of Chochmah within Binah protects one's thoughts from straying. Otherwise, when rationaliz-ing with Binah, we may become carried away by the details and lose focus of the thought as a whole. By having the holistic view of Chochmah in mind, the thoughts that are articulated in Binah will remain loyal to the original inspiration. Additionally, a measure of Binah nested within Chochmah allows for the fleeting intuitions of Chochmah to become grounded and settled in the mind (Rebbe Rashab, *Sefer HaMa'amarim, ATeReS* (5679), p. 226. Rebbe Rayatz, *Sefer Ha-Ma'amarim, 5702*, p. 16).

DIRECT LIGHT VS. REFRACTED LIGHT

Up until this point, only the ordinary mode of creative thought processes has been discussed. This mode of thinking is called *Ohr Yashar* / direct light. The thought begins as a flash of intuitive insight, a total 'vision', and then it descends into the world of Binah and begins percolating, slowly evolving into a fully comprehensive thought, one that can be properly articulated and linguistically expressed. The term Ohr Yashar suggests a straight and smooth course and line of development. An epiphany arises, an inner light is turned on, and the entire issue at hand becomes illuminated. An example of this would be to walk into a dark room and immediately, before groping to find the way around, turn on the lights and allow them to illuminate the darkness. This is a 'top-down' process.

There is also a thought process called *Ohr Chozer* / reflected, refracted, or 'returning' light. In this pathway, Binah precedes Chochmah. The holistic creative spark is ignited through a process of dissecting and analyzing details. For example, one begins with an intellectual dilemma, examining and probing into it. As the mind becomes engrossed in the subject, it becomes highly focused until new insights and sparks of creativity are revealed. *Chazal* / our sages describe Binah as a deduction process: "A person understands one thing *from* another" (*Chagigah*, 14a. Rashi, *Shemos*, 31:3). The mind may even be engaged in reverie, dreamily deducing one idea from the next, when suddenly the power of innovation and intuition is activated, and greater, penetrating insights gush forth. These innovative and creative thoughts are called 'reflected lights' because when flashes of insight arise through probing into detailed understandings, it is a 'bottom-up' movement from Binah below to Chochmah above. It is as if we are digging in the earth, and suddenly, a spring comes bursting up toward the sky.

In the mode of Ohr Chozer, Binah entails more than just deductively extracting a specific thought form from the original generic thought of Chochmah. Here, Binah exercises a hidden ability to elicit an insight from Chochmah that is greater than Chochmah's 'top-down' illumination. Through meditating in Hisbonenus (Binah), a higher level of creativity and profundity of thought is attained, beyond what Chochmah could have offered on its own (Rebbe Rayatz, *Sefer HaMa'amarim, 5701,* pp. 52-53. See also Rashab, *Sefer HaMa'amarim, RaNaT* (5659), p. 3 and onward. The Rebbe, *Sefer Ha-Ma'amarim Melukat,* Shavuos 5728, Os 8).

The sensation we have when operating in the Ohr Chozer mode is similar to that of a stranger entering a dark and unfamiliar room. Entering the room, he begins to stumble around, bumping into the furniture, and learning through trial and error where each object in the room is located. Gradually, he discovers the layout of the room, the 'bigger picture'. When he finds the light switch and turns it on, everything that he came to know in the darkness is at once illuminated. Ohr Chozer usually occurs only when there is a dilemma that needs to be made clear. As there is no re-solve on the horizon, it feels as though one is stumbling in darkness and confusion. With arduous labor, an elusive an-swer begins to form, and then, finally, an intellectual break-through occurs, and all becomes illuminated. This dynamic is the inner meaning of העם ההלכים בחשך ראו אור גדול / "A people who walked in darkness saw a great light" (*Yeshayah*, 9:1. *Tanchuma*, Noach, 3).

THE WORLD OF DA'AS

Chochmah and Binah are the first two capacities that make up the acronym *ChaBaD*. The third letter of the word *ChaBaD* stands for *Da'as*. But what is Da'as, and what is its place in this process of contemplation?

Traditionally, Da'as is translated as 'knowledge'. But what exactly is knowledge? Knowledge is commonly perceived to be a function of the intellect, associated with an activity of mind, but in fact, Da'as is more an act of identification with the wisdom and understanding, the Chochmah and the Binah. *LaDa'as* / 'to know' means to be completely intimate with and identify with the information and wisdom birthed through Chochmah and Binah.

Da'as is the attachment of the mind — and thus, by extension, the full self — to the idea it is contemplating. A thought becomes fully absorbed in the world of Da'as. Hence, דדא ביה כולא ביה, דלא דא ביה מה ביה / "If one has this type of intelligence (Da'as), in him, he has everything, and one who does not have this type of intelligence in him, what is then within him?" (*Nedarim*, 41a. *Tanchuma*, Vayikra). Indeed, there is no thorough and complete understanding of an idea until the thought is brought down into Da'as. For this reason, the Mishnah says, אם אין בינה, אין דעת. אם אין דעת, אין בינה / "If there is no *Binah* / understanding, there is no Da'as, and (conversely,) if there is no Da'as there is really no Binah" (*Avos*, 3:17). Without Da'as, ideas of the mind are transient and purely abstract. In Da'as, an idea is internalized, and one becomes completely identified with it.

Sometimes, the Torah uses the word *Da'as* as a euphemism for physical intimacy, as in "And Adam *Yada Es* / 'knew' Chavah / Eve, and she conceived" (*Bereishis*, 4:1). Da'as is a type of intimate attachment, connection and union with the information delivered by Chochmah and Binah. With Da'as, we can internalize a concept and become intimately joined to it (*Tikkunei Zohar,* Tikkun 69. Ramak, *Pardes Rimonim,* Sha'ar 23:4. *Eitz Chayim,* Sha'ar HaKelipos, 2. *Tanya,* Chap. 3. *Tanya, Iggeres HaKodesh,* 15. The Chayit on the *Ma'areches Elokus,* 4. p. 63a. *Agra DePirka,* 132, p. 15a).

Deep connection with a subject matter occurs on the level of Da'as, as the Alter Rebbe (*Tanya,* Chap. 42) expresses, regarding the experience of Da'as in contemplating the vastness of the Creator: "The essence of Da'as, however, is not the 'knowing' alone (in this context) that we should know of the greatness of Hashem from inspired authors or books, rather, it is to immerse one's mind deeply in the greatness of Hashem, and to affix one's thought on Hashem with all the strength and vigor of the heart and mind, until one's thought shall be bound to Hashem with a strong and powerful bond, as it would be bound to a physical object or subject that he sees with his physical eyes and on which he concentrates his thought. For it is known that *Da'as* means 'union', as in the verse, "And Adam knew Chavah" (אך עיקר

הדעת, אינה הידיעה לבדה, שידעו גדולת ה' מפי סופרים ומפי ספרים, אלא העיקר הוא, להעמיק דעתו בגדולת ה', ולתקוע מחשבתו בה' בחוזק ואומץ הלב והמוח, עד שתהא מחשבתו מקושרת בה' בקשר אמיץ וחזק, כמו שהיא מקושרת בדבר גשמי שרואה בעיני בשר ומעמיק בו מחשבתו, כנודע, שדעת הוא לשון התקשרות, כמו: "והאדם ידע וגו'").

On the level of Da'as, the provisional boundary that separates the 'knower' from the 'known' is somewhat removed, as we become one, as much as humanly possible, with our knowledge.

In the Garden of Eden, in the state where Adam and Chavah, and essentially all of humanity in their primordial condition, ate from *Eitz HaDa'as Tov v'Ra* / the Tree of Knowing (the duality) of Good and Evil, there was an identification with, and attachment to, evil. Prior to eating from The Tree of Knowledge, Adam and Chavah intellectually understood that good and evil exist, yet their understanding remained abstract and naive. Good and evil were like drawings on a blackboard; they recognized objectively that one was the correct way of being, and the other was incorrect, and they had a choice between them. By eating from the tree, they internalized it and became intimately identified with it. From that moment, the evil of the Tree of Knowing Good and Evil ceased existing as an external, objective entity, and it became an internal subjective interpretation. From then on, mankind knew and *identified* with both good and evil — the 'good' resides within us, and so does the potential to do 'evil'. Evil is no longer an *objective* fact but rather a subjective idea dependent on personal bias. This is what became part of our constitution (Alter Rebbe, *Torah Ohr*, Bereishis, 5c-5d. *Nefesh HaChayim*, Sha'ar 1:6:7. Before eating from the Tree of Knowledge, Adam and Chavah 'understood *Emes* / truth and *Sheker* / falsehood'. Following their eating, they 'knew *Tov* / good and *Ra* / evil'. Truth and falsehood are objective, while good and evil are subjective: Rambam, *Moreh Nevuchim*, 1:2).

THE RIGHT AND LEFT HEMISPHERES & THE FRONTAL LOBES

As the right and left hemispheres are connected with Chochmah, and Binah, Da'as too occupies a particular region in the brain. Some sources associate Da'as with the back of the brain, while many other sources specifically associate Da'as with the front part of the brain 'against' the *Metzach* / forehead (In the back, in the middle, and behind the forehead: *Torah Ohr*, Tetzaveh, p. 83d. *Toras Chayim*, Tetzaveh, p. 358b. p. 377c. Rebbe Rashab, *Sefer HaMa'amarim, 5678*, p. 146).

There is a large area toward the front of the brain on the right and left sides, which is called the frontal lobes. The frontal lobes serve to identify an objective, project a goal, and help forge plans to reach that goal. These have also been called the 'executive brain', the brain that controls our judgment, and social and ethical behavior. Technically called the 'prefrontal cortex', this region is located just behind the forehead, and in terms of neurology, it is the region that most clearly distinguishes the human brain from that of animals. The prefrontal cortex is said to intelligently regulate thoughts, actions, and emotions through its abundant connections with other regions in the brain. It helps regulate high-level functioning such as modulation of fear, planning, critical thinking, understanding the consequences of behavior, inhibition of impulsive behaviors, morality, empathy, and emotional balance. In other words, this part of the brain is the storehouse of our Da'as (Interestingly, in the back of the brain is the cerebellum, which assists and coordinates movement and helps with physical balance. Balance is a function of Da'as, perhaps connected to emotional and physical balance).

DA'AS IS AWARENESS & FREEDOM

Da'as, 'awareness', is the prism through which a person sees and apprehends the world around him; it is the means whereby information can guide choices and transformative actions. In this way, 'awareness is everything.' A person who has highly developed Chochmah and Binah but lacks Da'as has nothing, for he has no interface with the world. Wholesome self-awareness, and awareness of our surroundings, are crucial for a meaningful life.

A person who lives with unclouded Da'as lives freely, openly, and expansively. Conversely, without clear Da'as of oneself, others, and the world, an individual lives in an internal exile, a world filled with strife, anxiety, estrangement, and misalignment.

Our collective exile in Egypt was ultimately an exile of Da'as, and Moshe was the embodiment of Da'as, and hence the instrument of redemption. "The גלות מצרים / Egyptian Exile happened because the enslaved were lacking Da'as.

They lacked correct Da'as: the knowing and awareness that there is One Creator, who creates and recreates Creation anew, every moment. When Moshe, who embodied the quality of Da'as, came along, and when the miracles happened, it became revealed in the world that there is One Creator who creates the world anew every moment" (*Toldos Ya'akov Yoseph*, Vayishlach).

When Klal Yisrael was enslaved in Egypt, they lacked the tangible awareness of the Creator of all Life, who continually manifests existence from infinite no-thing-ness. If they would have never lost their Da'as and connection with that ultimate truth, they never would have become stuck, for they would have known that freedom and re-creation were a constant potential. When we have Da'as, we know that every moment is a new moment, and past conditioning, therefore, need not enslave us in the present. With complete Da'as, we actually have the choice of whether or not we will be enslaved to a person, nation, situation, substance, or thing.

On the deepest level, awareness itself is freedom. Da'as, as the Baal Shem Tov teaches, is "the secret of *Olam HaBa* / the World to Come, and the Resurrection, and Moshiach" (וזהו ענין תחית המתים ומשיח שהוא סוד הדעת והוא סוד עולם הבא: *Toldos Ya'akov Yoseph*, Lech Lecha. Da'as is *Ruach HaKodesh* / holy and clear vision... ואמלא אתו רוח אלקים בחכמה ובתבונה ובדעת / "And I will fill him with the Spirit of Hashem, with Chochmah, Tevunah and Da'as": *Shemos*, 31:3. Says Rashi, ובדעת, רוח הקדש / 'with Da'as': this is Ruach HaKodesh).

A person who lives with Da'as — both aware of their es-

sence and aware of the 'film' of their life story as it is projected onto the 'screen' of their consciousness — remains
forever free. This is because they have the ability, at any time,
to turn off the film, to choose another film, or to choose another way to see that same film, as it were. A person who
lives with this level of awareness tends not to get stuck in
negative patterns and reactive attachments, and even when
they do, they can just as easily extricate and detach themselves. Living with Da'as is thus the key to living a redemptive, open, fluid, life-affirming existence. Essentially, awareness is redemption. Through Hisbonenus, we develop the
redemptive power of Da'as.

FROM DA'AS TO EMOTIONS & AC-
TIONS

As we practice Hisbonenus, we first conceive and perceive
an idea within our faculty of Chochmah. Then, we analyze
it, develop it, and expand upon it with our Binah. Finally,
we absorb and internalize it with our power of Da'as. Once
a thought has been internalized and etched in our mind,
our Da'as transforms the information into an expression of
our heart. Da'as is the space where abstract ideas begin to
be 'felt'. Da'as is *Hargasha* / sensing. It is a type of knowing
that is *Murgash* / sensed and tangible (Rebbe Rashab, *Kuntres
HaTefillah*, Chap. 5. In the words of the Tanya, וכנודע, שדעת הוא לשון
הרגשה בנפש: *Tanya*, 46. See also, *Likutei Sichos* 9, V'Zos HaBerachah 1,

note 45. Note, *Nachlas Dovid*, Derashos, 3. Da'as is הכרה והרגשה. *Likutei Torah*, Va'eschanan, 4a).

Da'as is the bridge that moves cold, detached, abstract thoughts into our emotional center. When it carries a concept of the mind into the heart, then the concept can be embodied and transform our outer behavior.

In addition to its association with the frontal lobes of the brain (and/or the back of the brain), Da'as is also connected with the spinal cord (*Pardes Rimonim*, Sha'ar 31, 8. Note Sha'ar 23, 8). Our spinal cord serves as a conduit for messages of the brain to reach the entire body and, in reverse, messages from the body to reach the brain. Composed of nerve bundles and cells, it sends motor commands from the brain to the entire body and also sends sensory information gathered by the body to the brain. In other words, it is a connector, much like Da'as that connects the mind with the heart and thus with the entire functionality of self.

The Zohar calls Da'as 'the key to all emotions' (מפתחא דכליל שית: *Zohar* 2, p. 177a. Tzemach Tzedek, *Derech Mitzvosecha*, HaAmonas Elokus, 2). Da'as ensures that comprehension does not remain in the domain of the theoretical but rather affects our emotions and, as a consequence, our practical behavior. Da'as "fills the halls and passageways," as it were (*Zohar* 3, Idra, 295b).

The seeming divide between the heart and the mind is magnified in an individual who lacks Da'as. An example of a person lacking Da'as is a thief who, while stealing, cries out to Hashem for assistance in the theft (*Ein Ya'akov*, Berachos, 63a). He understands intellectually that there is a Creator who is watching over him and worthy of being prayed to. He even understands that the Creator has forbidden theft, yet all of this understanding lacks internalization and the personal practical significance afforded by Da'as. He behaves immorally, though he knows it is wrong, and he pleads with Hashem for help in doing what Hashem 'pleads' with him not to do. There is no connection between what he knows in his mind, how he feels in his heart, and what he does with his limbs. Da'as is thus the completion of the entire cycle of manifestation, from the initial inspiration to the detailed thought process to the felt emotion and the final physical action which was originally conceived in Chochmah.

Da'as is a מחבר / *Mechaber* / connector; in the words of the Alter Rebbe, שדעת הוא לשון התקשרות / "*Da'as* means connection" (*Tanya*, Chap. 3: כי דעת, פירושו התחברות, כידוע: *Nefesh HaChayim*, 1:6). Da'as connects the mind with the heart, and the heart and body with the mind.

A young child could score high in an IQ exam and be a prodigy with the mental capacity to understand concepts that adults have trouble comprehending. Yet, children are not deemed responsible, according to *Halachah* / Torah law, for their own actions or inactions. This is because they lack Da'as; their brain does not yet have the full ability to connect what they intellectually know to their actual behavior. Reward and punishment are only applicable with a certain level of mental and emotional maturity. This level is only attained when the child develops full Da'as, which doesn't generally happen before the age of twelve for girls and thirteen for boys.

Maturity means integration, the ability to correlate reality to experience, action to thought. Da'as is when our knowledge and understanding becomes personal, relevant and transformational, as opposed to abstract, theoretical and inconsequential (Rayatz, *Sefer HaMa'amarim*, 5706, p. 77-78).

Da'as is therefore also a מבדיל / *Mavdil* / separator (אם אין דעה הבדלה מניין / Without Da'as there is no possibility of separation": Yerushalmi, *Berachos*, 5:2. *Tikunei Zohar,* Tikkun 13). Once we have reached an age of maturity, of mental and emotional integration, and we connect with what we know, then we become responsible beings and can make real choices. Da'as allows us the 'separation' to step back and make decisions based on real data. Da'as gives us the ability to truly decipher, distinguish and and hence properly decide (Rebbe Rashab, *Sefer HaMa'amarim, ETeR* (5670), p. 113. *Sefer HaMa'amarim, 5678*, p. 147. See also *Pri HaAretz*, Vayigash).

Da'as give us the ability to make moral, ethical and spiritual *distinctions*, and then it empowers us to choose and act accordingly. Da'as is also connected specifically with speech since speech implies choice — through language we define our reality and proclaim decisions and intentions (*Dibbur /* speech is connected with *De'ah /* awareness: Rashi, *Bereishis*, 2:7).

TWO LEVELS OF DA'AS

There are two levels within Da'as itself: *Da'as Elyon /* higher Da'as and *Da'as Tachton /* lower Da'as. Da'as Tachton acts as a bridge and interface between abstract, aloof, 'cold' intellect and 'hot', embodied emotions. Da'as Elyon also connects, but not between the brain and the heart, rather most notably between the Chochmah and Binah (*Pardes Rimonim*, Sha'ar 3:8, Sha'ar 8:17, Sha'ar 9:6. *Tanya*, Igeres HaKodesh, 15. *Torah Ohr*, Mishpatim, 75a. *Likutei Torah*, 3:88c). In this way, higher Da'as facilitates unification between the masculine and feminine qualities of the mind by alleviating their intrinsic differences and distinctions. It acts as a conduit, causing the 'seminal' infusion of Chochmah to impregnate the womb of Binah.

In an overall map of Divine attributes, the level of *Keser /* Crown, a level of consciousness which is above the 'head' of the Divine intellect, is interchangeable with the *Sefirah /* attribute of Da'as (There are ten Sefiros, although if you count both Da'as and Keser there are eleven. This is because when Keser is counted among the ten, Da'as is not counted, and when Da'as is counted, Keser is not counted: *Pri Eitz Chayim*, Sha'ar 42, Sha'ar Derushei A'b'y'a, 1. *Sha'ar Mochin DeTzelem*, 5. *Eitz Chayim*, Sh'ar 23:8. Alter Rebbe, *Likutei Torah*, Emor, p. 39b. Rebbe Rashab, *Sefer HaMa'amarim*, *5665*, p. 408. *Sefer HaMa'amarim*, *5708*, p. 242, and in the notes of the

Rebbe therein. See also Rebbe Yoseph Gikatalia, *Sha'arei Orah*, Sha'ar 5. *Pardes Rimonim*, Sha'ar 3:8. *Shomer Emunim* (Kadmon), part 1:67. This is because when the Sefiros are counted on the level of externality (with vessels), then Keser is counted among them, but not Da'as. And when the Sefiros are counted on their internal level (the *Ohr* / light) then Da'as is counted among the 10 and not Keser. The Rebbe Rashab writes that Da'as is not counted, since Da'as is Ohr without a *Kli* / vessel: *Sefer HaMa'amarim, 5668,* p. 68. The 'external' part of Keser is counted among the 10 Sefiros, not the 'internal' and higher parts: see the Rebbe, Ma'amar on Mishpatim, 5723).

Higher Da'as is a level that transcends intellect, like a crown that sits above the head. In this way, Da'as and Keser are interchangeable, as they represent alternative expressions of the same force that enables a person to endure and sustain diametrically opposed states concurrently. Keser is the meta-level that allows the person to house the fundamental paradoxes of life, as it encompasses and connects the various opposing dimensions of reality. Da'as bridges and connects the various opposing forces of the intellect, and those of the intellect and heart.

'CONTEXT' OR 'CONTENT' CHOICES

Da'as reveals the bigger picture in a way that allows us to differentiate and make choices. Lower level Da'as does this in the world of 'content', whereas higher Da'as does this in the world of 'context'. Higher Da'as is, in its nature, creative and contextual. Choices based on a wider context make it possible to form decisions of content.

An example of a 'context choice' is what type of life path a person wants to invest in and follow; is he a future Torah scholar, or is he a future doctor? There is an encompassing quality to such higher Da'as choices, and there is a spiritual impetus within their soul that pushes them to make such a choice. Lower Da'as is rooted in higher Da'as, yet it chooses options for the *implementation* of the context choices. For example, if through higher Da'as someone has chosen to be a doctor, their lower Da'as may facilitate choosing the universities that they will apply to. This kind of choice is made at the level of 'content', or options which are aligned with the broad 'context' established by higher Da'as.

Since, on the level of higher Da'as, there is a spiritual calling or soul-stirring that drives our choices, these choices may seem irrational. When challenged about a higher Da'as choice, a person may simply state, "I just 'know' that this is the path I will follow; there's no question in my mind." Often, what we cannot fathom with logic, we can feel with higher Da'as. Yet, although outwardly, these choices may appear to be irrational, there is a vast difference between stubborn irrationality and functioning from a pure state of higher Da'as.

Stubborn unwillingness to listen to other people's feedback

is a sign of rigidity and an indication of fear, internal weakness and ego fragility (*Sefer HaMa'amarim, 5688,* p. 85). Clearly, a person with a healthy sense of self can be effortlessly open to other people's perspectives and suggestions. Yet, Da'as is of a higher order, beyond ego. A person who makes creative choices from higher Da'as senses a higher guiding force and a vision that is beyond intellect (*Sefer HaMa'amarim, ETeR* (5670), pp. 133-134). Often it is only much later, if at all, that we understand the 'reason' for our choices (*Sefer HaMa'amarim, 5700,* p. 156).

Having secured a working definition of these capacities of the mind, we can now proceed to understand the amazing benefits that can manifest once these capacities are harnessed and utilized in Hisbonenus.

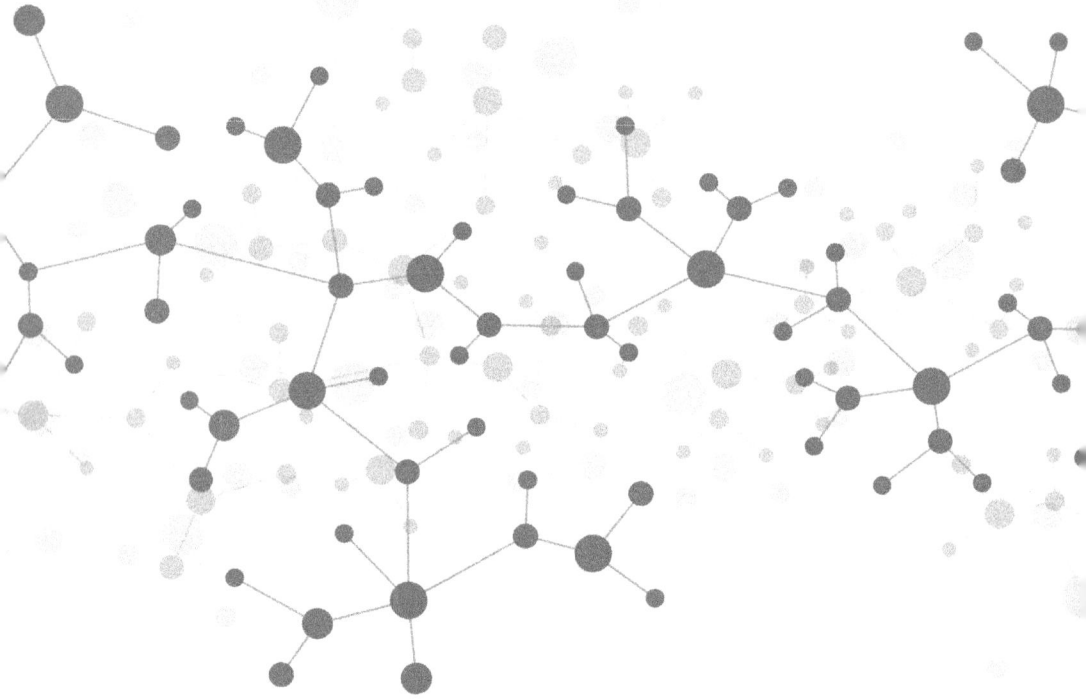

CHAPTER 7

FROM ILLUMINATED THOUGHTS TO INFLAMED EMOTIONS

TO REVIEW, THE PRACTICE OF HISBONENUS BEGINS BY CHOOSING, PROACTIVELY, A THOUGHT OR IDEA. The idea or thought we choose to meditate on and contemplate must be one that we have a deep *Cheishek* / desire for, pleasure in, or connection to. Typically, a Chasidic thought or *Ma'amar* / discourse is chosen to ponder. One begins by simply reading and studying the words, yet while contemplating the idea with Cheishek, one activates his creative capacity of Chochmah. This experience draws him in to delve deeper and develop the idea with his Binah, analyzing, deciphering, drawing parallels, in a way that deepens and broadens the idea. Then, the idea settles into the world of Da'as, intimate 'knowing' and identification. There, the knowledge is 'felt', and so it can descend further into the heart and emotions, where it leads to behavioral changes and personal transformation.

Essentially, the movement of contemplation flows from intellectual abstraction to passion and love. The Hisbonenus of the mind arouses the emotions of the heart and guides all of the emotions of the heart towards the Source of all Life. We begin by merely thinking 'about' HaKadosh Baruch Hu, yet we end up suffused by visceral, tangible feelings of love and awe for HaKadosh Baruch Hu, giving rise to a virtually unshakable sense of connection to Him.

At a Chasidic gathering over one hundred years ago, a *Chasid* / disciple quoted before the Rebbe Rashab an idea from the Alter Rebbe: 'Everyone has a natural love and awe of Hashem.' "True," the Rebbe Rashab retorted, "but not Chasidim. For Chasidim to have true love and awe of Hashem, they need understanding and Hisbonenus" (*Toras Shalom*, p. 233).

In other words, someone who wishes to have true and lasting love and awe, which come only through *Avodah* / toil and spiritual work, needs to practice Hisbonenus.

INTELLECT RESIDES IN SOLITUDE; EMOTIONS EXIST WITHIN A CONTEXT OF OTHERS

There are two opposite ways to live in the world: through the perspective of the mind and through the perspective of the heart. We can approach life through the mind, intellectually and conceptually, always analyzing and trying to understand, or we can approach it through the heart, emotionally and passionately, always trying to gauge experience by how we are feeling.

Living in a 'mental reality', we may over-rationalize experiences, but we can also make conscious choices in response to them. Living in a 'heart reality', we may respond more reactively and viscerally, but we can also be more empathetic and compassionate, and moved by beauty.

Intellect has the ability to gather and process external information and stimuli for the purpose of drawing conclusions and creating choices. Emotions react to external stimuli and these reactions are themselves external. Intellect gathers data from the outside, brings it inward, and then chooses to emote outwardly or not; this is, in general, an outside-in movement. While emotions may be very deeply and inwardly felt, they are triggered by outside events and objects, and their outward responses can be immediate; this is, in general, an inside-out movement.

Another way of defining this distinction is that intellect, the ability to think, functions in solitude. Even if there are no other people around, so long as there is some information to process, intelligence can be expressed. Emotions generally arise in the presence of others; they are nourished in relationships with others and are expressed towards others.

As emotions function in the world of 'others', a person who has a certain emotion percolating within his or her heart desires to have another person be a recipient of it. If, for some reason, a person does not find another human being to whom they can offer their love, they might seek out other recipients such as pets or an online 'community'; however, ultimately, human love wants in-person interaction with another human being.

As a whole, when someone has emotions bottled up inside, they have a tremendous urge to find an outlet. The Torah describes Avraham as a loving person, a man who embodied the Divine attribute of *Chesed* / loving-kindness (*Sefer HaBahir,* 101: מדת החסד כל ימי היות אברהם בעולם לא הוצרכתי אני לעשות מלאכתי שהרי אברהם עמד שם במקומי / "The attribute of Chesed (said), 'All the days that Avraham was alive in the physical world, I did not need do my task, as Avraham was standing in my stead.'" Ramak, *Pardes Rimonim*, Sha'ar 22:4). Avraham would invite all the passersby and travelers to enter his tent to have something to eat and be refreshed. And so, after going through a difficult circumcision at the age of ninety nine, the Torah tells us that Hashem created a heat wave so that Avraham could rest and not need to host anyone. Nevertheless, he was sitting at the opening of his tent, tending to his wound in the sweltering heat of the desert sun, waiting anxiously to invite passersby. He only longed to be able to share hospitality and kindness (*Bereishis*, 18:1, Rashi). The attribute of Chesed within Avraham demanded an outlet, a recipient, so even though he was physically in agony, his urge to give was stronger.

The realm of intellect exists outside that of interpersonal relationships. Love or awe, emotional attraction and repulsion, only exist in dialogue with others. If no one else existed, feelings of love and the need to hold another person would not exist (Rebbe Rashab, *Sefer HaMa'amarim, 5669*, p. 169).

COLD INTELLECT, INFLAMED EMOTIONS

Intellect is solitary and hence it can be cold, calculated, and detached. Emotions are participatory, and hence they are warm, involved and passionate. Intellect is likened to water and emotions to fire. Water is naturally cold, and fire is hot (Rambam, *Hilchos Yesodei HaTorah*, 4:2. *Shevilei Emunah*, Nesiv 2, p. 62). Cerebral people and intellectuals are commonly calm, cool and collected, whether by nature or by cultivated habit. Emotional people, on the other hand, brim with energy and vitality (Rebbe Rayatz, *Sefer HaMa'amarim, 5701*, pp. 126-127. Thus the Mishnah says, אבל זקני תורה אינן כן, אלא כל זמן שמזקינין, דעתן מתישבת עליהן / "But when it comes to aged scholars, it is not so. On the contrary, the older they get, the more their mind becomes settled": *Kinim*, 3:6. The reason being, as they become older and their physical energy and vitality lessens, their intellect becomes more settled. As the Rambam, in his Pirush to this Mishnah writes, תלמידי חכמים שבשעת שהם מזקינין ונחלשין ויפסיד גופם תרבה חכמתם ויתחזק שכלם / "Torah scholars as they age and their physical strength is weakened, their wisdom increases and their minds are strengthened." See also *Bartenura* and *Tosefos Yom Tov*, ad loc).

Yet, although intellect and emotion seem diametrically opposed, there is a direct link between the two. For the most part, intellect, when brought inward and contemplated deeply, births emotions. How we feel about the world and how we feel about ourselves in relation to the world and those around us is born out of thinking, whether consciously chosen thoughts or subconscious ruminations.

In the unfolding process of Hisbonenus, in order to birth holy, noble, transcendent emotions, it is not sufficient to simply think casually and tangentially about an issue. Intense and focused concentration is required. Complete dedication and commitment to the practice is necessary if higher emotions are to be awakened and sustained over time (Alter Rebbe, *Ma'amarei Admur HaZaken*, Inyanim, p. 127).

INTERNAL EMOTIONS THAT ARE
ROOTED DEEPER THAN MIND

Before delving further into the mind-heart dynamic, it is important to understand that while our mind, intellect, and opinions create our emotions, the way we understand the world and interpret our reality fashions our emotional responses to life. This is true with regard to our 'external' emotions; however, there is another type of emotion, one that is more deeply seated than thoughts and the mind.

There are 'emotions', proclivities, and inclinations that are more existential, fundamental, or primary than our intellect, whether they are conscious or subconscious. Essential emotions, such as the drive to survive and perpetuate oneself, are deeper than any intellectual decision based on information gathered from the outside world. Intellect does not create such essential emotions; it can only guide these emotions and modulate their expression.

Take the emotional need for security as an example. In a child, this emotion is directed towards his or her parents. An adult who has a more developed mind and greater spiritual maturity may direct his sense of security toward the Source of All Life. However, in both examples, the mind is not creating the emotions; rather, it is directing them toward a literal parent or toward our Parent in Heaven.*

---

* Generally, the principle is, as the Alter Rebbe explains, מוח שליט על הלב / *Moach Shalit al HaLev* / "The mind controls the heart." This in

fact, is the fundamental principle of Chasidus, as explained in *Hay-om Yom*: ר׳ משה מייזליש סיפר, דער רבי (רבינו הזקן) האט אונז געלערענט, אז דער אלף פון חסידות איז, אויסצוניצען די טבעיות אין עבודה. און ראשית העבודה זאל זיין אויסצוניצען די טבע הכחות, ווי למשל די טבע פון מוח שליט על הלב / "Reb Moshe Meisels related: The (Alter) Rebbe taught us that the *Aleph* (the first and fundamental teaching) of Chasidus is to use our natural traits and instincts in the service of Hashem. The beginning of spiritual work is to employ the natural characteristics of our powers, for example, the natural dominion of mind over heart": *Hayom Yom*, 19th Adar The heart that is under the control of the mind is the external heart, yet, there is a deeper, more internal level of the heart, which is much deeper than intellect. In the *Siddur*, regarding the intentions for blowing the Shofar, the Alter Rebbe teaches, הנה ענין השופר הוא שהוא קול פשוט שנמשך מהבל הלב ואינו כמו בחי׳ הדבור שהוא בחי׳ אותיות שנמשכים מן המוח כי אותיות הדבור נמשכים מאותיות המחשבה ואותיות המחשבה נמשכים מהשכל כו׳ משא״כ הקול פשוט הוא נמשך מן הבל הלב והוא למעלה מהשכל כי בלב יש חיצוניות ופנימית והנה חיצוניות הלב הוא למטה מהשכל ומקבל ממנו כמ״ש לפי שכלו יהולל איש שהתפעלות המדות שבלב הוא לפי השכל וכנודע אך התפעלות אלו הוא רק בחי׳ חיצונית הלב ונק׳ רצון התחתון שהוא בחי׳ רעותא דליבא הנולד ונמשך מבחי׳ התבוננות השכל אבל פנימית הלב שהוא הנק׳ רצון העליון אינו מקבל ונמשך מהשכל כלל אלא הוא גם למעלה מהשכל / "Indeed, the blowing of the Shofar, which is a simple sound that emanates from the breath of the heart, is unlike speech, which comes in the form of letters originating in the mind. The letters (language) of speech originate in the letters (language) of thought, and the letters of thought originate in the thought itself. Yet, the simple sound (that is produced by the Shofar) originates in the breath within the heart, and is thus higher than thought. In the heart there are in fact two levels, the external and internal. The external heart is 'lower' than thought, and draws from it, as it says, "According to his intellect he will praise." In other words, his emotions are aroused according to his intellect, as is known. Yet, these aroused emotions are only from the external part of the heart, also called 'lower will', the aroused heart born out of Hisbonenus of the mind. But the internal heart, which is called 'higher will', does not receive from the intellect at all, nor is it born from intellect, rather, it is higher than intellect."

COMMITTED INTELLECT
BIRTHS & UNBIRTHS EMOTIONS

Besides forming and directing our emotional states, our mind also has the ability to circumvent situations that would normally arouse particular emotions. In this way, the mind can prevent specific emotions from arising in the first place, and if they have become established, the mind can discontinue or retract them. Even instinctive, primal emotions can be preempted or canceled by consciously choosing what to think about. You can dissipate a negative reaction by simply and firmly 'changing the channel' of your mental focus.

Fear in battle is instinctive since the innate desire to survive is primal, yet even in battle, a soldier can use his mind to control his heart. In fact, the Torah directs him to do so. In *The Laws of Kings and Wars*, the Rambam writes of a soldier who needs to shift his attention during battle so as not to experience fear, for letting himself get pulled into fear would be violating a Mitzvah: ומאחר שיכנס בקשרי המלחמה ישען על מקוה ישראל ומושיעו בעת צרה וידע שעל יחוד השם הוא עושה מלחמה וישים נפשו בכפו ולא יירא ולא יפחד ולא יחשב לא באשתו ולא בבניו אלא ימחה זכרונם מלבו ויפנה מכל דבר למלחמה. וכל המתחיל לחשב ולהרהר במלחמה ומבהיל עצמו עובר בלא תעשה / "Once a soldier enters the throes of battle, he should rely on 'the Hope of Israel' and 'their Savior in times of need'. He should realize that he is fighting for the sake of the Oneness of Hashem's Name. Therefore, he should place his soul in His hands, and he should not fear or become afraid. He should not think about his wife or children. On the contrary, he should wipe their memory from his heart, removing all thoughts from his mind except the war. Anyone who begins to feel anxious and worry in the midst of battle to the point where he frightens himself violates a negative commandment" (Rambam, *Hilchos Melachim*, 7:15. See also Alter Rebbe, *Likutei Torah*, VaEschanan, 6d. Rebbe Rayatz, *Sefer HaMa'amarim*, 5703, p. 78. The Rebbe, *Sefer HaMa'amarim Melukat* 1, p. 245).

Through the power of his mind, his natural tendency to fear can be interrupted, and he can induce a state of mind where לא יירא ולא יפחד / "he will not be afraid nor fearful." Not only will he not 'show' outward fear nor display any emotions of freight, but through fixing his attention upon his purpose and upon HaKadosh Baruch Hu, he will not experience any fear at all.

THE MITZVAH OF AHAVAS HASHEM / LOVING HASHEM

As explained, if we wish to birth a particular emotion and not merely to guide or direct an emotion, we need to do more than casually think about a subject matter related to that emotion. We need to summon up a strong focus and intellectual commitment.

There is a Mitzvah in the Torah to love Hashem, yet this is puzzling: how can there be a commandment to love? Love, it seems, is an emotion that one either feels or does not. Can a person be coerced into loving someone or something? They can be coerced to do something or say something, but certainly not to 'feel' (A Mitzvah involves free choice; thus, man can be commanded to 'do' or not 'do', to 'speak' or not 'speak': Rebbe Chasdai Cresces, *Ohr Hashem*, Hatza'ah, in the beginning. See also Rambam, *Shemonah Perakim*, Chap. 2. Abarbanel, *Rosh Amanah*, Chap. 4. *Mifalos Elokim*, Ma'amar 1:3. Shemos, 20:2).

One answer to this question is that to perform the Mitzvah to love Hashem, the action required is not the love, but rather, the thought process, the contemplation that will awaken and arouse the love. The actual Mitzvah is thus to contemplate in a way which produces love, for this is an action that can be commanded (*Mifalos Elokim*, Ma'amar 1:3. Chasidus brings this answer in the name of the Maggid and Baal Shem Tov: כך" :בזה הלשון [אדמו"ר הזקן] שמעתי פנים אל פנים מאדמו"ר נ"ע Shem Tov קבלתי מהרב המגיד דמעזריטש וכך קבל הוא ז"ל מהבעל שם טוב, שמצות 'ואהבת' היא לתקוע מחשבתו ודעתו (ובלשון אידיש: מען זאָל זיך אריין טאָן) בדברים המעוררים את האהבה". Reb Eizik Homiler, *Shenei HaMeoros* 2, Chap. 2. Rebbe Rayatz, *Sefer HaMa'amarim, 5701*, p. 116. The Rebbe, *Sefer HaMa'amarim Melukat* 1, p. 245. See also *Yesod HaAvodah* 2:6. *Michtavei Kodesh*, p. 76. The Rambam writes that through meditating on the vastness of nature, one's love for Hashem is aroused — הא-ל הנכבד והנורא הזה מצוה לאהבו וליראה אותו ...והיאך היא הדרך לאהבתו ויראתו. בשעה שיתבונן האדם במעשיו / וברואיו הנפלאים הגדולים ויראה מהן חכמתו שאין לה ערך ולא קץ מיד הוא אוהב "It is a Mitzvah to love and fear this glorious and awesome G-d...When a person contemplates Hashem's wondrous and great deeds and creations and appreciates His infinite wisdom that surpasses all comparison, he will immediately love…": *Hilchos Yesodei HaTorah*, 2:2, 4:12. *Moreh Nevuchim*, 3:28. והיאך הוא הדרך לאהבתו וליראתו בשעה שיתבונן האדם במעשיו של הקב"ה הגדולים והמופלאים אשר אין להם ערך ולא קץ מיד אוהב / And which is the way in which to love Him and be in awe of Him? When the individual *Yisbonen* / contemplates the great and wondrous works of the Holy One, blessed be He, which are beyond assessment and limit, he immediately loves…: Rebbe Yehudah HaChasid, *Sefer Chasidim*, 14).

In this way, we are commanded to think about subjects such as the vastness and majesty of the Creator, or the *Hashgacha P'ratis* / Divine providence in our life, times when we sensed the guiding Hand of HaKadosh Baruch Hu. The more we recognize and contemplate how our lives are guided, and how small 'coincidences' lead to important chapters in our lives, the more our love grows. If we contemplate, for example, that we just 'happened' to bump into someone and because of that, we landed a good job, or we 'happened' to see someone after a long time, and because of that, we ended up meeting our spouse, we realize that the Creator loves us and is intimately orchestrating our life.

By contemplating the greatness and majesty of the Creator of natural beauty or the wonderful *Hashgacha* / providence that is manifest in our lives, the more we awaken emotions of love.

Love itself cannot be 'commanded', yet we can be commanded to create the vessels, conditions, or a context in which love can sprout and flower. This is precisely what the Mitzvah of loving Hashem requires; the Mitzvah is to focus thought in a way that can cultivate love.

All relationships function within the same dynamic. Our relationship with Hashem is similar to our relationship, for example, with our spouse. If a relationship feels stale or hollow of love or affection, there are methods to jumpstart and ignite the love. Sometimes, people just need to 'go back to the drawing board' and ponder why they are in this relationship in the first place. Contemplate the qualities within your spouse that sparked the original attraction, and feel the feelings come back. Methodically remembering what you loved about them, the goodness, kindness, and blessings that they have brought into your life, causes a renewal of that original love. The same holds true in our relationship with HaKadosh Baruch Hu.

Sometimes, love comes naturally and effortlessly, and other times not. This is why the Mitzvah is to meditate and methodically recount the goodness and blessings in your life, as well as the gifts, support, and salvations that could only have been given by the One who created you. The more you contemplate them with gratitude, the more your love will grow and flourish until, perhaps, a fire of passion for Divine love will glow within you day and night.

ABSTRACT VS. CONCRETE CONTEMPLATION

In the practice of Hisbonenus, mental contemplation stimulates and arouses the heart. Yet, the contemplation required to arouse robust, steady emotions needs to include a detailed and embodied focus and not only abstract or aloof modes of thought. It is fine to think about your chosen idea in a philosophical or heady way, but it needs to descend into tangible feelings and practical applications, as well. The more concrete the thought is, the more the thoughts will penetrate your heart and infuse your actions.

Once, the Alter Rebbe asked his son, Reb DovBer, "With what did you Daven?" Assuming that his father was asking him about his *Kavanah* / intention or Hisbonenus that he was focused on while praying, Reb DovBer responded, "With the idea of *Ein Od Milvado* / 'There is nothing else besides Him.'" "Very well," the Alter Rebbe retorted, "I, however, Davened with the *Shtender* / lectern."

What the Alter Rebbe was telling his son is that Ein Od Milvado is an exalted mental construct, but what is required to unleash the transformative power of this construct is to draw it down from the abstract level into a felt sense and actual life experiences. In this context, to hold the Shtender in one's hands and Daven with it means to sense the presence of Hashem's light even in the wooden furniture.

Meditating on the immense loftiness of Ein Od Milvado is admirable, but what is of greater importance is 'the lectern one leans on' — realizing that everything is included in Ein Od Milvado, even the inanimate furniture and the floor we stand on. Hashem's glory and Light permeates and enlivens everything, and nothing exists outside of this enlivening force. The Divine Presence is here and now, not just in transcendent, timeless Inner realms.

DETAILED CONTEMPLATION

Focused concentration can cause paradigm shifts when it absorbs all of our capacities and attributes, holistically re-orienting our consciousness. An intellectual contemplation of Ein Od Milvado evokes and stimulates our emotions, tet, to arouse more persistent and tangible emotions, deeply contemplating the details and implications, rather than just the general idea, is necessary (General conceptual contemplation usually remains abstract and aloof. When one contemplates the fine details of the concept, the meditation has a stronger and more lasting effect: Rebbe Rashab, *Kuntres HaTefillah*, Chap. 2).

Continuing to use Ein Od Milvado as the example, we can contemplate that "There is nothing else besides Hashem" as a general truth, or we can envision with our mind's eye how Hashem's glory and Light fills the universe, animating and giving life to every detail of Creation, from a drop of water to a tiny grain of sand. Then, since a main purpose of Hisbonenus is to meet G-d in a real and personal way, we can delve into concrete personal details, turning the contemplation inwards: how Hashem's guiding Light permeates and is vested in the very minutia of our own life experiences, sense perception, and body.

שימת לב / SIMAS LEV / PLACING IT UPON THE HEART

In order to move a holy idea from the mind, from Chochmah, Binah to Da'as and then from Da'as into our hearts, we need שימת לב / *Simas Lev* / 'placing (the idea) upon our heart' (Rebbe Rayatz, *Sefer HaMa'amarim*, 5701, p. 116).

Turning the focus of our Hisbonenus inwards toward our own experience, perception, and action is the ultimate goal. This occurs when we begin to identify personally with the concepts that we are thinking about. Ein Od Milvado is not merely a mental construct nor a cosmological or 'theological' concept of the Oneness of Hashem; rather, it is a declaration of the fact of our own existence and experience. However paradoxical it might seem, we need to sense that everything has its being in Hashem, including ourselves. This is true שימת לב / *Simas Lev* (*Sefer HaMa'amarim, 5700*, p. 165).

"You shall know this day and take it into your heart" (*Devarim*, 4:39) — it is not sufficient to know a truth in our mind, rather the Torah requires us to 'take it into our heart.' When the Torah commands us to love Hashem, it also says, ושמתם את־דברי אלה על־לבבכם / "And you shall place these words upon your heart" (*Ibid*, 11:18). In other words, the concepts revealed in the Torah need שימת לב / *Simas Lev* in order to become living truths and produce real and lasting love in us. To ensure that these ideas are placed upon our hearts and that they will penetrate our hearts, we need to make the words and ideas personal and relevant to our own lives.

If we only ponder the concept of Ein Od Milvado without stressing its relevance to our own life circumstances and physical senses, our understanding will remain mere theory, an idea 'about' the Oneness of Hashem. Thinking 'about' this may be relevant in some philosophical discussions, but Simas Lev means pointedly asking ourselves, 'What do these words have to do with me, personally, right now?' If we take Ein Od Milvado to heart, we are not just *thinking about* this truth; rather, we are sensing its truth in our daily work, in our relationships, and even in our sleep. We are becoming aware of the fact that our physical body itself is revealing and declaring the Majesty of Hashem: ומבשרי אחזה אלוקה / "....and from my flesh I will see Divinity" (*Iyov*, 19:26).

For example, we can keep in mind Ein Od Milvado while looking at the homeostasis mechanisms of our own bodies.

All of our physiological systems are miraculously designed
for precise self-regulation, causing continuous microscopic
internal adjustments to optimize stability and comfort in
the face of constantly changing external conditions. If we
are healthy, when the body's temperature rises a little bit too
high, sweat is 'automatically' released to cool it down. This is
one small demonstration of the unfathomable wisdom and
providence that surround and fill all creatures, and a hint
at the fact that there is no presence other than the Divine
Presence.

Meditating on the abundant kindness that Hashem be-
stows upon the world in general arouses vague, mild feelings, while meditating on specific kindnesses that Hashem
has shown you, in your own life, arouses passionate and fiery emotions.

CONNECTING OR DISCONNECTING & THE BRIDGE BETWEEN THE MIND & HEART

The physical form of the body resembles and parallels the
inner and spiritual meta-structure of the cosmos. In the
body, the brain is connected to cosmic Chochmah, Binah,
and Da'as, whereas the emotions (although emotions, too,
are a function of the brain) are associated with the heart.
Between the head and the torso is the neck, the passageway

or bridge that connects our mind to our emotions, transmitting information from the brain to arouse emotions in the heart (Arizal, *Likkutei Torah*, Vayeshev. Alter Rebbe, *Torah Ohr*, p. 58b. Mitteler Rebbe, *Biurei HaZohar* (5715) p. 37c. When the 'Seichel/ thoughts are in the 'neck' they are neither Seichel nor (yet) 'emotions'. Rebbe Rashab, *Sefer HaMa'amarim, Ateres, 5679*, p. 347. *Sefer HaMa'amarim, 5655*, p. 73).

This bridge enables the heart to feel what the mind is thinking. By moving through this passageway, an aloof, 'cold' objective theory transforms into a warm or passionate emotion. Yet, at the moment the thought is being channeled through the neck, it is no longer pure intellect. In this in-between state, the thought relinquishes its status as being a thought but it has not yet become an actual emotion.

INFORMATION GETTING STUCK IN THE PASSAGEWAY

Sometimes we hear or see something and it registers in our brain as bits of information, and it does not trickle down into our hearts or inform our way of feeling and acting. Sometimes we have a new experience but feel little reaction to it. There can be many different reasons for this. As one example, when one has had a traumatic experience (*Chas VeShalom*), the heart may be protected from feeling the emotional impact of the event through a dissociation response. It is as if the event has not yet 'sunk in' to the heart. The data is 'stuck in the neck', so-to-speak, lingering in an in-between state and has not yet trickled down into an emotional expression.

In another metaphor, we 'ingest' information from our experiences, and it can take time to 'digest' it. There is often a period between gathering of the information and the point when it is fully absorbed and processed. This digestion process can be effortless and without blockages, and sometimes something can be 'difficult to swallow', again, alluding to the neck.

While common sounds and sights are processed more instantaneously, if we hear or see something out of the ordinary, such as overwhelming or negative news, it can take time for the experience to become real to us and produce feelings. We may be initially 'stunned' until we can begin to understand what happened, and only when we have digested it, we may have a 'delayed reaction' and shed a tear, for example. As a subtler example, we may break out in a smile as we are walking down the street because of something we had heard hours earlier; only now do we feel its impact on our emotions and body (Rebbe Rayatz, *Sefer HaMa'amarim, 5700*, p. 41).

Our 'neck' or information passageway, can at times be impaired to the extent that our ability to feel in the heart what we know is true in our minds is all but absent. We can 'know' that a certain choice is right for us, but just not feel it. This occurs when there is clutter or a blockage in the path from the mind to the heart. On a physical plane, there are two passageways in the throat: the trachea, the 'windpipe', and the esophagus, the 'food pipe'. Just as there can be a physical obstruction inhibiting one's ability to breathe or swallow, there can be an obstruction in the healthy flow of thoughts to emotions.

In fact, the flow of physical digestion and the flow of information is interdependent. If one overeats, their esophagus or digestive process can become clogged, and this can clog the spiritual sensitivity of the mind and inhibit the movement of the meaning of their contemplation into their heart and action.

If the trachea or breathing is obstructed, it can mean that one is not in a conducive 'air' or environment or location for arousal of spiritual emotions. For example, it can be challenging (though not impossible) to quietly meditate in a large market, at a rowdy game, or in a place where people are smoking. Both the physical air we are breathing and the spiritual environment around us can play an integral role in the effectiveness of our contemplation and our Avodah of drawing thoughts down into emotions and actions.

TIMTUM HALEV / CLOSING OF THE HEART

If both of the passageways mentioned above are clogged, then the ideas of the mind will have no avenue to penetrate to the heart. Thoughts will not be able to evolve into emotions, and so they will remain in the mind, as merely intellectual ideas (Rebbe Rayatz, *Sefer HaMa'amarim, 5703*, p. 21).

Timtum HaLev is the term employed for this phenomenon, classically translated as 'closing or dullness of the heart'. This condition is a spiritual predicament caused, at least in part, by past actions, foods consumed, and other stimuli imbibed. In it, one suffers from spiritual insensitivity and an inability to feel and respond with the heart. In the context of Hisbonenus, it is an inability to arouse holy and wholesome emotions, perhaps even despite meditating and contemplating Ein Od Milvado for long hours. In this predicament, a person seems incapable of feeling any type of transcendent emotion or being spiritually moved, despite lofty contemplations of the mind. Such spiritual numbness can arise from having overindulged in pleasures (as in 'clogging the esophagus') and from living in an unhealthy or unholy environment (as in 'clogging the trachea').

Egoism is actually the greatest cause for Timtum HaLev. An over-identification as a separate individual, or an infatuation with, or indulgence in, self-centered needs and desires, causes extreme forms of Timtum HaLev. An unchecked ego desires more and more, in a never-ending loop of self gratification and craving. As a result, the person loses access to any level of experience beyond this narrow loop of addiction. All that one can feel is their own sense of self, their narrative, their need, and there is no room for anything or anyone else, certainly, no opening into transcendence. As such, try as one may to meditate on Ein Od Milvado, even if with deep intellectual understanding, it will be exceedingly difficult for the contemplation to stimulate and open the heart; there will be no movement 'below the neck'.

In simple words, preoccupation with coarse bodily indulgences does not allow for genuine sensitivity to anything spiritual. In this state of numbness, the ego refuses to allow any of the light of intellectual comprehension to illuminate the heart with any emotion.

Now the question is, how does one rid themselves of the dullness of Timtum HaLev? Changing one's eating habits and ensuring that one spends time in environments where they are taking in the 'air' and ambiance of holiness and purity is key, but how can one deal with Timtum HaLev more immediately? How can a person who is trying to practice Hisbonenus crack open his heart to feel what he or she understands mentally?

Speaking of Timtum HaLev, the holy Zohar offers a solution based on a metaphor (3, p. 168a): "A wooden beam that does not catch fire is splintered until it finally ignites. Similarly, a body into which the light of the soul does not penetrate must be (in a manner of speaking) crushed" (אעא דלא סליק ביה נהורא מבטשין ליה כו'. גופא דלא סליק ביה נהורא דנשמתא מבטשין ליה). As the Alter Rebbe comments in Tanya, "This reference to the 'light of the soul' means that the light of the soul *and of the intellect*, does not illuminate to such an extent as to prevail over the coarseness of the body. For although one understands and contemplates the greatness of Hashem in his mind, it is not grasped and implanted in his mind to a degree that would enable him to prevail over the coarseness of the heart, due to this coarseness and crassness. The cause is the arrogance of the 'other side', which exalts itself above the light of the holiness of the Divine soul, obscuring and darkening the light thereof. Therefore, one must crush it and cast it down to the ground, that is to say, by setting aside appointed times for humbling oneself...."

In other words, rather than increasing the flame of intellectual contemplation, one must first remove the Timtum HaLev, through the breaking down the underlying cause of this dullness. This is done by humbling the ego, one's illusionary sense of separateness (*Tanya*, Chap. 29. "Where ego exists, Hashem cannot." *Ibid*, Chap. 6. Chap. 22. Regarding an arrogant person, Hashem says, He and I can not simultaneously exist in the same place. *Sotah*, 5a. *Erchin*, 15b).

Once our hearts are open and the blockages unclogged, then the thoughts we entertain can begin to illuminate the mind and eventually inflame the heart as well.

A REVIEW

This is a review of the steps of Hisbonenus as discussed up until this point:

1. Make sure you have the *Cheishek* / desire to practice, since without Cheishek your mind will simply wander off to the place of its desire.

2. Some time before Davening, choose a thought or text to study and contemplate such as *Ein Od Milvado* / "There is nothing but Hashem."

3. Sit calmly as you study or contemplate, and allow your entire spectrum of intellectual capacity, from your intuitive, creative Chochmah, to your analytical Binah and your practical Da'as, to understand and develop the implications and applications of the thought.

4. In Da'as, sense the aliveness, the light, and the *Elokus* / Divine quality of the thought.

5. Allow the aliveness, light and Elokus of the thought to filter down into the heart, digesting it emotionally and opening the heart to respond emotionally. The deeper you receive Ein Od Milvado into your heart, the more your heart will be aroused, and the more you can enter into ecstasy, the heart burning with joy and love.

6. If the above steps were performed before Davening, e.g.,
   Shacharis / the Morning Service, you would stay in this
   state of ecstasy while you proceeded to Daven. You would
   allow yourself to 'feel' the words and phrases in the Siddur as hinting at the truth of Ein Od Milvado and the
   implied 'experiences' of Bitul and Deveikus.

As you praise the One, you will lose yourself in the One,
and reveal yourself and all reality as One with the Only
One.

CHAPTER 8

FROM AWARENESS
TO NON-AWARENESS

UP UNTIL THIS POINT, THE ECSTATIC EXPERIENCES
EXPLORED ABOVE ARE ONES THAT ARE AROUSED IN
THE HEART AND FELT AS A PALPABLE EMOTION. This is
an admirable level indeed, however, a higher goal of Hisbonenus is the attainment of 'non-self awareness', even beyond any type of felt ecstasy.

Overall, there are three layers of ecstasy and progressive
states of unity. The lowest layer is an ecstasy that is felt in
the heart as a physical sensation. Classically, the intellectual

contemplation of Ein Od Milvado arouses rapture within the heart; a pang of love or intimacy may arise from the soul, or a deep yearning to connect and be close to HaKadosh Baruch Hu. In some individuals, this rapture can feel blissful and it can also spread from the heart to fill the entire body and head. As sublime as these bodily sensations may sound, a more elevated, albeit more subtle, level of ecstasy is one which manifests within the mind. On this second level, as one's contemplation of Ein Od Milvado becomes more and more refined, abstract and quiet, one releases focus on physical sensations of rapture, and the mind itself is pulled toward closeness or Oneness with Hashem. This produces a sensation of deep happiness within the mind, and this is called an 'emotion of the mind'. The concentration and absorption in Divine Oneness is greater than the first level, yet there is still a subtle sense of 'self', a person experiencing this state. The most exalted, pure form of ecstasy is a state that is beyond sensations of the heart, body and mind, and beyond any subject-and-object split and self-awareness altogether.

On this highest level, the practitioner of Hisbonenus attains an absence of self-awareness and becomes one with the contemplation itself, and one with that which is being contemplated: Hashem. As there is no experience of distinction between the 'subject' of the contemplation (the contemplator) and the 'Object' of the contemplation (the Contemplated), this state is referred to as *Deveikus* / adhesion, meaning being consciously 'attached' or fused', as it were, with HaKadosh Baruch Hu.

VISCERALLY SENSED EMOTIONS

On the first level, emotions are awakened and viscerally sensed. As we contemplate the Oneness of Hashem, we may sense, within ourselves and within the world at large, a vitality emanating from the Source of Life. This level, in which emotions draw from the intellect and the intellect gives birth to and sustains the emotions, is also called _Yenikah_ / suckling.*

* Yenikah is where our emotions are expressed outwardly. Prior to Yenikah is the level of _Ibbur_ / pregnancy. The Alter Rebbe explores this topic in _Tanya_ at great length. With regard to the love of Hashem, there is an _Ahavah Mesuteres_ / a natural, albeit 'hidden', love. This love exists on the level of Ibbur, like a fetus still enclothed within her mothers womb. The act of Hisbonenus draws this fetus out to become a child, into a state of Yenikah, existing outwardly as a full emotion, albeit one that is dependent for sustenance on the intellect — דזהו מ"ש ואהבת את ה' אלקיך, דהגם שכל אחד מישראל בטבעו אוהב את ה', וכתורת אדמו"ר הזקן-שכל אחד מישראל אינו רוצה בשום אופן ואינו יכול כלל להיות נפרד ח"ו מאלקות, מ"מ ישנו ציווי על זה, כי אהבה טבעית התעוררותה היא ע"י התבוננות ועל זה הוא הציווי שיתבונן בדברים המעוררים את האהבה: The Rebbe, _Ma'amar Basi L'Gani_, 5728. Generally, the stages of Ibbur, Yenikah and Mochin are explained in the following way. _Ibbur_ is the way the emotions exist still undefined or revealed within the mind. _Yenikah_ is the way the emotions are felt in the heart, but dependent on the mind. _Mochin_ is the way the emotions are expanded in a flourishing manner as independent, stand alone emotions. This is explained in the Ma'amar cited above: וביאור הענין בפרטיות יותר, יובן ע"פ מ"ש אדמו"ר האמצעי בתורת חיים דבמדות יש (בכללות) ג' מדריגות, עיבור יניקה ומוחין. דזהו שהמדות נק' בשם צומח...כי צמיחת והגדלת המדות הם באופן דשינוי מדריגא לדרגא, עיבור ואח"כ יניקה ואח"כ מוחין. בחי' עיבור היא המדות כמו שהן נעלמות עדיין בהשכל, דוגמת עובר שבבטן האם. ובחי' יניקה היא המדות כמו שהן נמשכות בלב, שגם אז הן גדילין מהמוחין, ואדרבא אז הוא עיקר ההגדלה שלהם. בדוגמת התינוק, שגם לאחרי שנולד ונעשה מציאות בפ"ע, הוא יונק מחלב אמו שעי"ז נגדלים אבריו (ועד שעיקר הגדלת הולד הוא בזמן הינקה). ובחי' מוחין היא המדות כמו שהן בגדלות (בדוגמת הולד שלאאחרי זמן הינקה), וגם מדות אלו מקבלות מהמוחין, מבחי' גדלות

המוחין, כמבואר בתו"ח שם / "And to explain the matter in more detail, it will be explained according to the Mittler Rebbe in *Toras Chayim* that in *Midos* / personal attributes there are (generally) three levels: Ibur, Yenikah and Mochin. It is said that the Midos are called 'growth' because the growth and maturation of the Midos are in a manner of changing from one level to another: first Ibur, then Yenikah, and finally Mochin. The level of Ibur is the Midos as they are still concealed in the intellect, like a fetus in its mother's womb. The level of Yenikah is the Midos as they are drawn into the heart, for then they are also nurtured by the Mochin, and this is the essence of their maturation. And according to this metaphor of a baby, even after he is born and becomes an entity in his own right, he suckles from his mother's milk, and by means of this his limbs grow (just as the main growth of a baby is during his stage of nursing). At the level of Mochin, the Midos as are in a state of maturity (in the metaphor of a baby, after he has been weaned), and these Midos are also received from the Mochin, in the paradigm of *Mochin D'Gadlus* / expanded (or mature) consciousness, as explained there in *Toras Chayim*." Normally, certainly in Chasidus HaKlali, and in the way it is generally understood, the holy emotions of Ahavah and Yirah rest with the heart; they are emotions expressed in the heart, and the more התלהבות / excitement felt in the heart the stronger they are. The Alter Rebbe teaches that especially today, ואנחנו צריכים להתפלל יותר ויותר בהתלהבות מאד וכן בכל דור ודור למטה צריך להתפלל בהתלהבות גדולה, ולא כי אכשר דרי, אדרבה, מפני גודל הרע אשר נתערב ונתרבה בכל דור ודור צריך להפרידו ע"י אש חזק בתפלה ולברר הרע אשר בקרבו ולהביאו אל שרשו / "We need to Daven with more and more excitement and enthusiasm. And in each and every subsequent generation, we must Daven with even greater enthusiasm, not because we are today on a higher level, on the contrary, because of the magnitude of the negativity with which we mingle, and which multiplies in each and every subsequent generation. Thus (the negativity) must be separated (dissolved) by a strong fire in Davening, to cleanse and refine the negativity within us and bring it to its Root": *Likutei Torah*, Chukas. And if a person cannot arouse inflamed emotions of the heart, at least he should do so in his mind, as the Alter Rebbe writes in *Tanya* (Chap. 16), ויתר על כן, צריך לידע לידע כלל גדול בעבודה לבינונים, שגם אם אין יד שכלו ורוח בינתו משגת להוליד מאהבת ה' בהתגלות לבו, שיהיה לבו בוער כרשפי אש וחפץ בחפיצה וחשיקה ותשוקה מורגשת בלב לדבקה בו, רק האהבה מסותרת במוחו ותעלומות לבו

Just as mammals receive nourishment through suckling their mother's milk, these emotional and sensory states are nourished and nurtured by the intellect. The character and intensity of the feelings are contingent on the character and intensity of the person's thinking and mental focus. Spiritual emotions can only suckle from the intellect as much as the intellect generates profound insights into one's relationship with the Divine Presence (Alter Rebbe, *Torah Ohr,* Bereishis, p. 4b. Yisro, p. 68c. Rebbe Rashab, *Sefer HaMa'amarim, ETeR* (5670), p. 134). This kind of emotion is 'external' to the person, and it exists as an 'object' separate from intellect, the 'subject'. Yet, as sucklings, emotions do remain closely attached to their parent, the intellect. Their survival and thriving is dependent on what they can draw from the intellect, and so

/ "Furthermore, one must know an additional important principle in the life of the *Beinoni*: even if one's intellect and understanding are incapable of producing a revealed love of Hashem in his heart, to make it burn as it should with fiery flames, with desire and longing and passion manifestly felt in the heart, to cleave to Him — instead, the love is hidden in his mind and in the recesses of his heart." In other words, the ideal would be to experience revealed fiery emotions in the heart and that will help eradicate (transform) any negativity and evil within, but the innate natural love will also suffice. See also *Ma'amarei Admur HaZaken*, Parshiyos 2, p. 832. But other times, the Alter Rebbe seems to suggest that Hisbonenus in the 'mind' is actually a type of Ahavah and Yirah and the more we can contemplate and meditate in our minds (and the mind is something that we have control of; we can choose to think or not to think about a particular idea or not), and the stronger we hold these thoughts, the more the inner negativity and evil will dissolve and be transformed. The 'fire' of the contemplation, understanding that the Root of the fire of passion, of the ego, is the Divine holy attribute of 'fire' (in a distorted, perverse manifestation), will burn away and ultimately transform this negative fire to holy fire: See *Likutei Torah*, Ki Seitzei.

the attachment and nurturance must be continuously maintained.

Emotions that are aroused and expressed are those of passion and ecstatic desire for the Divine; this is an important stage but it is not yet full *Deveikus* / collapsing of the sense of separate self within the Light of Hashem. In this state, as there still exists a 'you' who is in love with the Holy 'Other', it is not yet a state of *Ein Od Milvado* / "There is nothing but the One." 'You' still have a sense of your own existence; there is still a 'you' separate from Existence Itself. You may feel great, rapturous love for HaKodesh Baruch Hu, but an identification remains, a belief in being an individual who is feeling that love. This is not true *Achdus* / Oneness.

SUBTLE EMOTIONS

A more elevated, subtle level of ecstasy is the experience of emotions within the mind itself. These emotions are called *Midos D'Mochin* / emotions within intelligence (not to be confused with 'emotional intelligence'). We can experience these 'intellectual emotions' prior to the stage of thoughts arousing emotions in the heart, or after the heart's arousal. In the latter, as we sit with the emotions that have been aroused in the heart, the external intensity of the emotions begins to recede, they rise up into our minds and become more and more subtle. In other words, in a more settled, 'mature' form, the emotions of the heart move up into the mind (Mitteler Rebbe, *Imrei Binah*, p. 69).

On the level of 'intellectual emotions', these emotions are not expressed as burning passion or desire, rather as a subtle and collected inclination of the mind (*Sefer HaMa'amarim, ETeR* (5670), p. 134. See also *Tanya,* Chap. 16). These emotions manifest as inclinations toward the subject matter we were contemplating. However, the main characteristic of this stage is the attainment of a more profound level of Deveikus and absence of ego. Our *Yeshus* / sense of separate self is now much less pronounced than in the state where our emotions were fully felt and expressed through the heart and displayed externally.

No matter how subtle our Yeshus may be, there will always be a slight sense of separateness. When emotions ascend to the brain, the feelings are refined, becoming luminous 'movements' within the mind — yet they are still being *felt* in the mind, and thus, there is still a sense of a self, a feeler of these feelings.

BEYOND SENSED EMOTIONS

Deveikus is the ultimate objective of Hisbonenus. It is to lose yourself, to lose the sensation of separateness and become completely consumed in the *Ohr* / Light of your contemplation, and through that in the Light of the Creator, the Ohr Ein Sof. In Deveikus, there is an absence of feelings and sensations. On the contrary, the experience is so all-absorbing that the sense of self vanishes in the act of contemplation, and one no longer feels himself as a separate existence. There is only *Havayah* / One Being.

Emotions, by their very definition, function in a world of separation and multiplicity. They call for other people who will receive them and respond. Emotions are generally 'movements' towards another person or away from another. They require 'otherness' to exist (Rebbe Rashab, *Sefer HaMa'am-arim, 5678,* p. 12). The emotion of hate reinforces separateness between people, magnifying the idea of 'me *or* you.' The emotion of love, on the other hand, expresses our willingness and desire to overcome separateness and alleviate the boundaries that exist between people. Once love is activated and expressed, it magnifies the idea of 'me *and* you'. The same holds true within the world of Hisbonenus. When contemplation stimulates strong emotions, even ecstasy, separateness still exists, and a clear distinction between the contemplator, the contemplation and the Divine 'object of contemplation', still functions. Once a deeper state of Hisbonenus is attained, the contemplator becomes one with the Contemplated. The contemplator is transcended; the Ohr, *Chayus* / vitality and *Koach* / power of the individual (in the language of the *Tanya,* Sha'ar HaYichud v'haEmunah, 12. *Siddur Im Dach,* pp. 1-2. *Likutei Levi Yitzchak,* Igros Kodesh, p. 327), connects with the Ohr, Chayus, and Koach of the Oneness of HaKadosh Baruch Hu.

In due course, both the intellect and the emotions implode, and the contemplator is left in a state of *Bitul* / transparency and Deveikus. All feelings, thoughts and self-perception become, in a 'revealed' way, one with the *Ohr Ein Sof* / the Infinite Light of Hashem.

The more *Ayin* / no-thing we become, as it were, the more still and unexpressive, inward and quiet our form becomes. We tap into the Ayin within the Yesh, within the structure of the words and thoughts we are contemplating until there is just contemplation without a 'contemplator' doing it. Eventually, we immerse completely and non-separately in the Ayin of the Ein Sof, Itself.

To arrive at this destination, we first need to 'overstimulate' our rational, intellectual mind, until it 'implodes' and is absorbed into *Elokus* / Divinity. First, we contemplate the intellectual idea to its maximum, in its רוחב / *Rochav* / breadth, אורך / *Orech* / length, and עומק / *Omek* / depth, and even in its *Omek Lifnim M'Omek* / depth within the depth, the core and essence of the idea. Finally, we burrow into the Ayin within the thought, where the thought exists beyond words and language, and then even beyond that; we connect to the Elokus within the thought. This is where the mind is released into Divine Light.

BREADTH, LENGTH, DEPTH

Intellectually pondering the *Rochav* / breadth of a lofty idea means making it 'widely applicable'. Expanding the idea in this way involves associating it with similar or parallel concepts, and contrasting it with dissimilar and opposite ideas. This 'broadens' the idea to include many other ideas, revealing how it can illuminate a variety of topics.

Pondering a lofty idea's *Orech* / length means making it universally accessible. One can draw it down into various analogies and parables until even a child will understand it. 'Extending' it in this manner also includes bringing it all the way from an abstraction to practical wisdom, revealing how this idea can be utilized in day to day life.

Pondering the *Omek* / depths of an idea means extracting its deepest essence. This is a process of 'mining', putting aside the surface meanings and stripping away the layers of conventional understandings and assumed definitions that cover it. One can ask 'what does this really mean in its own right?' until the idea's unique essence shines like gold.

Contemplating *Ein Od Milvado* / "Nothing truly exists except Hashem" in its Rochav means broadening it to apply to everything in your life. You gain an understanding, for example, of how all the egoic pleasures one could pursue are in reality "nothing" (*Ein*) — imaginary and devoid of any "truly existing" (*Od*) content, for there is really no source of pleasure "except Hashem" (*Milvado*). Rather than contemplating a single application alone, you apply it to a multitude of ideas and values until Ein Od Milvado expands to incorporate and synthesizes all details into an entire worldview. For example, 'There is no one to fear but Hashem,' or 'This experience of Chesed is nothing other than Hashem's Chesed,' or 'It is ultimately not me who is reciting the words of the Davening, it is Hashem's speech alone...'

Contemplating Ein Od Milvado in its Orech means to draw analogies from life that bring it down from the realm of abstract, spiritual concepts into a clear, simple illustration that anyone could understand. For example, there seem to be countless separate waves, but they are really inseparable from the one vast ocean. When you look at a wave, you are seeing none other than the ocean. In the same way, there seem to be countless separate beings, but they are really inseparable from the One Infinite Being. When you are looking at a creation, you are really seeing none other than the Undivisable Creator.

Contemplating Ein Od Milvado in its Omek means contemplating deeper and deeper, until you not only 'know' that there is nothing except Hashem, but you directly sense the essential core of its Ohr and its Ayin, and directly identify with its essential truth. The surface understanding of the Pasuk remains valid: 'There is no other G-d but Hashem,' but to mine the essence, we need to dig deeper.

Every thought, as every creation, has a particular letter formation, a specific combination of Divine letters or sounds that serve as its 'DNA'. Beyond the surface layers of every thought, idea, and entity, and beyond the letters and sounds that give rise to it, is the *Ayin* / the limitless 'non-thing-ness' (as perceived from the perspective of our *Yesh* / limited 'something-ness'). 'Within' this Ayin, there is a revelation of the Ohr Ein Sof, the Endless Divine Light that shines through all the letters, structures, words, ideas, and entities in Creation. Through Omek, which moves from Binah to Chochmah, we 'dig' into the world of an idea before it descends into the world of 'words and letters'. This is the experience of the 'Ayin' of the idea. If we continue digging beyond that as well, we finally connect to, and merge with, a revelation of the Ohr Ein Sof.

The layers of conceptuality that cover over the essence of Ein Od Milvado, which need to be stripped away, may include subconscious assumptions such as there *are* many g-ds (powers) but Hashem Alone is the only 'true' G-d. When we finally refute any and all such limited beliefs, we discover, intellectually, that Hashem is not just the only Divinity and Power there is, but Hashem must be the *only reality*, the only existence there is, period. At this point, the Ohr of the idea begins to suffuse our minds. If we then look into our direct experience, we will be forced to sense and admit that 'I, too, do not exist in my own right; there is no "me"; only Hashem exists.' This is an example of 'sensing' the Ayin. The essence at the core of all these deeper recognitions is simply living in identification with the Only 'I', the Ohr Ein Sof.

THREE ASCENDING LEVELS

As mentioned, there are three ascending steps in Hisbonenus. To begin with, we should first, in the words of the Rebbe Rayatz, establish proficiency in *Hisbonenus Limudis* / Hisbonenus in Torah study: התבוננות למודית, אחר שמבין / העניין על בוריו, הוא מתבונן בעומק העניין ההוא, עד שהשכלי מאיר אצלו "Hisbonenus Limudis (is established when) after mastering the concept thoroughly, one meditates on its profundity until the intellectual element *shines forth* for him."

After understanding the concept correctly, in its Chochmah, Binah, and Da'as, and its breadth, length, and depth, we sit with the idea until it becomes illuminated in the heart — and then more subtly yet powerfully 'illuminated', or comes alive in the mind. Then, הרגש חיות העניין שלמד ולא הרגש השכלי כמו בהתבוננות למודי / "the vitality of the concept that one learned is *felt*, although not how it was sensed intellectually in intellectual Hisbonenus." In other words, rather than understanding the idea like we did in the beginning, we now begin to connect with the *Ohr* / light, *Chayus* / vitality, and *Koach* / power within it.

Finally, we arrive at the third level, הרגש האלקות שבהעניין שלמד / "to sense the Divine Transcendence (Ayin) within the idea contemplated." This means we penetrate deeper than the facade of the intellectual ideas, sensing the Light and Divinity within the contemplation, until we 'collapse' into mental and physical stillness. There is a total *Bitul* / nullification of the sense of separate self in which we are not even aware of being in this state (Mitteler Rebbe, *Kuntres Ha-Hispa'alus*, Chap. 4. *Derech Chayim*, Sha'ar HaTefillah, p. 176).

In other words, the practice of Hisbonenus evolves in stages, organically moving from one level into the next. First, we begin to ponder an idea until the concept becomes secure and 'fastened' in our minds, and fully absorbed in its breadth, length, and depth. Then, the idea enters the heart where profound emotion is awakened. As the thought rises back up into Binah and Chochmah, we sit with the idea until we feel the vitality, the life force, the inner energy, and the aliveness of the subject matter. Finally (especially in Davening) we begin to feel and sense the *Elokus* / Divinity within the idea, and indeed, by extension, the Elokus within everything, until we ourselves become absorbed within the Ayin, the Bitul in the Ohr Ein Sof.

Every weekday, my illustrious grandfather would be seen bent over a book of Chasidus, deeply absorbed in Hisbonenus Limudis for hours. Sometimes he would seem to be straining to understand something, sometimes he was weeping with awe or love, and sometimes he was completely motionless in Deveikus, his head resting in his hands. The *Sefer* / book that he had been studying before and during Davening was a cherished volume of *Hemshech Samech Vov* by the Rebbe Reshab, and he would scratch with his fingernail underneath the lines that he would learn each day, slowly moving his nail along the lines. Years later, when his family observed the nail marks, it became clear that he had been studying just a sentence or two of this Sefer each day! This anecdote demonstrates something of the depths of absorption in the Ein Sof that a person can reach through textual contemplation.

ACQUIRED LOVE, NATURAL LOVE, AND 'LOVE OF BEING'

An analogy for the three states of Hisbonenus, while not absolutely precise, may be drawn from three general levels of love: 'acquired love', 'natural love', and 'love of being'. 'Acquired love' is the feeling one feels toward a spouse or close friend. 'Natural love' is like one's love of his family, in particular, like a parent's natural love for his or her children. 'Love of being' is the innate love of oneself.

'Acquired love' is generally a passionate emotion, a love that burns like fire. The beauty of such love is that despite the two parties' differences, their distinct genetic makeups, backgrounds, and upbringings, affection binds them and allows them to transcend their 'otherness'. It is a love that bridges 'opposites'. In fact, the greater their differences, the stronger their attraction. Yet, since acquired love overcomes their distance and otherness, it thus requires continuous renewal and rekindling. Being that there are always two separate people involved in the relationship, renewal of passion is required to ease their sense of separation. Without this renewal, their differences may resurface, obscuring their love and causing at least a temporary separation.

'Acquired love' corresponds to the first level of Hisbonenus, in which emotions are birthed outwardly from one's intellectual contemplation. On this level, the emotions are felt tangibly, intensely, and passionately. These emotions bridge the abyss separating the finite contemplator from the Infinite subject matter being contemplated. The feelings aroused are the exhilaration of having overcome this apparent divide. Since these are still 'exterior' manifestations, they need to be renewed by returning to intellectual contemplation.

'Natural love' is less passionate and more cerebral; it is love within the mind. As a more innate love, it is always present and thus does not need to be aroused or rekindled. Whether the love of family or love for a child, this love is much calmer than spousal love. It is less exciting and less overtly passionate, although since it is more innate, it is deep, real, and ever-present. There is little or no distance that needs to be overcome, and therefore, it is more subdued, subtle, and inward.

Natural love relates to the more elevated level of Hisbonenus, the state of Mind. In this level, the emotions are not 'externalized' in effusive expressions or tears, etc., rather, they remain quiet, enclothed within the mind. This is a result of the greater level of Deveikus and diminished *Yeshus* / sense of independent existence.

The third form of love is 'love of being', or 'divine self-love'. Of course, 'loving oneself' seems to be a paradoxical statement, for if love is a bridge that unites that which is separate, there is no separation from oneself to be bridged. In this context, this is, in fact, a love of overcoming a divide within oneself; there was some perceptual 'distance' from one's true self and then a love that caused a return to it in a new state of unification and wholeness. Nonetheless, this 'self-love' is a state of being, not a feeling. Feelings are contingent on movement towards another or retracting from another; they are temporary arisings and need to be sustained or repeatedly rekindled. A 'state of being' is constant and contextual and is actually the un-felt source of feelings.

This highest state of love corresponds to the most advanced stage of Hisbonenus. It is the level of total *Bitul* / nullification of the sense of being a separate 'I', which is the gate to Deveikus (Rebbe Rayatz, *Sefer HaMa'amarim, 5701*, p. 126-127). The intensity of the love and ecstasy of Deveikus is such that one cannot 'sense' it, as the Mitteler Rebbe explains at great length in *Kuntres HaHispa'alus* / "Tract on Ecstasy." On this deep level of Hisbonenus, there is an eclipse of self, as it were, including self-based feelings, perceptions, and thoughts. Nothing registers in the mind. Without the egoic sense of self, there is no room for 'individualized' awareness (Mitteler Rebbe, *Derech Chayim*, Sha'ar HaTefillah, p. 176). There is no 'feeler', 'perceiver', or 'thinker'.

AYIN OF THE THOUGHT & THE EIN SOF

These three levels of Hisbonenus are ordinarily ascended one rung at a time. We begin by harnessing the entire apparatus of the mind, Chochmah, Binah, and Da'as, in contemplation until the sensations of the mind stimulate the heart, and we begin to feel in the heart what the mind comprehends. Then, the emotions become more refined and subtle, and we begin to sense a type of emotion within the mind. At some point, we transcend this sense, as well, and are left in a state of complete stillness, referred to as Ayin.

Emotions are our wings; they compel us to grow and elevate ourselves, assisting us in taking steps toward living a more meaningful, purposeful, and Divinely-charged life. They are wings that allow us to fly and journey, but they are not the destination. They get us to the door, not through the door. Our destination is our 'home', our being. To get there, we need to walk through the door and just be, to abide in a state of Deveikus.

While we become less and less of a 'separate individual', and experience more and more Deveikus, we also grasp the essence of thought, the 'Ayin within thought', and bask in the Light of the Ein Sof.

The 'Ayin within a thought' is the thought in its pure essence, prior to descending into and being enclothed in the *Tzurah* / form of letters and words. For the most part, our thoughts arise from sense perception and stimuli or from other thoughts and abstract ruminations. The way we hold thoughts in our mind is by engaging *Tzurah* / form, whether through imagery, symbols, or actual letters. Usually, we think in images or in language, which are defined, finite, and limited 'vessels' that allow abstract thoughts to be tangibly accessed and digested, whereas thought itself is 'limitless', so to speak. In itself, thought is really *Ayin* / transparent and self-empty. When we connect with the Ayin within a thought, the Chochmah of the thought also manifests, and our mind and heart release all objectified sense perceptions and felt sensations. We become motionless both internally and externally as we enter the Ayin of the thought and connect to the cosmic Ayin, the radiant emptiness and transparency of all form, until we become absorbed within the Light of the Ein Sof (See *Igros Kodesh*, Alter Rebbe, Miluim).

LOOKING, SEEING & GAZING: THREE LEVELS OF SEEING

Living with Deveikus brings us to a new way of seeing reality, which is called *Histaklus* / gazing. Histaklus is deeper than 'glancing at' or 'seeing' something (Rosh, see *Beis Yoseph*,

Orach Chayim, 229: כי המסתכל מוסיף ומדקדק בהבטתו יותר מהרואה / "For the one who 'gazes' augments and refines his perspective beyond that of the one who (merely) 'sees'"). Each thought process consists of a 'body' and 'soul'. The 'body' of a thought is grasped in intellectual Hisbonenus, whereas the 'soul' of the thought is perceived in *Histaklus* / gazing upon the thought (Rebbe Rayatz, *Sefer HaMa'amarim, 5701*, p. 99. See also *Torah Ohr*, Terumah, where the Alter Rebbe explains the idea of learning Torah as coming to 'see and be seen' in intimate Divine embrace).

The manner through which we apprehend reality occurs on three levels, three ways of seeing. The first is 'glancing', which is purely a biological, mechanical function, almost involuntary. Our eyes can be open to the world around us, yet not consciously 'seeing'. This is a superficial way of perceiving reality.

The second level is 'seeing', in which that which is viewed is interpreted through the prism of the viewer's prejudices and personal context. We 'create' the nature of the event or object in our mind and project it upon the visual field; we see things the way *we* are, not the way things are. This is also true on the first level, yet here, we can be more conscious of the way we interpret, create, and project our perceptions.

The third way of perceiving reality is Histaklus, in which we see the object being observed in itself, for itself. We see things as they are, without filters, as much as is humanly possible. To observe this way demands *Bitul* / transcendence of egoic prisms and presumptions. In the condition of Bitul, having quieted the static of the inner filter of *Yesh* / ego, we can now see ourselves accurately as one with all of life, and deeply, one with the Creator of all Life.

When the ego asserts control over perception and apprehension, every sight, sound, and sensation is colored by the ego. It casts a shadow of self-interest over everything. It never lets us see or sense anything without bias and an agenda: 'What can I take from this encounter? How can I benefit?' As such, the more the ego is out of the way, the more we see other people and objects for what they are, and the more we can truly 'be' with them. The act of Histaklus is born out of a way of being that allows 'the seen' to be just as it is. Histaklus is an ability to see without the clouded lenses of Yesh.

Histaklus in *Avodah* / inner work, and particularly in the practice of Hisbonenus, prevails when we have attained a measure of genuine Deveikus through a loss of the sense of separate selfhood. In Deveikus, we come to live in a state of revealed unity with HaKadosh Baruch Hu. There is no longer an object looking at a subject, an observer observing an observed; rather, the two have collapsed into a singularity.

THE PLEASURE OF SEEING, AND BEING WITH, ANOTHER

In *Shir HaShirim* / "The Song of Songs," Shlomo HaMelech / King Solomon sings of the passion between lovers.

The song is interpreted by our sages as an analogy of the love between us and HaKadosh Baruch Hu (Mishnah, *Yadayim*, 3:5. *Medrash Rabbah*, Shir HaShirim, 1:11. Rambam, *Hilchos Teshuvah*, 10:3). At one point, Hashem addresses us: "O my dove, trapped in the clefts of the rock!"(2:14) Doves derive pleasure from gazing at their mate, and also arouse great desire in the other. When we practice Hisbonenus and attain a measure of Histaklus, gazing lovingly upon Hashem's Light and His glory that fills Creation, we experience immeasurable spiritual delight in this state of Deveikus (ובבחי' לאסתכלא

ביקרא דמלכא, דלשון לאסתכלא היינו כמו מי שמסתכל על דבר הפלא ופלא שלא תשבע עינו מהסתכל בו כך ויותר מזה לאין קץ כשיתבונן המשכיל בעין השכל בגדולתו ית' שהוא למעלה עד אין קץ כו' ובנפלאותיו הגדולים ואשר ברא עולמות עליונים לאין קץ ותכלית ורגלי החיות כנגד כולן כו'.... אזי לא תשבע עין השכל מלהסתכל ולהתבונן בזה היטב ולהתענג תענוג נפלא לאין שיעור מזה. וזהו בחי' יונתי כמו יונים מסתכלים זה בזה וזהו אסתכלא / התענוג שלהם ממה שמסתכלים זה בזה

...(Regarding) the level of ביקרא דמלכא / "Gazing upon the preciousness of the King": The word אסתכלא / 'gazing' (alludes to the fact that) when a person gazes at something wondrous, his eyes will not be satiated by looking at it (rather he will desire to continue gazing and feasting his eyes upon it). This is even more so when a wise person looks with the eye of the intellect at Hashem's greatness, He who is infinitely above all the wonders of the world... The eye of the intellect will not be satisfied with looking at it intently and contemplating it and delighting in an infinitely more wonderful pleasure. This is the level of *Yonasi* / 'my dove', as doves gaze at each other and experience pleasure from doing so": Alter Rebbe, *Likutei Torah*, Shir HaShirim, p. 41d. Note that certain birds are hatched by the Histaklus of their loving mother — אבל עכ"ז מצינו קצת כח בהסתכלות

העין כנראה בחוש העין בטבע כעניין ביצת בת היענה שנולד האפרוח על ידי הסתכלותה

זמן מה בלתי שתשב על הבצים לחממם כמו שאר העופות וזה יורה היות כח ממשית

בהסתכלות העינים :Eitz Chayim, Sha'ar 8:1. Sefer Chareidim, 66:137).

It may seem paradoxical, but the deepest and truest form of *Ta'anug* / pleasure is experienced when the separate self is absent. The more absence of ego, the more pleasure. The more a person is aware of the technical or theoretical side of beautiful music being played, for example, the less joyful it may be for them. This is because the self-awareness in listening to the music can separate them from the experience; the music is objectified and reified and 'held at arm's length' where it can be 'seen'. Only when you let go, lose yourself, and merge in music until you have no awareness of yourself as 'the listener', can you experience the deepest musical pleasure.

The peak of pleasure is the collapse of self within something or someone else. Sadly, people mistake indulging a craving for pleasure itself, but indulgence is actually a form of suffering caused by identifying as a separate self. If you are eating ice cream and you desire to eat more and more of it, you are probably trying to use the ice cream to fill a sense of *Cheser* / lack within yourself. As a separate self consuming a separate substance, you can never overcome Cheser and be satisfied. Consuming it in that way is a barrier to true enjoyment, and in fact, the craving and the Cheser are only exacerbated because the sense of being a separate self is strengthened.

If you were to taste even a small bit of food while ceasing to focus on yourself or your desires, you could lose your sense of separate self in the experience of taste. You could become lost in the experience, absorbed in the Light within the taste, and even in the Creator of the taste. Only afterward would you become aware that 'you' had the experience, for there was not a person plus a bite of food; there was only oneness. This is true pleasure and satisfaction. Even after this experience, there is no sense of lack and no requirement for more of the food.

Pleasure is collapsing your identity into someone or something else — *Bitul* / selflessness equals *Ta'anug* / pleasure. And the deepest pleasure of all is that of the ego merging with and becoming one with the Source of All Life (Hence, the opposite of *Oneg* / pleasure is *Nega* / a lesion on the skin that causes separation).

Such spiritual Ta'anug, pleasure, and bliss is so overwhelming that one can reach a mystical state of *K'los HaNefesh* / soul expiration, in which the soul 'ascends' from the body until mundane life and corporeality no longer have any pull. Ascending from the body can mean that the person experiences no negativity or attachment to the trivialities of life, or it can mean that the person is ungrounded and dissociated from the body in an unhealthy and unstable way. If one is not properly anchored in the physical world (which is not a problem for most people, as most are too tied up in physicality), the intensity of the experience may cause the soul to leave the body and actually pass away, G-d forbid (Alter Rebbe, *Ma'amarei Admur HaZaken,* Inyanim, p. 134. This occurs through Histaklus: Rebbe Rashab, *Kuntres HaTefillah,* Chap. 1. Here, "passing away" can mean literally, but also "expiration" on a mental or emotional level as well, such as in a 'mental breakdown', a state of in-coherence or a lack of integration between the mind and emotions).

Histaklus / gazing is Deveikus attained in Bitul in the Ta'anug of Ohr, and this is the eventual objective of Hisbonenus. In order to 'get there', we first need to travel through the entire spectrum of intellectual consciousness. In other words, from Chochmah, our intellectual focus descends into Binah and then Da'as and holy emotion. From there, we settle our minds on the level of Binah and, through Binah, elevate to higher Chochmah, and then beyond into Bitul in Ayin and Deveikus with the *Ma'or* / Source of Light.

CHOCHMAH, BINAH, DA'AS — DA'AS, BINAH, CHOCHMAH, AYIN & BEYOND

To review: Chochmah must precede Binah, and Binah must precede Da'as. Once the initial germ of a thought is revealed in Chochmah, developed into fine details in the world of Binah, and then absorbed in Da'as and felt as outward or inward emotion, the thought is fully absorbed and even felt in the heart. Then, the procedure can move in reverse in the mode of *Ohr Chozer* / reflected light. One contemplates the "emotion of the mind" in Binah, and through Binah, one reaches Chochmah. Ultimately, via Binah, one attains the highest degree of Chochmah and beyond.

In the words of the Rebbe, in a Ma'amar on Shavuos, ובעומק יותר יש לומר דע"י העבודה בהפרטים מגיעים לבחינת עצם האור, שלמעלה גם מהאור שלמעלה מעולמות...והענין הוא, דשרש הפרט הוא למעלה מהכלל וכמו חכמה ובינה, דהגם שחכמה היא הכלל שממנה נמשכים כל הפרטים דבינה, מ"מ מצד זה גופא, שרש הבינה הוא למעלה משרש החכמה. שלכן, על ידי העיון בהפרטים דבינה ניתוספים (לפעמים) ענינים חדשים שלא היו בנקודת החכמה / "And in greater depth, we could say, that through the *Avodah* / spiritual inner work in the realm of details, we reach the Essence of the Light, which is beyond even the (Infinite) Light that is beyond our world... and this is the concept of the root of *P'rat* / details being deeper than the *Klal* / general principle,* much like with Chochmah (*Klal*) and Binah (*P'rat*). Although Chochmah is the Klal *from which arise* the details of Binah (first there is an initial conception or intuition of the thought, the 'right' side of the brain, and then the idea descends into the 'left' side of the brain, which begins to analyze and decipher it), yet, because of this (because Binah is the realm of P'rat) the root of Binah is *deeper* than Chochmah, and therefore, through contemplating deeply with Binah, with comprehension and diligence, sometimes new ideas are revealed to him that did not even exist in the world of Chochmah" (*Sefer HaMa'amarim Melukat* 3, Shavuos, p. 331).

---

* As the Rebbe Rashab explains at great length. See *Sefer HaMa'amarim, 5640*, Chap. 17. *Sefer HaMa'amarim, RaNaT* (5659), p. 3.

Through Ohr Chozer, we connect to the level of Ayin beyond Chochmah, the no-thing-ness beyond all things (Rebbe Rayatz, *Sefer HaMa'amarim, 5701,* p. 52). Not only do we connect with the Ayin of the thought, but with the Ayin of life itself. This *Ayin* / no-thing-ness is the Divine animating force that enlivens and sustains all of life and which is beyond human comprehension and imagination, even beyond any conception of the higher intellect.

TO CONNECT WITH AYIN, WE NEED TO BE, NOT JUST CONTEMPLATE, AYIN

In order for us to truly connect with the ultimate Ayin, we ourselves must 'be' *Ayin* / as nothing, in a state of Bitul. If not, the connection is impossible (Rebbe DovBer, the Maggid of Mezritch, *Maggid Devarav l'Ya'akov, Likutei Amarim, Or Torah*, Chap. 151, p. 34b). We cannot even authentically 'think' of Ayin if we are not ourselves Ayin. Certainly, we cannot grasp, cleave to, or become one with Ayin if we are still identified as Yesh. A Yesh cannot grasp Ayin because Ayin does not have an interface; a Yesh feels and perceives only Yesh; an entity can only relate to other entities.

To reach the Ayin within a thought and the Ayin beyond thoughts, phenomena, and experiences, we must be in the same category; we must enter the mode of *Bitul HaYesh* / nullification of our Yesh-nature.

Experientially, living as Ayin means living in great humility. On a deeper level, it is living as the witness self, the unobserved observer of experience, which is, by definition, disengaged from experience and untouched by sensation. And even deeper, to live as Ayin is to be the pristine quiet and stillness 'behind' all bodily sensing, emoting, thinking, acting, and 'existing'. Living from this 'no-thingness', the Yesh itself becomes more still and quiet. The body, emotions, and mind become tranquil and non-reactive. The more we are Ayin, the more we 'feel' the peaceful ease and 'weightlessness' of Ayin.

THE 'MORE' AYIN WE ARE, THE MORE ALIVE THE WORLD IS

The less Yesh we are, the 'more' Ayin we can be. The less our attention is tangled in external concerns, the more internal depths of experience we can perceive. The less we identify with our coarse sensations, emotions, and thoughts, the more our *Ayin*, our clarity, our soul, becomes revealed. And the more that our inner dimension of Ayin is revealed to us, the more we are connected with the 'Ayin' of the *Ohr Ein Sof* / Infinite Light.

When we are consciously connected to the 'Ayin' of the Ohr Ein Sof, both ourselves and the world we perceive are extraordinarily alive, vibrant, harmonious, intentional, and soulful. Our relationship with HaKadosh Baruch Hu and our perception of the continuous recreation of existence become ever more vitalized when we are Ayin.

We are, as Ayin, in constant intimacy with the Ultimate Ayin from which all existence emerges. Creation is a *Yesh* / existence that is continually being created and recreated from the Divine Ayin anew. In this way, there are two dynamics present within Creation: the Ayin and the Yesh, and we always have a choice with which to connect. We can either sense ourselves and the world around us as Yesh, 'created' in the past tense, or we can connect with the continuous Divine unfolding of Ayin into Yesh and sense the renewal and re-creation of everything in the present tense. Yesh is stale and stagnant; Ayin is fresh and flowing. The most extreme state of Yesh is 'heresy', having no revealed connection to the Creator. A person in this state, sadly, does not sense or even think, Chas V'Shalom, that there is a Source of All Manifestation.

When we feel ourselves as Yesh, a separate entity who has been created from Ayin but is now 'solidified' as a Yesh, then the act of creation is perceived as having happened in the past. Our relationship with the Creator is also stale and in the context of the past: 'Hashem created me, and now I exist as an independent creation. Even if I am still connected to the Creator, it is because He set me in motion when I was conceived, and my life now is just a consequence of that personal "genesis" moment.' However, the truth remains that we and all manifestations are continually being created out of Ayin.

If we regard ourselves as emerging out of Ayin at every moment, experientially living as the flow of Divine Ayin, then every moment of our existence feels like a *Chidush* / novelty, and the world always feels new. This places our relationship with the Creator in the present tense and in a state of constant regenesis. It is not a worn-out relationship dependent on memory and past, as if Hashem just 'created' the world long ago; rather, it is a fresh and exciting relationship with the *Elokim Chayim* / Living G-d, Who is creating the world and myself right now. This is the most authentic way to live, in closeness with Living Presence, in the eye-opening, awe-inspiring unfolding of this moment.

Practicing Hisbonenus and attaining Ayin, both intellectually and experientially, our sense of Yesh becomes entirely absorbed in the Ayin of the Ein Sof. In this state, there is 'no-thing' to contemplate, and 'no-one' is contemplating (Mitteler Rebbe, *Sha'ar HaYichud*, Ner Mitzvah v'Torah Ohr, Chap. 5). This state can also be summed up as "No-thingness meditating upon Itself."

AN EXPERIMENT IN HISBONENUS PRACTICE

To train yourself in Hisbonenus, it is important not just to study it theoretically but to experiment with putting it into practice. Before practicing, ensure that you have the Cheishek, the desire and deep will to practice the Hibonenus. If you do have the desire, set aside a place and some amount of time to practice. As an alternative to Ein Od Milvado, experiment with focusing on a parallel idea that is also a prevalent theme in Chasidic Ma'amarim: the mystery of how the world (including yourself and your body) is being created as *Yesh MeAyin* / something from Nothing. Allow your entire intellectual capacity, your Chochmah, creativity and intuition, your Binah, understanding and analysis, and your Da'as, intimate awareness, feeling, and practical know-how, to understand and develop the stream of thought. How is it possible that finite existence could even *appear* to emerge from an absolutely infinite, borderless, indivis-ible, Omnipresent Being? Since Hisbonenus is a spiritual quest to know and to feel in both the mind and heart, let your thoughts trickle down into your heart, arousing your emotional center to feel the greatness and majesty of the Creator and the beauty of the unfathomable mystery of cre-ation Yesh MeAyin.

Once the heart is awakened, a deep yearning to connect with HaKadosh Baruch Hu is aroused. Spend some time just being present with such emotions, allowing them to grow and expand. At first, they are felt in the heart, palpably and viscerally, but if the depth or intensity of the emotions gradually becomes too intense to be expressed in the heart, they will begin to be felt as subtle, 'intellectual' states of longing in the mind. Gradually, ascend higher and higher into this subtlety, letting your body and mind become more and more still, until you have at least a moment of merging into Ayin, your sense of *Yeshus* / separateness dissolving and melting into the inner Light of the Ein Sof. Even if this lasts just an instant, you have become one with the Ayin, and for that moment, Ayin is consciously meditating on itself. Rest in this Divine Deveikus for however long it remains, and repeat it again and again.

When you reemerge from this practice session, notice if, in the final stages, there were any emotions, any bodily mobility, or inner sensations, or if these seemed to collapse and cease. If you were connected to the Ayin within the thought and the Ayin within and beyond everything, you became, to some extent, one with Ayin. Did you touch into an ecstatic state of quiet and stillness without any sense of self-awareness? Make mental notes of your Hisbonenus journey each time you attempt the practice; build on your successes and remain positive, non-judgmental, and experimental. Even the briefest moment of Bitul or Deveikus can change your life forever.

CHAPTER 9

EIN OD MILVADO
& CREATION
YESH MEAYIN

WHILE CONTEMPLATING HOW ALL OF CREATION EMERGES FROM THE DIVINE AYIN, ONE CAN ATTAIN THE AYIN WITHIN THE SUBJECT MATTER AND THE AYIN WITHIN ONESELF. This offers the contemplator a clear, intuitive sense of the fact of Ein Od Milvado.

This chapter may be utilized as an intellectual contemplation for Hisbonenus practice. Take your time with it and let yourself become absorbed in the mysteries, intricacies, and depths within the ideas.

CREATION OF YESH FROM AYIN

Bereishis Bara / in the beginning (Hashem) created. The word *Bara* / ברא / 'creates' suggests creation *Yesh MeAyin* / 'ex nihilo' / something from nothing (as the Ramban explains, *Bereishis*, 1:1. הקב"ה ברא כל הנבראים מאפיסה מוחלטת. ואין אצלנו בלשון הקדש. בהוצאת היש מאין אלא לשון ברא / "The Holy One, blessed be He, created all things from absolute non-existence. We have no expression in *Lashon Kodesh* / the Sacred Language for bringing forth something from nothing other than the word *Bara* / created." Rebbe Shlomo Ibn Gabirol wrote a few hundred years prior, למשוך משך היש מן האין: *Keser Malchus*. This is the first clear and published Torah source of creation *ex nihilo*). The world of substance, form, and physicality is created from a Divine No-thing-ness, which is beyond all physical form and substance. The Divine enlivening, animating force within all of creation is referred to as Ayin (it is called no-thing-ness from our perspective, since it is beyond our grasp and conception). Hence, reaching the Ayin within and without translates as piercing the veil of physicality and connecting to the Divine animating 'No-thing force'.

OHR EIN SOF / INFINITE LIGHT

The Creator, or the creative force that emanates from the Creator, is called the *Ohr Ein Sof* / the Infinite Light.[*]

---

[*] The first (revealed, published, or recorded) references to the Ohr Ein Sof (or *Ein Lo Tichla* / with no end) appear in the writings of Rebbe Shlomo Ibn Gabirol. It shows up years later in many of the teachings of the early *Mekubalim* / Kabbalists of Catalonia, Aragon. See Rebbe Az-

When we call the Light (which is a metaphor) 'Infinite', we do not mean the mathematical or philosophical definition of infinite, which is something that is merely unmeasurable or non-dimensional. We do not mean an 'infinite' amount of something finite, such as an unending extension of dimensional space or an infinite quantity of finite numbers. These types of 'infinity' are actually finite since they can be defined. True Infinity is beyond all limitation, qualification, dimension, quantification, and definition. The Infinity of the *Ohr* / light is *Ein Sof*, infinitely boundless, unlimited, indivisible, and without any comparison whatsoever with which to define It.

Ein Sof defies all linguistic formulations and distinctions that we use to interpret reality. The best way to facilitate our own discourse (the only discourse we know) and indicate the Creator's Light is to describe what It is not. This is known as *Derech Shelilah* / the path of negation, or 'negative

---

riel of Gerona, *Biur Eser Sefiros*. Rebbe Moshe ben Nachman, the Ramban (*Talmid Chaver* of Rebbe Azriel), Pirush *Sefer Yetzirah*, 1:1. *Kisvei HaRamban*, Vol. 2, p. 453. *Ma'areches Elokus*, Chap. 7, p. 82b. Rebbe Yoseph Gikatalia (a Talmid of Reb Avraham Abulafia), *Sha'arei Orah*, Sha'ar 1, p. 8. There was a great debate about whether the term *Ein Sof* refers to Hashem Himself (as it were) or to Hashem's will or manifestation. The Ramak, Rebbe Moshe Cordovero, asserts that *Ein Sof* applies to Hashem's Essence, as it were, as He is for Himself: *Pardes Rimonim*, Sh'ar 3:1. *Ohr Ne'erav*, 6:1. Rebbe Menachem Azaryah De Fano argues that *Ein Sof* applies to Hashem's will, to the Divine first cause: *Pelach HaRimon*, Sha'ar 4:4. *Yonos Elim*, Hakdamah MeInyan Ein Sof. See the Rebbe Rashab, *Sefer HaMa'amarim, 5660*, p. 166.

theology'; we indicate the Infinite by saying what It is not. On the other hand, even this description is a 'definition' of Infinity; it is a description of being beyond description. The Ohr Ein Sof transcends this definition as well, for It is also beyond any idea of transcendence.

FINITUDE EMERGING FROM INFINITY

Hashem desires for us to understand and know Him and His process of creation as much as is humanly possible ("The foundation of all foundations and the pillar of wisdom is to *know* that there is a Primary Being who brought into being all existence...וידיעת דבר זה מצות עשה / and *knowing* this idea is a positive Mitzvah" (Rambam, *Hilchos Yesodei HaTorah*, 1:1:6), as the Pasuk says, וידעת היום והשבות אל לבבך כי ה' הוא האלקים). But this leaves the mind with a profound quandary: if the Ohr is Ein Sof, if the Divine Light is Infinite, how can a finite existence emerge into existence at all? How can there be a transformation from the *Ein Sof* / Infinity to *Sof* / end, from absolute unified Oneness to multiplicity and diversity? This idea violates our normal pattern of thinking, and the mind is left with an intolerable paradox.

Of course, this question is not directed toward Hashem's 'capabilities', as it were. After all, Hashem is able to create, form, and manifest existence instantaneously, without any process, devolution, or division at all. Furthermore, as Infinity itself is a definition, and Hashem is beyond (while also inclusive of) all definitions, Hashem can simultaneously manifest within Infinity as in finitude. For Hashem, paradoxes are not paradoxes. The question, however, remains: from our process-oriented and finite perspective, *how* do finite entities emerge from the Infinite Oneness? And then, how can multiple and finite entities maintain their existence in the presence of Infinite Oneness? In our world-view, Infinity cannot coexist with finite entities; Oneness should overwhelm multiplicity and not allow finite phenomena to emerge — certainly not as separate entities.

TZIMTZUM / CONTRACTION / WITHDRAWAL

To overcome this difficulty and allow the creative process to be more humanly and rationally comprehensible (Rebbe Rashab, *Sefer HaMa'amarim*, 5658, p. 120. See also: Rebbe Yoseph Ergas, Shomer Emunim (HaKadmon) 1, Chap. 53), the Arizal revealed that Hashem created the world of finitude through a construct called *Tzimtzum* / 'contraction' or withdrawal, in a sense, a 'self-abandonment' (though the roots of the idea of Tzimtzum are found in *The Zohar* 1, 15a. *Zohar Chadash*, VaEschanan, 57a. It was the holy Arizal, Rebbe Yitzchak Luria, who was the first to expound and explain the Tzimtzum. See, e.g., *Eitz Chayim*, Mevo Shearim, Sha'ar HaAkdamos. See also Medrash *Tanchuma*, Vayakhel 7. *Medrash Rabbah*, Vayikra, 29:4, where the word *Tzimtzum* is used with regard to a Divine revelation. Note the Alter Rebbe, *Torah Ohr*, Terumah: וכדי להיות המשכה מבחי' ח"ע להתלבש בתורה דבריאה ...., צ"ל ע"י צמצום.

וזהו שארז"ל צמצם שכינתו בין בדי ארון / "In order to draw from the level of higher Chochmah (Atzilus) and enclothe it in the Torah of *Beriah* / Creation…, it must be done by means of a contraction, a withdrawal, and this is what our sages say '(Hashem) contracted his Shechinah (Light and Presence) between the two poles of the Aron.'")

Creation was and is, in fact, not based on a gradual or progressive process of devolution from Infinite to finite, from spiritual to physical, from no-thing-ness to some-thing-ness. The only possible basis is a quantum leap: the Creator must have radically withdrawn from His own Omnipresence, figuratively speaking, and thereby 'concealed' the Ohr Ein Sof. Through this cosmic withdrawal, a so-called *Chalal* / 'vacated space' was revealed, in which the basic properties of time, space, and finitude could eventually emerge.

As Hashem withdrew Himself into Himself, folding Infinity into Itself, there was an unprecedented *Chidush* / novelty: the potential for a finite manifestation. Through this Tzimtzum, a sense of otherness came into focus, as finitude can only exist when it is not overwhelmed by Infinity (הן הן גבורותיו של הקדוש־ברוך־הוא, אשר כל יכול, לצמצם החיות והרוחניות הנשפע מרוח פיו ולהסתירו, שלא יבטל גוף הנברא במציאות / "This [Tzimtzum] is the very 'restraining power' of the Holy One, blessed is He, Who is Omnipotent, לצמצם / to 'condense' the life-force and spirituality which issues from the 'breath of His mouth' and to conceal it, so that the body of the created being shall not become nullified": *Tanya*, Sha'ar HaYichud VeHaEmunah, 4). Once a finite form of Light was revealed, the 'vessels' were revealed, and then a gradual process and course of devolution from pure Light to dense matter could begin. This process of devolution is called *Seder Hishtalshelus* / 'the great chain of staged descent'. In the culmination of this descent, pure Divine energy is miraculously converted into form and matter. Our perceived physical world is the last link in this great 'chaining down' process, and therefore, it is spiritually the 'furthest removed' from the Infinite Source of Light. However, the chain metaphor also implies that matter is, in effect, a compressed and contracted version of the Divine Light or Energy. It is only due to the fact that we humans are also included in the category of 'furthest removed' (insofar as we are identified with form and matter) that all we perceive with our physical senses is form and matter and not the endless brilliance of Divine Light.

IS TZIMTZUM REAL?

With closer intellectual contemplation, we will realize that the solution of Tzimtzum is not complete, and a fundamental question still remains unresolved. If the Tzimtzum actually occurred (albeit in a spiritual sense, and not in any physical manner), then we are compelled to admit that there was a limitation to the Ohr Ein Sof, in that it could not coexist with finitude, nor create a finite entity that could coexist with It. And if the Tzimtzum did not actually occur but was rather an illusion based on a human perspective, then we still need to face the dilemma of how it is that a finite world (and a human perspective) can now exist and not be overwhelmed by Infinity.

To begin to answer this, we must inspect the 'relativity' of perspectives. Tzimtzum is only real or not relative to the perspective of the observer. In the eyes of the Infinite One, as it were, all that exists is always and forever only Itself. Hence, the Tzimtzum is not an *actual* withdrawal, leaving a chasm and empty space devoid of Divinity; rather, always and forever, there is Ein Od Milvado, nothing other than the Divine 'I'. In this way, Omnipresent Infinity is the context in which everything and nothing are contained. There is no contradiction because Infinity is, so to speak, 'big enough' to maintain every contradiction, paradox, and seeming anomaly. There are no contradictions or paradoxes from the 'viewpoint' of the Ohr Ein Sof — in the panoramic Infinite perspective, there is no separate existence. Only the human being perceives the Tzimtzum as a real Divine contraction, because our evaluative and discerning powers are tuned to physicality. We think and access spatially, and thus, our minds interpret the Tzimtzum as if the Ein Sof really shrank and pulled away, leaving a void. We can only imagine existence in a context of limitations and separations, requiring an actual withdrawal of the Infinite light and the world emerging within a *Chalal HaPanui* / cosmic 'Vacated Space'.

What is more, to a person of flesh, only what is tangible to the senses of flesh is real. If we can see it, touch it, or smell it, then it is a Yesh, a verifiable existence. The creative animating force which lies beyond our senses is thus called *Ayin* / nothingness because, for us, it is not tangibly real, and in that sense is as if 'nothing'. Conversely, in the Creator's 'perspective', the Divine, creative, animating force is the *only* true Yesh existence, and the physical world is Ayin.

What we call Ayin, from the Supernal perspective, is Yesh. The world, which seems to operate as an independent and separate existence, is thus an illusion of man's perception and is really Ayin (And even the "Light" that creates and animates this world is merely a הארה דהארה / "a glimmer of a glimmer" of the Infinite Light of Hashem. Certainly, the actual Creation is considered as a nothing of nothing. This idea is expressed in Chasidus countless times. See, for example, *Likutei Torah,* Behar, 41c. Keep in mind, this paradigm of the world being merely an Ayin of an Ayin, 'a nothing of a nothing' in comparison to its Source, is true from the perspective of the higher Ayin (in other words, the world 'exists', but in comparison to true existence, it is like 'nothing'. This means, *for us* the world definitely *does* exist as a separate existence), yet, from an even higher perspective, from the 'view' of *Atzmus* / Essence, there is *literally* "nothing else besides Him"). In the end, we must conclude that *Tzimtzum Lo K'P'shuto Hu* / "The Tzimtzum is not literal." In this way, contemplating the subject of 'creation Yesh MeAyin' has led us back to a contemplation of Ein Od Milvado; the only *literal* reality is HaKadosh Baruch Hu.

TURNING 'YESH MEAYIN' & 'EIN OD MILVADO' INWARDS

An exhaustive contemplation of creation Yesh MeAyin is ultimately answered by the truth of Ein Od Milvado, and this is where the seemingly two subject matters become one. Yet, in the first stages of the practice, we only pondered the ideas of Yesh MeAyin and Ein Od Milvado on a purely objective, analytical level, for example, by studying a *Ma'amar* / Chasidic discourse with all our Chochmah and Binah. As we received the idea in our Da'as, we began to turn the information inwards and see and feel its relevance in practical life. Explored earlier, this stage is called שימת לב / placing upon the heart. This is where information becomes a catalyst for transformation, for it is now sitting at the gate to the heart, ready to ignite the emotion and yearning for active implementation.

There is a difference between how information and knowledge sits in the mind as an objective theory and the way it is known at the feeling level of Da'as, 'placed' at the gate of our emotional and motivational center. In a Chasidic tale, a wealthy scholar and teacher owned a timber factory. One day, a fire broke out in his factory and destroyed his entire inventory and fortune. His students, uncertain how to inform him of the bad news, decided to ask him, as a 'theoretical question', what he would say to someone who lost all his worldly possessions. He replied, "Surely, I would remind that person of the saying by our sages, 'Whatever the Merciful One does, He does for the good.'" Upon hearing his reply, they gently informed him of the fire. Upon hearing what had happened to his fortune, he collapsed and fainted. When he revived and was reminded of his predicament, he fainted again. This happened over and over again. Once he was fully revived, he declared, "Up until now, the teachings of our sages were nice and empowering theories. Now, I need to truly understand them."

Once the knowing of the mind becomes the knowing of the heart, and we fully *feel* what we know, emotions are aroused with an unstoppable desire to cleave and unite with the *Milvado* / 'Him Alone' of *Ein Od Milvado*. Like a diving board, this bounces the focus back upward and inward to the mind, where it manifests as 'mental emotion'. In the process, the Ayin of Ein Od Milvado becomes not merely theory nor emotion but inherent, experiential knowing. This is what pulls one's consciousness into a collapse of perception and sensation, a stilling of bodily and mental movement, and a sense of Deveikus with and within the Divine Ayin. The 'small i' of self collapses within the Infinite I, the only True Self.

It should be clear that *Bitul* / nullification of the sense of separate I does not translate as 'self-negation' in the sense of self-deprecation. It does not mean thinking less of oneself; rather, it means thinking less *about* oneself. Certainly, it does not mean denying one's purpose or power; on the contrary, when a person is radically less self-obsessed, it *liberates* their purpose and power. It means recognizing that our 'Yesh' comes from Ayin at every instant, making us transparent to our Creator.

Bitul, 'transparency' to Ayin, is where our entire 'i' becomes absorbed, on a revealed and lived level, into the Ultimate I of the Ein Sof. Yet, it should be emphasized that the deepest level of living is not 'no-self', but rather recognizing the Ultimate I within our own i. It is allowing the fullness of self to be a transparent medium through which the Ultimate I of Hashem is revealed. It is where we 'recognize' that the entirety of our unique personhood is created by the Creator and exists to express something even greater than ourselves. This will be explored in more detail further on.

In this state of transparency and Deveikus, although we are not experiencing or knowing anything as a separate individual, we 'experience' the knowledge that there is nothing else besides Hashem, *Mamash* / literally.

HISBONENUS K'LALIS VS. HISBONENUS P'RATIS: GENERAL VS. DETAILED HISBONENUS

In a state of Deveikus, 'our' knowing and sensing (which is beyond personal knowing and sensing) of the fact of Ein Od Milvado is miraculously birthed from the seed of intellectual thought. Through thinking about the creation of Yesh from Ayin, we 'experience' Ayin. This is the way of Hisbonenus that was initiated, forged, and developed by the Alter Rebbe.

In a short Ma'amar, or Chasidic discourse, the Alter Rebbe laid out the path of detailed mindful Hisbonenus in contrast to the practice of merely circumventing the mind and imagining the emergence of Yesh from Ayin without thinking it through (See the appendix for a full translation of this Ma'amar).

There are generally two ways, says the Alter Rebbe, in which we can meditate on a subject such as the emergence of creation from Ayin to Yesh. One way is to focus on the core concept in a very general sense until our Yesh is experientially subsumed by the Ayin. This is a *Hisbonenus K'lalis* / general Hisbonenus. In this path, one harnesses the power of imagination and creativity to envision how a physical object, for example, implodes into pure energy and merges into the Divine Ayin. On a personal level, one pictures their own Yesh being absorbed into the Ayin, and then filling the mind completely with this image.

In the Alter Rebbe's definition of Hisbonenus K'lalis, one meditates on the overarching idea, for example, envisioning the Glory of Hashem filling the universe and imagining how all Yesh is constantly emerging and being enlivened and animated by the Divine Ayin.

The other way is to meditate on the details of the issue in the method called *Hisbonenus P'ratis* / 'detailed Hisbonenus'. This is the method that we have been exploring at length. We meditate on the details of the 'evolution' of Yesh from Ayin, and analyze how every single detail of our life is filled with Hashem's guiding 'hand' and Presence. Seeing how the idea is reflected in detail in our own life makes it less abstract and more real than an image. This "detailed" method uses and employs the intellect, while the "general" method bypasses the intellect, utilizing the right side of the brain more prominently, and the power of imagination and imagery (*Ma'amarei Admur HaZaken*, Inyanim, Hisbonenus, pp. 133-134).

Hisbonenus P'ratis exercises our G-d given power of Binah, expanding the idea into its length, breadth and width, and this way we arrive to the deepest levels of Chochmah, to the Ayin of Chochmah, and eventually to the Ayin itself.*

*Mitteler Rebbe, *Ner Mitzvah VeTorah Ohr, Sha'ar HaYichud*, p. 5b. The Mitteler Rebbe also writes (*Ibid*, Chap. 4) a *Kabbalah* / tradition he heard from his father, the Alter Rebbe, who heard it from the Maggid of Mezritch, that it is always important to practice Hisbonenus P'ratis, whether you are learning the *Zohar*, Arizal or any other time: אך הנה מי שלא העמיק דעתו ביחודי' פרטי' ומתחיל מבחי' הכלל גם שבא לו ביגיעה רבה בהשגות רבות באיכות ענין הביטול בכלל כמו כשלהבת כו' וכה"ג לא יוקבע בנפשו אמיתית ענינו כ"כ כמו אחר עיון היטב בכל פרטיי' עד שמהם יבוא לבחי' הכלל... מ"מ מי שהוא מעמיק בכל לבו ובכל חפצו לעצמו' האלקו' דוקא הנה גם בעיונו בפרטיות יכוין הכל אל המח' הכללי' דעצמות דוקא ולא יפול מכללות הכונה כלל מחמת צמצום הכונה הפרטיות מאחר שכל הפרטים אינם נמשכים והולכים רק אחר הכלל דוקא... ענין ההתבוננו' בפרטי מדותיו הוא רק רק כדי שיבא לעצמותו ומהותו דוקא... גם בעיונו בס' הזהר ובכתבי האריז"ל צ"ל עד"ז דוקא ודל "But one who has not deepened his Da'as in the specifics, and starts from the general analysis, even though he has come to it with great labor, and has achieved levels of Bitul, such as "when a flame (is drawn to

Clearly, Hisbonenus K'lalis may be easier. However, in His-bonenus P'ratis, when we meditate on the details of the Yesh nullified within the Ayin, when we eventually reach the Ayin, we will 'sense' it in a more tangible and real way. As the concept of Yesh MeAyin is contemplated meticulously and the details digested more gradually, one level at a time, it brings the awareness of Ayin, and thus the actual felt experience of Ayin, closer to our reality. When, through the Klalis approach, we contemplate the general concept of the Yesh absorbed within the Ayin, it may be less transformative. Although we may arrive at the core of the issue more directly and pierce the essence of the Ohr within the thought more comfortably and quickly, still, the experience of the idea will remain more aloof and abstract.

---

its Source Above)" etc., yet, the truth of the idea will not be established in his soul so much as after delving deeply in all of its details, until from the details he comes to the level of the general idea… In any case, one who deepens (contemplation) with all his heart and desire to the Divine Essence itself, so also in his delving into the various Details, he will intend everything (all his intention, to and) in the general analysis of Essence, and he will then not fall from the the general intent at all, even though all his contraction of the (mind in the) intent in on the details, since all the details are drawn from and progressing to just the one general principle…. The idea of Hisbonenus on the details of the Attributes is only to come to the Divine Essence and Being…even as you do study *The Zohar* or *Kisvei Arizal* / "The Writings of the Arizal", it has to be in the exact same way (as explained, the idea of focusing on the details) — וכאשר מקובל היה א״א מו״ר ז״ל נ״ע בדבר זה מפי הה״מ ז״ל בפי׳ גמור וכך שמעתי מפיו ל״ז / "as I have received from my father, my teacher, of blessed memory, who heard it from the Maggid of blessed memory, so I heard from his mouth": See also *Sefer HaMa'amarim Melukat*, 6, p. 97.

Furthermore, the Alter Rebbe explains, when a truth is attained without the full involvement of our intellectual capacities, then those truths are merely imagined, and in this sense, they are illusory. The insights that we gained and the clarity we perceived were, in effect, just projections of our own imagination. Consequently, when emotions are aroused, they tend to be more egoic, the proof of this being that they are coupled with a sense of spiritual superiority and sometimes even followed by a frivolous pursuit of bodily pleasures. In other words, even if we do seem to pierce the ego through general contemplation and attain Bitul and 'experience' Ayin, since this was attained by bypassing the intellect, the impression will not be permanent and the feelings aroused will fade.*

---

*Or, as the Mitteler Rebbe writes, כי בהתבוננות דרך כלל יוכל להטעות א"ע עד שנדמה לו כי כי מאד קרוב אליו הדבר ובאמת מרחוק מאד ה' נראה לו בהיותו דרך כלל לבד משא"כ ההתבוננות דרך פרט שכל פרט בהשגה בדבר פרטי הרי יוקבע בנפשו בבחי' הקירוב ביותר וממנו יבא להשגת דבר פרטי העליון הימנו בהדרגה עד שיבוא לכלל ההשגה בכלליות שאז מתאמת יותר בלתי הטעאת א"ע כלל / "For in general contemplation, he can deceive himself until it seems to him that it is very close to him these ideas (which he is contemplating) when in truth 'from a great distance he (is seeing) Hashem', since it is a very general contemplation. In Hisbonenus in the path of details, however, where he ponders all the details in detail, these ideas will be cemented in his soul and be (authentically) close to him, and from there, he will be able to further contemplate even higher, until he comes to the general understanding of the general idea, and then this truth will be fully ingrained into his consciousness, without fooling himself at all": *Sha'ar HaYichud*, Chap. 4. See also *Toras Chayim*, Bereishis, p. 112b. When Ayin and Bitul are gained via intellect and meditation on the details, the impact is more lasting and transformative, as the truth (of the insight and experience) can even be explained to the animal soul: the Rebbe, *Igros Kodesh*, 19, p. 195.

ACTIVELY OR PASSIVELY
SEEKING AYIN

Besides the fact that Hisbonenus K'lalis may not have as much durability, the meditator may falsely assume he has attained a high level of growth when, in actuality, he may be simply having pleasant sensations or a pleasant imaginative trip.

This is one overarching issue with Hisbonenus K'lalis, and generally, when trying to meditate on or visualize or imagine the emergence of Yesh from Ayin. Furthermore, trying to reach the level of Ayin through visualization or imagination is an oxymoron. An objective to directly become 'nothing' is doomed, for the person, the Yesh, is the one seeking to become Ayin. In this mode, the meditator will always perpetuate himself, and no matter how long or arduously he tries to eliminate his separateness, it survives; the Yesh is the meditator. If there is a 'self' who is seeking or meditating, then by definition, separateness is maintained. Seeking always affirms or creates distance from that which is sought.

Circumventing the intellect and attempting to directly become Ayin only causes us to attain another version of our Yesh, a 'spiritual ego' and a grandiose imagination. Seeking, and the individual seeker himself, must collapse. If not, then one's contemplation was really focused on an idea of Ayin that is tainted with ego.

One reason that it is crucial to clear contemplation of any taint of ego is that "Wherever a person's thoughts are, that is where he is — all of him," as the Baal Shem Tov teaches. Everything is in the mind, for the mind creates our reality. The thoughts we think color our experience. The depth of this idea is not simply in the fact that the main part of our experience is a reflection of our thoughts, but even deeper, that is actually *where you are* — all of you. If your thoughts are focused on *Ruchniyus* / spirituality and higher worlds, *you* are, in fact, in those higher worlds, not just your mind, but also your body and your entire self. If you are authentically thinking of the selfless Ayin within thought, as opposed to projecting your ego's vision of it, you can *really* be in a state of selfless Ayin.

In Hisbonenus P'ratis, one meditates and thinks through in elaborate detail the ideas of Yesh and Ayin, and how, through incremental steps and processes, there was a movement from Divine Ayin into the world of Yesh. Focusing, thinking, and remaining in this state of contemplation requires painstaking effort and patience, but this helps eliminate ego from the mind, allowing us to attain Ayin in a holistic manner. In fact, Ayin is attained almost as a side effect — in a sense, 'accidentally' or indirectly. We do seek intellectual understanding, but we are not directly seeking to find or become the Ayin. Rather, our seeking, thinking mind eventually implodes, and Yesh gives way to Ayin.

Our ambition is to *comprehend* the idea of Ayin as much as possible, while reaching the actual state of Ayin within the thought and within ourselves is a spontaneous consequence.

AYIN AWARENESS

With Hisbonenus P'ratis, we begin with contemplating and employing our own *Yesh* / limited mind — the realm of Yesh that emerges from limitless Ayin — and then we move, intellectually and maybe even experientially, gradually into the realm of Ayin. Perhaps this means reaching a point where we find ourselves meditating on the Ayin itself, or simply Ayin meditating on Itself.

Meditating on the Ayin is a highly advanced state of Hisbonenus and demands expansive states of consciousness. Within the evolving stages of Hisbonenus, this occurs after fully developing and pondering the thought of Yesh from Ayin with our Binah; the thoughts rise back into a pure, subtle, refined, unformed Chochmah state. And with Chochmah, one can access Ayin, as Chochmah is from and yet united with Ayin.

"Who is a *Chocham* / wise person? Someone who can see the נולד / what is going to be born" (in the future)." Yet, this statement also means that a Chocham is someone who can see the power of the נולד, the Divine life force and creative power within Creation (איזהו חכם הרואה את הנולד / "Who is wise? someone who can see what will be born (the future)": *Tamid*, 32a. A wise person is someone who can see the power of the נולד, the 'birthing' of Creation. In the words of the holy Tanya: ,"איזהו חכם הרואה את הנולד פירוש, שרואה כל דבר איך נולד ונתהוה מאין ליש, בדבר ה' ורוח פיו יתברך / "Who is wise? He who sees that which is being born." That is to say, he sees how everything originates and comes into being *Yesh meAyin* / 'ex nihilo' by means of the word of Hashem and the breath of His mouth, blessed be He": *Tanya*, 43. See also *Tzava'as HaRivash*, Chap. 90).

The essence of meditating on the Ayin is "knowing how things are being born", or coming into being. When we function on a level of Chochmah, we come to 'gaze', with our inner eye, the Divine enlivening force that sustains, animates, and fills all of created existence. Part of attaining Ayin within Hisbonenus and 'gazing' at the Ayin within all of life is that we then attain a radical state of Ayin, Bitul, loss of separateness, and certainly, loss of self-awareness. There is a cessation of all senses; even emotions are stilled, the body becomes motionless (or not, whatever comes naturally), and we collapse into the experience of Ayin.

A distinguishing criterion of whether we have attained a measure of Ayin or merely another level of more subtle Yesh is if we are 'feeling' any tinge of excitement or, for that matter, any 'feelings' at all. If we are sensing the Ayin within Yesh but because of that we feel ecstatic or elevated, this is proof that our ego, our Yesh, is still involved in the experience. Only when there is no sense of self and the absence of all self-awareness does it indicate that the ecstasy is truly Divine (Mitteler Rebbe, *Kuntres HaHispa'alus*, Chap. 1. Rebbe Rashab, *Sefer HaMa'marim, 5672*, 1, Chap. 214. Rebbe Rayatz, *Sefer HaMa'amarim, 5706*, pp. 118-119).

Following the path of Hisbonenus and tapping into the Divine Ayin will serve as a guiding light that allows us to re-engage with the world with a higher and more meaningful perspective and mindset. Being meditatively connected to the Transcendence will give us the wisdom and clarity to meet the unfolding drama of existence with a sense of peace and inner harmony.

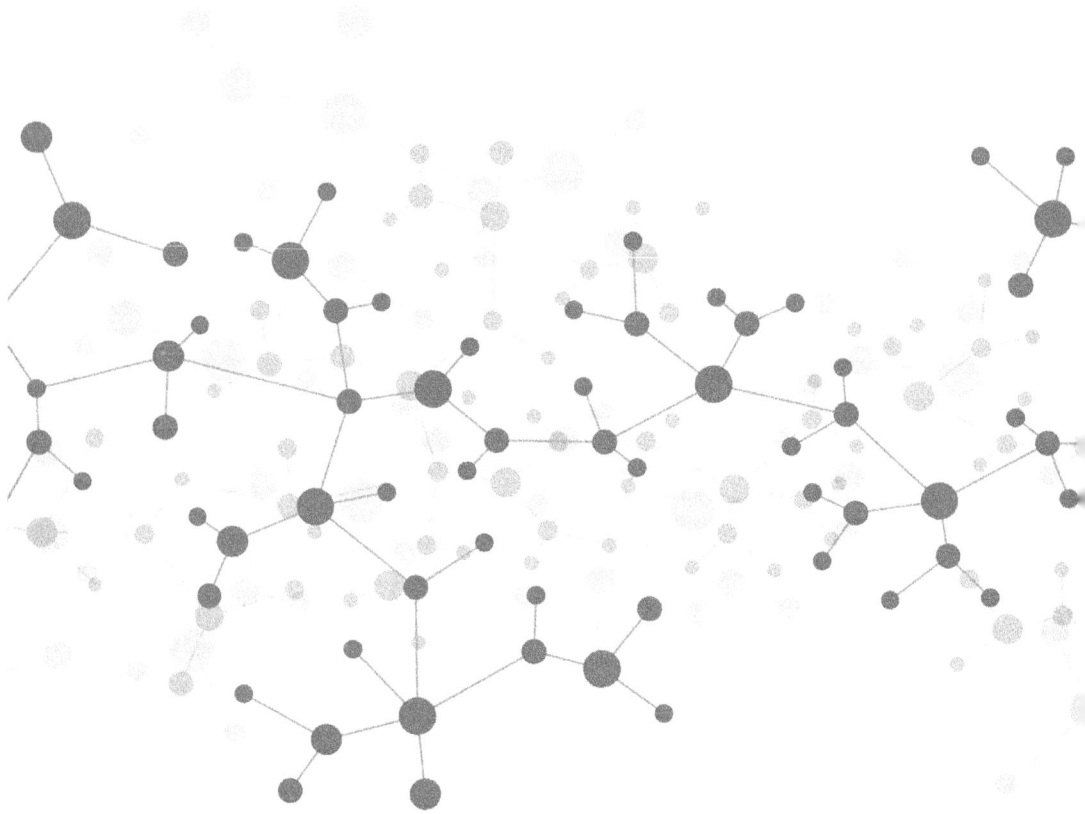

CHAPTER 10

NO-THING-NESS & BEYOND

TO REALIZE AYIN, WE MUST BE AYIN, AS ONLY AYIN CAN EXPERIENCE AYIN. When we attain a measure of Bitul, both a Bitul of sense of separate self, and a Bitul of all sensations and thoughts, only then can we tap into the Ayin. By being Ayin and connecting to our inner Ayin, we can attach ourselves to the cosmic Ayin.

In our *Avodah* / inner work, Bitul means to nullify ego; to align our desires, thoughts, emotions, and activities with our higher or deeper Divine soul. Yet, amazingly enough, the 'less' we are, the 'more' we become. We become 'greater' by being less egocentric, as more of our deepest, infinite self can then be revealed. Since our innermost consciousness, our Divine soul, is actually "part of the One Above", Bitul of the ego does not negate our existence. On the contrary, we find our true selves through Bitul. Bitul renders transparent our lower, finite self (what we ultimately are not), allowing us to shine as what we ultimately are: 'infinite' soul one with its Infinite Creator.

Through Bitul, we untangle ourselves from the trap of our animal soul, our ego-driven, reactive, fight-or-flight state of consciousness. Through Bitul, we take leave of this narrow, petty, competitive, and constricted way of living and being and become a truly alive, open, present, free, and empowered human being.

In a state of Bitul, where we are connected to the part of self that is one with the Infinite Creator, our actions are in revealed alignment with the Ultimate Will of the Creator. We are effective co-creators dedicated to actively making this world a better, brighter, and holier place.

This is a Bitul of Ayin, in which the fullness of our lower 'i' is eclipsed, and the self becomes submerged in the Ultimate 'I' of the Ein Sof. The small 'i' has collapsed within the Infinite 'I', and the small 'i' has been hollowed out and emptied.

Yet, there is an even deeper level than Ayin (as will be explained), in which Bitul is not the absence of the fullness of self; rather, it is the alignment of our uniqueness (Yechidah), the fullness of our 'I', within the Ultimate 'I'. This means recognizing that there is *only* the Ultimate 'I' expressed in the entire fullness of Creation, and the fullness of each individual person's 'I'. Here, the totality of who we are expresses itself fully and does so as a perfect conduit through which the Ultimate Divine 'I' is manifest in the world.

In other words, up until this point, we have mostly treated the Ayin as the pinnacle of Hisbonenus practice, connecting to the Ohr and the Ayin within thought and within all of Creation. Yet, there are levels beyond the Ayin — Ayin is not the ultimate reality. The ultimate is beyond both form and formlessness; it is beyond emptiness, as emptiness is also a limitation and a definition.

The following sections are more material that you can contemplate in your Hisbonenus practice.

MEMALEH KOL ALMIN: SOVEV KOL ALMIN

In general, there are two forms of Divine manifestation: a Divine Light that creates all substance although remains utterly transcendent of Creation, and a Light that permeates all existence, enlivening and animating all matter. These two emanations, metaphorically referred to as 'Light' are called *Memaleh Kol Almin* / 'filling all worlds' and *Sovev Kol Almin* / 'surrounding all worlds'. Memaleh Kol Almin (*Memaleh* for short) is a Divine finite Light that permeates and infuses all of Creation. It is the force that animates and sustains the universe in an intimate way, similar to the soul that is vested in the body. Sovev Kol Almin *Sovev* for short) is a Divine Infinite Light that creates existence and then encompasses or hovers above it.

In the process of creation, the transcendent Sovev gives rise to the substance of things, while the imminent Memaleh forms the substance into a particular structure and configuration. Sovev allows something to be, while Memaleh articulates and animates its existence.

Clearly, these terms, such as 'surrounding' and 'filling', are mere metaphors and should not be taken literally, much like Light itself is a metaphor. The distinction between Memaleh and Sovev is in their degrees of revelation, both in the cosmos and in our own life and experiences. The Light of Sovev is called 'surrounding the world' because it is indirectly revealed and experienced. The Light of Memaleh is called 'filling the world' because it can be directly experienced in this world. Sovev is experienced as a moment of trembling and awe, a moment in which we behold the mystery or transcendence that lies beyond comprehension and certainly beyond articulation. It is a sense of being in the presence of the Ineffable, Unfathomable Transcendence. The Light of Memaleh is felt when we sense the unifying Divine Presence orchestrating and 'filling in' the details of our lives. In the first, we sense the Beyond, and in the second, we sense the Immediate.

Both these expressions of Light are 'Ayin' from the viewpoint of the physical existence of Yesh. It is also important to recognize that they are both manifestations and revelations of HaKadosh Baruch Hu, but are not Hashem Himself.

ATZMUS / ESSENCE

Hashem Himself, or 'the Essence of Hashem', so to speak, is referred to as *Etzem* or *Atzmus* / Essence. Atzmus is beyond Yesh and finitude, but it is also beyond Ayin and Infinity. It is beyond even being called 'beyond', as 'beyond' is a definition and hence a limitation.

From our limited, finite, three-dimensional perspective, we can only describe Hashem through the manifestations with which we identify Him, as in Infinite Light or Memaleh Kol Almin, when in truth, any description or word, even 'Hashem' or 'Atzmus' falls short. As Atzmus is completely beyond description, we cannot actually describe *what* It is, only *how* It manifests, such as 'Sovev' and 'Memaleh', for example.

Atzmus is the ultimate context and totality of reality. Although this Divine Essence is beyond the polarity of finite and Infinite, it paradoxically embraces and 'includes' both.

It is the Ultimate 'I' within all finitude, but also beyond even Infinity. It transcends these categories and concepts (and even the term 'It'), but it also paradoxically includes them. Unlike the Infinite or *Ohr Ein Sof* / Infinite Light, Atzmus is not exclusive, for there is nothing outside of Atzmus to exclude or transcend. As a provision to the binary mind, Divine Essence can be likened to the two sides of a coin, as well as the circumference that connects and includes them both as One.

The 'existence' of Yesh and the 'non-existence' or formlessness of Ayin, the perceptual fullness of dimensionality and the imperceivable emptiness of Infinity, are merely 'expressions' of Atzmus.

Atzmus is nothing and everything, and both and neither. It cannot be thought, yet it includes all thoughts. It is all form and yet remains utterly formless. For this reason, Atzmus cannot be spoken about or even 'experienced' consciously. Descriptions do not apply to Atzmus, and even the descriptions 'the Ultimate', 'the Essence' and 'the Paradoxical' are limitations. It is not possible to understand It, because understanding requires separation from It, and we are not separate from Atzmus.

Hashem's Light is expressed in both finitude and Infinity simultaneously. It shines as Yesh and Ayin, form and formlessness, fullness and emptiness, without being divided or compartmentalized. While the Divine power of *Gevul* / boundedness is displayed in the Yesh of existence and finite form, and the power of *Bli Gevul* / unboundedness is expressed in the Ayin, still there is only One Source of Power, which is inseparable from Its powers.

Indeed, both Ayin and Yesh, *Ohr* / light and *Kli* / vessel, Infinity and Finitude, Spirituality and Physicality, are but manifestations of the Creator, and not the Creator. And yet, 'in Essence', there is no separation between manifestation and the Manifestor.

עלמא דשיקרא /
THE FALSENESS OF THIS WORLD

With our understanding of Atzmus (meaning only our understanding that It exists), we can begin to decode the enigma of the presence of a physical Creation.

A question that has been asked and reasked for millennia is whether the world of appearances, the world apprehended by our senses, is a true reality or is just an illusion of the senses. Is there a purely objective reality outside of our experience of an object? Or is all reality merely subjective, a 'perception' of objectivity, created by the subject, the observing self?

This is a philosophical question, a theological question, and today, it is even a scientific question. Are 'the observer' and 'the observed' actually a singularity; are there no separate subjects and objects? In the context of Ein Od Milvado, the fundamental question is, is the world that is perceived with the naked eye observed as an objective and seemingly separate reality from Source an illusion of the Truth or somehow part of the Truth as well?

Chasidic texts refer to *Olam HaZeh* / 'this world' as עלמא דשיקרא / *Alma D'Shikra* / a world of fallacy, as opposed to *Olam HaBa* / the World to Come is called in the Zohar "the World of Truth" (*Zohar* 1, 192b). This reference seems to be saying that since we are matter, our apparatus of perception is matter, and so we perceive the world as matter; matter and Yesh is what is real to us. What we experience is what is real to us, what we see and touch, the world of Yesh. In truth, from the Creator's 'perspective', as it were, the world is Ayin and the Divine animating and sustaining life-force is Yesh. This is why the world is called *Alma D'Shikra*; it is concealing the very Divine Light that sustains it. It is an *Olam Hafuch* / "upside-down world," in which the true Yesh appears to be Ayin, and the true Ayin appears to be Yesh.

If this is so, the physical world apprehended by our physical senses is a figment of our imagination, a grand illusion. Yet if this world is merely a mirage, it violates the opening Pasuk of the Torah: "In the beginning, *Elokim* / G-d created the heavens and the earth." By stating this, the Torah is unequivocally confirming the authenticity of the physical world. As Hashem created the world, it is real.

How can we reconcile these opposite perspectives, the 'falsity' of the physical world and the 'reality' of the physical world? The answer is that the falsity of this world is in the fact that it does not exist the way we perceive it — as a separate entity, a Yesh independent of the Ayin of the Ein Sof. The reality of the world is that it is an expression of Atzmus, the Just as the inner, spiritual realms manifest the Divine's 'Infinite' power, the physical world manifests Divine 'finite' potential. We experience the Creation as real because it is a Divine manifestation of the Yesh HaAmiti / the Absolute True Existence, Atzmus.

Our physical universe exists with all the finite limitations and dimensions of time and space, but it is not an entity separate from its Creator. It is a revelation of Hashem's Infinite Light in a finite expression.

ATZMUS & PHYSICALITY

"The end is wedged in the beginning" (*Sefer Yetzirah*, 1:7). Surprising as it may seem, physical reality ('the end') is the layer of reality most directly wedged in Atzmus, the Essence of *Elokus* / Divinity.

Seder Hishtalshelus / 'the Great Chain of Causality' is the pathway of the unfolding of Creation, the externalization of the Infinite Light into finite form. All upper and lower worlds, realms, and states between Atzmus and physical matter are links in this chain. Every link is tied to the link above it and the link below it; all phenomena in this great unfolding are interlaced and interdependent in a process of mutual development.

Among all worlds, realms, and states, our physical reality is unique in that it is perceptually separate from the other links in the Great Chain. Our world does not, on its own, sense its connection to its highest Source. It does not automatically declare, "I am a creation of Infinite One, a devolution of Infinite Light." Every other link in the chain recognizes, so to speak, where it came from. Only in this physical world is one able to think that 'This world was always here,' or 'The world created itself,' or even, "I am my own creator." Atheism and skepticism only exist here at the 'end' of the chain. The sensation that מציאותו מעצמותו / "My existence comes from my own self" is possible only in this state of Yesh (לפי שהיש בהרגשתו הוא מציאותו מעצמותו: the Rebbe, Ma'amar *Lehavin Inyan Rosh Hashanah, 5716,* Chap. 6).

And so, since the world senses that it is independent, with nothing above it, it must be a reflection of עצמות / *Atzmus* / the Independent Essence of HaKadosh Baruch Hu, 'above' Whom there is no other. Only Atzmus, the Uncaused

Cause, has the power to create a reality which senses that it caused itself.

Only Atzmus Itself, Whose being is an imperative and Whose Being is 'from' Itself, has the ability to manifest a level of Creation that can seem to deny that its existence depends on itself rather than on a Creator (In the words of the Alter Rebbe: הוא מהותו ועצמותו של המאציל ברוך־הוא, שמציאותו הוא מעצמותו, ואינו עלול מאיזה עילה שקדמה לו חס ושלום, ולכן הוא לבדו בכחו ויכלתו לברוא יש מאין ואפס המוחלט ממש, בלי שום עילה וסיבה אחרת קודמת ליש הזה / "The nature and essence of the Emanator, blessed is He, Whose Being is of His Essence, and He is not, Heaven forfend, caused by some other cause preceding Himself. He alone, therefore, has it in His power and ability to create something out of absolute naught and nothingness, without this "something" having any other cause preceding it": *Tanya*, Igeres HaKodesh, 20. This is perhaps also alluded to in the Rambam, וכל הנבראים משמים וארץ ומה שביניהם לא נמצאו אלא מאמתת המצאו / "All the beings of the heavens, the earth, and what is between them came into existence only from the truth of His Being." *Hilchos Yesodei HaTorah*, 1:1. In other words, physicality comes into existence by the Essence of HaKadosh Baruch Hu: the Rebbe, *Toras Menachem*, 5746, 1, p. 347).

The uniqueness of physical beings is that they can entertain the illusion that they can exist on their own, without sustenance from Elokus (*Chas v'Shalom*). Only Atzmus Itself, the Alone, the Self-Sufficient, infuses created beings with the notion of self-sufficiency and free choice. Freedom of choice can only be exercised where there is some sense of separation and independence from the Source of All Life.

In a time of *Galus* / exile, estrangement, a time of concealment, and alienation, the ultimate truth of Atzmus, reflected within Creation, can be expressed in agnosticism and even atheism, a world that thinks it alone exists. When redemption, however, is revealed and everything is realigned with their deepest truths, and there is no longer any alienation and estrangement, the world, the Yesh of existence will, in a revealed way, show itself to be nothing less than an 'expression' of Atzmus, the *Yesh Amiti* / True Existence, the True Being of all existences.

In a redeemed world and consciousness, everyone will see and experience how the Yesh of physicality is derived from and is, in fact, nothing more than the Yesh Amiti. It will be revealed precisely how the *Yesh HaNivrah* / the created Yesh, is nothing but a revelation of the Yesh Amiti (Rebbe Rashab, *Sefer HaMa'amarim*, 5678, p. 113. See also Alter Rebbe, *Ma'amarei Admur HaZaken*, Ma'amar Razal, p. 483. Mitteler Rebbe, *Biurei HaZohar*, Beshalach, p. 43c).

As such, the ultimate *Kavanah* / intention of Creation, the way the Kavanah exists within Atzmus (as it were) is revealed specifically in this 'lower' and completely 'Yesh' world. In the realms within the *Seder Hishtalshelus* / Great Chain of Causality, the lower the rung, the lower the revelation of Divinity. As the level of revelation in a lower rung is a diminishment of the Divine Light in relation to the rung above, less of the ultimate intention of Creation can be expressed there. With this in mind, one needs to ask: what could be the purpose of creating lower realms if the revelation of Divine intention is expressed in higher realms? Indeed, it seems there would be no point in creating lower realms, for they do not serve the Divine revelation occurring in higher realms, as the Alter Rebbe teaches: תכלית השתלשלו העולמות וירידתם ממדרגה למדרגה אינו בשביל עולמות העליונים הואיל ולהם ירידה מאור פניו יתברך / "The purpose of the chain of worlds and their descent from level to level is not for the sake of the higher worlds, since for them, this would constitute a descent from the light of His Countenance" (*Tanya*, Chap. 36). Yet, it is impossible that Hashem did not have a purpose in creating the lower realms, and the lowest realm of all, this physical world. The only solution to this dilemma is that the ultimate intention of Creation is realized specifically in this physical and 'lowest' most dense realm, in the world where there is the greatest diminishment of גילויים / *Giluyim* / revelations of Divinity. Only in a place where creations feel that they are the only Yesh can the real Only Yesh, the Yesh HaAmiti, be revealed. This is because, in higher spiritual realms, the simplicity and self-sufficiency of Yesh HaAmiti is 'concealed' by the great light of higher realms, which cannot help but 'acknowledge' their Cause. The purpose of creating the physical world can only be to make a דירה בתחתונים / *Dirah b'Tachtonim* / "dwelling place for Hashem in the lower worlds" and to demonstrate that physical existence is the ultimate revelation of the True Existence (it is not that the Yesh HaNivra "is" Hashem, Chas V'Shalom, rather that Atzmus is everything *including* the Yesh HaNivra).

It is precisely in the world of Yesh where it can be revealed that סוף מעשה עלה במחשבה תחילה / "the final act is connected to the original thought" and that "the beginning is wedged in the end." This is the only realm where the יש האמיתי / *Yesh Amiti* / True Yesh, and the יש הנברא / *Yesh HaNivrah* / the created Yesh, are unified. This revelation is incomparably deeper than the luminous revelation of Divinity in higher realms; that is only a revelation of Light or 'emanation', whereas in the physical world, the Essence Itself can be revealed. And this is ultimately the meaning of Ein Od Milvado. Even a world of Sheker and concealment is not separate from Hashem.

PHYSICALITY AS SPIRITUALITY; THE BELOW IS ONE WITH THE ABOVE

Understanding the above, it is clear why Chasidus emphasizes עבודה בגשמיות / *Avodah b'Gashmiyus* / physical Divine service, and the approach of בכל דרכיך דעהו / *B'chol Derachecha Da'eihu* / "In all your ways know Him" (*Mishlei*, 3:6. *Berachos*, 63a. *Tzava'as HaRivash*, 94. For general sources in Chasidus HaKlali regarding עבודה בגשמיות see *Toldos Ya'akov Yoseph,* Naso. *Ben Poras Yoseph,* 92. *Degel Machaneh Ephrayim,* Ki Sisa).

Everything we do, not only sacred pursuits such as prayer or learning Torah, is an opportunity to connect and unify with the One Above. Every action can be transformed into a sacred action.

No 'mundane' activity is merely a means to an end. Eating, sleeping, and working do not exist only to support higher ends, such as to give us the strength and resources to learn Torah and perform other Mitzvos (Rambam, *Hilchos De'os*, 2:3. Tur, *Orach Chayim*, 231). Rather, these acts can be ends in themselves. Every action we do, and every moment we are alive, is another opportunity to become aware of and consciously unify with the Divine Essence that pervades our 'mundane' world.

Eating is perhaps the most elementary and universal act of a physical creature; every living being needs to eat. Eating can be mechanical, pedestrian, and self-serving, or it can be transformative, depending on one's intention. We can eat *L'sheim Shamayim* / 'for the Sake of Heaven', with the intention of giving us strength to serve the Creator through subsequent Torah study and Tefillah, for example. This approach to eating corresponds to the paradigm of the Light of the worlds that are higher on the Chain of Causality. However, we can also eat in a way that the act of eating itself is connection with the Creator, as an act of *B'Chol Derachecha Da'eihu* / "In all your ways know Him." This *Avodah b'Gashmiyus* / physical Divine service, makes a microcosmic Dirah b'Tachtonim for the Creator — the Divine Presence resides in the physical act of eating, here, in the lowest world. This is an actualization of the truth of Ein Od Milvado.

B'Chol Derachecha Da'eihu means that every act becomes an end unto itself, not merely a precursor to some future Mitzvah. Through intending *Yichud* / unification in a physical act, we can turn every action into a 'Divine' activity (*Likutei Sichos*, 3, 907. Other general Chasidic sources speak about this type of *Avodah* / spiritual work and mindset as an Avodah for Tzadikim. *Sefas Emes*, Shavuos, 5656. Yet, the Rebbe (*ibid*, and in many places) explains that this *Atzmiyus* / Essential Avodah is one that is applicable to and possible by all, by everyone, and at any time. This paradigm is specifically connected to Atzmus).

The teaching of Atzmus is one of the great revelations of *Chasidus* / the teachings of the Baal Shem Tov and the subsequent Rebbes, masters, and teachers who developed and articulated Baal Shem Tov's teachings. As the arch of history moved closer and closer toward a world of unity, Moshiach, and redemption, the profound Light of Atzmus began to be more and more revealed.

In this vein, Alter Rebbe once remarked that the teachings of Kabbalah, before the Baal Shem Tov, discussed the Names, meaning, the revelations of Hashem's Infinite Light, whereas Chasidus is נגילה ונשמחה בך – בא"ס עצומ"ה / "to be gladdened and rejoice in *You* — in the Atzmus of the Ein Sof" (Rebbe Maharash, *Toras Shmuel*, 5638, p. 452. Rebbe Rashab, *Toras Shalom*, Yud Tes Kislev, Samach Tes. Note, א"ר אבין אין אנו יודעים במה לשמוח אם ביום אם בהקב"ה בא שלמה ופירש נגילה ונשמחה בך בהקב"ה. *Medrash Rabbah*, Shir HaShirim, 1:32). In other words, whereas the teachings of Kabbalah prior to Chasidus were primar-

ily interested in explaining and drawing down the גילויים /
Giluyim / revelations of Hashem's Infinite Light (which is
a movement from Above to Below, drawing down the Ohr
from Above into the vessels below) Chasidus comes to reveal Atzmus, the ultimate implication of Ein Od Milvado.
Chasidus reveals that there is only *Achdus Hashem* / Divine Oneness, only Atzmus, and our deepest Avodah is to
live with this awesome, life-changing, profound, but simple
truth. In contrast to drawing down revelations of the Infinite Light from higher worlds to this earth, this Avodah
reveals that earth is *already* one with Divine Essence.

While this truth is utterly simple, sometimes to understand,
internalize, and digest sheer simplicity is quite complicated.

YESH / AYIN AND DEEPER YESH: THREE WAYS OF SEEING THE WORLD

Overall, there are three stages or levels of perceiving the
world. The first level is empirically verifiable perception via
our physical senses. This perception suggests to us that the
Yesh HaNivra / physical existence is the true reality of the
world. A deeper level of perception comes about through
inner work, expanded states of consciousness, and a 'third
eye' or 'intuitive' form of knowing, which is that objects are
paradoxically Ayin, empty of independent existence or substance. This perception suggests that the *Ein Sof* / Infinite
Light of Hashem is the true reality. In this conception, the

drama-ridden world of form is insubstantial and transparent, having no intrinsic value other than being a means of revealing Infinite Light. The deepest level of perception, which essentially includes both the above perceptions, is the realization that True Existence, the *Yesh Amiti*, Atzmus is equally 'expressed' in the Yesh HaNivrah and the Ayin. When we live with this level of perception, the world is an end unto itself; it is already transformational, just the way it is.

These three evolving stages of perception, collectively revealed over the course of the unfolding of history and human consciousness, can and are also experienced within every Hisbonenus practice. (The Mitteler Rebbe writes, כללות ענין ההתבוננות בפרטי מדותיו הוא רק כדי שיבא לעצמותו ומהותו דוקא...גם בעיונו בספר הזוהר ובכתבי האריז"ל צ"ל עד"ז דוקא וד"ל. וכאשר מקובל היה א"א מו"ר ז"ל נ"ע בדבר זה מפי הה"מ ז"ל בפירוש גמור וכן שמעתי מפיו / "The general principle of Hisbonenus on the specifics of Hashem's 'Attributes' is only to bring us to *Atzmus* and *Mahus* / Essential Being... Also, when we delve deeply into the teachings of the *Zohar* or the writing of the holy Arizal, this should be our intention, as my master, my father, and my teacher would repeat in the name of his teacher, the holy Magid, and he would clearly explain this. I also heard this from his mouth." *Ma'amrei Admur HaEmtza'i,* Sha'ar HaYichud, p. 112. See also *Magid Devarav L'Yaakov,* Hosafos, 118).

On the level of perception that we live with pre-Hisbonenus (or prior to any other spiritual Avodah), the world appears to us as it is observed with the naked eye. This outer perspective tends to solidify the belief that we are physical selves in a physical world. Through Hisbonenus and other deeper states of consciousness, we come to realize that the Yesh of this world is nothing but a facade that had concealed from us the light and vibration of the Divine animating force that sustains all Creation at every moment. This inner perspective affirms the belief that the world is continuously manifesting from the Unmanifest, arising from selfless formlessness into form. After deep engagement with Hisbonenus, as we reopen our eyes and view the world, we see the world the way Atzmus sees it, as it were. We see beyond the self-emptiness of the world and realize that Hashem is both within physicality and above it. We come to understand something of the incredible miracle that the Yesh NaNivrah is one with the Yesh Amiti, the Divine Self.

Revealing the Yesh of physicality as being one with the Yesh Amiti of Atzmus is to come full circle. After even a lifetime of spiritual journeying into selfless transcendence, we arrive where we began: in a personal, earthly life, but now with a whole new way of seeing it and engaging with it. In this way, Hisbonenus opens us up to true life, allowing us to finally be present with 'what is' rather than rising above it. We come to rest in the pristine clarity of the here and now, grounded in who we are, and naturally flowing with mindful and effective action in this world.

EVERYTHING IS ALIVE

Through the practice of Hisbonenus, we come to behold our surroundings as if for the very first time. Everything seems to have come alive. The colors of the world are more vibrant and rich; red is redder, and green is greener. The sounds in our environment are more vivid and melodious. The scents and aromas are more delicious. The universe seems to be *more.*

In our pre-Hisbonenus state, the Yesh of the world was merely a Yesh; mountains were mountains, and rivers were rivers. In the process of Hisbonenus, while connecting to Ayin and elevated states of consciousness, mountains cease to be mountains, and rivers cease to be rivers. Once we connect with Atzmus and re-engage with the world in a post-Hisbonenus state, mountains are once again mountains, but now they are *real* mountains (expressing the Yesh HaAmiti), and rivers are *real* rivers, alive, vibrant, and *Glantzik* / sparkling.*

---

* The path of Atzmus in Avodah is to live with this third level of awareness. As explained earlier, although the Avodah of *B'Chol Derachecha Da'eihu* / "In all your ways know Him" is the loftiest path of Atzmus, it is also the Avodah B'Gashmiyus, in this world. And precisely due to this, and being connected to Atzmus, this Avodah is applicable to everyone and at any time. In this way, this injunction of Shlomo HaMelech in Mishlei alludes to the revelation of Chasidus, which makes the highest levels of Deveikus accessible to anyone who will commit to it. It is a prominent teaching of the Baal Shem Tov that comes into fruition with the teaching of the Seventh Rebbe, the embodiment of Malchus (the lowest level, without its own light), and hence it is also Atzmus (the 'highest' level, beyond light). In the Avodah of (Malchus and) Atz-

mus, devotion and presence are most dominant, not intellectualism. In fact, intellectualism can separate one from their actual experience. The path of Atzmus is being in total presence and mindfulness with every experience. It is being fully present and engaged in a holy way with every individual person and every area of life. Whoever you are encountering, you are fully present for them, and whatever you are doing, you are there fully. This posture of Atzmus can be reflected in Avodas HaTefillah, especially in this generation, as revealed in the living teachings of the Rebbe. The Rebbe once said, regarding Avodas HaTefillah, the inner work of prayer, which is deeply connected with Hisbonenus, that א איד שטעלט-זיך צו דאוונען / "A Jew *stands up* to *Daven* / pray" (Heard from Reb Yoel Kahan). In Yiddish, שטעלט-זיך צו actually means more than just 'standing up'; it means to ready yourself, to gather yourself, like a soldier who straightens himself out as the commanding officer enters the room. Standing up is a posture of complete presence and focus. Contemplative Tefillah in the Avodah of Atzmus is not an intellectual form of contemplation. Nor is it necessarily to be practiced in the context of protracted or lengthy prayer, although that can be praiseworthy and very helpful. The distinguishing attribute of this Avodah is rather the total presence, unwavering focus, and depth of being. In many private audiences (*Yechidus*), the Rebbe told various Chasidm that as they go on Shelichus into the various parts of the world, they should not forget the importance of Avodas HaTefillah. (Note, *Hayom Yom*, Iyyar 23. "The beginning of one's decline…is the lack of Avoda in Tefillah. Everything becomes dry and cold…The atmosphere itself becomes crass. Needless to say, one is totally incapable of influencing others"). Yet, the Rebbe instructed, Avodas HaTefillah does not always have to involve איבעריקע אריכות / excessive length (*Shelichus K'Hilchasah*, p. 26). In other words, in the Avodas HaTefillah of the earlier generations, the length of Hisbonenus and Davening was a hallmark of their dedication and achievement, and indeed, many Chasidim Davened for hours on end. However, now, the most crucial element is simply to stand in the reality of Atzmus with presence and awareness, no matter the length of Davening. Here are the Previous Rebbe's words on the subject. גזע חב"ד מיינען אז עבודת התפלה מיינט אז מען בא‎דארף מאריך זיין שעות ארוכות, אבער באמת איז / דער חסידות'ר דאוונען ... מאנט ניט דעם כמות פון דאוונען נאר דעם איכות פון דאוונען "Chabad Chasidim think that 'Davening' means that you need to spend long hours, but really, Chasidic Davening…is not the quantity of prayer but the quality of prayer": *Sefer HaSichos 5701*, p. 42.

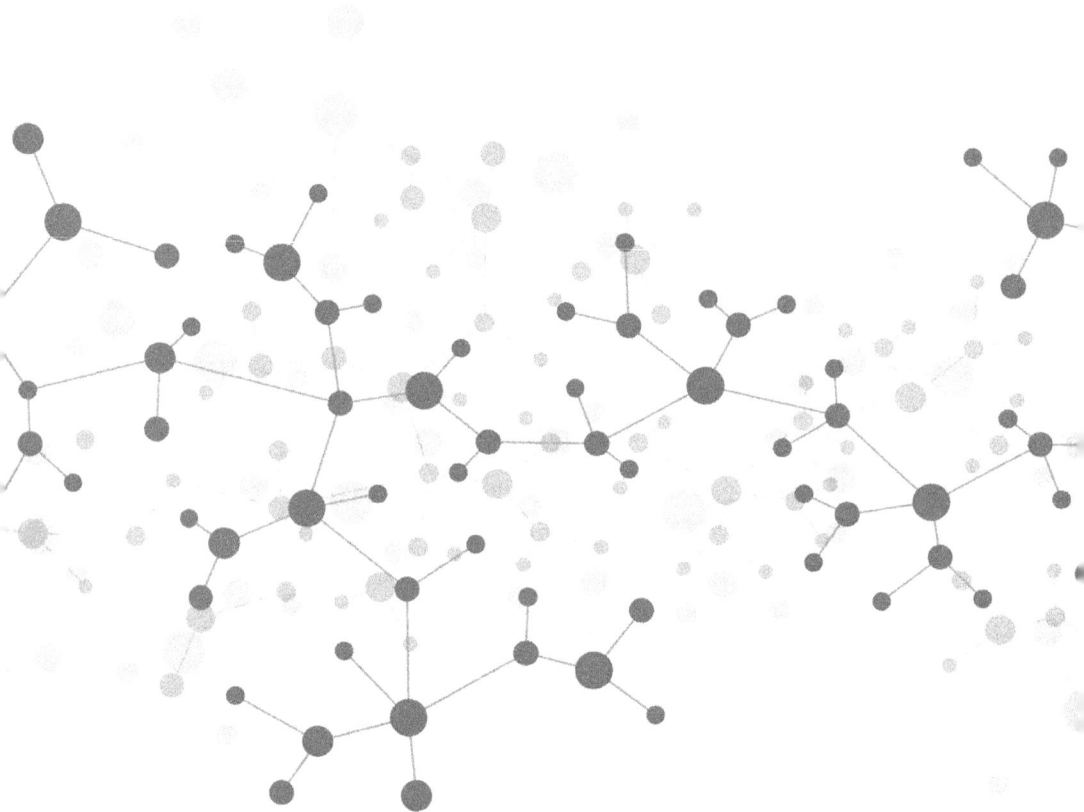

CHAPTER 11

THE ACTUAL HISBONENUS PRACTICE

THE PRACTICE OF HISBONENUS CAN BE A STAND-ALONE ACTIVITY, OR PRACTICED BEFORE DAVENING / PRAYING, or even while Davening. Following are practical guidelines for Hisbonenus, culling from everything that was explored above.

Keep in mind that the importance of this practice, as with all spiritual practices and paths of self-development, lies not only in the destination but also in the journey itself. Chances are that the deepest levels of Deveikus will be elusive, yet the milestones on the road are also highly essential. Whether your contemplation just arouses emotions in the heart, or the effect extends all the way into emotions of the mind, whether you experience subtle feelings or dramatic ones, or even transcend all feelings and emotions, each level and quality has its own reward and should serve to encourage your progress. If you throw yourself into refining your capacity for this practice, after some time, כולי האי ואולי / maybe, just maybe, you will slip into a state of genuine Deveikus.

STEP ONE

The first thing you must do is check your level of commitment. The degree of your success will be commensurate with your investment of focus, energy, and your will to take the Hisbonenu session as far as possible within the given timeframe. You must dedicate yourself anew before each individual Hisbonenus session, as well as dedicate yourself to your long-term goals. This sacred discipline requires yearning, willpower, mindfulness, and presence. Confirm your ability to commit before moving on to Step Two.

STEP TWO

Establish an opportune time to practice Hisbonenus. Normally, it is performed around Davening times, and particularly before *Shacharis* / morning prayers. Regardless of the time of day, it is important that you are not tired, overwhelmed, or unfocused and that no internal or external conditions will cause distractions. Ensure that you can be available mentally and energetically during the length of the session.

The time period allocated could be five minutes or five hours; the main thing is to dedicate a certain block of time completely to the practice and aspire to practice consistently within that duration.

STEP THREE

Find a location that is conducive to conducting a process that is incompatible with disturbances and interruptions. Make it 'your' space by familiarizing yourself with it and establishing it as safe and comfortable.

If done in a *Shul* / synagogue, try to use your *Makom Kavua* / your established seat within the Shul where you pray. Make sure that the building is open and available for a period of time before the beginning of the communal service, without other activities in the sanctuary, such as classes or cleaning or maintenance work that would interrupt you.

Before you begin, make sure there are no internal or physical distractions, such as needing the restroom or needing to think about an outstanding problem in life or at work. Certainly, eliminate any distractions from electronic devices. If you have a phone, put it on 'silent' or shut it down — if possible, it would be best not to have your phone with you at all.

STEP FOUR

Choose a *Ma'amar* / Chasidic discourse, or a topic within a Ma'amar, that you wish to contemplate. Select a text that speaks to you and resonates since "A person should always learn Torah in a place where his heart desires." The topic you choose does not have to be etched in stone; if today it is not speaking to you, move on and try another Ma'amar or another topic.

STEP FIVE

Take the topic of the Ma'amar you have chosen, or a section or the entire Ma'amar, and delve into it with the goal of fully understanding it intellectually, letting the words and the insights fill your mind completely. Then zero in on the kernel of the idea (Chochmah) and ponder it in finer detail, using your power of *Binah* / understanding. Explore the thought in its breadth or implications, and in its length or examples and parables.

As your entire mind is engaged, allow any innovative, creative, or intuitive understandings to arise; utilize your entire mind to fully internalize its meanings, perhaps in relation to world history and the needs of Klal Yisrael, and definitely in relation to your own life. Think about the personal implications of the idea and what it demands of you in terms of your actions and perspective. To the best of your ability, identify emotionally, mentally, and even physically with the idea.

STEP SIX

Find a sentence or idea that summarizes the idea or that strongly draws you (such as Ein Od Milvado), and allow the ideas that you have been contemplating to be distilled into that one thought. Now *feel* the quality of that thought; let it take hold of you, and move from an intellectual focus to the felt experience of the insight. Let the feeling of the energy or light of the insight envelop you. Let yourself be suffused and permeated by it.

STEP SEVEN

Now, turn the contemplation even further inwards with *Simas Lev* / placing the energy or light of the insight upon your heart, specifically. Allow that energy or light to drop or filter down into the heart, and stay alert to sensing any emotion, ecstasy, or rapture that is aroused in response. Let the heart feel whatever it feels, allowing emotions to flow and move through you.

STEP EIGHT

Stay present with your emotions, letting go of any associated dramatic feelings, imagery, words, melodies, or physical expressions until the external layer of emotion subsides and recedes, leaving a quieter, lighter, more subtle, refined, or ethereal sense of ecstasy or emotion. Place your attention on this 'emotion of the mind' and lose yourself in it.

Continue to follow these 'emotions of the mind' as they become more and more quiet and subtle and draw you more deeply inward toward silence or stillness. At some point, even this subtle experience should disappear, leaving you in a state of pure awareness. This is the doorway into the utter immobility and timelessness of *Bitul* / 'selfless being' and *Deveikus* / union, mystical union.

Nothing should be done to enter Bitul and Deveikus; these states will happen without any form of human choice or agency. There is no need for anxiety or concern about the passage of time; the self, along with its sense of time, space, and cognition, will remain quiescent until Divinely guided, at the right moment, to come back.

STEP NINE

Emerge gently from Bitul, and ground yourself in the body. Feel the seat under you, the weight of the Siddur, or the solidity of the *Shtender* / lectern. Notice that the Divine Presence is within all of these physical and perceptual phenomena as *Atzmus* / Essence. Now Deveikus is revealed in words and physical actions, as a *Dirah b'Tachnonim* / a dwelling for the Infinite in this material world.

If it is time to Daven, begin slowly, remaining open to 'invitations' from the text of the Siddur back into spiritual absorption. During Davening, there may be countless movements of *Ratzo v'Shov* / 'running' into transcendent stillness, and 'returning' back into the physical expressions and Divine actions of Atzmus. A word or associated teaching may trigger a sudden shower of rapture or emotion, the white space on the page may somehow draw you into silence, you may become immobilized in Deveikus again, and you may simply Daven without spiritual feeling or drama, but from the deep realization of omnipresent Essence. Whether you are ascending or descending or simply Davening, *be* that Essence as you Daven.

Traversing the nine steps outlined above, you may have experienced all three states of 'emotion'. The initial emotional state, after fully contemplating Ein Od Milvado, for example, comes from the thoughts of your mind arousing your heart. These are 'external emotions' that may be dramatic or rapturous.

A second, more elevated, and subtle state of emotion or ecstasy is experienced when emotions are experienced not primarily in the heart or body but in the mind. Then, if you slip into Deveikus, you enter the third level of emotion in which you do not actually 'experience' them. In this level, the self has become lost in thought and ecstasy, to the point that there is no sense of separate existence. Without an individual to feel or be aware, there is no 'feeling' of ecstasy. Only af-

238 THE MEDITATION SERIES

ter emerging from this state, when the 'feeler' returns, is this recognized as a sort of emotion. This is similar to waking up from sleep; in deep sleep there is no sense of being a person who is asleep, for 'you' are unconscious. Only after waking, when the mind and sense of self and separation comes back, can we say, 'I slept soundly.'

The path of any form of contemplation begins with Chochmah, the kernel of the idea that was studied, to Binah, in which we analyze the idea, and then to Da'as, application and identification with the idea, and then aroused emotions (whether *Chesed* / love, *Gevurah* / awe, *Tiferes* / beauty, *Netzach* / confidence, *Hod* / humility, or Yesod / a gathering or focused unification of the above emotions).

After the external energies of these emotions play out and recede, the movement is reversed as *Ohr Chozer* / reflective light. From the aroused state in the heart, the emotions return to the mind as more subtle and quiet experiences. They ascend through Da'as and Binah, until they are exceedingly subtle and transparent thought-forms in 'higher Chochmah'. Here, we 'feel' the Ayin within the thought, the transparency and light of the idea 'before' it descends into language, the primal 'substance' of the thought prior to letters and words. This empties out into the Divine animating force, the luminous, formless, unbridled no-thing-ness, that gives rise to all vessels, forms, and thoughts. Then, all trace of thought and form vanishes into pure awareness until our very sense of existence vanishes into a selfless, transcendent state of Ayin. *Im*

Yirtzeh Hashem / If the Creator wills, we are then absorbed into motionless Divine Deveikus.

STEP TEN

When it is the Divine will that we return from Deveikus back into physical and mental 'existence', we begin to live, think, emote and act 'within' the open Beingness of Essence. With this final stage comes a new way of seeing the world, called *Histaklus*. Having rendered the internal static of *Yesh* / ego, which usually prevents people from being with life, others, and Hashem, you can now experience and be at one with the object you are viewing. Having lost your sense of separateness, you have unified with the unity of HaKadosh Baruch Hu.

Through Hisbonenus, you have become unified with Divine Ayin within thought and within Creation itself. Yet, this condition does not negate your existence; on the contrary, you *find yourself* through that *Bitul* / egolessness. Reaching a state of Ayin is submitting your natural animal instincts to your selfless Divine Self, trading limitations for limitless illumination. Through this submission, you have become truly free and empowered as an effective co-creator, making this world a better and brighter place; co-creating a dwelling for Hashem in this world.

Hisbonenus has come full circle. Having implemented the power of this practice, you have discovered and aligned your being with actions that express who you really are. You have become one with your true self, the Divine soul that animates your life, decisively having let go of the false self that manifested as the ego and which derived its identity from externalities such as possessions, titles, money, power, and so forth. You have become more authentic.

Now, you can truly open your eyes and see the world for the very first time.

APPENDIX A

TWO MODES OF HISBONENUS:

GENERAL / PASSIVE VS. SPECIFIC / ACTIVE

Below is a short Ma'amar / discourse by the Alter Rebbe (Ma'amarei Admur HaZaken, Inyanim, Hisbonenus, p. 133-134) on the nature of Hisbonenus, in Hebrew with a loose translation.

התבוננות כללית ופרטית

בנידון ההתבוננות מהותה ואיכותה, יש ב' דרכים בה הא' התבוננות בכלל להעמיק הדעת רק בתמצית ענין כללי דהיינו רק היוצא מן תוכן הדבר איך שהוא בטל כו' והעמקה זו היא דייקא צמצום המוח ולא הרחבות כלל כי צריך לשהות כחצי שעה על דיבור א' כמו מאין ליש וכיוצא איך ומה הוא עד שיבא לכלל דמיון מפני שמיגע דייקא כוחות חיצוני' כדי להפשיט הענין מן ההגשמה עד שיהי' בבחי' רוחני' ממש כלומר דברי רוח ממש ורוח תשאם

והתעיף עיניך בו ואיננו כו' ובשיבוש זה נשתבשו רבים מההמון בדמיונות
שוא כו' ולזה הדרך א"צ שמיעה בה כי די בב' וג' דברים בלבד. וד"ל,
סימנים גשמי' לדרך זו תנועת הגופני' בדחיקה וקצת רתיחה בלב, והעדר
.טרדת המחשב' וביטולה ועוצם הרגשת העניין בעצמו

Regarding the essence and the quality of Hisbonenus, there are generally two paths. A) The first path involves settling one's mind on the external general idea, that is (for example) on the consequence of the thoughts of how beingness does not truly exist (independently). In this mode, the contemplator contracts his mind, and in no way does he attempt to increase the breadth of the understanding. Here, he needs to settle and fixate his awareness for approximately a half hour on one singular point, such as creation *ex nihilo*, until he comes to a condition where he experiences imaginary airy-like visions — a result of utilizing only the superficial prowess of the intellect, his surface levels, to divest the contemplation of any concrete definition. (This continues) until (in the later stages of this process, he) perceives the concept as pure spirit (which is related to what the prophet says,) "And they will be swept away by the wind," and "When you set your eyes on it, it is already gone" (*Mishlei*, 23:5). It is (due) precisely to this delusional condition that many have blundered, having become confused by their own imagination and the like (that is, confusing imaginary movements with genuine ones). This path does not need further detailing. With the slightest of indications, this type of Hisbonenus is recognizable, such as the physical manifestations of this method are A) bodily tensions (such as jerking or nervous twitching), B) a slightly faster heartbeat (escalating and decreasing), C) less disturbances of thoughts (an emptiness of thoughts), D) thoughts that do arise dissipate immediately, and E) an increased measure of feeling about the topic of contemplation.

והדרך הב' הדעת באמת והוא התרחבות המוח ולא צמצומה, ואופן העמקה זו בהעמקת הפשט ממש בנגלה דהיינו דייקא טרדת המחש' ממש שזהו אינו אלא הרחבת ענינים רבים ופרטי' ולא בענין א' כלל וסימן לזה הוא ההיפוך מעניין תנועת כוחות חיצוני' שבגוף אלא רק תנועת כחות הנפש בשכל דייקא ועוצם טרדת המח' עד שלא ירגיש בעצמותו, ומאד רחוק מן הדמיון באיכות הדבר אלא אדרב' ילביש במשלים הרבה עד כי יתפס הדבר גם בעין השכל האנושי כו', וגם הסימן לזה תשוקת התחדשות השגות ובכל תיבה ותיבה יש כוונה מיוחדת פרטיית דייקא ואז ישכח על עצמותו לגמרי מפני שהמוח שליט על הלב לגמרי וד"ל.

The second path demands genuinely deep comprehension, a broadening of the intellect, and not a withdrawal of it. This process increases one's awareness of the simple and revealed meaning of the contemplation, meaning, specifically and literally exerting the mind fully, which can only occur when one elaborates on the concepts in their many details and ramifications rather than settling on one single point. A sign of this is the opposite of external bodily movement (or nervous twitching), rather an internal movement of the mind within the thought process. The intensity of this contemplation is such that one does not experience any sensation of self, and he is very distant from any imaginary vision (in stark contrast to the first, more passive mode of

Hisbonenus, which was replete with imaginary visions and futile delusions). Here, he draws the idea into many metaphors until it is thoroughly comprehended, even to the eye of the human (educated) mind. In addition, another indication (that one is truly and deeply involved in this second path of Hisbonenus) is the great desire and yearning to unveil new insights and to expose in very fine detail other implicit and specific meanings. And then (through this method), he will become entirely oblivious to the self since the mind's total preoccupation with the idea completely overshadows any sensations of the heart. (This is all) based on the principle that the mind naturally controls the heart.

בנידון ההתפעלות מן ההתבוננות לפי הדרך הראשון ההתפעלות מורגשת מאד כי מייגע להביא הדבר בעצמותו דייקא מפני שהשמוח פנוי וא״כ התפעלות זו באה בשיתוף מב' דברים מעניני אלקי' ומעצמותו במה שמידבק כו' ואזי נעש' יש גדול ורחוק ממש היפוך אלקי' כו' וקרוב זה לדרך הישן וד״ל. ולפי הדרך הב' ההתפעלות באה רק מצד אלקים בלבד כי אינו מייגע כלל להדביק א״ע אלא טרוד בהתבוננות בלבד וממילא מתפעל במוחו והשגתו מפני ההשגה ולא מפני הקירוב כו' ואינו מרגיש כלל התפעלות זאת מצד שאין לעצמו חלק בה כלל כו' והוא ענין לאסתכלא ביקרא דמלכא ולא יתיר, שהחיצוני' בורחים מזה לפי שנא' לא יחפוץ כסיל בתבונה עצמה להתפעל מחמתה בלבד רק כשבאה בהתפעלות מורגשת שהוא בהתגלות לבו לפי שזהו רחוק מאלקות כו'. והסימנים לב' התפעלות הללו להתפעל' הראשונה נידבק כל מיני גסות והוללות ותאוות רעות וכו', ולהתפעלות הב' נדבק כל מיני שפלות אמיתית שלא להרגיש בעצמו בשום מעלה ורחוק מאד מהגשמה גופני' במדות הרעות בכעס ונצחון ולילך אחר הוללות כו' ותמיד נבזה בעיניו נמאס ולא מחזיק טיבותא לנפשי' ומשים א״ע כאלו אינו כו' וד״ל.

The ecstasy and the arousal that arises via the first path of Hisbonenus is quite powerful and charged, with strong feelings. This occurs because the meditative process is purposely geared toward bringing elation to the self. Since, in this case, the mind (the intellectual capacity) is empty, as a result, the ecstasy that is generated is sourced in an admixture of both the self (the ego) and the Divine. Thus, he becomes even more egoistic and self-centered, and ultimately he is isolated and comes in direct opposition to Divinity. On some level, this is similar to that of a sleeping state (when the conscious, rational mind is as asleep, it does not mean one is closer to spirit; often, the subconscious mind continues to burp up all sorts of detritus that it needs to unburden itself from). In the second path, however, the ecstasy is purely transcendent and Divine. Here, he is not involved in seeking to become "one" (seeking to experience ecstasy); rather, his sole occupation is the Hisbonenus, and as a *by-product*, he becomes intellectually (and emotionally) aroused. Consequently, he is not enthralled by the experience of ecstasy since he (his sense of self) was never part of the equation. This is the idea of "gazing at the Glory of the King and nothing else," from which the superficial shy away. As it is written, "The fool does not desire [true] comprehension" and to be aroused accordingly. What he seeks is to 'feel' ecstasy in an open, revealed heart, which is distant from Divinity (as there is still separateness).

Another indication of their differences is that in the first path, the Hisbonenus (may) cause him to become more arrogant and flippant, with an increased appetite for sensual pleasures (while the converse is true in the second path). In the second path, the Hisbonenus calls forth and brings to him all forms of humility; he will no longer esteem himself higher than anyone else, and he will become more removed from bodily over-indulgence. He will distance himself ever more from negative character traits like anger, oppressiveness, callousness, and the like. In addition, he will (from then onwards) regard (negative characteristics within himself) as repulsive and deplorable. He will not glorify himself for personal accomplishments; in fact, he will consider himself as if non-existent (a genuine level of Bitul. Yet, keep in mind that the idea of Bitul does not translate into denial or loss of individuality. To the contrary, Bitul liberates the spirit, allowing for genuine spontaneity and unlimited creativity. Bitul is not thinking of yourself as less, but rather, 'thinking less' about yourself).

APPENDIX B

YISHUV HADA'AS /
SETTLED CONSCIOUSNESS

FOR THE MOST PART, THE QUALITY OF OUR DA'AS IS DEFINED BY OUR PERSONAL PERSPECTIVE AND CHOICES REGARDING THE 'CONTENT' OF OUR LIFE. This is *Da'as Tachton* / the lower level Da'as that we live with in the minutiae of day to day existence. There is a deeper part of ourselves that 'observes' Da'as Tachton. Hence, Da'as is interchangeable with *Keser* / Crown, 'superconsciousness' knowing. Da'as on the level of Keser is called *Da'as Elyon* / higher level Da'as. It is the detached witness above all states, perspectives and experiences (the word *Keser* has the same letters as *Kares* / cut off, removed, detached; also, the highest level of Keser is *Atik*, which comes from the word 'ancient' or *Ne'etak* / removed). It is the uninvolved experiencer, the witness of all states, contents and contexts.

An insightful term for Da'as Elyon is *Da'as HaNe'elam* / hidden Da'as, because as the 'unseen seer', the 'unknown knower', it is always hidden from view. It is the all-transcending pure consciousness above all *Yesh* / self, world, and all observable phenomena, and even all theoretically observable phenomena. As the observer of everything, it cannot be observed as a thing; it is *Ayin* / no-thing. Yet, it can be known, not as an object, but by *being* it, as the pure subject.

The word Da'as has the same letters as the word *Eid* / witness; from the standpoint of Da'as HaNe'elam we are always witnessing life as the 'Eid' of our life. By witnessing both the state of undistracted presence and the state of distraction, Da'as HaNe'elam is the impartial, unaffected common ground for both. Yet, it is of a different order as well. It is off the map. It is not part of worldly struggles or spiritual games.

Since Da'as HaNe'elam is 'above' all perspectives, choices, parts, identification, and sense of agency, self-awareness as this level has to be given, imparted from Above. We cannot cultivate it or tune into it from our perspective as a Yesh, as Yesh can only grasp Yesh. The opening words of the prayer for Da'as in the Amidah point to this fact: *Atah Chonein le-Adam Da'as* / "You grace the human being with knowing...." The final letters of these words, *Atah* (Hei) *Chonein* (Nun) *le-Adam* (Mem) *Da'as* (Tav), spell the word *Matanah* / gift. Our knowingly viewing life from the essence of consciousness is a gift that only HaKadosh Baruch Hu can give. Only the Ultimate Knower, the Creator of awareness itself, can endow a creature with the *Koach* / power of consciously 'being' the detached witness and 'awareness' over his life and world.

YISHUV HADA'AS

The Torah's definition of Da'as is 'intimate connection', as in, "And Adam 'knew' Chavah." This is clearly not the detached, uninvolved observer of Da'as but rather a more inclusive type of Da'as. The Torah describes the observer of life not as outside of life but both outside and *inside* life. It is not only an aloof, detached state of mind but also an *engaged* observer. From this perspective, *Yishuv HaDa'as* / 'settled consciousness' means the impersonal Da'as is *Yishuv* / 'dwelling' or settling within the world and personal relationships. It is a type of relaxed presence of 'knowing' that unifies the witness self with the present moment that is arising and this moment's content and context. This Da'as is both transcendent and intimate with phenomena, it is a revelation of the *Etzem HaDa'as* / the essence of consciousness', or *Da'as HaAmiti* / the true Da'as.

Wherever there is a duality, such as 'being present' vs. 'not being present', we ourselves are the Da'as HaAmiti, the 'essential' third dynamic that reconciles those two opposites by transcending and including them both. *Da'as* a general term for "the third that reconciles the two"; it is our selfless Self, our authentic nondual state which reconciles all conflicts by transcending yet intimately engaging with objects of knowledge, unifying them in the simple fact of witnessing them.

A state of mind that is settled, disentangled from the drama of life, and yet also unified with life, is a paradox. To be both detached and attached is to be viscerally attuned to whatever is happening in the here and now, in unity with the experience — and yet in a sense also outside experience, for the subject of experience is not an object in experience. Even while being 'intimate' with the content and the context of life, Da'as HaAmiti is not submerged nor exiled in the world of Yesh; it remains ever pure and free, the *'Ayin'* beyond *Hasagah* / comprehension, as it were. Whereas there is an aspect of Da'as that is *Mavdil* / disconnective, and there is an aspect of Da'as that is *Mechaber* / connective, Da'as HaAmiti, is not one of these polarizations; it is both.

On the one hand, Da'as as a power *beyond* one's intellect (*Sefer HaMa'amarim ETeR* (5670), pp. 133-134. Rebbe Rayatz, *Sefer HaMa'amarim, 5688*, p. 85. Hence, sometimes, much later, one finally understands the reasons for one's choices. *Sefer HaMa'amarim, 5700*, p. 156). It is beyond 'human' faculties, so to speak. And yet, on the other hand, Da'as is connected with Yishuv — in fact, Da'as *is* Yishuv, as Chazal tell us, בעשרה דברים נברא העולם: בחכמה ובתבונה ובדעת / "With ten things Hashem created the world: with Chochmah, Tevunah and Da'as" (*Chagigah*, 12a).... Rashi comments, דעת – ישוב / 'Da'as means Yishuv, being settled.' If it is *only* transcendent, it is not 'true' Da'as.

Yishuv HaDa'as is exemplified by Yoseph HaTzadik. As the viceroy of Egypt, and having earlier conquered his lusts, he is aloof, undisturbed, and *Ne'elam* / hidden from his brothers when they arrive at the palace. Yet, when the time is right, he descends from this 'transcendent' state and reveals himself as *Mechaber* / intimately connected with his brothers, crying, "I am Yoseph! Is my father alive?" and embracing them and weeping with them. He is able to gather and reconnect with his family precisely through his separation from them as the viceroy of Egypt.

This is why Yoseph symbolizes the *Tikun* / healing of Da'as. When human beings are from *Eitz HaDa'as Tov v'Ra* / the Tree of Da'as that is entangled in 'good' and bad', they internalize a perspective of being a separate Yesh, enmeshed in the struggle of clashing opposites, without transcendence or presence. Chavah became greatly unsettled and said, "The snake *Hishi'ani* / deceived me!" *Hishi'ani* has the letters of *HaYesh Ani* / 'I am the separate ego.' In other words, 'The snake convinced me to see myself as if I am an object of experience, I am content, not a being of Da'as or with access to Ayin.' Yoseph HaTzadik, through his Yishuv

HaDa'as, allows humanity to see ourselves as whole and undivided, including both Yesh and Ayin, both peacefully disengaged and compassionately engaged at the same time.

There is an oral tradition that a great ambition of the holy Baal Shem Tov was to teach people how to be in a state of perfect Da'as, how people can untangle themselves from emotions and even bodily sensations so that they could be present and mindfully, peacefully observe life. However, he did not wish to guide people to become totally detached, aloof, inert or impersonal, rather how to attain *Yishuv Ha-Da'as* / settled mind. He knew that only by becoming free from psycho-physical entanglements, people can have the inner freedom to experience real *Yishuv HaDa'as* / settling of the mind and to apply it in action in the world.

LEARNING THE ART OF
BEING PRESENT

Let us explore the true Da'as that the Baal Shem Tov taught, and that the path of Chasidus continues to facilitate in people. How can we at once step into full presence with the world from a place of freedom from entanglement in the world?

It is easy for human beings to get entangled in thoughts and lose all sense of Yishuv HaDa'as; thoughts of anxieties, angers, worldly desires and self-importance all draw us into an unconscious state of reactivity. Our thoughts, like the snake, can suggest that we are a Yesh, a being without Da'as. However, the truth is, *Machshavah* / thought is nothing but a *Levush* / a 'garment' that enclothes and lightly covers the 'content' of our Chochmah, Binah and Da'as.

Again, by nature, Da'as is linked to our 'superconsciousness', which is *Keser* / Crown, and our subtle inner space of Atzilus, above all opposites. From this open space of knowing, we see that all is one, empty of all thought, our inner dimension of *Ayin* / no-thing-ness and perfect, selfless serenity. From this perspective, we are completely untangled and free of conflict and desire. And yet, we are disconnected from the world and other people.

How is this serene presence and Yishuv HaDa'as cultivated? It is actually not through practices of letting go of distractions, nor is it trying to 'force' the mind to stop thinking, settle down, and be present. Trying to stop 'not being present', and trying to strengthen presence directly, both just intensify the swing between opposites. Every time you become powerfully present, distraction comes swinging back with equal power.

The only way off this pendulum and this exhausting clash of opposites is A) to acknowledge the fact that thoughts are just a garment, B) to simply go off the map to Da'as HaNe'elam, the knowingness that sees both presence and distraction — and finally, C) to settle back into life and re-engaging intimately with people and thoughts, carrying the calm into the world.

Whenever you feel that you are not being present, stop, turn inward and take notice. Look at your sense of being you. Who is looking at 'you'? It is *Da'as* / pure knowingness. This is *Da'as HaNe'elam*, the unmanifest *Eid* / witness prior to all manifestations. Here, there is no entanglement with thoughts, emotions, or relationships; it is a form of *Bitul* / ego-nullification. All is peaceful, yet you are not connected and engaged with people. Thus, the final step is to turn outwards again. Carry your peace into connection with people, the world, and your thoughts.

This 'practice' is not something you need to believe in. Verify it for yourself through direct experience.

APPROBATION

Letter from Rabbi Shlomo Zarchi,
head Mashpia /spiritual teacher and mentor of 770,
the Central Chabad Yeshivah of Tomchei Temimim
Lubavitch

לכבוד ידידי ...העוסק בהפצת המעיינות הרה"ח... דובער שי' פינסאן

ראיתי דפי ספרו בענין ההתבוננות ובודאי יביא הדבר תועלת ויעורר
התמימים ואנש לעסוק בהתבוננות בדא"ח בפרט שהרבה מבקשים זה
לכן אמינא לפעלא טבא יישר חילא ויחזק ה' את ידו להמשיך לפעול
פעולות טובות לתועלת מבקשי ה' לנח"ר ורצו"ק אדמו"ר ויתברך ממעון
הברכות על פועלו הטוב ויחיש גואלנו ויעמידנו בקרן אורה

בכבוד ובברכה
בידידות שלמה הכהן זרחי

ENGLISH TRANSLATION

To my dear friend … who is engaged in spreading the wellsprings of Chasidus, the honorable Rabbi …DovBer Pinson

I have seen the pages of your book on Hisbonenus / contemplation, and it will surely be beneficial and inspire the students and people to engage in contemplation of Chassidic teachings, especially since many are seeking this.

Therefore, I say to you, may you be firm in your strength, and may Hashem strengthen your hand to continue performing good deeds for the benefit of those who are Mevakshei Hashem / seekers of Hashem, to the satisfaction and will of the Rebbe.

May you be blessed from the source of blessings for your good work, and may our Redeemer hasten and place us in a bright place.

With respect and blessings, and in friendship,
Shlomo HaKohen Zarchi

Other Books by Rav Pinson

Rav Pinson on the Torah

AWAKENINGS:
Drawing Life from the Weekly Torah Reading

The deeper teachings of the Torah reveal to us that the weekly Torah reading is connected to the unique energetic properties of that week. Every Torah portion, and thus every week, radiates with a particular quality, a distinct energy that, when understood and received, can bring tremendous guidance and assistance to every facet of our lives.

Delving into the weekly Torah reading and uncovering its overarching theme allows us to apply the power available on that week in our practical life.

We can learn how to harness the Ko'ach, power, of each unique Torah reading to expand consciousness, overcome challenges, gain control of our lives, and come to learn how to serve Hashem, self and others more mindfully, productively and effectively.

Weaving together the various facets of Torah interpretation, from the most esoteric (Kabbalah) and mystical (Chassidus) to the straightforward literal meaning (Peshat), this book is a multi-dimensional tapestry of practical, allegorical, philosophical, and mystical ideas and implications.

Rav Pinson on the Life Cycle

A BOND FOR ETERNITY
Understanding the Bris Milah

What is the Bris Milah – the covenant of circumcision? What does it represent, symbolize and signify? This book provides an in depth and sensitive review of this fundamental Mitzvah. In this little masterpiece of wisdom – profound yet accessible —the deeper meaning of this essential rite of passage and its eternal link to the Jewish people, is revealed and explored.

UPSHERNISH: THE FIRST HAIRCUT
Exploring the Laws, Customs & Meanings
of a Boy's First Haircut

What is the meaning of Upsherin, the traditional celebration of a boy's first haircut at the age of three? Why is a boy's hair allowed to grow freely for his first three years? What is the deeper import of hair in all its lengths and varieties? What is the meaning of hair coverings? Includes a guide to conducting an Upsherin ceremony.

THE JEWISH WEDDING:
A Guide to the Rituals and Traditions
of the Wedding Ceremony

The Jewish Wedding: A Guide to the Rituals and Traditions of the Wedding Ceremony.
This guide is based on the teachings of Torah, Talmud, Medrash, Zohar, Halacha, Poskim, Kabbalah and Chassidus. By quoting these teachings, we actively draw down the 'presence' of these holy souls who revealed these teachings, thus extending blessings to the bride and groom and all in attendance at the Chupa.

THE MYSTERY OF KADDISH
Understanding the Mourner's Kaddish

The Mystery of Kaddish is an in-depth exploration into the Mourner's Prayer. Throughout Jewish history, there have been many rites and rituals associated with loss and mourning, yet none have prevailed quite like the Mourner's Kaddish Prayer, which has become the definitive ritual of mourning. The book explores the source of this prayer and deconstructs the meaning to better understand the grieving process and how the Kaddish prayer supports and uplifts the bereaved through their own personal journey to healing.

THE BOOK OF LIFE AFTER LIFE

What is a soul? What happens to us after we physically die?
What is consciousness, and can it survive without a physical brain?
Can we remember our past lives?
Do near-death experiences prove immortality?
What is Gan Eden? Resurrection?
Exploring the possibility of surviving death, the near-death experience and a glimpse into what awaits us after this life.
(This book is an updated and expanded version of the book; Jewish Wisdom of the Afterlife)

Rav Pinson on Kabbalah

REINCARNATION AND JUDAISM
The Journey of the Soul

A fascinating analysis of the concept of Gilgul / Reincarnation. Dipping into the fountain of ancient wisdom and modern understanding, this book addresses and answers such basic questions as: What is reincarnation? Why does it occur? And how does it affect us personally?

INNER RHYTHMS
The Kabbalah of Music

Exploring the inner dimension of sound and music, and particularly, how music permeates all aspects of life. The topics range from Deveikus/Unity and Yichudim/Unifications, to the more personal issues, such as Simcha/Happiness and Marirus/ sadness.

THIRTY–TWO GATES OF WISDOM
Into the Heart of Kabbalah & Chassidus

What is Kabbalah? And what are the differences between the theoretical, meditative, magical and personal Kabbalistic teachings? What are the four paths of interpreting the teachings of the ARIzal? What did Chassidus teach? These are some of the fundamental issues expanded upon in this text. And then, more specifically, why are there so many names of G-d and what do they represent? What are the key concepts of these deeper teachings?

The book explores the grand narrative of the great chain of reality, how there was and is a movement from the Infinite Oneness of Hashem to a world of (apparent) duality and multiplicity.

———————

PASSPORT TO KABBALAH
A Journey of Inner Transformation

Life is a journey full of ups and downs, inside-outs, and unexpected detours. There are times when we think we know exactly where we want to be headed, and other times when we are so lost we don't even know where we are. This slim book provides readers with a passport of sorts to help them through any obstacles along their path of self-refinement, reflection, and self-transformation.

———————

THE SEVEN PRINCIPLES:
Towards a Life of Meaning and Purpose
A book on the Seven Mitzvos of Noach

These seven principles will open you up to a new and empowering way of thinking and being in this world.

It will inspire you to engage in life proactively with openness, care, clarity of consciousness and attachment to the Source of life and fulfillment. Overflowing with thought provoking insights, Divine guidance and practical exercises, The Seven Principles is a manual to leading a life of purpose and joy.

———————

THE GARDEN OF PARADOX:
The Essence of Non - Dual Kabbalah

This book is a Primer on the Essential Philosophy of Kabbalah presented as a series of 3 conversations, revealing the mysteries of Creator, Creation and Consciousness. With three representational students, embodying respectively, the philosopher, the activist and the mystic, the book, tackles the larger questions of life. Who is G-d? Who am I? Why do I exist? What is my purpose in this life? Written in clear and concise prose, the text, gently guides the reader towards making sense of life's paradoxes and living meaningfully.

––––––––––

THE POWER OF CHOICE:
A Practical Guide to Conscious Living

It is the essential premise of this book that we hold the key to unlock many of the gates that seem closed to us and keep us from living our fullest life. That key we all hold is the power to choose. The Power of Choice is the primary tool that we have at our disposal to impact the world and effect change within our own lives. We often give up this power to outside forces such as the market, media, politicians or peer pressure; or to internal forces that often function beyond our conscious control such as ego, anger, lust, greed or jealousy. Making conscious, compassionate and creative decisions is the cornerstone of living a mature and meaningful life.

––––––––––

MYSTIC TALES FROM THE EMEK HAMELECH

Mystic Tales of the Emek HaMelech, is a wondrous and inspiring collection of stories culled from the Emek HaMelech. Emek HaMelech, from which these stories have been taken, (as well as its author) is a bit of a mystery. But like all good mysteries, it is one worth investigating. In this spirit the present volume is being offered to the general public in the merit and memory of its saintly author, as well as in the hopes of introducing a vital voice of deeper Torah teaching and tradition to a contemporary English speaking audience

Rav Pinson on Meditation

MEDITATION AND JUDAISM
Exploring the Jewish Meditative Paths

A comprehensive work encompassing the entire spectrum of Jewish thought, from the sages of the Talmud and the early Kabbalists to the modern philosophers and Chassidic masters. This book is both a scholarly, in-depth study of meditative practices, and a practical, easy to follow guide for any person interested in meditating the Jewish way.

TOWARD THE INFINITE

A book focusing exclusively on the Chassidic approach to meditation known as Hisbonenus. Encompassing the entire meditative experience, it takes the reader on a comprehensive and engaging journey through this unique practice. The book explores the various states of consciousness that a person encounters in the course of the meditation, beginning at a level of extreme self-awareness and concluding with a state of total non-awareness.

BREATHING & QUIETING THE MIND

Achieving a sense of self-mastery and inner freedom demands that we gain a measure of hegemony over our thoughts. We learn to choose out thoughts so that we are not at the mercy of whatever belches up to the mind. Through quieting the mind and conscious breathing we can slow the onrush of anxious, scattered thinking and come to a deeper awareness of the interconnectedness of all of life.

Source texts are included in translation, with how-to-guides for the various practices.

SOUND AND VIBRATION:
Tuning into the Echoes of Creation

Through our perception of sound and vibration we internalize the world around us. What we hear, and how we process that hearing, has a profound impact on how we experience life. What we hear can empower us or harm us. A defining human capacity is to harness the power sound -- through speech, dialogue, and song, and through listening to others. Hearing is primary dimension of our existence. In fact, as a fetus our ears were the first fully operating sensory organs to develop.

This book will guide you in methods of utilizing the power of sound and vibration to heal and maintain mental, emotional and spiritual health, to fine-tune your Midos and even to guide you into deeper levels of Deveikus / conscious unity with Hashem. The vibratory patterns of the Aleph-Beis are particularly useful portals into our deeper conscious selves. Through chanting and deep listening, we can use the letters and sounds to shift our very mindset, to induce us into a state of presence and spiritual elevation.

VISUALIZATION AND IMAGERY:
Harnessing the Power of our Mind's Eye

We assume that what we see with our eyes is absolute. Yet, beyond our ability to choose what we see, we have the ability to choose how we see. This directly translates into how we experience life. In a world saturated with visual imagery, our senses are continuously assaulted with Kelipa/empty/fantasy imagery that we would not necessarily choose. These images can negatively affect our relationship with ourselves, with the world around us, and with the Divine. This volume seeks to show us how we can alter that which we observe through harnessing the power of our mind's eye, the inner sanctum of our imagination. We thus create a new way to see and experience the world. This book teaches us how to utilize visualization and imagery as a way to develop our spiritual sensitivity and higher intuition, and ultimately achieve Deveikus/Unity with Hashem.

Rav Pinson on The Holidays

THE HAGGADAH:
Pathways to Pesach and the Haggadah

"In every generation a person must regard oneself as having gone out of Mitzrayim / Egypt." This means that when recalling the Exodus, which occurred thousands of years ago, we also need to envision ourselves as being taken out of Mitzrayim and freed from enslavement.
Introducing the Haggadah and the themes of Pesach, this book delves into the greater context of the Festival and the Seder, allowing us to tap into the profound inspiration and Koach / power that Pesach and Seder Night offers.

EIGHT LIGHTS
8 Meditations for Chanukah

What is the meaning and message of Chanukah? What is the spiritual significance of the Lights of the Menorah? What are the Lights telling us? What is the deeper dimension of the Dreidel? Rav Pinson, with his trademark deep learning and spiritual sensitivity guides us through eight meditations relating to the Lights of the Menorah, the eight days of Chanukah, and a fascinating exploration of the symbolism and structure of the Dreidel. Includes a detailed how-to guide for lighting the Chanukah Menorah.

THE PURIM READER
The Holiday of Purim Explored

With a Persian name, a masquerade dress code and a woman as the heroine, Purim is certainly unusual amongst the Jewish holidays. Most people are very familiar with the costumes, Megilah and revelry, but are mystified by their significance. This book offers a glimpse into the hidden world of Purim, uncovering these mysteries and offering a deeper understanding of this unique holiday.

The High Holiday Series:

A CALL TO MAJESTY:
The Mysteries of Shofar & Rosh Hashanah

The Shofar is the preeminent symbol of Rosh Hashanah, waking us up to a time of deep introspection and celebration. But why do we blow the Shofar on this most special of days? While the Torah decrees that the Shofar must be blown, it does not provide a reason. On the deepest level, the Shofar is of course beyond reason altogether, and yet, from within its shape, sound and story, a constellation of "reasons" emerge. Rebirth. Responsibility. Radical Amazement. On a primal vibrational level, the Shofar calls each of us to a place of deeper consciousness and community as we crown the King of All Creation.

A CALL TO MAJESTY delves deeply into the world of Rosh Hashanah and its primary Mitzvah, the sound of the Shofar. Weaving together a multi-dimensional tapestry of practical, allegorical, philosophical, and mystical ideas and implications, the teachings collected herein empower us all to answer the higher calling of the Shofar.

———————

A LIGHTNESS OF BEING:
Your Guide to Yom Kippur

Yom Kippur is unabashedly transformative; the power of the day beckons us to work toward fundamental transformation and Teshuvah / return to who we really are. Often, the word Teshuvah is unfortunately translated as 'repentance'. It is more accurately rendered as 'return', meaning both a return 'from' our states of spiritual alienation and exile, as well as a 'turning to' experiencing our deepest selves. Yom Kippur empowers us to return to our essence, reclaim who we truly are, and live from that place.

A LIGHTNESS OF BEING delves into the powerful and transformative day of Yom Kippur. Weaving together a multi-dimensional tapestry of practical, allegorical, philosophical and mystical ideas and implications, the teachings gathered herein empower us all to enter Yom Kippur and truly feel enlightened, elevated, lighter and transformed.

———————

THE FOUR SPECIES
The Symbolism of the Lulav & Esrog

The Four Species have inspired countless commentaries and traditions and intrigued scholars and mystics alike. In this little masterpiece of wisdom both profound and practical - the deep symbolic roots and nature of the Four Species are explored. The Na'anuim, or ritual of the Lulav movement, is meticulously detailed and Kavanos,, are offered for use with the practice. Includes an illustrated guide to the Lulav Movements.

Rav Pinson on Prayer

INNER WORLDS OF JEWISH PRAYER
A Guide to Develop and Deepen
the Prayer Experience

While much attention has been paid to the poetry, history, theology and contextual meaning of the prayers, the intention of this work is to provide a guide to finding meaning and effecting transformation through the prayer experience itself.
Explore: *What happens when we pray? *How do we enter the mind-state of prayer? *Learning to incorporate the body into the prayers. *Discover techniques to enhance and deepen prayer and make it a transformative experience.
This empowering and inspiring text, demonstrates how through proper mindset, preparation and dedication, the experience of prayer can be deeply transformative and ultimately, life-altering.

ILLUMINATED SOUND:
The Baal Shem Tov on Prayer

In the year 1698 a great light was revealed to the world with the descent of the holy soul of the Baal Shem Tov. In time, the Baal Shem Tov became one of the most important and influential teachers of Torah in all of history, and the founder of Chassidus.

Amongst the vast repository of profound and revolutionary teachings of the holy Baal Shem Tov, the teachings on the path of Tefilah / Prayer are the most elaborate. The teachings of the Baal Shem Tov on Tefilah include some of his most innovative expressions, or Chidushim. Tefilah is the essential and central tenet from which all other teachings flow. In this masterful and practical text, Rav Pinson revives the awe-inspiring and transformational teachings of the Baal Shem Tov, and illuminates his unique path to Tefilah.

Rav Pinson on Jewish Practice

RECLAIMING THE SELF
The Way of Teshuvah

Teshuvah is one of the great gifts of life. It speaks of a hope for a better today and empowers us to choose a brighter tomorrow. But what exactly is Teshuvah? How does it work? How can we undo our past and how do we deal with guilt? And what is healthy regret without eroding our self-esteem? In this fascinating and empowering book, the path for genuine transformation and a way to include all of our past in the powerful moment of the now, is explored and demonstrated.

WRAPPED IN MAJESTY
Tefillin - Exploring the Mystery

Tefillin, the black boxes and leather straps that are worn during prayer, are curiously powerful and mysterious. Within the inky black boxes lie untold secrets. In this profound, passionate and thought-provoking text, the multi-dimensional perspectives of Tefillin are explored and revealed. Magically weaving together all levels of Torah including the Peshat (literal observation), to Remez (allegorical), to Derush, (homiletic), to Sod (hidden) into one beautiful tapestry. Inspirational and instructive, Wrapped in Majesty: Tefillin, will make putting on the Tefillin more meaningful and inspiring.

SECRETS OF THE MIKVAH:
Waters of Transformation

A Mikvah is a pool of water used for the purpose of ritual immersion; a place where one moves from a state of Tumah; impurity, blockage and death— to a place of Teharah; purity, fluidity and life.

In SECRETS OF THE MIKVAH, Rav Pinson delves into the transformative powers of the Mikvah with his trademark all-encompassing perspective that ranges from the literal, Pshat observation and Halachic implications of the texts, to the allegorical, the philosophical, and finally, to the deep secrets of the Mikvah as revealed by Kabbalah and Chassidus.

This insightful and inspirational text demonstrates how immersion in a Mikvah can be a transformative and life-altering practice, and includes various Kavanos—deep intentions—for all people, through various stages of life, that empower and enrich the immersion experience.

THE MYSTERY OF SHABBOS
Shabbat Rediscovered

Delving into the transformative power of Shabbos. With an all-encompassing perspective that ranges from the literal, Pshat observation and Halachic implications of the texts, to the allegorical, the philosophical, and finally, to the deeper secrets as revealed by Kabbalah and Chassidus, creating an elegant tapestry of thought and experience. THE MYSTERY OF SHABBOS is a profound meditation on the meaning of Shabbos and demonstrates the physical, emotional, mental and spiritual possibilities available and given to us with the gift of Shabbos. Studying and contemplating this inspired text on the depths of Shabbos will unveil a redemptive light in your experience of the Seventh Day -- and by extension, every day of your life.

Rav Pinson on Time

THE SPIRAL OF TIME:
A 12 Part Series on the Months of the Year

VOL 1: THE SPIRAL OF TIME:
Unraveling the Yearly Cycle

Many centuries ago, the Sages of Israel were the foremost authority in the fields of both astronomical calculation and astrological wisdom, including the deeper interpretations of the cycles and seasons. Over time, this wisdom became hidden within the esoteric teachings of the Torah, and as a result was known only to students and scholars of the deepest depths of the tradition. More recently, the great teachers, from R.Yitzchak Luria (the Arizal) to the Baal Shem Tov, taught that as the world approaches the Era of Redemption, it is a Mitzvah / spiritual obligation to broadly reveal this wisdom.

"The Spiral of Time" is volume 1 is a series of 12 books, and serves as an introductory book to the basic concepts and nature of the Hebrew calendar and explores the special day of Rosh Chodesh.

VOL 2: THE MONTH OF NISAN:
Miraculous Awakenings from Above

The month of NISAN is the first month of the lunar cycle of the year, a month that brings in the spring and a month of redemption. Spring represents a time of plenty, abundance, sunshine, hope, and possibility. Redemption, on whatever level, feels palpable and accessible. In spring, the world is redeemed from the cold winter, the flower is redeemed from the tree, the grass from the earth, and we too feel that redemption is possible. A whole complex of ideas, including newness, redemption, going out of Egypt, and being freed from slavery, is intricately bound with the idea of Aviv / spring and the powerful month of Nisan.

VOL 3: THE MONTH OF IYYAR:
EVOLVING THE SELF
& The Holiday of LAG B'OMER

The month of IYYAR is the second month of the spring, a month that connects the Redemption from Egypt in Nissan with the Revelation of Torah in Sivan. The Chai/ Eighteenth day of the Month is the day we celebrate the Rashbi (Rabbi Shimon Bar Yochai) and the revealing of the hidden aspects of the Torah. This is the 'Holiday' of Lag b'Omer. The book explores the unique quality of this special month, a month that has a Mitzvah of counting the Omer every day. In addition, the book explores the roots and significance of the mystical 'holiday' of Lag b'Omer. Including the customs & Practices of Lag b'Omer, such as, bonfires, bows & arrows, parades, Upsherin, and more.

VOL 4: THE MONTH OF SIVAN:
The Art of Receiving: Shavuos and Matan Torah

Sivan is the third month of the lunar cycle. One is a singularity. Two is division. Three is harmony, a unity that synthesizes individuality and multiplicity, Heaven and Earth, Spirituality and Physicality. During this month we celebrate Shavuos and the giving of the Torah, the ultimate expression of the unity of the Above and Below and we aspire to connect with the Keser/Crown of Torah that Transcends and yet includes all Worlds. Learning how to truly receive Higher wisdom in our Lower faculties is the mental, emotional, and spiritual exercise of the month.

VOL 5: THE MONTHS OF TAMUZ AND AV:
Embracing Brokenness -
17th of Tamuz, Tisha B'Av, & Tu B'Av

Each month and season of the year, radiates with distinct Divine qualities and unique opportunities for growth and Tikkun.
The summer month of Tamuz and Av contain the longest and hottest days of the year. The raised temperature is indicative of a corresponding

spiritual heat, a time of harsher judgement and potential destruction, such as the destructions of the first and second Beis HaMikdash, which began on the 17th of Tamuz and culminated on the 9th and 10th of Av. A few days later, on Tu b'Av, the darkness is transformed and reveals the greatest light and possibility for new life. During these summer months of Tamuz and Av we embrace our brokenness so that we can heal and transform darkness into light.

VOL 6: THE MONTH OF ELUL:
Days of Introspection and Transformation

Each month of the year radiates with a distinct quality and provides unique opportunities for growth and personal transformation. Elul, as the final month of the spring/summer season is connected to endings. Elul gives us the strength to be able to finish strong, to end well. Elul also serves as a month of preparation for the New Year/Rosh Hashanah.

We inhale our past year, ending with wisdom and then we also gain the wisdom to begin anew and exhale a positive year into being. The mental, emotional, and spiritual objective of this month is introspection and the reclaiming of our inner purity and wholeness.

VOL 7: THE MONTH OF TISHREI:
A Time of Rebirth & Upward Movement

Each month of the year radiates with distinct Divine qualities and unique opportunities for growth and spiritual illumination. As Tishrei begins the new yearly cycle, it is an appropriate month to introspect, reflect and resolve to move forward and preserve moving forward into the more inward months of the winter. This month creates the space to unburden ourselves from our negativities, and enter a more sacred, grounded sacred space. In Tishrei we are given the gift of forgiveness and then the ability to truly regain our space and inner joy.

VOL 8: THE MONTH OF CHESHVAN:
Navigating Transitions, Elevating the Fall

Directly on the heels of the inspiring and holiday-filled month of Tishrei, Cheshvan is a month that is quiet and devoid of holidays. In the month of Cheshvan we use the stored up energies of the previous months to self-generate our inspiration and creativity and provide ourselves with the strength to rise up after a fall. In Cheshvan we are entering into a stormier, wetter and colder season. It is a month of transition. The mental, emotional and spiritual objective of this month is to weather the transitions, learn to self-generate and stand tall. And if we do fall, we use the quality of this month to get back up and do so with more conviction, strength, wisdom and clarity.

VOL 9: THE MONTH OF KISLEV:
Rekindling Hope, Dreams and Trust

Kislev is the final month of the fall. Throughout this month, daylight progressively shortens, and the temperatures drop. Towards the end of the month, at the darkest hour, the winter solstice arrives and we begin the celebration of Chanukah. We commemorate the miracle of a small jug of oil that burned for eight nights, and as we celebrate, daylight expands. In the month of Kislev-despite the darkness, or perhaps because of it-we have the ability to tap into the Ohr HaGanuz, the hidden light of hope that rekindles our dreams and aspirations.

VOL 10: THE MONTH OF TEVES:
Refining Relationships, Elevating the Body

The quality of Teves is generally harsh—much like its counterpart Tamuz in the summer, thus the tendency for many is to hunker down, retract, curl up and wait for the month to pass by, only to reemerge when the harshness has dissipated. Think for a moment about the 'easier' months of the year, which, like gentle waves in the ocean, carry us where we want to go. We can ride these energies easily and they can propel us forward effortlessly, we just need to go with the overall flow, so to speak. The harsher months, on the other hand, can be compared to the more powerful waves that emanate from the belly of the ocean, which come forcefully crashing down and can easily drown a person before they even realize what has happened. However, those who want to utilize the momentum of the powerful energy that is available during such times can, with caution and creativity, harness these intense waves and ride them higher and farther than other, more gentle circumstances may allow. However, harnessing the power of Tohu, the raw energy of the body, does in fact need to be approached with great care and attention.

VOL 11: THE MONTH OF SHEVAT:
ELEVATING EATING
& The Holiday of Tu b'Shevat

Each month of the year radiates with a distinct Divine energy and thus unique opportunities for growth, *Tikkun* and illumination. According to the deeper teachings of the Torah, all of these distinct qualities, opportunities and natural phenomena correspond to a certain data set. That is, the nature of each month is elucidated by a specific letter of the Aleph Beis, a tribe, verse, human sense, and so forth. The month of

Shevat is particularly connected to food and our relationship to bodily intake. During this month we celebrate Tu b'Shevat, the New Year of the Tree, and aspire to create a proper and physically/emotionally/spiritually healthy relationship with food.

_____

VOL 12: THE MONTH OF ADAR:
Transformation Through Laughter & Holy Doubt

Each month of the year radiates with distinct Divine qualities and unique opportunities for growth and spiritual illumination. As Adar concludes the monthly cycle of the year, as well as the solar phenomena of the winter, it is an appropriate month to think about our essential identity, before moving out to meet the world come spring. This month we strive to create a healthy relationship with holy humor, unbounded joy, and a general sense of lightness of being. Through the work of Adar we transform negative, crippling doubt and uncertainties into radical wonderment and openness.

New Release!

_____

PROCESS AND PRESENCE
Life in Balance

In the world of process, the self and the world are broken, and we ambitiously strive to improve and to better.
In presence reality, all is now, everything is perfect, and there is nowhere to progress and certainly no reason to fight or strive.
This book offers the gift of a balanced life, wherein the path of process and the pathless path of presence are lived in unison.

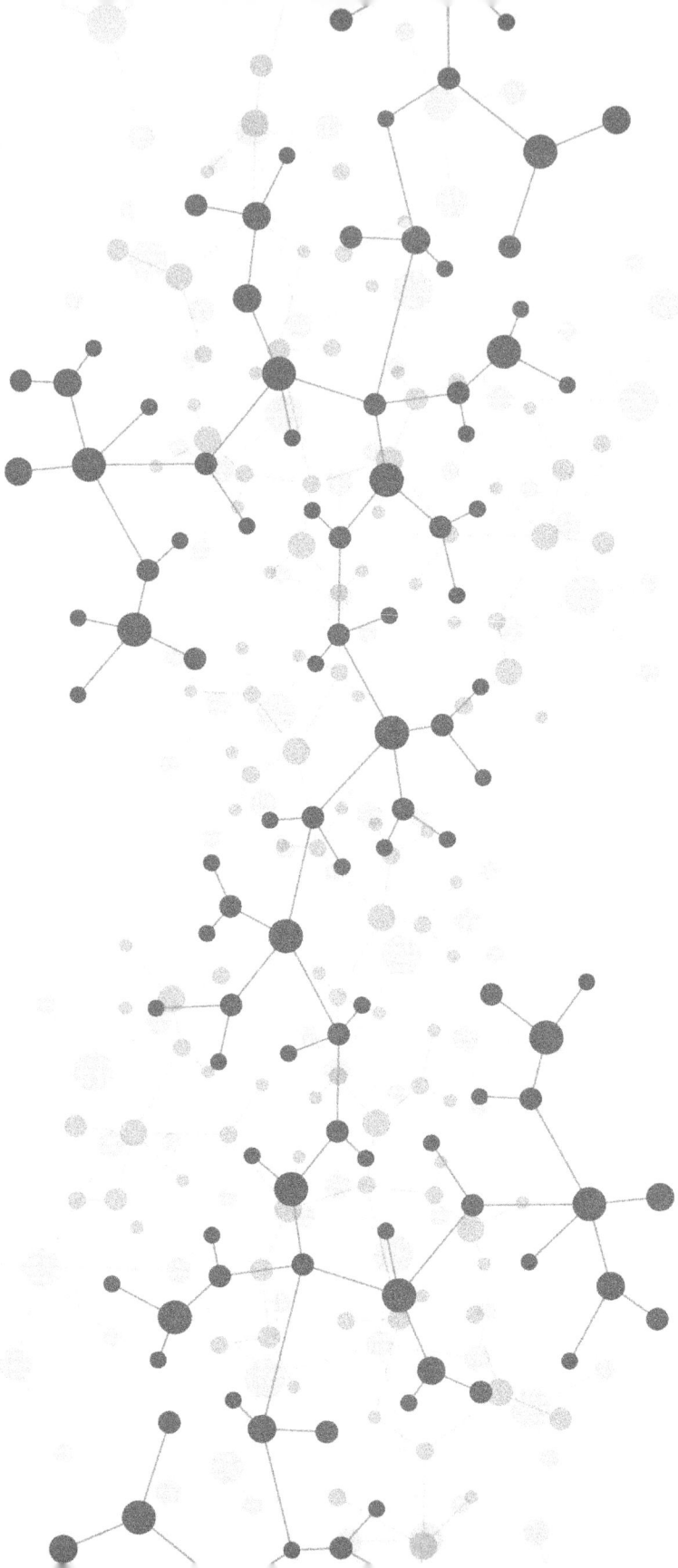